Interlibrary Loan Practices Handbook

Second Edition

Virginia Boucher

American Library Association

Chicago and London

1997

Cover by Tessing Design

Text design by Dianne M. Rooney

Composed by the dotted i in Times and Optima
on Xyvision

Printed on 50-pound Victor Offset, a pH-neutral stock, and bound in 10-point C1S cover stock by Victor Graphics, Inc.

The paper used in this publication meets the minimum requirements of American National Standard for Information Sciences—Permanence of Paper for Printed Library Materials, ANSI Z39.48–1992. ∞

Library of Congress Cataloging-in-Publication Data

Boucher, Virginia, 1929–
    Interlibrary loan practices handbook / Virginia
Boucher. — 2nd ed.
        p.   cm.
    Includes bibliographical references and index.
    ISBN 0-8389-0667-2
    1. Interlibrary loans—United States—Handbooks, manuals, etc. I. Title.
Z713.U6B68   1997
025.6′2—dc20   96-18419

Printed in the United States of America.

01 00 99 98 97   5 4 3 2 1

For
America's interlibrary
loan and document
delivery workers,
who valiantly supply
what is wanted,
when it's needed,
at the least cost.

CONTENTS

FIGURES

PREFACE

I T ALL BEGAN WITH Sarah Katharine Thomson's *Interlibrary Loan Procedures Manual,* published by the American Library Association in 1970, which offered librarians new to interlibrary loan an understanding of just how interlibrary loan should be accomplished. Next came the first edition of the *Interlibrary Loan Practices Handbook,* published by the American Library Association in 1984. Here is the second edition, coming when there is still a paucity of formal instruction for interlibrary loan and document delivery librarians. The need to understand the complexities of getting materials for patrons from outside the library quickly and at reasonable cost is even greater today because the volume of requests for such service has mushroomed. More than ever library workers need to do interlibrary loan efficiently and effectively while faced with a rapidly changing environment.

Change has always been a way of life for interlibrary loan service. What is done today could be done very differently tomorrow. Uncertain, often decreasing, financial support for the purchase of library materials, the frequent inability to hire new staff to meet the challenges, the sheer numbers of ever-increasing requests, and the explosive growth of electronic sources and ways of doing business have all contributed to the ongoing change that interlibrary loan faces.

This manual is intended, first of all, for those without interlibrary loan experience who seek advice on how to proceed. It is a place to start. It can be used to teach oneself or to train new staff. It is also designed to refresh the memory of those who do not spend all their time doing interlibrary loan or who have been away from it for a time. It can be referred to for procedures infrequently used. The chapters on special areas can be consulted when necessary. Knowing the traditional steps required to achieve an interlibrary loan can help in designing and increasing the use of electronic management for the service. Recorded knowledge need not be lost to the patron when paper reference tools are used to supplement the online sources (not everything is listed online). An interlibrary loan and document delivery service can be commenced, expanded, or improved by using the information in this book.

This manual describes the procedures for implementing the policies outlined in interlibrary loan codes. It sets forth the character of sound interlibrary loan practices, though not every library will carry out all the procedures described because of individual circumstances. Chapter 1, "Instructions for Borrowing Libraries," chapter 2,

"Instructions for Lending Libraries," and chapter 3, "Interlibrary Loan, Reproduction, and the Copyright Law," should be read and assimilated by all who engage in inter-library loan. Chapter 4, "Dissertations and Masters' Theses," chapter 5, "Interlibrary Cooperation," and chapter 6, "International Interlibrary Loan," should be read quickly as an overview and then consulted carefully when the need arises. Chapter 7, "Man-agement of Interlibrary Loan," is primarily for larger libraries, although there are many useful suggestions for smaller ones too. Those who supervise interlibrary loan while others do the day-to-day work will find this chapter useful.

Though a seamless electronic interlibrary loan function tends to be the present goal, *people* are still what make the difference in interlibrary loan service. Acting as a manager, bibliographic reference practitioner, legal advisor, automation counselor, network consultant, teacher, and defender of rights, the interlibrary loan librarian has a stellar contribution to make in the modern and changing world of librarianship.

ACKNOWLEDGMENTS

A GREAT MANY PEOPLE contributed time and energy to the perusal of this work. Several librarians read much of the manuscript and offered many helpful suggestions: Noelene P. Martin (who performed a similar service for the first edition), Mary E. Jackson, Margaret W. Ellingson, Una M. Gourlay, and Sheila A. Walters. A number of people offered additional advice on the first two chapters: Eva D. Calcagno, Allison A. Cowgill (who also turned in a stellar performance as proofreader), Yem Fong, Monica Ortale, Barbara G. Preece, Franca Rosen, Mary L. Williamson, and N. J. Wolfe, who commented from their various perspectives.

Individual chapters received extra help from other generous professionals. Advice on government publications was rendered by Timothy L. Byrne and Margaret M. (Peggy) Jobe of the University of Colorado at Boulder Libraries (UC-Boulder) and Daniel P. O'Mahony of Brown University Library. Jody Gehrig and Daniel Pagliasotti of the Denver Public Schools, Lisbeth B. Lord of the St. Vrain Valley School District, and Maureen G. Van Camp of UC-Boulder explained the intricacies of audiovisual materials. Laura N. Gasaway, University of North Carolina, kindly read and corrected the chapter on the copyright law as well as contributing the chart to help determine duration of copyright. Carol Smale, National Library of Canada, and Mary Samson, Canada Institute for Scientific and Technical Information, responded to many questions regarding Canadian practices. Margaret M. Barwick and Graham P. Cornish answered numerous queries put to the IFLA Office for International Lending. Richard Walker graciously read and commented upon the parts of the manuscript dealing with the British Library Document Supply Centre. Expertise was offered on mailing requirements of the U.S. Postal Service by Dave Reedy. Carol Ann Hughes of the Research Libraries Group and Linda A. Naru of the Center for Research Libraries helped with information about their organizations. Susan Dueis sent a description of the Traverse des Sioux Library System.

Staff at UC-Boulder gave assistance in many ways. Keith Gresham, Fred (Skip) Hamilton, and Ellen E. Robertson of the Reference Department were particularly helpful where electronic sources were concerned. William A. Garrison of the Cataloging Department shed light on current cataloging practices. Joan S. McConkey translated a French periodical article, and Eugene E. Petriwsky translated several Russian articles.

Special help came from John Dziadecki, UC-Boulder, who designed and produced the paper patron request forms, and Julie Wessling, Colorado State University, who provided the electronic patron request forms. Dudley Emmert, UC-Boulder, checked bibliography and World Wide Web addresses as well as giving other assistance.

Though great care was taken to be accurate, errors have no doubt crept in, and those are mine, not my helpers'.

Employees, patrons, and workshop participants have contributed in many ways to my understanding of interlibrary loan and document delivery. The students who attended my seminars on "Managing Interlibrary Loan," given at the University of Wisconsin-Madison School of Library and Information Studies, stimulated my thinking on many interlibrary loan topics.

No acknowledgment would be complete without a mention of my spouse, Stanley W. Boucher, who once again put up with encroachment on his domestic felicity and who once again turned in a noteworthy performance as editorial advisor and proofreader.

Last and certainly least, Needlepoint T. Boucher has gone to his reward and no longer purrs raucously in my ear. Zorro Boucher Baillie did come to visit on occasion and was prone to chew and claw my hands as they attempted to fly over the keyboard. This book was written in spite of his well-meant help.

Instructions for Borrowing Libraries

Some Basic Definitions
What is interlibrary loan?
Why is interlibrary loan done?

Interlibrary Loan Codes

Interlibrary Borrowing Policies
Who can use interlibrary borrowing?
When should interlibrary borrowing be used?
What can be borrowed or obtained?
Will there be any fees?
How long will it take? Can requests be rushed?
How will notification of the material's arrival be given?
Where can material be borrowed or obtained?

Supplies
Minimum supplies needed
Additional supplies recommended

Interlibrary Borrowing Procedures
Interview interlibrary borrowing patrons
Take applications for borrowing
Verify borrowing requests and find where material is located
Books and pamphlets
Periodical articles
Chapter in a book or paper in a proceedings
Newspapers
Dissertations and masters' theses
Government publications and technical reports
Microforms

Interlibrary loan has always meant change. In 1967 the big change was the sending of interlibrary loan requests by the use of teletype equipment and thus taking days off the time for a request to be processed. Today it is the emergence of the World Wide Web with its rapidly changing topography and implications for libraries. No one knows what the library patron will do using the Web in the pursuit of information. No one knows every Web site that is useful for libraries. No one knows what sort of equipment will be required in the future. No one knows what will develop in terms of publication, copyright, and the delivery of documents. Keeping up with what happens next is vital.

A knowledge of the details of interlibrary loan in today's environment—part paper, part digital—is useful as a way of learning the tasks that will have to be accomplished for a long time to come. Changes do not happen all at once. Knowing each step in the operation can promote an intelligent transition from paper to electronic means. The traditional ways can act as "pointers" for the future.

SOME BASIC DEFINITIONS

What is interlibrary loan?

Interlibrary borrowing is used to describe the policies and procedures necessary for the requesting library. Interlibrary lending is used to describe the policies and procedures necessary for the supplying library (see chapter 2, "Instructions for Lending Libraries"). The term *interlibrary loan* encompasses both borrowing and lending—the requesting of materials and the sending of materials, including provision of reproductions. In essence, the purpose of interlibrary loan is to borrow or obtain copies of library materials not found in a local collection on behalf of that library's clientele, and to lend or provide copies of library materials requested by other libraries. A formal definition and statement of purpose for interlibrary loan can be found in sections 1 and 2 of the National Interlibrary Loan Code for the United States, 1993, presented in appendix A.

Libraries today are moving beyond traditional interlibrary loan to tap the resources offered by electronic databases and commercial services. *Document delivery* is one of the terms frequently used to describe the procurement of materials from fee-based library services and from commercial document suppliers. The best name for today's augmented service might be "interlibrary loan and document delivery," thus using the term familiar to library patrons coupled with the one that may not be so well known. Wherever possible, this handbook uses interlibrary loan to mean not only borrowing and lending but borrowing, lending, and document delivery.

Other ways to explain interlibrary loan are:

- Expansion of traditional reference service to include resources in other libraries, electronic databases, or commercial services
- Method for obtaining materials, subject information, or answers to reference questions not found in your library
- Sharing library resources—books, periodicals, records, films, and other materials
- The lifeline to the outside world of knowledge
- What you do when material cannot be found in your own library

Why is interlibrary loan done?

The basic premise for interlibrary loan is that no library can be completely self-sufficient in meeting the needs of its patrons. As the introduction to the National Interlibrary Loan Code for the United States, 1993, explains, "the exchange of material between libraries in the United States is an important element in the provision of library service" and it is "in the public interest to encourage such an exchange. Interlibrary loan is essential to the vitality of libraries of all types and sizes. . . ." In addition, "libraries have an obligation to obtain materials to meet the informational needs of users when local resources do not meet those needs." We live in an age of expanding information, growing technology for sharing that information, and ever-increasing demands for scholarly and scientific endeavor.

INTERLIBRARY LOAN CODES

No one can operate an effective interlibrary loan service in the United States today without first becoming familiar with the basic codes that in effect govern interlibrary loan procedures among virtually all libraries. These codes are (1) the National Interlibrary Loan Code for the United States, 1993 (hereafter referred to as "the Code"), and (2) state, regional, network, consortia, or other interlibrary

loan codes adhered to by a defined group of libraries. These codes are designed to regulate borrowing and lending among all types of libraries throughout the country.

The codes spell out the responsibilities of the borrowing library and the lending library. The codes represent detailed interlibrary loan policies for the guidance of all. Abiding by these codes, exercising common sense, and establishing goodwill among librarians will accomplish the task of getting library and other resources to those who need them.

The Code is reprinted in appendix A. Throughout the first three chapters, references are made to specific sections of the Code to show the policy basis for the instructions on how to do interlibrary loan. The Code, as well as any other codes that apply to your particular library, should be read carefully before beginning a perusal of this manual.

INTERLIBRARY BORROWING POLICIES

Interlibrary borrowing is used here to describe the policies and procedures necessary for the requesting library. Once you have mastered the necessary codes, you need a policy statement for your interlibrary borrowing service. (For more information about the necessity of developing an interlibrary loan policy, see chapter 7, "Management of Interlibrary Loan," "Organizational Climate and Planning," "Policies.") Such a statement should be developed, approved, and made available for use by the library staff (see appendix B). Consider policy statements for the following questions:

Who can use interlibrary borrowing?

All primary clientele of a library should be able to use interlibrary borrowing. While the amount of material available for purchase continues to increase, libraries are experiencing decreased acquisitions funding. Fewer new books on the shelves and the cancellation of periodical titles are the result. At the same time, there is ready access to bibliographic information either by using CD-ROMs or online sources. Under these circumstances it is very difficult to justify refusing interlibrary borrowing. Some libraries, however, attempt to regulate the number of requests being submitted by denying service to undergraduates or some other part of the library's primary clientele. Such a policy may dampen rather than foster the pursuit of knowledge. To avoid ambiguity, spell out who has access to interlibrary loan services.

When should interlibrary borrowing be used?

Each library strives to develop its collection to meet the ordinary needs of its patrons. Changes in the last decade have forced "a shift in the very nature of interlibrary cooperation" (the Code, Introduction). Today, "interlibrary borrowing is an integral element of collection development for all libraries, not an ancillary option" (the Code, Introduction). Whether the requested material should be purchased rather than borrowed can be considered. The collection development policy of the library, recurring demand, resource-sharing agreements, the time available to the patron, and the cost of the material compared to the cost of interlibrary borrowing are guidelines to help make this decision.

Full use of the library's collection should be made before interlibrary borrowing is attempted (the Code, 2.1). The library patron should be urged to recall circulated material or place a hold request for such material. If material is on reserve, then access is available to the patron and interlibrary borrowing is not necessary.

Items from the library's collection may not be available. If a periodical is at the bindery or the pages needed are torn out, interlibrary borrowing should be a viable option for getting the material. If a book has been declared missing or lost, after being formally searched, interlibrary borrowing should be used. If the book is long overdue or on extended loan, a decision must be made as to whether or not interlibrary borrowing is appropriate.

Some libraries have an agreement to circulate materials to each other's clientele. Such an agreement, usually called a reciprocal borrowing agreement, allows a patron to borrow library materials directly at the reciprocating library rather than having to use interlibrary borrowing. Some states or consortia have "universal" borrowing cards that allow the library patron to borrow at a wide variety of libraries. Because the cost is less for material processed through circulation than for material processed through interlibrary loan, such agreements should be fostered. The patron should be urged to circulate materials from *nearby* libraries with which there are reciprocal borrowing agreements. Sometimes travel to a library containing noncirculating or large amounts of material needed by the patron is actually more practical than interlibrary borrowing. Providing such information as the name of the library, the address, the telephone number, hours of service, conditions of on-site use, the name of the person in charge of a special collection, and the method of travel to get there can be very helpful.

What can be borrowed or obtained?

A loan or copy of any kind of library material may be requested on interlibrary borrowing when it is in accordance with the policy of the lending library (the Code, 3.2). Often a library will provide a reproduction of material that does not circulate, and this possibility should be discussed with the patron. The intricacies of borrowing or copying dissertations is another topic about which patrons have many questions. (For more information about this topic, see chapter 4, "Dissertations and Masters' Theses".) Because the purpose of interlibrary loan "is to obtain, upon request of a library user, materials not available in the user's local library" (the Code, 2.1), another library's book should not be put on reserve for *many* users. The wear and tear resulting from this sort of use can cause serious damage. Reserve material should be purchased by the library, remembering reprint, microform, and second-hand sources. Sometimes an arrangement can be worked out with the publisher in which you can copy a substantial portion or all of a book that is out of print. In rare cases when putting a borrowed item on reserve seems the only option, the full consent of the lending library must be obtained.

There are always certain "heavy" users of interlibrary borrowing. These are usually people working on a very current or an obscure topic in an area in which the library does not purchase materials. They are often working against a book, dissertation, or other deadline. They tend to submit a large number of requests at one time or a constant stream of requests. Rather than limit a patron to a number of submissions per day, week, or semester (necessitating additional record keeping), all requests can be taken at once. It is often easier to do the verification and location work on a whole group of similar requests. The patron should be told that these requests will be processed steadily as time permits because other patrons' requests must be sent out as well.

Will there be any fees?

A policy concerning pass-along fees and other charges to the library patron needs to be developed. Should fees for processing requests be levied? Should charges for special service, such as rushing a request, levied by the lending library or by a commercial document supplier be passed on to the library patron? Should the total cost of an interlibrary borrowing transaction be charged? Or should the library consider interlibrary borrowing an integral part of library service and pay for it out of the acquisitions or operations budget? Should fines be levied for overdue material?

How long will it take? Can requests be rushed?

A plan for time is useful for both the patron and the interlibrary borrowing service. A goal for in-house processing time can be established (the Code, 4.2). A knowledge of common transaction time from patron submission of the request to receipt of the material helps the patron decide what to do. The feasibility of rushing a request to meet a particular deadline needs to be established. Policies concerning priorities, peak loads, and backlogs can be stated.

How will notification of the material's arrival be given?

The decision must be made as to how flexible the borrowing service can be when notifying the patron. The method of notification, be it telephone, internal mail, U.S. Postal Service, electronic mail (e-mail), voice-mail, or the like, can be a real service when tailored to the individual need. A decision might be made to deliver certain kinds of material to the patron, thus skipping this task altogether.

Where can material be borrowed or obtained?

Make clear to your patrons that interlibrary borrowing is a library-to-library transaction, except where commercial document delivery services are used. An individual's direct request to borrow from another library will not be honored except where reciprocal borrowing agreements exist. All types of libraries—academic, public, school, special, and governmental—participate in interlibrary loan. Explain that your library abides by the National Interlibrary Loan Code for the United States, 1993, and any other applicable codes and resource-sharing agreements. Photocopy agreements that do away with charges or reduce them for the patron are of particular interest. Point out that in terms of the codes and agreements, the fastest and least expensive library will be used in each case. Inform the patron of the procedures for patron-initiated online purchase of a copy of a periodical article or request to borrow from another library, if such services are available.

An interlibrary borrowing brochure (see appendix C) can be designed once the policies of interlibrary borrowing are set, with information presented in a straightforward, concise way for the use of library patrons.

SUPPLIES

Minimum supplies needed

ALA Interlibrary Loan Request forms as revised in November 1988 (see figures 1–7 and 13). It is recommended that the name and full address of the borrowing library be imprinted for clarity and to prevent inadvertent reversal of borrowing and lending libraries.

Shipping labels, self-addressed, for return, your library as receiver, gummed (see appendix D)

Packing materials (see chapter 2, "Instructions for Lending Libraries," "Ship material")

Policy statements from lending libraries on interlibrary loan, photocopy charges, and other practices

Additional supplies recommended

Interlibrary borrowing brochure (see appendix C)

Patron request forms, paper: book, periodical article, dissertation and thesis, newspaper (see appendix E). There could be one form for all types of requests. There may also be an electronic system for patron requests (see appendix F)

Patron response forms (see appendix G)

Shipping labels, address section blank, your address as sender, gummed (see appendix D)

Window envelopes with return address

Forms for requesting materials from libraries that require special ones

Printer paper and ribbons or toner

Typing paper and ribbons

Rubber stamps for commonly needed instructions or identifications

Book bands or sleeves (see appendix H)

Patron notification forms (see appendix I)

INTERLIBRARY BORROWING PROCEDURES

A variety of procedures is required to accomplish interlibrary borrowing. First, the patron should be made aware of interlibrary borrowing by publicity about the service, explanation of the service during the course of a reference interview, or information given during bibliographic instruction. Second, an interlibrary borrowing interview can be conducted with the patron while accepting the application for borrowing. Next comes the most difficult and interesting step: verifying the bibliographic information and finding which library holds the material or determining which document delivery service to use. Preparing the request and transmitting it to a lender or other supplier follow. Then the material is received, unwrapped, and presented to the patron. Eventually the borrowed materials are returned, problems are solved, and any follow-up activities accomplished. Last of all, reports on interlibrary borrowing are sent to the library administration.

Interview interlibrary borrowing patrons

The interlibrary borrowing interview is of vital importance as an information and teaching opportunity and as a significant means of saving preparation time. The exchange between the patron and the staff person provides an excellent opportunity for the patron's basic questions to be answered, for background information on interlibrary borrowing to be imparted, and for essential facts concerning a patron and a particular request to be gathered. It may be necessary to do such an interview only once in order to encourage patrons to turn in complete requests in the future. Especially well-designed forms are needed if the interview process is skipped. There should be ample help screens for patrons sending requests electronically, and it may be necessary to have a training session to ensure that complete electronic requests are submitted. Information for the patron about ordering his or her own document online can be imparted during the interview process. Staff taking requests must be trained in providing answers to questions most commonly asked and in giving basic information, as well as collecting data needed to process an interlibrary borrowing request.

Background information on interlibrary borrowing, based on the policy statements, can be given during an initial interview. Such questions as the following can be answered:

What is interlibrary loan?

Who can use interlibrary loan?

When should interlibrary loan be used?

What can be borrowed or obtained?

Where can material be borrowed or obtained?

Answers to basic questions patrons most commonly ask about interlibrary borrowing should be supplied:

How long will it take? Can requests be rushed?

How much will it cost me?

How many requests can I submit at once?

How will I know when it gets here?

How long can I use it?

What must I do?

What has happened to my request? (in subsequent interviews)

Special interlibrary borrowing information on the following can be furnished as necessary:

Common restrictions on use

Other libraries that will circulate materials directly to the patron (reciprocal borrowing)

Travel to other libraries for on-site use of materials

Photoduplication and the copyright law (see chapter 3, "Interlibrary Loan, Reproduction, and the Copyright Law")

Dissertations and theses, borrowing and buying (see chapter 4, "Dissertations and Masters' Theses")

The patron can be handed a copy of your interlibrary borrowing brochure for future reference (the Code, 4.1; see appendix C). This brochure can cover the following topics:

Purpose of interlibrary loan

Location of interlibrary loan, telephone number, fax number, e-mail address, hours open

Who may use the service (eligibility)

Materials available through interlibrary loan

How interlibrary loan works; submitting requests

Correct data for a bibliographic citation

Cost

Time it takes for material to arrive; possibility of rushes

Notification procedures

Loan period

Restrictions

Returning materials

Reciprocal borrowing privileges

Take applications for borrowing

The staff person continues the interlibrary loan borrowing interview while accepting applications for borrowing. Determine that the patron is eligible for service according to your library's policies. Ask the patron if the online public access catalog, the card catalog, or the serials records were checked to see if the item was in your library (the Code, 2.1). An opportunity to teach better search techniques often presents itself in this way. Give instructions for filling out a patron request form (see appendixes E and F). These forms can be used by staff when verifying and locating the item and when typing or transmitting the interlibrary borrowing request. Ascertain whether the patron wants information that your library might be able to provide or a specific title. Suggest substitutions from material in your collection. Sometimes, it is necessary to ask what foreign languages the patron reads. When necessary, patrons can be referred to other library personnel for further advice on research needs. For example, the patron may be referred to a reference librarian specializing in U.S. government publications to find online sources for statistics not yet in printed form.

The bibliographic citation must be checked for completeness and accuracy. Definitions for the bibliographic terms used below, as well as other information on the structure of interlibrary loan, can be found in *Interlibrary Loan Data Elements*.[1] Information that is needed follows:

Book
    author
    title
    edition (if a particular one is needed)
    place of publication
    publisher
    date of publication
    series (if there is one)

Periodical article
    title of periodical
    volume
    issue number or issue date
    year
    author of article
    title of article
    pages to be copied

Newspaper
    title of newspaper
    place of publication
    date: month, day, year

and if pertinent:
    author of article
    title of article
    pages to be copied

Dissertation or master's thesis
    author
    title
    institution (sometimes the department helps)
    degree granted
    year

Government publication
    information for book *or*
    information for periodical article
    issuing country and agency
    report number
    Superintendent of Documents classification number (for U.S. documents)
    contract number

Subject
    (see "Subject Requests" later in this chapter for information on general requirements and appropriateness)
    nature of the subject
    type of material needed

Other facts are needed from the patron. A source of information can be helpful, for many times this information can make a difference in unscrambling a difficult request. Insisting on a source of reference, however, is not reasonable with so many electronic means of verifying bibliographical information. Ascertain the "last use" date (sometimes called the "need before" date, "not needed after" date, or "cannot-use-it-if-it-comes-the-next-day" date). Get the patron to clarify such phrases as "rush" or "as soon as possible." It might be necessary for the patron to specify delivery time or delivery method. Be sure to put "today's date" on the request. When photocopy is being requested, make sure the "Order Warning of Copyright" is read (see appendix E, "Periodical: Warning"). Be certain the patron understands the library's policy for passing on fees and charges. Obtain an authorization to charge the patron for photocopy and monographic

---

1. National Information Standards Organization, *Interlibrary Loan Data Elements: American National Standard for Interlibrary Loan Data Elements*, National Information Standard Series ANSI/NISO Z39.63–1989 (New Brunswick, N.J.: Transaction Publishers, 1990). (Revised edition in press)

loans when needed. Get complete patron information: name, patron number (if required), address (including e-mail address, should there be one), and telephone number. Department or affiliation, status, or age group might also be needed.

Explain that in fairness to other patrons, a large number of requests may not be processed immediately. Ask the patron to prioritize requests in batches of five or ten, to be processed over a period of time. With the patron, consider spacing out the requests so that they do not all arrive at once, allowing too little time for use.

An alternative way for a patron to submit a request is by using an electronic message or e-mail. The patron needs access to e-mail and the ability to transfer a request to the interlibrary borrowing mailbox. A template can be designed that asks for the same information that is required on the paper patron request form (see appendix F). There may need to be separate templates for different kinds of requests. Each request for photocopy must include the "Order Warning of Copyright" (see appendix E, "Periodical: Warning"). Require that certain fields be filled in before the request is sent in order to get all the information that is needed. It is helpful if the system used can verify the patron's status. It is even more helpful if the system can determine that the item is not available in your library. Details of your e-mail patron request system, such as the abilities to reply to the sender, upload bibliographic references, and include in-office processing data, have to be worked out with the computer staff who manage the e-mail service. Electronic interlibrary borrowing patron requests are gaining in popularity because of convenience and the automatic transfer of repetitive data that must be entered by hand on paper forms.

Patrons using OCLC's FirstSearch reference system can send interlibrary borrowing requests to their local interlibrary loan service's review file and thereby avoid manually filling out forms. The interlibrary borrowing service must activate this procedure. Not all databases available on FirstSearch have this option as yet.

Patron-initiated document delivery is becoming more common. When a patron orders his or her own document online for which the library pays,

there are a number of problems to be resolved: (1) How is payment handled? (2) How will you satisfy the auditor that something was received? (3) How will you handle nonreceipt of the item or the receipt of the wrong item? (4) How will the electronic records be managed? These questions should be carefully considered before patron-initiated document delivery in which the library handles the finances is undertaken.

Verify borrowing requests and find where material is located

Very often today, the verification and location process can be accomplished using only one source that lists the correct bibliographic citation *and* the library or document delivery service that has the material. For those requests that require a two-step process, several sources may have to be used. Remember that much material exists that may not be included in online bibliographic databases. Print verification and location sources still have their place in meeting interlibrary borrowing needs.

Sloppy, inaccurate requests often come back to the borrower unfilled. Requested items should be verified and the verification source noted before the interlibrary borrowing request is sent. To verify a bibliographic citation means to

- Confirm or substantiate the existence of the item by finding it in an authoritative bibliography, bibliographic database, CD-ROM, or indexing source.
- Describe the citation completely and accurately, following accepted bibliographic practice.

For verification, the best general advice is to draw on a number of avenues of approach. Verification is made more challenging for interlibrary loan librarians today for several reasons: (1) cataloging may or may not have been done using new (AACR2) cataloging rules,[2] (2) local contributions to bibliographic databases may not be cataloged according to national standards, and (3) electronic databases and online public access catalogs have changed the way in which bibliographic informa-

---

2. Michael Gorman and Paul W. Winkler, eds., *Anglo-American Cataloguing Rules,* 2nd ed., 1988 rev. (Chicago: American Library Association, 1988).

tion is searched. There are, however, authoritative sources for the verification of each type of material. These are listed later in the chapter under headings for specific types of material.

Critical to a correct citation is the avoidance of abbreviations, acronyms, and initials. Initials or abbreviations should be used only if they are officially part of the main entry or access point of the item. If the main entry or title is a series of initials, it should be so cited, but subsequently spelled out in full within parentheses, especially for scientific, technical, and foreign-language publications. An acronym should be spelled out within parentheses also. However, if the citation is abbreviated in the source of reference and the borrowing library has no tools to determine what the abbreviation stands for, it is necessary to send the request exactly as given. Guessing only leads to difficulties. To avoid mistakes, include a copy of the source of information or add a note explaining that the citation is exactly as given in the source of reference.

Misspelled names (and other words) and typographical errors on request forms cause more trouble than any other mistakes in the citations libraries receive. For typed forms, this problem continues to require constant vigilance. With electronic transfer of bibliographic information, the problem has largely been circumvented. Care must still be taken, however, to see that all the important information has been transferred and not omitted. Remember that electronic information was created by humans and therefore is subject to error.

The correct author (main entry or main access point) for the needed work is still of importance because the borrowing library rarely knows intimately the cataloging practices of the lender—how the item will be entered in the lender's catalog. Which set of cataloging rules was used to build the catalog or what can be searched electronically by subject or key word is information about a lender not usually known. With such a variety of approaches possible, and such uncertainty about the lender, the need for complete and accurate bibliographic description, based as well as one is able on established cataloging norms, remains. Requests will usually be searched in

routine fashion by interlibrary lending staff (sometimes lacking in bibliographic training) who must find the entry in the online public access catalog, general card catalog, or serials records, which may contain millions of entries. If you make the checking process as easy as possible for the lending library, you are more likely to get what you want. Rarely does a library with a large lending volume have time to unscramble citations.

The correct author (main entry or main access point) can be, in fact, any of several entities:

> The person or group responsible for the intellectual content of an entire work. This may be an author, composer, creator, or originator. This may take the form of a personal name, a pseudonym, a corporate body, a government agency, or an association.[3]

A personal author is easily recognized. A corporate body may be a business, a government, a society, or an institution. A corporate author may include a committee, department, bureau, or other subdivision of an organization. Titles, on the other hand, are being used with greater frequency as the main entry or main access point. With exact titles, the lender's online public access catalog can be readily searched.

Using online union catalogs, such as OCLC (Online Computer Library Center), RLIN (Research Libraries Information Network), and WLN, as well as sources available on the Internet, one can often determine correct citations as well as provide locations. The variety of possible search strategies makes using these sources a top priority.

For those hard-to-find citations, develop a search strategy for verifying and completing the information in a citation. Decide whether to try an author, title, or subject approach; more than one approach is frequently required. Consider the language of the material, the format of the material, and the date. Think about reference books covering a specific language or a specific locality, state, region, or country. "National" bibliographies can be very helpful. Sometimes a bibliography of a particular library's holdings can be used. Reflect about

3. National Information Standards Organization, *Interlibrary Loan Data Elements: American National Standard for Interlibrary Loan Data Elements,* National Information Standard Series ANSI/NISO Z39.63–1989 (New Brunswick, N.J.: Transaction Publishers, 1990), 7. (Revised edition in press)

what the most appropriate reference tool in your library might be. Using a subject approach, look in the online public access catalog or the card catalog under a particular subject with the subdivision —Abstracts, —Bibliography, —Indexes, or Bibliography—Catalogs or Periodicals—Indexes to discover reference tools that may have slipped your mind. For older print catalogs and other sources see Ruth Freitag's "Bibliography of Verification Sources."[4]

Remember that for a particular subject you may have to go to a more general overview, or conversely, a more specific aspect. For example, checking unsuccessfully in *Social Sciences Index* may indicate that the more specific *Sociological Abstracts* should be consulted next.[5] Examine *Guide to Reference Books* for additional pertinent titles.[6] Be imaginative in looking at bibliographies, abstracts, indexes, and other reference tools because the arrangement of each will vary.

The elements of correct citations, common bibliographic tools and services, and illustrative figures are shown below as an approach to verification. "Verification Sources: Standard Abbreviations" can be found in the OCLC's *Interlibrary Loan User Guide*.[7] During the verification process, correct the patron request form so that the information will be ready for transmission. Whether your library's card catalog, online public access catalog, or serials records are checked before or after verification is a matter of choice. Remember, though, that your own library's records must be checked, and they must be checked using the correct cataloging information (the Code, 2.1). You may wish to check your library's order and processing files as well to see if the material is expected to arrive shortly or if it is being cataloged.

The key to harmony in interlibrary loan relationships is to ask another library only for what it owns (the Code, 4.3). Determining in advance which library owns the wanted item will do more to increase the proportion of requests filled than any

other preparation the borrowing library can make. Requests for materials that the lending library does not own wastes the time and money of the borrowing library and the lending library, as well as delays filling the request for the patron. Of particular importance is the use of union lists, whether online or in paper format, to determine that a lender actually owns the *volume* of a periodical that is needed. It may well be necessary to consult both print and online sources to verify and locate the needed item. Not all libraries have all of the sources listed below. It is important to make full use of the ones that you do have for verification and location purposes.

Books and Pamphlets

The elements of a correct citation for books and pamphlets include author, title, edition, place of publication, publisher, date of publication, and series. The discussion below will help in understanding the importance of a correct citation. For an example of a complete book citation correctly typed on an ALA Interlibrary Loan Request form, see figure 1.

ELEMENTS OF A CORRECT CITATION
Author

Individual personal author's names should be given in full: surname, followed by a comma and then by first names. Author's birth and death dates for relatively common names may be helpful and should be included when searching indicates there is more than one author with the same name. For multiple authors, citing the first one is sufficient. Remember that foreign authors' names may not be given in the same order as in English. Entries for corporate authors, anonymous classics, etc., should follow the Library of Congress and Anglo-American cataloging norms and be given in their entirety.

---

4. Ruth Freitag, "Bibliography of Verification Sources," in *Interlibrary Loan Practices Handbook,* by Virginia Boucher (Chicago: American Library Association, 1984), 183–91.

5. *Social Sciences Index,* vol. 1– (New York: Wilson, 1974–); *Sociological Abstracts,* vol. 1– (San Diego, Calif.: Sociological Abstracts, 1952–). Check for these also in online and computer disk format.

6. *Guide to Reference Books,* 11th ed., ed. Robert Balay (Chicago: American Library Association, 1996).

7. OCLC Online Computer Library Center, *Interlibrary Loan User Guide* (Dublin, Ohio, 1992), appendix D.

Request no.: | Date: 022696 | Need before: 040196 | Notes:

Call No.

INTERLIBRARY LOAN SERVICE
UNIVERSITY LIBRARIES, CAMPUS BOX 184
UNIVERSITY OF COLORADO
BOULDER, CO 80309

BORROWING
LIBRARY

FILL IN LEFT
HALF OF FORM
INCLUDING
BOTH LIBRARY
ADDRESSES
IN FULL

FOLD
HERE

Patron information:
Book author; OR, Serial title, volume, issue, date, pages; OR, Audiovisual title:
Gailey, Christine Ward

Pobble, Henrietta

Book title, edition, imprint, series; OR, Article author, title: ☐ This edition only
Kinship to kingship. Austin, TX: Univ. of Texas Press, 1987.
(Texas Press sourcebooks in anthropology; no. 14)

recycled paper

SEND SHEETS
A, B AND C
TO LENDING
LIBRARY, AND
ENCLOSE
SHIPPING
LABEL

Verified in; AND/OR, Cited in: CARL, OPAC:CSU
ISBN, ISSN, LCCN, or other bibliographic number: ISBN 02927245X

Interlibrary Loan Department
Colorado State University Library
Ft. Collins, CO 80523

LENDING
LIBRARY

FILL IN PER-
TINENT ITEMS
UNDER
REPORTS.
RETURN SHEETS
B AND C TO
BORROWING
LIBRARY

Request complies with
( ) 108(g) (2) Guidelines (CCG)
( ) other provisions of copyright law (CCL)

Authorization: V. Boucher

Telephone: (303) 492-6176

REV 11/88

A

TYPE OF REQUEST:
(X) LOAN: WILL PAY FEE Up To $20.00
( ) PHOTOCOPY: MAX. COST $
( )

LENDING LIBRARY REPORT: Date
Date shipped _____ Shipped via _____
Insured for $ _____ Charges $ _____
DUE _____ ( ) Return insured
Packing Requirements
RESTRICTIONS: ( ) Library use only
( ) Copying not permitted ( ) No renewals

NOT SENT BECAUSE: ( ) In use ( ) Lacking
( ) Not owned ( ) At bindery ( ) Cost exceeds limit
( ) Non Circulating ( ) Not found as cited
( ) Not on Shelf ( ) Poor Condition ( ) Lost
( ) Lacks copyright compliance ( ) On order
( ) Vol/issue not yet available ( ) On reserve
( ) In process ( ) Rerequest on
( ) Hold placed
( ) Estimated Cost of Loan $
Photocopy $ _____ Microfilm/fiche $
( ) Prepayment required

BORROWING LIBRARY RECORD:
Date received 3/6/96 Date returned 3/20/96
Returned via _____ Insured for $ _____
Payment provided $ _____

RENEWALS:
Date requested _____
New due date _____
Renewal denied _____

ALA INTERLIBRARY LOAN REQUEST FORM

FIGURE 1.   ALA Interlibrary Loan Request Form: Book (Note "Borrowing Library Record")

Title

Give the title in full unless it is exceedingly long. In that case, give an understandable portion followed by an ellipsis to indicate missing words. Accuracy in giving the exact words in the proper sequence is particularly important for searching titles. (A lender may use the title as a first choice for searching an online public access catalog.)

Edition

Indicate which edition is required, if appropriate. Indicate that "This edition only" is needed when necessary. State "Any edition" if that is acceptable. Not all works have edition statements.

Place of publication

This information is helpful in determining the country in which a work was published and for matching what is found with what is desired, especially when a particular edition is required.

Publisher

This is also important for matching what is found with what is desired and in sorting out editions.

Date of publication

This date is very important in distinguishing between similar materials and in some cases indicating where a lending library is to search its records. Be certain to include this.

Series

A series is "a group of separate bibliographic items often related to one another by subject and usually issued by the same publisher in a uniform style—bearing a collective title of each item. May be known as a monograph series." [8] This often neglected piece of information can be of vital importance in finding library materials. Where parts of a series are not cataloged separately, looking for a call number under the series entry is the only way to locate material. Do include this information and include it in the format established by cataloging rules when possible. On cataloging

records, the MARC (machine-readable cataloging) tag 440 indicates a series that has an added entry as a title. The 490 tag indicates a series that has an added entry different from the way it appears in this field. Check the 800, 810, 811, or 830 MARC tags for correct entry. Not all works are issued in a series.

SUGGESTED REFERENCE TOOLS FOR BOOKS AND PAMPHLETS

- **Online union catalogs (a first choice for verification and location)**

OCLC (Online Computer Library Center)

RLIN (Research Libraries Information Network)

WLN

- **Online public access catalogs and using the Internet to find library catalogs (for verification and location)**

For help finding online public access catalogs and using the Internet, consult the following:

OPAC Directory: An Annual Guide to Internet-Accessible Online Public Access Catalogs. Westport, Conn.: Mecklermedia, 1994– .

Gale Directory of Databases. 1993– . Detroit: Gale, 1993– . Available online: Data-Star, ORBIT, and Questel.

Krol, Ed. *The Whole Internet User's Guide and Catalog.* 2nd ed. Sebastopol, Calif.: O'Reilly & Associates, 1994.

Newby, Gregory B. *Directory of Directories on the Internet; A Guide to Information Sources.* Westport, Conn.: Meckler, 1994.

Thompson, Hugh A., comp. *Internet Resources: A Subject Guide.* Chicago: American Library Association, 1995.

- **United States national catalogs (for verification and location)**

National Union Catalog, Pre-1956 Imprints. 685 vols. London: Mansell, 1968–80.

---

8. National Information Standards Organization, *Interlibrary Loan Data Elements: American National Standard for Interlibrary Loan Data Elements,* National Information Standard Series ANSI/NISO Z39.63–1989 (New Brunswick, N.J.: Transaction Publishers, 1990), 22. (Revised edition in press)

———. *Supplement.* Vols. 686–754. London: Mansell, 1980–81.

National Union Catalog. Washington, D.C.: Library of Congress, 1953–83.
1953–57, 28 vols.
1958–62, 54 vols.
1963–67, 72 vols.
1968–72, 119 vols.
1973–77, 135 vols.
1978, 16 vols.
1979, 16 vols.
1980, 18 vols.
1981, 15 vols.
1982, 21 vols.

National Union Catalog: Books. Washington, D.C.: Library of Congress, 1983– , microfiche.

National Union Catalog: Register of Additional Locations. Washington, D.C.: Library of Congress, 1969–80.
1963–67, vols. 60–67 of NUC
1968–72, vols. 105–119 of NUC
1973, 2 vols.
1974, 2 vols
1975, 2 vols.
1976, 2 vols.
1977, 2 vols.
1978, 2 vols.
1979, 2 vols.

National Union Catalog: Register of Additional Locations. Cumulative microform edition, 1968/79– . Washington, D.C.: Library of Congress, 1980– , microfiche.

Library of Congress Information System (LOCIS). Via the Internet, *LOCIS* includes more than 26 million records in 35 different files. *LOCIS* URL: <telnet://locis.loc.gov>. These files include LC's MARC (machine-readable cataloging) files; copyright files, 1978 to the present; and federal bill status files. See *LOCIS* manuals for information about searching these files.[9]

Dictionary Catalog of the National Agricultural Library, 1862–1965. 73 vols. New York: Rowman & Littlefield, 1967–70.

National Agricultural Library Catalog. Vol. 1– , Jan. 1966– . Totowa, N.J.: Rowman & Littlefield, 1966– . Quinquennial cumulations; 1971– quinquennial cumulations issued in index forms.

AGRICOLA (AGRICultural OnLine Access) [database online]. Beltsville, Md.: National Agricultural Library, 1970– . Available on CD-ROM. Available online: DIALOG, OCLC EPIC, OCLC FirstSearch, etc.

National Library of Medicine Catalog, 1948–1965. Washington, D.C.: Library of Congress, 1949–66.
1948, 1 vol.
1949, 1 vol.
1950–54, 6 vols.
1955–59, 6 vols.
1960–65, 6 vols.

National Library of Medicine Current Catalog. Washington, D.C.: U.S. Government Printing Office, 1966– .
1965–70, 7 vols.
1971–75, 5 vols.
1976–80, 72 microfiche
1981– .

■ **Other national or international catalogs (for verification and sometimes location)**

Examples:

The British Library General Catalogue of Printed Books to 1975. 360 vols. London: C. Bingley; New York: K. G. Saur, 1979–87.

———. *Supplement.* 6 vols. London and New York: K. G. Saur, 1987–88.

The British Library General Catalogue of Printed Books. London and New York: K. G. Saur, 1983–90.
1976–82, 50 vols.
1982–85, 26 vols.

---

9. *LOCIS, Library of Congress Information System: Reference Manual* (Washington, D.C.: Library of Congress Cataloging and Distribution Service, 1994); *LOCIS, Library of Congress Information System, Quick Search Guide* (Washing-ton, D.C.: Library of Congress Cataloging and Distribution Service, 1994). Search guides are available online. URL: <gopher://marvel.loc.gov:70/11/locis/guides>.

1986–87, 22 vols.
1988–89, 28 vols.

British Library Catalogue: Document Supply Centre (Monographs) [database online]. Boston Spa, Wetherby, West Yorkshire, U.K.: British Library Document Supply Centre, 1980– . Corresponds to microfiche and *Boston Spa Books on CD-ROM.* Available online: BLAISE-LINE.

■ **Center for Research Libraries (for verification and location)**

CRLCATALOG [database online]. Chicago: Center for Research Libraries, 1993– . URL: <telnet:// crlcatalog.uchicago.edu>. At log-in and password prompts, enter "guest."

Center for Research Libraries. *Catalog.* Microfiche edition. Chicago: Center for Research Libraries, 1982.

———. *Catalog: Supplement.* Chicago: Center for Research Libraries, 1989, microfiche.

———. *Handbook.* Chicago: Center for Research Libraries, 1990.

■ **Large research library catalogs (for verification and location)**

Example:

University of Texas at Austin. Library. Latin American Collection. *Catalog of the Latin American Collection.* 31 vols. Boston: Hall, 1969.

———. *Supplements 1–4.* 19 vols. Boston: Hall, 1971–77. Continued by *Bibliographic Guide to Latin American Studies.* Vol. 1– , 1978– . Boston: Hall, 1979– .

■ **Bibliographies (for verification)**

Example:

Shoemaker, Richard H. *Checklist of American Imprints for 1820–1829.* 10 vols. New York: Scarecrow, 1964–71.

■ **Databases online or on computer disk (for verification)**

Example:

ERIC (Educational Resources Information Center) [database online]. Rockville, Md.: U.S. Office of Educational Research and Improvement, ERIC Processing and Reference Facility,

1966– . Contains indexing from *Current Index to Journals in Education* and *Resources in Education.* Available on CD-ROM. Available online: CDP Online, DIALOG, OCLC EPIC, OCLC FirstSearch, etc.

■ **Other sources (for verification)**

Cumulative Book Index. 1928/32– . New York: Wilson, 1933– . Available on CD-ROM. Available online: WILSONLINE, and planned for CDP Online, OCLC EPIC, OCLC FirstSearch, etc.

Books in Print. 1948– . New York: Bowker, 1948– . Also issued as microfiche, 1982– .

Books in Print Online [database online]. New York: Bowker. (current information) Corresponds to *Books in Print, Subject Guide to Books in Print, Forthcoming Books, Books in Print Supplement,* and other Bowker bibliographies. Available online: CDP Online, DIALOG, OCLC FirstSearch, etc.

Books in Print Plus [computer disk]. New York: Bowker, 1979– . Corresponds to *Books in Print, Subject Guide to Books in Print, Forthcoming Books, Books in Print Supplement,* and other Bowker bibliographies.

Whitaker's Books in Print. 1988– . London: Whitaker, 1988– . Continues *British Books in Print.*

Bowker-Whitaker Global Books in Print Plus. 1993– . [computer disk]. New York: Bowker, 1993– . Includes *Books in Print, Bookbank, International Books in Print, Australian Books in Print, New Zealand Books in Print,* and the *Canadian Telebook Agency.*

Forthcoming Books. Vol. 1– . New York: Bowker, 1966– . Included in *Books in Print Online* and *Books in Print Plus.*

Paperbound Books in Print. 1971– . New York: Bowker, 1971– . Included in *Books in Print Online* and *Books in Print Plus.*

Scientific and Technical Books and Serials in Print. 1972– . New York: Bowker, 1972– . Included in *Books in Print Online* and *Books in Print Plus.*

Children's Books in Print. 1980/83– . New York: Bowker, 1983. Included in *Books in Print Online* and *Books in Print Plus.*

Books and Periodicals Online. Edited by Nunchine Nobari. New York: Library Alliance, 1994.

Fulltext Sources Online. Needham, Mass.: Biblio-Data, 1988– .

Guide to Reprints: An International Bibliography of Scholarly Reprints. 1967– . Kent, Conn.: Guide to Reprints, 1967– .

Books in Series 1876–1949. 3 vols. New York: Bowker, 1982.

Books in Series. 1st ed.– . New York: Bowker, 1977– .

Children's Catalog. 16th ed. New York: Wilson, 1991.

———. *Supplement.* 1992– . New York: Wilson, 1992– .

Fiction Catalog. 12th ed. New York: Wilson, 1991.

———. *Supplement.* 1992– . New York: Wilson, 1993– .

Middle and Junior High School Library Catalog. 7th ed. New York: Wilson, 1995.

Public Library Catalog. 9th ed. New York: Wilson, 1989.

———. *Supplement.* 1989– . New York: Wilson, 1989– .

Senior High School Library Catalog. 14th ed. New York: Wilson, 1992.

———. *Supplement.* 1993– . New York: Wilson, 1993– .

Use a search strategy such as that outlined above to discover many others.

Periodical Articles

The elements of a correct citation for periodical articles include title of periodical, volume, issue number or issue date, year, author of article, title of article, and pages to be copied. The discussion below will help in understanding the importance of a correct citation. For an example of a complete periodical article citation correctly typed on an ALA Interlibrary Loan Request form, see figure 2.

ELEMENTS OF A CORRECT CITATION

Title of periodical
Use no abbreviations, if possible. If the periodical has changed its name, the entry should be under the name it had at the time of the issue needed, with the latest name given in brackets. If several periodicals have similar names, include issuing body (very important) and the place of publication. The International Standard Serials Number (ISSN) can be included for help in identifying the exact title needed.

Volume, issue number or issue date, year
Always give the volume number, issue number or issue date, and the year. The complete date is especially helpful for recent issues or for periodicals issued with great frequency. When the volume and the year do not "match" for a given title, the request is usually returned unfilled. Indicating when the needed material is located in a supplement is important.

Author of article, title of article, pages
Give the author's last name with the initials for the first names. Multiple authors are usually not necessary. Give enough of the title so that there can be no doubt about what is wanted. If this is not possible, mention the subject of the article. Give inclusive pagination. If the ending page is not known, give a beginning page and a dash to indicate that the entire article is wanted, put "eoa" (end of article) after a dash, or add a note, "entire article needed." Remember that replacement pages for periodicals may not correspond to an entire article. Inaccurate requesting of pages often results in an unfilled request.

Serial item and contribution identifier
This identifier, where available, is a code for the exact periodical article citation. It includes the ISSN of the journal, volume, issue, page number (or screen location), and article or contribution title.

SUGGESTED REFERENCE TOOLS FOR PERIODICAL TITLES

■ **Periodical title abbreviations (for verification of correct titles)**

Periodical Title Abbreviations. 1st ed.– . Detroit: Gale, 1969– .

OCLC Online Computer Library Center. *Interlibrary Loan User Guide.* Dublin, Ohio: OCLC, 1992, appendix D.

A

TYPE OF REQUEST:
( ) LOAN: WILL PAY FEE
(X) PHOTOCOPY: MAX. COST $ $15.00
( )

LENDING LIBRARY REPORT: Date
Date shipped _____ Shipped via _____
Insured for $ _____ Charges $ _____
DUE _____ ( ) Return insured
Packing Requirements _____

RESTRICTIONS: ( ) Library use only
( ) Copying not permitted ( ) No renewals
( )

NOT SENT BECAUSE: ( ) In use ( ) Lacking
( ) Not owned ( ) At bindery ( ) Cost exceeds limit
( ) Non Circulating ( ) Not found as cited
( ) Not on Shelf ( ) Poor Condition ( ) Lost
( ) Lacks copyright compliance ( ) On order
( ) Vol/issue not yet available ( ) On reserve
( ) In process ( ) Rerequest on
( ) Hold placed
( ) Estimated Cost of Loan $
Photocopy $ _____ Microfilm/fiche $ _____
( ) Prepayment required

BORROWING LIBRARY RECORD:
Date received _3/11/96_ Date returned _____
Returned via _____ Insured for $ _____
Payment provided $ _No charge_

RENEWALS:
Date requested _____
New due date _____
Renewal denied _____

ALA INTERLIBRARY LOAN REQUEST FORM

DEMCO
Madison, Wis.
Fresno, Calif.
NO. 165-270

Request no.: _____ Date: 2/26/96 Need before: 4/15/96 Notes:

Call No.

BORROWING LIBRARY

→ FILL IN LEFT HALF OF FORM INCLUDING BOTH LIBRARY ADDRESSES IN FULL

INTERLIBRARY LOAN SERVICE
UNIVERSITY LIBRARIES, CAMPUS BOX 184
UNIVERSITY OF COLORADO
BOULDER, CO 80309

Patron information: Counterpoint, Annamaria
Book author; OR, Serial title, volume, issue, date, pages; OR, Audiovisual title:

Astronomy, V.22, April 1994: 30-7.

FOLD →
HERE

♻ recycled paper

Book title, edition, imprint, series; OR, Article author, title: ☐ This edition only

Robinson, M.S.   Exploring Small Volcanos on Mars

SEND SHEETS A, B AND C TO LENDING LIBRARY, AND ENCLOSE SHIPPING LABEL

Verified in; AND/OR, Cited in: RG 1994: 2323,   OCLC# 1787772
ISBN, ISSN, LCCN, or other bibliographic number:

LENDING LIBRARY

→ FILL IN PERTINENT ITEMS UNDER REPORTS, RETURN SHEETS B AND C TO BORROWING LIBRARY

Interlibrary Loan Department
Colorado State University Library
Ft. Collins, CO 80523

Request complies with
(X) 108(g) (2) Guidelines (CCG)
( ) other provisions of copyright law (CCL)

Authorization: V. Boucher
Telephone: (303) 492-6176

REV 11/88

FIGURE 2. ALA Interlibrary Loan Request Form: Periodical Article (Note "Photocopy; Max. cost $," copyright representation—"Request complies with . . . ," and "Borrowing Library Record")

Chemical Abstracts Service Source Index, 1907–1989. 3 vols. Columbus, Ohio: Chemical Abstracts Service, 1990.

———. *Annual Cumulation*. 1990– . Columbus, Ohio: Chemical Abstracts Service, 1990– . Available online: ORBIT.

■ **Online union catalogs (a first choice for verification and location)**

OCLC (Online Computer Library Center). The MARC tag 245 field is the best choice for a periodical title. The MARC tag 510 field lists where that periodical is indexed.

RLIN (Research Libraries Information Network)

WLN

■ **Online public access catalogs and using Internet to find library catalogs (for verification and location)**

For help in finding online public access catalogs and help in using the Internet consult the following:

OPAC Directory: An Annual Guide to Internet-Accessible Online Public Access Catalogs. Westport, Conn.: Mecklermedia, 1994– .

Gale Directory of Databases. 1993– . Detroit: Gale, 1993– . Available online: Data-Star, ORBIT, and Questel.

Krol, Ed. *The Whole Internet User's Guide and Catalog*. 2nd ed. Sebastopol, Calif.: O'Reilly & Associates, 1994.

Newby, Gregory B. *Directory of Directories on the Internet; A Guide to Information Sources*. Westport, Conn.: Meckler, 1994.

Thompson, Hugh A., comp. *Internet Resources: A Subject Guide*. Chicago: American Library Association, 1995.

■ **Union lists of periodicals (for verification and location)**

OCLC (Online Computer Library Center) Union Lists

New Serial Titles: A Union List of Serials Commencing Publication after December 31, 1949, 1950–1970 Cumulative. 4 vols. New York: Bowker, 1973.

New Serial Titles. Washington, D.C.: Library of Congress, 1976–89.
1971–75, 2 vols.

1976–80, 2 vols.
1981–85, 6 vols.
1986–88, 6 vols.

New Serial Titles. 1990 Annual Cumulation– . Washington, D.C.: Library of Congress, 1991– .

Union List of Serials in Libraries of the United States and Canada. 3rd ed. 5 vols. Edited by Edna Brown Titus. New York: Wilson, 1965.

Chemical Abstracts Service Source Index, 1907–1989. 3 vols. Columbus, Ohio: Chemical Abstracts Service, 1990.

———. *Annual Cumulation*. 1990– . Columbus, Ohio: Chemical Abstracts Service, 1990– . Available online: ORBIT.

British Union-Catalogue of Periodicals: A Record of the Periodicals of the World, from the Seventeenth Century to the Present Day, in British Libraries. 4 vols. London: Butterworths, 1955–58.

———. *Supplement to 1960*. London: Butterworths, 1962.

British Union-Catalogue of Periodicals, Incorporating the World List of Scientific Periodicals; New Periodical Titles. 17 vols. London: Butterworths, 1964–80.

Serials in the British Library Together with Locations and Holdings of Other British and Irish Libraries. No. 1– . London: British Library, Bibliographic Services Division, 1981– . Also available in microfiche.

Boston Spa Serials on CD-ROM [computer disk]. Boston Spa, Wetherby, West Yorkshire, U.K.: British Library Document Supply Centre, 1989– . Corresponds to *Keyword Index to Serial Titles* available on microfiche.

Current Serials Received. Boston Spa, Wetherby, West Yorkshire, U.K.: British Library Lending Division, 1977–85.

———. Boston Spa, Wetherby, West Yorkshire, U.K.: British Library Document Supply Centre, 1986– .

National Union List of Current Japanese Serials in East Asian Libraries in North America. Compiled by Yakuko Makino and Mihoko Miki. n.p.: Subcommittee on Japanese Materials,

Committee on East Asian Libraries, Association for Asian Studies, 1992.

Smits, Rudolf. *Half a Century of Soviet Serials, 1917–1958* . . . 2 vols. Washington, D.C.: Library of Congress, 1968.

■ **Other catalogs (for verification and location)**

National Union Catalog, Pre-1956 Imprints. For details, see "Books and Pamphlets," above.

■ **Center for Research Libraries (for verification and location)**

CRLCATALOG [database online]. Chicago: Center for Research Libraries, 1993– . URL: <telnet: //crlcatalog.uchicago.edu>. At log-in and password prompts, enter "guest."

Center for Research Libraries. *Catalog.* Microfiche edition. Chicago: Center for Research Libraries, 1982.

———. *Catalog: Supplement.* Microfiche edition. Chicago: Center for Research Libraries, 1989.

———. *Handbook.* Chicago: Center for Research Libraries, 1990.

■ **Other sources (for verification)**

Faxon Guide to Serials. Westwood, Mass.: Faxon, 1992– .

Hudson's Subscription Newsletter Directory. Rhinebeck, N.Y.: Hudson's Subscription Newsletter Directory, 1989– .

National Directory of Magazines. 1st ed.– . New York: Oxbridge Communications, 1988– .

Newsletters in Print. 4th ed. 1988/89– . Detroit: Gale, 1988– .

Oxbridge Directory of Newsletters. 1979– . New York: Oxbridge Communications, 1979– .

Serials & Newspapers in Microform. 1992/93– . Ann Arbor, Mich.: UMI, 1992– .

Serials Directory: An International Reference Book. Birmingham, Ala.: EBSCO, 1986– . Available on CD-ROM.

Standard Periodical Directory. 1st ed.– . New York: Oxbridge Communications, 1964– .

Ulrich's International Periodicals Directory. 1st ed.– . New York: Bowker, 1932– . (Entries include the following information of particular interest: ISSN, language of publication, format,

where indexed, document suppliers, and CCC registration notation.) Available as *Ulrich's Plus* on CD-ROM. Available online: DIALOG.

Ulrich's Update. Vol. 1, no. 1– . New York: Bowker, 1988– .

UMI Article Clearinghouse. Ann Arbor, Mich.: UMI, 1984– .

Working Press of the Nation. Vol. 2., *Magazine Directory.* 1st ed.– . New York: National Register Publishing, 1945– .

Books and Periodicals Online. Edited by Nunchine Nobari. New York: Library Alliance, 1994.

The Directory of Electronic Journals, Newsletters and Academic Discussion Lists. 1st ed.– . Washington, D.C.: Association of Research Libraries, Office of Scientific and Academic Publishing, 1991– .

On Internet 94; An International Guide to Electronic Journals, Newsletters, Texts, Discussion Lists, and Other Resources on Internet. Edited by Tony Abbott. Westport, Conn.: Mecklermedia, 1994.

Ulrich's International Periodicals Directory. 34th ed., 1996. Vol. 5, *Indexes, U.S. Newspapers and Newspaper Index.* New Providence, N.J.: Bowker, 1995. "Serials Available on CD-ROM," 9097–136. "Serials Available Online," 9141–262.

Canada Institute for Scientific and Technical Information. *Serials List/Liste des périodiques.* Ottawa, Canada: National Research Council Canada, CISTI, 1995.

Canadian Serials Directory=Répertoire des publications seriées canadiennes. 3rd ed. Edited by Gordon Riley. Toronto: Reference Press, 1987.

Journals in Translation. 5th ed. Boston Spa, Wetherby, West Yorkshire, U.K.: British Library Document Supply Centre, 1991.

Use a search strategy such as that outlined above to discover many others.

SUGGESTED REFERENCE TOOLS FOR PERIODICAL ARTICLES

When the periodical article information given by the patron is incomplete, it may be necessary to verify this information before sending out the request. Incomplete requests frequently come back unfilled. There is an abstracting or indexing service that will cover nearly any subject. Remember that government publications are also a source for abstracts and indexes.

■ **Compact disk and online sources for indexing and abstracting services**

CD-ROM Databases [database online]. Boston: Worldwide Videotex, 1988– . Available online: DIALOG, Newsnet, etc.

The CD-ROM Directory with Multimedia CD's. 1st ed.– . London and Washington: TFPL, 1986– .

CD-ROMs in Print. 1987– . Westport, Conn.: Meckler, 1987– .

Database Directory [database online]. White Plains, N.Y.: Knowledge Industry Publications. (current coverage) Available online: CDP Online.

■ **Subject databases on computer disk or online (for verification and ordering [sometimes])**

Example:

Medline [database online]. Bethesda, Md.: U.S. National Library of Medicine, 1964– . Corresponds to *Index Medicus* and in part to *Index to Dental Literature* and *International Nursing Index.* Available on CD-ROM. Available online: CDP Online, DIALOG, OCLC EPIC, OCLC FirstSearch, PaperChase, etc.

■ **Abstracting and indexing services (for verification)**

Examples are drawn from a multitude of abstracting and indexing services that could be used:

Biological Abstracts. Vol. 1– . Philadelphia: BioSciences Information Service, 1926– . Available on CD-ROM. Available online as *BIOSIS Previews* on CDP Online, DIALOG, OCLC EPIC, OCLC FirstSearch, etc.

Chemical Abstracts. Vol. 1– . Columbus, Ohio: Chemical Abstracts Service, American Chemical Society, 1907– . Available as *CAS-Collective Abstracts* on CD-ROM. Available online as *CA File* on STN International.

Humanities Index. Vol. 1– . New York: Wilson, 1974– . Available on CD-ROM. Available online: WILSONLINE, CDP Online, OCLC EPIC, OCLC FirstSearch.

Psychological Abstracts. Vol. 1– . Arlington, Va.: American Psychological Association, 1927– . Available as *Psychlit* on CD-ROM. Available online as *Psych INFO* on CDP Online, DIALOG, OCLC EPIC, OCLC FirstSearch, etc.

Readers' Guide to Periodical Literature. Vol. 1– . New York: Wilson, 1900– . Available on CD-ROM. Available online: WILSONLINE, CDP Online, OCLC EPIC, and OCLC FirstSearch.

Social Sciences Citation Index. 1972– . Philadelphia: Institute for Scientific Information, 1973– . Available on CD-ROM. Available online as *Social SciSearch* on CDP Online, Data-Star, DIALOG, etc.

Canadian Index. Jan. 1993– . Toronto: Micromedia, 1993– . Merger of *Canadian News Index, Canadian Business Index,* and the *Canadian Magazine Index.*

■ **Vendor periodical table of contents databases (for verification and location)**

Examples:

UnCover [database online]. Denver: UnCover Co., CARL Corporation, 1988– .

Current Contents Search [database online]. Philadelphia: Institute for Scientific Information. (current 2 years) Available online: CDP Online and DIALOG.

SUGGESTED REFERENCE TOOLS FOR THE INDEXING OF PERIODICALS

The following will be useful in discovering where a particular periodical title might be indexed.

OCLC (Online Computer Library Center): The MARC tag 510 field on a bibliographic record lists where a periodical is indexed.

Ulrich's International Periodicals Directory, 1994– 1995. 34th ed. Vol. 1, *Classified List of Subjects, A-D.* New Providence, N.J.: Bowker, 1995. "Abstracting and Indexing Services," xxxii–xliv. "Subject Guide to Abstracting and Indexing," xlv.

The Index and Abstract Directory: An International Guide to Services and Serial Coverage. 1st ed.– . Birmingham, Ala.: EBSCO, 1989– . Includes "Index and Abstract Service Title Listings." A list of all serial titles covered by each service appears under the index/abstract listing.

Katz, Bill, and Linda Sternberg Katz. *Magazines for Libraries*. 8th ed. New York: Bowker, 1995.

Chapter in a Book or Paper in a Proceedings

Special attention must be paid to chapters in books and papers in proceedings. They are frequently very difficult to verify and locate.

ELEMENTS OF A CORRECT CITATION

The elements of a correct citation for a chapter in a book include author (editor or compiler), title, edition, place of publication, publisher, date of publication, and series (if there is one) *and* the author of the chapter (if different from the editor or compiler), the title of the chapter, and the pages (if known). See "Books and Pamphlets," earlier in this section, for comments on the parts of the bibliographic citation and for sources in which to verify and locate the book itself. A photocopy can usually be ordered for a chapter if the book is not available for loan.

One of the elements of a correct citation for a paper in a proceedings is the main entry or access point, including name of the conference, congress, symposium, etc.; the number of the meeting; the place the meeting was held; and the date. In addition, the title, place of publication, publisher, date of publication, and series (if there is one) are required. Then the author of the paper, the title of the paper, and the pages are needed. See "Books and Pamphlets" and "Periodical Articles," in this section, for comments on the parts of the bibliographic citation and for tools in which to verify and locate the proceedings itself. A photocopy can usually be ordered for a paper if the proceedings are not available for loan. Papers can sometimes be obtained by writing to the author and requesting a copy. For an example of a paper in a proceedings correctly entered on an ALA Interlibrary Loan Request form, see figure 3.

SUGGESTED REFERENCE TOOLS FOR PROCEEDINGS

■ **Directories and indexes (for verification)**

Index of Conference Proceedings 1964–1988. Boston Spa, Wetherby, West Yorkshire, U.K.: British Library Document Supply Centre, 1989?, microfiche.

Index of Conference Proceedings. 1989– . Boston Spa, Wetherby, West Yorkshire, U.K.: British Library Document Supply Centre, 1990– . Available on CD-ROM as *Boston Spa Conferences on CD-ROM*. Available online as *Conference Proceedings Index:* BLAISE-LINE. Available on OCLC FirstSearch (PapersFirst, ProceedingsFirst).

Proceedings in Print. Vol. 1– . Arlington, Mass.: Proceedings in Print, 1964– .

Bibliographic Guide to Conference Publications. 1975– . Boston: Hall, 1976– .

Directory of Published Proceedings, Series SEMT —Science/Engineering/Medicine/Technology. Vol. 1– , 1965– . Harrison, N.Y.: InterDok Corp., 1967– .

Directory of Published Proceedings, Series SSH— Social Sciences/Humanities. Vol. 1/4– . Harrison, N.Y.: InterDok Corp., 1968/71– .

Index to Scientific & Technical Proceedings. Jan.-June 1979– . Philadelphia: Institute for Scientific Information, 1979– . Available on CD-ROM.

Index to Social Science & Humanities Proceedings. Jan.-March 1979– . Philadelphia: Institute for Scientific Information, 1979– . Available on CD-ROM.

■ **Online union catalogs (for verification and location)**

OCLC (Online Computer Library Center)

RLIN (Research Libraries Information Network)

WLN

Guide to Searching the Bibliographic Utilities for Conference Proceedings. Chicago: Association of College and Research Libraries, American Library Association, 1994.

Use a search strategy such as that outlined above to discover many others.

Newspapers

Although lending of original paper copies of newspapers is ordinarily precluded by the difficulty and expense of shipping them, many libraries regularly lend newspapers on microfilm. If you have a choice,

A

Request no.: _____ Date: 2/28/96 Need before: 5/15/96 Notes: If not available for loan please copy p.167-69. Our Copy Missing

TYPE OF REQUEST:
( ) LOAN; WILL PAY FEE _____
( ) PHOTOCOPY; MAX. COST $ _____
(X) Will Pay Up To $15.00

Call No.

BORROWING LIBRARY

FILL IN LEFT HALF OF FORM INCLUDING BOTH LIBRARY ADDRESSES IN FULL

INTERLIBRARY LOAN SERVICE
UNIVERSITY LIBRARIES, CAMPUS BOX 184
UNIVERSITY OF COLORADO
BOULDER, CO 80309

LENDING LIBRARY REPORT: Date _____
Date shipped _____ Shipped via _____
Insured for $ _____ Charges $ _____
DUE _____ ( ) Return insured
Packing Requirements

RESTRICTIONS: ( ) Library use only
( ) Copying not permitted ( ) No renewals

Patron information: Croissant, Andre
Book author; OR, Serial title, volume, issue, date, pages; OR, Audiovisual title:
Compilation, critical evaluation, and distribution of stellar data: proceedings of the International Astronomical Union Colloquium no. 35.

NOT SENT BECAUSE: ( ) In use ( ) Lacking
( ) Not owned ( ) At bindery ( ) Cost exceeds limit
( ) Non Circulating ( ) Not found as cited
( ) Not on Shelf ( ) Poor Condition ( ) Lost
( ) Lacks copyright compliance ( ) On order
( ) Vol/issue not yet available ( ) On reserve
( ) In process ( ) Rerequest on _____
( ) Hold placed
( ) Estimated Cost of: Loan $ _____
Photocopy $ _____ Microfilm/fiche $ _____
( ) Prepayment required

FOLD HERE

recycled paper

Book title, edition, imprint, series; OR, Article author, title: ☐ This edition only
Dordrecht, Holland, D. Reidel Pub. Co., 1977. (Astrophysics and space science library, v. 64) Need: Dixon, R.S. A master list of non-stellar objects, p. 167-69.

SEND SHEETS A, B AND C TO LENDING LIBRARY. AND ENCLOSE SHIPPING LABEL

Verified in; AND/OR, Cited in: Astronomy and Astrophys. Abst., v. 19: 002.033
ISBN, ISSN, LCCN, or other bibliographic number: OCLC# 2818094

BORROWING LIBRARY RECORD:
Date received _____ Date returned _____
Returned via _____ Insured for $ _____
Payment provided $ _____

University of Kansas Library
Interlibrary Loan
Watson Library
Lawrence, KS 66045

RENEWALS:
Date requested _____
New due date _____
Renewal denied _____

LENDING LIBRARY

FILL IN PERTINENT ITEMS UNDER REPORTS, RETURN SHEETS B AND C TO BORROWING LIBRARY

Request complies with
(X) 108(g) (2) Guidelines (CCG)
( ) other provisions of copyright law (CCL)

Authorization: V. Boucher
Telephone: (303) 492-6176

ALA INTERLIBRARY LOAN REQUEST FORM

REV 11/88

FIGURE 3. ALA Interlibrary Loan Request Form: Paper in a Proceedings (Note request to copy and copyright representation—"Request complies with . . .")

request the newspaper from a library not located in the city where the newspaper was published; local newspapers are often in high demand in the hometown. Requests for loans of long runs of newspapers on microfilm should usually be limited to a few reels at one time, with the next group to be sent when those reels are returned. Photocopies of pages can be requested from a newspaper. In that case, it is especially important to know the correct page on which the information is found.

The elements of a correct newspaper citation include title of newspaper, section (if known), place of publication, and date (author of article, title of article, and pages, if a photocopy is wanted). For an example of a complete newspaper citation correctly typed on an ALA Interlibrary Loan Request form, see figure 4.

ELEMENTS OF A CORRECT CITATION

Title of newspaper
Newspapers should be entered under the name of the newspaper.

Edition
Some papers specify an edition (e.g., "national edition").

Section
For very large papers, the section can be important.

Place of publication
The place of publication (city, state, and country) should be given if it is not in the title. There are many similar titles, so this is very important.

Date of publication
Give full date whenever possible: month, day, year.

Author of article, title of article, pages
When asking for a photocopy, include this information, if at all possible.

SUGGESTED REFERENCE TOOLS FOR NEWSPAPERS

■ **Online union catalogs (for newspapers in microform and newspaper titles; for verification and location)**

OCLC (Online Computer Library Center)
RLIN (Research Libraries Information Network)
WLN

■ **Additional major resources for newspapers in microform (for verification and location)**

Newspapers in Microform: United States, 1948–1983. Washington, D.C.: Library of Congress, 1984.

Newspapers in Microform: Foreign Countries, 1948–1983. Washington, D.C.: Library of Congress, 1984.

United States Newspaper Program National Union List. 4th ed. Dublin, Ohio: OCLC, 1993. 70 microfiches and 1 guide in binder.

Smets, Kristine, and Adriana Pilecky-Dekajlo, comps. *Foreign Newspapers Held by the Center for Research Libraries.* 2 vols. Chicago: Center for Research Libraries, 1992. Some are paper copies of newspapers only.

Underground Newspaper Microfilm Collection: Table of Contents, 1963–1984. Wooster, Ohio: Bell & Howell, Indexing Center, 1985.

■ **Additional sources for newspaper titles (for verification)**

IMS . . . Ayer Directory of Publications. 1983– . Ft. Washington, Pa.: IMS Press, 1980– . Supersedes *Ayer Directory of Publications.*

Serials and Newspapers in Microform. 1992/93– . Ann Arbor, Mich.: UMI, 1992– .

Working Press of the Nation. Vol. 1, *Newspaper Directory.* 1st ed.– . New York: National Register Publishing, 1945– .

Ulrich's International Periodicals Directory, 1994–95. 33rd ed. Vol. 5, *Newspapers.* New Providence, N.J.: Bowker, 1994.

■ **Sources for newspaper articles (for verification)**

Many newspapers have individual indexes. To find the index for an individual newspaper, consult:

Milner, Anita Cheek. *Newspaper Indexes: A Location and Subject Guide for Researchers.* 3 vols. Metuchen, N.J.: Scarecrow, 1977–82.

Some major newspaper indexes:

National Newspaper Index. 1979– . Los Altos, Calif.: Information Access Corp., 1979– . Index to *Christian Science Monitor, New York Times, Wall Street Journal, Los Angeles Times,* and *Washington Post.* Available on CD-ROM

DEMCO Madison, Wis Fresno, Calif. NO. 165-270

BORROWING LIBRARY

FILL IN LEFT HALF OF FORM INCLUDING BOTH LIBRARY ADDRESSES IN FULL

FOLD HERE

recycled paper

SEND SHEETS A, B AND C TO LENDING LIBRARY, AND ENCLOSE SHIPPING LABEL

LENDING LIBRARY

FILL IN PERTINENT ITEMS UNDER REPORTS, RETURN SHEETS B AND C TO BORROWING LIBRARY

REV 11/88

Request no.:   Date: 2/28/96   Need before: 4/1/96   Notes: Borrow Microfilm, Please.

Call No.

INTERLIBRARY LOAN SERVICE
UNIVERSITY LIBRARIES, CAMPUS BOX 184
UNIVERSITY OF COLORADO
BOULDER, CO 80309

Patron information: Ashford-Croft, Susan
Book author; OR, Serial title, volume, issue, date, pages; OR, Audiovisual title:

Washington Post, Washington, D.C.
August – September, 1991

Book title, edition, imprint, series; OR, Article author, title: ☐ This edition only

Verified in; AND/OR, Cited in: NIM 1948–83, 1:158
ISBN, ISSN, LCCN, or other bibliographic number:

University Of Utah Library
Interlibrary Loan
Salt Lake City, Utah   84112

Request complies with   Authorization: V. Boucher

( ) 108(g) (2) Guidelines (CCG)   Telephone: (303) 492-6176
( ) other provisions of copyright law (CCL)

ALA INTERLIBRARY LOAN REQUEST FORM

TYPE OF REQUEST:
(x) LOAN; WILL PAY FEE Up To $15.00
( ) PHOTOCOPY; MAX. COST $
( )

LENDING LIBRARY REPORT: Date
Date shipped ___ Shipped via ___
Insured for $ ___ Charges $ ___
DUE ___ ( ) Return insured
Packing Requirements

RESTRICTIONS: ( ) Library use only
( ) Copying not permitted ( ) No renewals
( )

NOT SENT BECAUSE: ( ) In use ( ) Lacking
( ) Not owned ( ) At bindery ( ) Cost exceeds limit
( ) Non Circulating ( ) Not found as cited
( ) Not on Shelf ( ) Poor Condition ( ) Lost
( ) Lacks copyright compliance ( ) On order
( ) Vol/issue not yet available ( ) On reserve
( ) In process ( ) Rerequest on
( ) Hold placed
( ) Estimated Cost of: Loan $
Photocopy $ ___ Microfilm/fiche $ ___
( ) Prepayment required

BORROWING LIBRARY RECORD:
Date received ___ Date returned ___
Returned via ___ Insured for $ ___
Payment provided $ ___

RENEWALS:
Date requested ___
New due date ___
Renewal denied ___

FIGURE 4.   ALA Interlibrary Loan Request Form: Newspaper

and microfiche. Available online: CDP Online, Data-Star, DIALOG, etc.

New York Times Index. Vol. 1– . New York: New York Times, 1913– . The *New York Times,* itself, is available from 1989 on as *New York Times Ondisc* and online on NEXIS.

Newspaper Abstracts Ondisc [computer disk]. 1985– . Ann Arbor, Mich.: University Microfilms International, 1987– .

Newsearch [database online]. Foster City, Calif.: Information Access Corp. (current two to six weeks) Available online: DIALOG.

Canadian Index. Jan. 1993– . Toronto: Micromedia, 1993– . Merger of *Canadian News Index, Canadian Business Index,* and the *Canadian Magazine Index.*

■ **Other sources**

Research libraries, local, state, and regional newspaper lists

Use a search strategy such as that outlined above to discover many others.

Dissertations and Masters' Theses

Requests for dissertations and masters' theses usually follow the format for "Books and Pamphlets." Be sure to indicate that the item is a dissertation or thesis. See chapter 4, "Dissertations and Masters' Theses," for more information.

Government Publications and Technical Reports

Special attention should be paid to government publications and technical reports, a baffling field at best. There are several guides that offer help.

Guide to U.S. Government Publications. Edited by Donna Andriot. 1953– . McLean, Va.: Documents Index, 1953– .

Robinson, Judith Schiek. *Tapping the Government Grapevine: The User Friendly Guide to U.S. Government Information Sources.* 2nd ed. Phoenix, Ariz.: Oryx Press, 1993.

Ross, John M. *How to Use the Major Indexes to U.S. Government Publications.* Chicago: American Library Association, 1989.

Sears, Jean L., and Marilyn K. Moody. *Using Government Information Sources, Print and Electronic.* 2nd ed. Phoenix, Ariz.: Oryx Press, 1994.

The elements of a correct citation for a government publication include the usual information for a book or a periodical article *and* the issuing agency, report number, and Superintendent of Documents classification number for United States documents, if known. The date of publication in all cases is absolutely essential. Corporate authors and contract numbers are helpful for technical reports. For examples of complete government publications citations correctly typed on ALA Interlibrary Loan Request forms, see figures 5 and 6.

ELEMENTS OF A CORRECT CITATION

Corporate author

Technical reports are often done on a contract basis. Tracking them down is easier with information concerning the corporate body responsible for the work.

Issuing agency

If the issuing agency is not the main entry or access point, it is especially important to include this information. Many lending libraries retrieve material using the issuing agency to find a call number.

Report number

Report numbers or other identifying numbers are always necessary for retrieving government publications. If in doubt, include the number, espccially in the case of technical reports.

Supt. of Documents classification number

Many libraries arrange their federal publications using this classification scheme. Supplying this number can lead to immediate retrieval from the shelf.

Contract number

Another good way to search for technical reports. Do include this information.

SUGGESTED REFERENCE TOOLS FOR GOVERNMENT PUBLICATIONS AND TECHNICAL REPORTS

■ **Online union catalogs (for verification and location)**

OCLC (Online Computer Library Center)

RLIN (Research Libraries Information Network)

WLN

DEMCO
Madison, Wis
Fresno, Calif.
NO. 165-270

BORROWING LIBRARY

FILL IN LEFT HALF OF FORM INCLUDING BOTH LIBRARY ADDRESSES IN FULL

FOLD HERE

♻ recycled paper

SEND SHEETS A, B AND C TO LENDING LIBRARY, AND ENCLOSE SHIPPING LABEL

LENDING LIBRARY

FILL IN PERTINENT ITEMS UNDER REPORTS, RETURN SHEETS B AND C TO BORROWING LIBRARY

REV 11/88

Request no.: | Date: 2/26/96   Need before: 3/5/96   Notes: Please Rush!

Call No.

INTERLIBRARY LOAN SERVICE
UNIVERSITY LIBRARIES, CAMPUS BOX 184
UNIVERSITY OF COLORADO
BOULDER, CO 80309

Patron information: Lemming, Gus

Book author: OR, Serial title, volume, issue, date, pages; OR, Audiovisual title:

Cadoree, Michelle

Book title, edition, imprint, series; OR, Article author, title: ☐ This edition only

Computer crime and security. Washington, D.C.: Science Reference Section, Science and Technology Division, Library of Congress, 1994.   (LC Tracer bullet)

Verified in; AND/OR, Cited in: MoCat Jan. 1995: 95-2476 OCLC# 31307372
ISBN, ISSN, LCCN, or other bibliographic number: SUDOC# LC33.10:94-1

Aurora Public Library
Interlibrary Loan
14949 E. Alameda Dr.
Aurora, CO 80012

Authorization: V. Boucher

Request complies with   Telephone: (303) 492-6176
( ) 108(g) (2) Guidelines (CCG)
( ) other provisions of copyright law (CCL)

TYPE OF REQUEST:
(X) LOAN: WILL PAY FEE Up To $20.00
( ) PHOTOCOPY: MAX. COST $
( )

LENDING LIBRARY REPORT: Date
Date shipped _____ Shipped via _____
Insured for $ _____ Charges $ _____
DUE _____ ( ) Return insured
Packing Requirements

RESTRICTIONS: (⟩ Library use only
( ) Copying not permitted ( ) No renewals
( )

NOT SENT BECAUSE: ( ) In use ( ) Lacking
( ) Not owned ( ) At bindery ( ) Cost exceeds limit
( ) Non Circulating ( ) Not found as cited
( ) Not on Shelf ( ) Poor Condition ( ) Lost
( ) Lacks copyright compliance ( ) On order
( ) Vol./issue not yet available ( ) On reserve
( ) In process ( ) Rerequest on
( ) Hold placed
( ) Estimated Cost of Loan $
Photocopy $ _____ Microfilm/fiche $
( ) Prepayment required

BORROWING LIBRARY RECORD:
Date received _____ Date returned
Returned via _____ Insured for $
Payment provided $

RENEWALS:
Date requested
New due date
Renewal denied

ALA INTERLIBRARY LOAN REQUEST FORM

A

FIGURE 5. ALA Interlibrary Loan Request Form: Government Publication

DEMCO
Madison, Wis
Fresno, Calif.
NO. 165-270

BORROWING LIBRARY

FILL IN LEFT HALF OF FORM INCLUDING BOTH LIBRARY ADDRESSES IN FULL

FOLD HERE →

recycled paper

SEND SHEETS A, B AND C TO LENDING LIBRARY, AND ENCLOSE SHIPPING LABEL

LENDING LIBRARY

FILL IN PERTINENT ITEMS UNDER REPORTS. RETURN SHEETS B AND C TO BORROWING LIBRARY

REV 11/88

Request no.: | Date: 022696   Need before: 032596   Notes: Microfiche O.K.

Call No.

INTERLIBRARY LOAN SERVICE
UNIVERSITY LIBRARIES, CAMPUS BOX 184
UNIVERSITY OF COLORADO
BOULDER, CO 80309

Patron information: Stalworth, Henry
Book author; OR, Serial title, volume, issue, date, pages; OR, Audiovisual title:

Clarke, N.   PB 95-267654GAR

Book title, edition, imprint, series; OR, Article author, title: ☐ This edition only
Evaluation of California's commercial driver license drive test. Sacramento, CA: Calif. State Dept. of Motor Vehicles Research and Development Section, 1995.

Report # CAL-DMV-RSS-95-149

Verified in: AND/OR, Cited in: GRAI 95 (Dec. 1, 1995):23-03,268
ISBN, ISSN, LCCN, or other bibliographic number:

California State Library
Interlibrary Loan
P.O. Box 2037
Sacramento, CA 95809

Request complies with
( ) 108(g)(2) Guidelines (CCG)
( ) other provisions of copyright law (CCL)

Authorization: V. Boucher

Telephone: (303) 492-6176

TYPE OF REQUEST: Up To $20.00 A
(X) LOAN: WILL PAY FEE
( ) PHOTOCOPY: MAX. COST $
( )

LENDING LIBRARY REPORT: Date
Date shipped _____ Shipped via _____
Insured for $ _____ Charges $ _____
DUE _____ ( ): Return insured
Packing Requirements
RESTRICTIONS: ( ) Library use only
( ) Copying not permitted ( ) No renewals

NOT SENT BECAUSE: ( ) In use ( ) Lacking
( ) Not owned ( ) At bindery ( ) Cost exceeds limit
( ) Non Circulating ( ) Not found as cited
( ) Not on Shelf ( ) Poor Condition ( ) Lost
( ) Lacks copyright compliance ( ) On order
( ) Vol/issue not yet available ( ) On reserve
( ) In process ( ) Rerequest on
( ) Hold placed
( ) Estimated Cost of: Loan $
Photocopy $ _____ Microfilm/fiche $ _____
( ) Prepayment required

BORROWING LIBRARY RECORD:
Date received _____ Date returned _____
Returned via _____ Insured for $ _____
Payment provided $ _____

RENEWALS:
Date requested _____
New due date _____
Renewal denied _____

ALA INTERLIBRARY LOAN REQUEST FORM

FIGURE 6.   ALA Interlibrary Loan Request Form: Technical Report and Microform

- **Online public access catalogs and using the Internet to find library catalogs (for verification and location)**

A particularly good database is that of the online public access catalog of CARL Corporation, "U.S. Government Publications," which contains the Superintendent of Documents cataloging from July 1976 onwards.

For help in finding online public access catalogs and help in using the Internet, consult the following:

OPAC Directory: An Annual Guide to Internet-Accessible Online Public Access Catalogs. Westport, Conn.: Mecklermedia, 1994– .

Gale Directory of Databases. 1993– . Detroit: Gale, 1993– . Available online: Data-Star, ORBIT, and Questel.

Krol, Ed. *The Whole Internet User's Guide and Catalog.* 2nd ed. Sebastopol, Calif.: O'Reilly & Associates, 1994.

Newby, Gregory B. *Directory of Directories on the Internet; A Guide to Information Sources.* Westport, Conn.: Meckler, 1994.

Thompson, Hugh A., comp. *Internet Resources: A Subject Guide.* Chicago: American Library Association, 1995.

- **Federal publications (for verification)**

Monthly Catalog of United States Government Publications. 1895– . Washington, D.C.: U.S. Government Printing Office, 1895– . Available on CD-ROM. Available online: CDP Online, DIALOG, OCLC EPIC, OCLC FirstSearch, etc.

Monthly Catalog of United States Government Publications, Periodicals Supplement. 1985– . Washington, D.C.: U.S. Government Printing Office, 1985– . Also available in microfiche.

Buchanan, William W. *Cumulative Subject Index to the Monthly Catalog, 1900–1971.* 15 vols. Washington, D.C.: Carrollton Press, 1973.

Cumulative Title Index to United States Public Documents, 1789–1976. 16 vols. Arlington, Va.: United States Historical Documents Institute, 1979–82.

GPO Sales Publications Reference File (PRF). Washington, D.C.: U.S. Government Printing

Office, 1977– , microfiche. Available on CD-ROM. Available online: DIALOG.

U.S. Government Books. Washington, D.C.: U.S. Government Printing Office, 1982– .

New Books. Washington, D.C.: U.S. Government Printing Office, 1982– .

C.I.S. Index to Publications of the United States Congress. Vol. 1– . Bethesda, Md.: Congressional Information Service, 1970– . Available on CD-ROM. Available online: DIALOG.

American Statistics Index: A Comprehensive Guide to the Statistical Publications of the U.S. Government. 1973– . Washington, D.C.: Congressional Information Service, 1973– . Also available as part of the *Statistical Masterfile* CD-ROM. Available online: DIALOG.

Government Reports Announcements and Index. 1975– . Washington, D.C.: U.S. Dept. of Commerce, National Technical Information Service, 1975– . Issued since 1946 with variant titles. Available on CD-ROM. Available online: DIALOG.

Index to U.S. Government Periodicals. 18 vols. Chicago: Infordata International, 1970–87. Available on CD-ROM.

U.S. Government Periodicals Index. Vol. 1– , Oct. 1993– . Bethesda, Md.: Congressional Information Service, 1994– .

Catalog of National Archives Microfilm Publications, with Supplementary List of National Archives Microfilm Publications, 1974–82 (bound in back). Washington, D.C.: U.S. General Services Administration, National Archives and Records Service, National Archives Trust Fund Board, 1974, 1982.

- **Older federal publications sources (for verification)**

Poore, Benjamin Perley. *A Descriptive Catalogue of the Government Publications of the United States, September 5, 1774–March 4, 1881.* Washington, D.C.: U.S. Government Printing Office, 1885. (U.S. 48th Congress, 2nd session. Senate. Misc. Doc. 67)

Checklist of United States Public Documents, 1789–1976. Washington, D.C.: United States Historical Documents Institute, 1976? Microfilm.

Checklist of United States Public Documents, 1789–1970: Indexes. Washington, D.C.: United States Historical Documents Institute, 1972.

Ames, John G. *Comprehensive Index to the Publications of the United States Government, 1881–1893.* 2 vols. Washington, D.C.: U.S. Dept. of the Interior, Division of Documents, U.S. Government Printing Office, 1905. (58th Cong., 2nd sess. H. Doc. 754)

U.S. Superintendent of Documents. *Catalog of the Public Documents of the Congress and of All Departments of the Government of the United States.* No. 1–25; March 4, 1893/June 30, 1895–Jan. 1, 1939/Dec. 31, 1940. 25 vols. Washington, D.C.: U.S. Government Printing Office, 1896–1945.

■ **Numerous other government abstracts and indexes (for verification)**

Examples:

Energy Research Abstracts. Vol. 1– . Oak Ridge, Tenn.: Technical Information Center, U.S. Dept. of Energy, 1977– . Available on microfiche and microfilm. Available online: DIALOG.

EPA Publications Bibliography. Vol. 1– . Washington, D.C.: Library Systems Branch, U.S. Environmental Protection Agency, 1977– . Available in microfiche.

INIS Atomindex. Vol. 1– . Vienna: International Atomic Energy Agency, 1970– . Continued in 1973– in microfiche.

Nuclear Science Abstracts. 33 vols. Oak Ridge, Tenn.: Oak Ridge Directed Operations, Technical Information Division, 1948–76.

Scientific and Technical Aerospace Reports. Vol. 1– . Washington, D.C.: National Aeronautics and Space Administration, Office of Scientific and Technical Information, 1963– . Available in microfiche. Available on CD-ROM. Available online: DIALOG.

■ **Patents (for verification and location)**

See appendix J for information on verifying and obtaining U.S. and foreign patents.

■ **State publications (for verification)**

U.S. Library of Congress. Exchange and Gift Division Processing Services. *Monthly Checklist of State Publications.* Vol. 1– . Washington, D.C.: U.S. Government Printing Office, 1910– . Available on microfiche.

Statistical Reference Index: A Selective Guide to American Statistical Publications from Private Organizations and State Government Sources. Washington, D.C.: Congressional Information Service, 1980– . Also available as part of the *Statistical Masterfile* CD-ROM.

■ **Municipal publications (for verification)**

Index to Current Urban Documents. Vol. 1– , 1972– . Westport, Conn.: Greenwood, 1972/73– . Provides access to *Urban Documents Microfiche Collection.*

■ **United Nations and international publications (for verification)**

UNDOC, Current Index: United Nations Documents Index. New York: United Nations Dag Hammarskjöld Library, 1987– . Began with vol. 1, no. 1, Jan./Feb. 1979.

UNDOC, Current Index Cumulative Edition. 1984– . New York: United Nations Dag Hammarskjöld Library, 1986– , microfiche. Continues annual cumulative printed edition of *UNDOC, Current Index.*

Directory of United Nations Information Sources. 1st ed.– . Compiled by Advisory Commmittee for the Co-ordination of Information Systems. New York: United Nations, 1984– .

Index to United Nations Documents and Publications [computer disk]. New York: Readex, 1990–94.

UNBIS Plus on CD-ROM [computer disk]. Alexandria, Va.: Chadwick Healey, 1975– .

International Bibliography, Information, Documentation. 10 vols. New York: Bowker/UNIPUB, 1973–82.

Guide to Official Publications of Foreign Countries. American Library Association, Government Documents Round Table. Bethesda, Md.: Congressional Information Service, 1990.

International Bibliography: Publications of Inter-governmental Organizations. 9 vols. New York: UNIPUB, 1983–91.

Index to International Statistics: A Guide to the Statistical Publications of International Inter-governmental Organizations. 1983/87– . Bethesda, Md.: Congressional Information Service, 1988– . Also available as part of the *Statistical Masterfile* CD-ROM.

See "Books and Pamphlets," "United States national catalogs," above, or use a search strategy such as that outlined above in "Verify borrowing requests and find where material is located" to discover many others. See "Choose a supply source," "Government Publications and Technical Reports Supply Sources," below, for information on how to obtain government publications.

Microforms

If it is not obvious, indicate that a microform is acceptable and which kind is expected, for example, microcard, microfiche, microfilm, or microprint. Indicate whether you want to borrow or purchase a copy. Some libraries do not have the equipment to read certain kinds of microforms. Micro-opaque cards, for example, require special equipment for reading. Paper copies can be made from micro-opaque cards. For information, contact

> University of Missouri Libraries
> 115 Ellis Library
> Columbia, MO 65201-5149
> Telephone: (314) 882-3398
> Fax: (314) 884-5004

For an example of a complete microform citation correctly typed on an Interlibrary Loan Request form, see figure 6.

ELEMENTS OF A CORRECT CITATION

Name of microform project, if there is one

Identifying number

Usual information for book or periodical

SUGGESTED REFERENCE TOOLS FOR MICROFORMS

Consider tools listed under previous categories. Take a look at the following:

Bibliographic Guide to Microform Publications. 1986– . Boston: Hall, 1987– .

Dodson, Suzanne Cates. *Microform Research Collections; A Guide.* 2nd ed. Westport, Conn.: Meckler, 1984.

Index to Microform Collections. Edited by Ann Niles. 2 vols. Westport, Conn.: Meckler, 1984–88.

Primary Sources in History: A Guide to Microform Collections at Arizona State University. Compiled by Elliot S. Palais. 2nd ed. Tempe, Ariz.: Arizona State University, 1991.

Research Collections. Ann Arbor, Mich.: University Microfilms Information Service, 1986– .

U.S. National Archives and Records Administration. *Microfilm Resources for Research: A Comprehensive Catalog.* Washington, D.C.: Published for the National Archives and Records Administration by the National Archives Trust Fund Board, 1996.

Guide to Microforms in Print: Author, Title, Incorporating International Microforms in Print. 1978– . Munich: K. G. Saur, 1978– . Latest publisher given.

Guide to Microforms in Print: Subject, Incorporating International Microforms in Print. 1978– . Munich: K. G. Saur, 1978– . Latest publisher given.

Guide to Microforms in Print: Supplement. Munich: K. G. Saur, 1979– . Latest publisher given.

Microform Market Place: An International Directory of Micropublishing. 1974/75– . Munich and New York: K. G. Saur, 1974– . Latest publisher given.

Micropublishers' Trade List Annual. 1975– . Alexandria, Va.: Chadwyck Healey, 1975– . Latest publisher given. Issued also as microfiche.

National Register of Microform Masters. 16 vols. Washington, D.C.: Library of Congress, 1965–83.

RLIN Register of Microform Masters. Stanford, Calif.: Research Libraries Group, 1989– , microfiche.

Use a search strategy such as that outlined above to discover many others.

Audiovisual Materials

Check the lending library's policy to see if loans will be made before sending an audiovisual request (the Code, 4.3). Audiovisual materials are usually not available for public performance. Copyright and licensing agreements may effect the loan of material; therefore, it helps the lender if the purpose for borrowing and the intended use are indicated. If it is possible to do so and you are planning to show the material, be sure to indicate the date the material is to be shown and alternative dates. Do not copy the audiovisual material without clearing the copyright and checking with the lending library. A telephone number for the borrower allows the lender to clear up problems quickly. For an example of a complete audiovisual citation correctly typed on an ALA Interlibrary Loan Request form, see figure 7.

ELEMENTS OF A CORRECT CITATION

The elements of a correct citation for audiovisual materials may include the following:

Format

Title

Date, if known

Author/composer/performer

Producer or distributor

Language or languages

Captioned: closed or open

Where the citation was found, the call number, and
the internal location can be useful

ADDITIONAL INFORMATION NEEDED

Sound recording
format (cassette tapes, compact disks, reel-to-reel tapes); stereo or monaural; running time

CD-ROM
hardware specifications so it will run on your equipment

Computer software
hardware specifications so it will run on your equipment

Motion pictures
format (8mm, 16mm, 35mm, 70mm); color or black and white; silent or sound; running time

Slides
size (2″ × 2″, 2¼″ × 2¼″, 3″ × 3″); designate format if accompanied by sound; designate type if contained in a projection tray

Videorecordings
format (8mm, high 8mm, VHS, compact VHS, super VHS, compact super VHS, ¾″ Umatic, Betamax, Beta SP, M-II, 1″, videodisc); other formats that are developed[10]

Other
art reproductions, costumes, filmstrips, globes, kits, realia, and any other "stuff" (whatever information you can think of that would help identify and retrieve the material)

SUGGESTED REFERENCE TOOLS
FOR AUDIOVISUAL MATERIALS

■ **Online union catalogs**

OCLC (Online Computer Library Center)

RLIN (Research Libraries Information Network)

WLN

■ **United States national catalogs**

Audiovisual Materials. Washington, D.C.: Cataloging Publication Division, Library of Congress, 1979–82.

Audiovisual Materials. Washington, D.C.: Cataloging Distribution Service, Library of Congress, 1983– , microfiche.

Books on Music and Sound Recordings. Jan./June 1973–89. Washington, D.C.: Library of Congress, 1973–89.

Music Catalog. 1981/90– . Washington, D.C.: Cataloging Distribution Service, Library of Congress, 1991– , microfiche.

Music Catalog on CD-ROM [computer disk]. Washington, D.C.: Cataloging Distribution Service, Library of Congress, 1994– .

AVLINE Catalog. Washington, D.C.: National Library of Medicine, 1975/76– .

---

10. The American Library Association Video Round Table is developing "Guidelines for the Loan of Video and Other Audiovisual Formats." Publication of the completed document was expected in 1996.

DEMCO
Madison, Wis
Fresno, Calif.
NO. 165-270

BORROWING LIBRARY
FILL IN LEFT HALF OF FORM INCLUDING BOTH LIBRARY ADDRESSES IN FULL

FOLD HERE →

recycled paper

SEND SHEETS A, B AND C TO LENDING LIBRARY, AND ENCLOSE SHIPPING LABEL

LENDING LIBRARY
FILL IN PERTINENT ITEMS UNDER REPORTS, RETURN SHEETS B AND C TO BORROWING LIBRARY

REV 11/88

Request no.: _____ Date: 022696 Need before: 031596 Notes: Need For Class Mar. 11-15!

Call No. _____

INTERLIBRARY LOAN SERVICE
UNIVERSITY LIBRARIES, CAMPUS BOX 184
UNIVERSITY OF COLORADO
BOULDER, CO 80309

Patron information: Halfacre, Gerald
Book author; OR, Serial title, volume, issue, date, pages; OR, Audiovisual title:

Momaday, N. Scott

Book title, edition, imprint, series; OR, Article author, title: ☐ This edition only

Storyteller. Santa Fe, N.M.: Sunset Productions, 1992.
Sound Recording: Analog Stereo

Cassette

Verified in; AND/OR, Cited in: OCLC# 30383203
ISBN, ISSN, LCCN, or other bibliographic number:

Aurora Public Library
Interlibrary Loan
14949 E. Alameda Dr.
Aurora, CO 80012

Request complies with
( ) 108(g) (2) Guidelines (CCG)
( ) other provisions of copyright law (CCL)

Authorization: V. Boucher Telephone: (303) 492-6176

TYPE OF REQUEST:
(X) LOAN; WILL PAY FEE Up To $20.00
( ) PHOTOCOPY; MAX. COST $ _____

LENDING LIBRARY REPORT: Date _____
Date shipped _____ Shipped via _____
Insured for $ _____ Charges $ _____
DUE _____ ( ) Return insured
Packing Requirements

RESTRICTIONS: ( ) Library use only
( ) Copying not permitted ( ) No renewals
( ) _____

NOT SENT BECAUSE: ( ) In use ( ) Lacking
( ) Not owned ( ) At bindery ( ) Cost exceeds limit
( ) Non Circulating ( ) Not found as cited
( ) Not on Shelf ( ) Poor Condition ( ) Lost
( ) Lacks copyright compliance ( ) On order
( ) Vol/issue not yet available ( ) On reserve
( ) In process ( ) Rerequest on _____
( ) Hold placed
( ) Estimated Cost of: Loan $ _____
Photocopy $ _____ Microfilm/fiche $ _____
( ) Prepayment required

BORROWING LIBRARY RECORD:
Date received _____ Date returned _____
Returned via _____ Insured for $ _____
Payment provided $ _____

RENEWALS:
Date requested _____
New due date _____
Renewal denied _____

ALA INTERLIBRARY LOAN REQUEST FORM

A

FIGURE 7. ALA Interlibrary Loan Request Form: Audiovisual Request

National Library of Medicine Audiovisuals Catalog. 28 vols. Bethesda, Md.: National Library of Medicine, 1977–93.

■ **Other sources**

A-V Online [database online]. Albuquerque, N.M.: Access Innovations, National Information Center for Educational Media, 1964– . Corresponds in part to NICEM *Film & Video Finder* and *Audiocassette Finder.* Available on CD-ROM. Available online: DIALOG and others.

Audiocassette & Compact Disc Finder. 3rd ed.– . Medford, N.J.: Published for the National Information Center for Educational Media by Plexus Publishing, 1993– . Available on CD-ROM as part of *A-V Online.*

Educational Media Catalogs on Microfiche. 1975– . Hoboken, N.J.: Olympic Media Information, 1975– , microfiche.

Educators' Guide to Free Films. 1st ed.– . Randolph, Wis.: Educators Progress Service, 1941– .

Educators' Guide to Free Filmstrips and Slides. Compiled and edited by John C. Diffor and Elaine Diffor. 55th ed. Randolph, Wis.: Educators Progress Service, 1995.

Educators' Guide to Free Health, Physical Education and Recreation Materials. 1st ed.– . Randolph, Wis.: Educators Progress Service, 1968– .

Film and Video Finder. 1st ed.– . Medford, N.J.: Published for the National Information Center for Educational Media by Plexus Publishing, 1987– . Available on CD-ROM as part of *A-V Online.* Available online: DIALOG and others.

Filmstrip and Slide Set Finder. 1st ed.– . Medford, N.J.: Published for the National Information Center for Educational Media by Plexus Publishing, 1990– . Available on CD-ROM as part of *A-V Online.*

Health Sciences Video Directory. 1977– . New York: Esselte Video, 1977– .

Index to Free Educational Material—Multimedia. 1st ed.– . Los Angeles: National Information Center for Educational Media, University of Southern California, 1978– .

Video Source Book. 1st ed.– . New York: Gale, 1979– . Latest publisher given.

When Not to Verify

Sometimes the local library is not required to verify. Careful attention should be paid to network agreements and practices that provide for verification of requests from the local library by channeling them to another library, the state library, or a network office. Some document delivery services, such as UnCover S.O.S., either verify requests or supply a document without a complete citation for an additional fee.

Requests in Non-Roman Alphabets

Foreign-language materials, including serial titles, should always be requested in the original language (do not translate the title). Requests in non-Roman alphabets present a problem. Librarians should consult their language specialists, if part of the staff, to help find a record that agrees with what the patron wants. If the request must be Romanized, correct standard Romanization is exceedingly important. Sometimes it is necessary to send an ALA Interlibrary Loan Request form with a copy of the source of information, which will usually give the author and title in the original script.

Citing a Source of Verification and Location

Enter the source of verification and location on the patron request form (see appendix E). You may need to refer to the source again for clarification or in the transmission process. Use the name of the online union catalog or the online public access catalog and a bibliographic record identification number or other unique number, provided a search can be made by that number. Such a number may be an OCLC number, RLIN number, WLN number, International Standard Book Number (ISBN), International Standard Serials Number (ISSN), or Library of Congress card number (LCCN). For bibliographic database searches, give the name of the database and the unique identification number for the record. Your library may provide now, or in the future, automatic transfer of bibliographic information from an electronic source to an interlibrary loan request form. In that case, the information provided should be correct. For printed sources, the citation should include a common abbreviation for the reference source and the page number on which the verification was found. If the source of location for the item is different from the verification, the location source should be cited as well. Unusual verification or location sources should be cited in full or with sufficient information so that there can be no doubt which work and page are meant. See figures 1–7 and 13 to see how verification and location sources have been noted.

Unable to Verify a Citation

For items not readily verified by the borrowing librarian, the source of citation given by the patron should be carefully checked to see if the information was correctly copied or if the source gives additional information to help identify the citation. Series notes are especially important. A library may own the series without having the various parts of the series in its catalog. Searching the series as a serial may lead to the item, making an interlibrary loan unnecessary. Remember that online union catalogs, online public access catalogs, the *Union List of Serials, New Serials Titles,* or local serials catalogs may provide locations for the series.

If the library, after a thorough search, is unable to verify a citation, it should include a note, "Cannot verify. Not in . . . " to the lending library. It is helpful to include information about where the item was found (source of information) (the Code, 4.4) including (for books) full author, title, edition, place of publication, publisher, date of publication, series, and page on which the citation appears. For periodical articles, give the title of the periodical, volume, issue number or issue date, year, author of the article, title of the article, and page on which the citation appears. The more complete the information given the lending library, the greater the chance the item will be found. In cases where the citation is very complex, has a long series note, is in a foreign language (especially a non-Roman alphabet), or is abbreviated, it may be necessary to request the material on a paper ALA Interlibrary Loan Request form and attach a photocopy of the page with the citation. When a periodical article citation cannot be found, a request can be made for a photocopy of the "Table of Contents" of a particular issue. Very often a patron can then determine what is needed.

Complete Verifying Procedures

Search under the correct main entry or access point in your online public access or card catalog, serials records, and the outstanding order and processing files. Do not overlook the possibility that the item may have been reprinted in a collection you already own. Listing the library's holdings in reference tools (CD-ROMs or online) can alert the patron to where materials are located in your library. Reference, serials, special collections, and other noncirculating materials owned by your library should not be requested from another library. "Reserve" materials (those with restricted use held for students) are also available in your library and should not be requested from another. If the material is not checked out, make certain it is on the shelf before reminding the patron where to find it. Some libraries pull the material and place it on hold for the patron. Check to see if the material can be printed out or downloaded from an online source. If the material is in use, see if a hold or recall can be placed. You may need to go ahead and borrow if the current user is very slow in returning the item. For materials not yet processed but in the library, a "rush" procedure may be used to speed the material to the patron. If the material is lost, at the bindery, on order, or not actually owned, another library can be asked to supply it. Keep in mind reciprocal borrowing privileges and the possibility of sending the patron to another library for on-site use. Return the patron request form together with a patron response form to the patron if the item is found in the library or if the patron needs to take some action (see appendix G).

Subject Requests

These requests can only be made to libraries that agree to fill them—usually those within a network or consortium. Follow any instructions given by the network or consortium regarding subject requests. Use any special forms supplied for that purpose.

- **Nature of the subject**

Be as exact, definite, and specific as possible

Define words when there is a chance of ambiguity

Include limiting data and special aspects, such as current view, historical or economic data, population, etc.

Give full personal name indicating dates of birth and death, whether living or dead if dates are not known, nationality, and occupation

■ **Type of material needed**

Book

Periodical article

Newspaper

Dissertation or thesis

Government publication

Nonprint, specify

Any type

■ **General requirements**

Purpose of the request, if volunteered by the patron (term paper, speech, club report, business use, research)

Degree of reading difficulty (school grade, college student, adult, health professional, etc.)

Degree of generality (basic, advanced, technical, etc.)

Currency of information

Amount of material needed

Photocopy okay; can pay cost or amount willing to pay

Material already used

Where information has already been sought

Choose a supply source

One of the more difficult and time-consuming tasks in interlibrary loan today is choosing a supply source. A wide variety of libraries and commercial document supply services are available for use. It is necessary to have a detailed knowledge of a number of supply sources and to keep up with the new developments by checking the Internet's interlibrary loan listserv (ILL-L), by reading, talking to others, and trying and evaluating new sources (see appendix GG). Barbra

Buckner Higginbotham and Sally Bowdoin devote a chapter to document suppliers that charge and classify the various services as follows:

Collection-Based Services
    General-Interest Services
    Subject-Specific Services
    Material-Specific Services

Cooperative Clearinghouses

Universal or On-Demand Services

Table of Contents Services (TOCs)

Library Fee-Based Services

Electronic Document Suppliers

Full-Text Online Files[11]

    Eleanor Mitchell and Sheila A. Walters discuss at length many ramifications of document supply in their book, *Document Delivery Services: Issues and Answers.*[12] Of particular interest are case studies of document suppliers' performance found in chapter 5.[13]

    It is wise to use a variety of libraries and services in order to deliver what the patron wants when the item is needed at a reasonable cost and in the desired format. Using a very large number of sources can greatly add to the time it takes to select a supply source. Choosing from a reasonable number of libraries and a select group of commercial document suppliers is a good mix for many libraries. Online union catalogs, where verification and location of material come by using the same source, may simplify choosing a potential supplier for a number of requests. Both the OCLC PRISM Interlibrary Loan system and DOCLINE offer the ability to customize lenders. Having a deposit account with a document supplier may help focus the choice of commercial sources. Separating requests into those that can be returned (books, microfilms, etc.) and those that are kept (photoduplication, microfiche to microfiche copies, etc.) may help in the decision-making process. The factors below must be considered.

---

11. Barbra Buckner Higginbotham and Sally Bowdoin, "Commercial Document Suppliers," in *Access versus Assets* (Chicago: American Library Association, 1993), 144–200.

12. Eleanor Mitchell and Sheila A. Walters, *Document Delivery Services: Issues and Answers* (Medford, N.J.: Learned Information, 1995).

13. Eleanor Mitchell and Sheila A. Walters, "Evaluating Document Delivery Service," in *Document Delivery Services: Issues and Answers* (Medford, N.J.: Learned Information, 1995), 117–47.

Important Considerations When Choosing a Supply Source

Not all conditions apply to all requests. The most important considerations for selecting a supply source follow:

Coverage

Does the supplier have the correct titles, years, current updates, and holdings information? Will the supplier lend or copy obscure items, if needed?

Delivery method

Do you have the equipment or service needed to receive the document? Can the document be sent directly to the patron, if necessary?

Cost

Can you determine the cost if it is passed on to the patron? Is the cost itself reasonable? Are there additional costs for special types of delivery?

Speed of delivery

Is distance a factor? Will the turnaround time be sufficient? Will negative responses be delivered in a timely fashion? Can a "rush" be done to meet a real deadline?

Lending partners

Can a consortial, network, or informal understanding arrangement be used? Is geography a factor in the lending pattern of potential library suppliers? Can the net lending load on a particular library be reduced?

Copyright compliance

Is it necessary to pay royalties? Does the supplier take care of that?

Other Considerations When Choosing a Supply Source

Other factors may come into play when choosing a supplier.

Quality of reproduction

Is the item complete and accurate (no missing pages)? Is it readable? Are the illustrations and graphics there?

Correction of mistakes

How are mistakes handled? Is reordering necessary?

Fill rate

Can the supplier be relied upon to fill most of the requests received?

Ease of access

Is it easy to order and accept delivery? Is re-keying of information necessary?

Ease of financial transactions

Are there deposit accounts, group, or volume discounts available? Can credit cards be used? Can borrowing and lending be balanced? Is the billing procedure especially cumbersome? Does the invoice contain a way to match it with the request? Can invoices be consolidated for larger payments?

Ease of fit with statistical systems

Can transactions be transferred electronically to the statistical system used? Are the transactions easy to read and to identify if keying is needed?

Confidentiality

Will an individual patron's name be retained in conjunction with what is requested?

Transaction support

Can someone respond to questions about how the system operates or what has happened to an individual request?

Libraries as Supply Sources

Unscramble symbols that identify libraries by using the codebooks provided by the online union catalogs or by consulting *Symbols of American Libraries*.[14] Keep in mind and comply with the National Interlibrary Loan Code for the United States, 1993 (the Code, 4.13). Remember local, state, and regional interlibrary loan codes that may apply. Check the lending policies of other libraries (the Code, 4.3), particularly the charges made for loans and the charges made for photoduplication and estimates of photoduplication. Those who use OCLC may consult its Name-Address Directory (NAD) online for interlibrary loan policies. Some interlibrary loan services mount their policies on a World Wide Web

---

14. *Symbols of American Libraries,* 14th ed. (Washington, D.C.: Library of Congress, 1994).

home page. Collect periodically individual policy statements not available online from libraries you use. A loose-leaf binder is a good way to keep these policies. Leslie R. Morris's *Interlibrary Loan Policies Directory* can be helpful.[15] Check any resource-sharing agreements or network arrangements of which you are a part before picking a location.

The best choice is to pick a library close to you that will give you quick and inexpensive service. Some lending libraries and networks limit the number of requests that can be made by one borrowing library at one time or for one individual. Spread requests among a number of libraries to avoid burdening a few (the Code, 4.5). Use a variety of libraries from an alphabetical list—not just those listed at the beginning. Be reasonable and use common sense in approaching very large research libraries, which customarily supply far more than they borrow. These libraries should be used as a last resort (the Code, 4.5).

The Center for Research Libraries will supply a limit of ten requests per year to libraries that are not members at a fee of $20 per request.

> Access Services Department
> Center for Research Libraries
> 6050 South Kenwood Avenue
> Chicago, IL 60637-2804
> Telephone: (312) 955-4545,
> ext. 313 or 314

Policies of the Loan Division—Interlibrary Loan and the Photoduplication Service of the Library of Congress, the National Agricultural Library, and the National Library of Medicine describe specific requirements, particular procedures, and acceptable forms to use when applying to them for service. Details of these policies are found in appendixes K–N.

Commercial Document Suppliers

Pertinent facts must be obtained and kept on hand for commercial document suppliers. The kinds of services available, the costs, and answers to the questions posed under "Important Considerations When Choosing a Supply Source," above, are all necessary pieces of information. The *Fiscal Directory of Fee-Based Research and Document Supply Services* provides information about commercial document suppliers and how to reach them.[16] Bradley J. Morgan's *Information Industry Directory* may also be of help.[17]

At an Interlibrary Loan Discussion Group meeting during the American Library Association midwinter conference in Los Angeles, February 1994, those attending identified the commercial document suppliers listed below as being commonly used by interlibrary loan services. Many of them can be reached by ordering through the bibliographic utilities such as OCLC and RLIN. Documents can often be ordered in conjunction with an online search through such services as DIALOG.

Here are some commercial document suppliers:

UnCover

Table-of-contents and an online periodical article delivery service. For information:

> The UnCover Company
> 3801 East Florida Avenue, Suite 200
> Denver, CO 80210
> Telephone: (800) 787-7979 or
> (303) 758-3030
> E-mail: uncover@carl.org
> Uncover World Wide Web/
> URL: <http://www.carl.org/
> uncover>

UMI Article Clearinghouse

University Microfilms International supplies photocopies from a range of periodicals, conference proceedings, and government documents. (OCLC symbol: UMI) For information:

> UMI Article Clearinghouse
> University Microfilms International
> P.O. Box 17
> Ann Arbor, MI 48106

---

15. Leslie R. Morris, *Interlibrary Loan Policies Directory,* 5th ed. (New York: Neal-Schuman, 1995).

16. *Fiscal Directory of Fee-Based Research and Document Supply Services,* compiled by Steve Coffman and Pat Wiedensohler for FISCAL, a discussion group of the Association of College and Research Libraries, 4th ed. (Chicago: American Library Association, 1993).

17. Bradley J. Morgan, *Information Industry Directory,* 11th ed. (Detroit: Gale, 1991– .)

Telephone: (800) 521-0600,
            ext. 2533 or 2534 or
            (313) 761-4700
Fax: (313) 665-7075

The Genuine Article

Document delivery from ISI (Institute for Scientific Information) articles. (OCLC symbol: TGA) For information:

The Genuine Article
Institute for Scientific Information
3501 Market Street
Philadelphia, PA 19104
Telephone: (800) 523-1850 or
            (215) 386-0100

Article Express International/Information on Demand

Locates and retrieves copies of any publicly available document regardless of subject, date, or publication type. (OCLC symbol: GET) For information:

Article Express International
Document Delivery
469 Union Avenue
Westbury, NY 11590
Telephone: (800) 238-3458 or
            (516) 997-0699
Fax: (516) 997-0890

BLDSC

British Library Document Supply Centre uses an enormous stock of books, periodicals, reports, conference proceedings, music scores, and theses to supply requests. (OCLC symbol: BRI) For information:

The British Library Document
  Supply Centre
Boston Spa
Wetherby
West Yorkshire LS23 7BQ
United Kingdom
Telephone: +44 937 546000
Fax CCITT Group III: +44 937 546333
E-mail: DSC-Customer-Services@
LONDON.BRITISH-LIBRARY.UK

CAS DDS

Documents from the Chemical Abstracts Service collection. (OCLC symbol: CAS) For information:

CAS
Marketing, Dept. 40891
P.O. Box 3012
Columbus, OH 43210-0012
Telephone: (800) 753-4CAS or
            (614) 447-3600

ERIC Document Reproduction Service

Supplier of ERIC (Educational Resources Information Center) documents. (OCLC symbol: EDR) For information:

ERIC Document Reproduction Service
Customer Service Manager
7420 Fullerton Road, Suite 110
Springfield, VA 22153-2852
Telephone: (800) 443-3742 or
            (703) 440-1400
Fax: (703) 440-1408

Engineering Information, Inc.

Supplies copies of nearly any engineering article, conference paper, or technical report. (OCLC symbol: EIO) For information:

Engineering Information, Inc.
Document Delivery Service
345 East 47th Street
New York, NY 10017-2387
Telephone: (212) 705-7600
Fax: (212) 832-1857

National Technical Information Service (NTIS)

Provides access to the results of U.S. and foreign-government-sponsored research and development activities in the form of technical reports. For information, see "Government Publications and Technical Reports Supply Sources," below.

New or expanded services for commercial document suppliers are developing rapidly. Constant vigilance is the best approach.

Government Publications and Technical Reports Supply Sources

A suggestion for the first source for obtaining federal government publications is libraries. This is particularly successful when a definite location can be found by using online union catalogs or other location devices. Another source is to try a library that is part of the Federal Depository Library Program. Fifty-three libraries are responsible for retaining material permanently and providing interlibrary loan and reference services in their regions. For the one closest to you, see the list in appendix O. Obtain the documents-lending policies of the strong depositories near you. As a start toward using the Internet to find government publications, see Blake Gumprecht's article, "Internet Sources of Government Information."[18]

United States senators and representatives will sometimes supply, without charge, popular recent government materials.

Federal issuing agencies have also been known to supply copies of their publications.

Libraries having depository collections of U.S. government documents and collections of United Nations and foreign documents are listed in the following publications:

Directory of Government Document Collections & Librarians. Edited by Judy Horn. 6th ed. Bethesda, Md.: Congressional Information Service, 1991.

GPO Depository Union List of Item Selections. Washington, D.C.: U.S. Government Printing Office, Superintendent of Documents, 1982?– , microfiche.

Directory of Special Libraries and Information Centers. Ed. 1– . Detroit: Gale, 1963– .

Ash, Lee, and William G. Miller. *Subject Collections: A Guide to Special Book Collections and Subject Emphases.* 7th ed., rev. and enl. New Providence, N.J.: Bowker, 1993.

Union List of Technical Reports, Standards and Patents in Engineering Libraries. Compiled by James A. Ruffner and Linda R. Musser. 2nd ed. University Park, Pa.: American Society for Engineering Education, Engineering Libraries Division, 1992.

Union List of Serials in Libraries of the United States and Canada. 3rd ed., 5 vols. Edited by Edna Brown Titus. New York: Wilson, 1965. Lists governmental periodicals.

Canadiana in United States Repositories: A Preliminary Guide. Compiled and edited by William A. Gosling. Occasional Papers Series, 57. Halifax, Nova Scotia: Dalhousie University, School of Library and Information Studies, 1994.

List of Serial Publications of Foreign Governments, 1815–1931. Edited by Winifred Gregory. New York: Wilson, 1932.

The U.S. National Archives has a wealth of material available in microfilm, including some U.S. census information. Reels of microfilm can be obtained through a rental program. There is a small per-reel charge for borrowing:

> Microfilm Rental Program
> National Archives
> P.O. Box 30
> Annapolis Junction, MD 20701-0030
> Telephone: (301) 604-3699

Another source provides government information of genealogical interest, including U.S. census information. There is a small per-reel charge for borrowing:

> American Genealogical Lending
>   Library
> P.O. Box 244
> Bountiful, UT 84011-0244
> Telephone: (801) 298-5446
> Fax: (801) 298-5468

Although federal government publications frequently do not stay in print for a long time, it may be possible to purchase an item. Remember that not all listings in the *Monthly Catalog of United States Government Publications* can be purchased. Refer to the *GPO Sales Publications Reference File (PRF)* for titles that can be bought. (Full information on these two publications can be found in this chapter under "Verify borrowing requests and find where material is located," "Government Publications and Technical Reports.") The Superintendent of Documents sells federal government publications:

> U.S. Government Printing Office
> Superintendent of Documents

---

18. Blake Gumprecht, "Internet Sources of Government Information," *College & Research Libraries News* 55 (January 1994): 19–22.

Mail Stop: SSOP
Washington, DC 20402-9328

Orders can be placed using the order form listed in appendix P or by telephone, (202) 783-3238. Payment can be made by establishing a deposit account or by credit card.

There are also 24 U.S. government bookstores located in major metropolitan areas. These bookstores carry the government's most popular publications and will sell any government book currently for sale. They accept credit cards and Superintendent of Documents deposit account orders. For a list of U.S. government bookstores, see appendix Q.

The National Technical Information Service (NTIS) is the central source for the public sale of government-sponsored research, development, and engineering reports and other analyses prepared by federal agencies, their contractors or grantees, or by special technology groups. NTIS sells subscriptions, technical reports, and other information products and services of specialized interest. An all-inclusive biweekly journal, *Government Reports Announcements and Index* (see "Verify borrowing requests and find where material is located," "Government Publications and Technical Reports," above in this chapter for details), is published for librarians, technical information specialists, and those requiring all summaries of research in a single source. Federal depository libraries may own report collections, but many of them are fragmentary. Sometimes special arrangements for interlibrary loan, photocopy, and reference service for technical reports can be made with such special libraries as professional scientific societies' libraries or libraries of firms that contract with the government. When definite locations cannot be found for borrowing a technical report, purchasing from NTIS can be a good choice.

NTIS reports can be ordered by fax, online via OCLC, by telephone, or by mail. An order form to be used for fax or mail requests can be found in appendix R. The telephone number and address listed there can be used to make inquiries. The quickest way to order is by using the NTIS order number. Payment can be made by check or money order, NTIS deposit account, charge card, or a bill can be sent for an extra fee.

Keep in mind commercial document suppliers that obtain government publications as part of their service.

When all else fails, ask a librarian at a federal depository library for help.

Contact the state library for help in finding state government publications, or try the issuing agency.

The United Nations has established depository libraries in many countries. These depository libraries can be found in the following publication:

List of Depository Libraries Receiving United Nations Material. ST/LIB/12/Rev.12, 5 April 1995. n.p.: United Nations Secretariat, 1995.

The same list can be found online:

URL: <http://www.un.org/MoreInfo/deplib.html>

European Community government publications can be found at the British Library Document Supply Centre (see chapter 6, "International Interlibrary Loan," "British Library Document Supply Centre"). A source for purchasing European Community documents, as well as other in-print United Nations publications, is UNIPUB:

UNIPUB
4611-F Assembly Drive, Dept. C
Lanham, MD 20706-4391
Telephone: (800) 274-4888 (U.S.)
Telephone: (800) 233-0504 (Canada)
Fax: (301) 459-0056

When a Supply Source Cannot Be Found

When locations cannot be found, requests for materials should be sent to libraries likely to have strong collections on that subject. The statement "cannot locate" and the original source of the reference should be included with the request (the Code, 4.4). If all else fails, look at Lee Ash and William G. Miller's *Subject Collections* for information on locations of strong collections on various topics.[19] As a last resort, it is possible to post a message on the Internet's interlibrary loan listserv (ILL-L) asking for help or to telephone another interlibrary loan librarian who may be able to provide assistance.

---

19. Lee Ash and William G. Miller, *Subject Collections,* 7th ed., rev. and enl. (New Providence, N.J.: Bowker, 1993).

Once a supply source is determined, this source should be indicated on the patron request form so that the person who will be doing the transmission will know where to send the request.

When Patrons Do Their Own Work

With rapidly expanding technology, the library patron has an increasing number of options for helping with the interlibrary loan and document delivery process—from submitting requests electronically to the proper library department (see appendix F), to receiving documents online, to taking care of the whole process without involving interlibrary loan and document delivery services in any way. In the latter case, the role of the librarian may be to design effective online information systems and to teach the patron how to satisfy his or her own needs. The role of advisor in such matters will become more important. Once again, keeping a sharp eye on developments in interlibrary loan and document delivery services is absolutely necessary in order to give the best possible service to the library patron.

Prepare and transmit borrowing requests

Add any notes that need to be transmitted, such as "Replacement pages, need wide margins," to the patron request form.

"Standard bibliographic format" (the Code, 4.6) should be used when transmitting borrowing requests. Look at "Take applications for borrowing" and "Verify borrowing requests and find where material is located," above in this chapter, for the correct bibliographic information needed for each kind of request. The form of transmission used will dictate the format, but the same complete and accurate information is needed on each request. Be sure to use the protocols dictated by the system chosen to transmit the request. If it is not obvious, note the transmission method to be used on the patron request form.

Put only one title on each request form. Even requests for two articles from the same volume should be sent on separate forms. All requests should be electronically produced or typed. Handwritten requests are generally not accepted. Typing should be neat with no strikeovers. Train staff carefully in the preparation of requests and have them

proofread their work. Instructions for filling out the different kinds of forms follow.

Bibliographic Utilities Requests

Follow carefully the instructions given by the automated interlibrary loan system used: OCLC (Online Computer Library Center), RLIN (Research Libraries Information Network), and WLN. DOCLINE is the automated system used by medical and other libraries for requesting medical materials. Abide by whatever particular network regulations apply. Be sure the user manual for the system you use is handy for training and reference purposes. Post information not to be forgotten for the persons transmitting requests. Remember to include correct and complete citations and the source of information for all requests. Watch for truncation of author's name or publication date, lack of series information, etc. Take care that a patron's personal information does not go to another library due to automatic transfer from an electronic source. For examples of OCLC interlibrary loan requests, see figures 8 and 9. See chapter 5, "Interlibrary Cooperation," for more information about the bibliographic utilities offering interlibrary loan services.

ALA Interlibrary Loan Request Form
(see figures 1–7 and 13)

Approval of this form was given by the Reference and Adult Services Division of the American Library Association in 1988. Each form comes in four parts and can be ordered from library supply firms. Leave the parts of the form attached to the stub at the left side. This form can be used for requesting books, periodical articles or other photocopies, and all other types of material, including government publications and subject requests. They should be typed (or electronically produced) and not handwritten.

Some libraries use a software package to print ALA Interlibrary Loan Request forms. While most commercial forms have been standardized as to content, spacing varies among manufacturers. Be sure that the form selected is compatible with your printer. Most suppliers will provide sample forms to test compatibility prior to bulk ordering. If continuous forms are used, get a sample with enough forms to test the spacing from one form to the next. Prior testing is critical when ordering forms preprinted

```
                                                      MOD   SID: 05401        OL
   Entire record displayed.

   ILL

   ► :ILL: NEW          :Borrower: TRN  :ReqDate: 920925 :Status: PENDING
     :OCLC: 6316335     :NeedBefore: 921104 :RecDate:        :RenewalReq:
     :Lender: ×SER,ACQ,OCL             :DueDate:           :NewDueDate:       ¶
   ► :AUTHOR:  Leiber, Fritz, 1910- ¶
   ► :TITLE:   A pail of air ¶
   ► :EDITION:     ¶
   ► :IMPRINT: New York : Ballantine, c1964. ¶
   ► :ARTICLE:   ¶
   ► :VOL:        :NO:      :DATE:                    :PAGES:              ¶
   ► :VERIFIED: OCLC ¶
   ► :PATRON:     ¶
   ► :SHIP TO:   ILL/Central Lights University Library/Central OH  43017 ¶
   ► :BILL TO:    ¶
   ► :SHIP VIA:                   :MAXCOST:          :COPYRT COMPLIANCE:    ¶
   ► :BORROWING NOTES:  ¶
```

FIGURE 8.   OCLC Interlibrary Loan Book Request

```
   Search  ►Edit  ►View  ►Actions  ►Options  ¶           SID: 05507        OL
   Entire record displayed.

   ILL

   ► :ILL: NEW          :Borrower: TRN  :ReqDate: 920925 :Status: PENDING
     :OCLC: 2868398     :NeedBefore: 921104 :RecDate:        :RenewalReq:
     :Lender: ×ACQ,SER,OCL,OZZ,OZZ         :DueDate:        :NewDueDate:     ¶
   ► :AUTHOR:     ¶
   ► :TITLE:   Online. ¶
   ► :EDITION:     ¶
   ► :IMPRINT: [Weston, Conn., Online, inc.] ¶
   ► :ARTICLE: Riehm, S. M. "A first look at FirstSearch" ¶
   ► :VOL: 16     :NO:      :DATE: May 1992           :PAGES: 42-44+        ¶
   ► :VERIFIED: OCLC/Lib Lit August 1992, p. 129 ¶
   ► :PATRON:     ¶
   ► :SHIP TO:   ILL/Central Lights University Library/Central OH  43017 ¶
   ► :BILL TO:    ¶
   ► :SHIP VIA: Library Rate         :MAXCOST: $6.00   :COPYRT COMPLIANCE: CCG ¶
   ► :BORROWING NOTES:  ¶
```

FIGURE 9.   OCLC Interlibrary Loan Periodical Article Request

with the library's address, because they cannot be returned.

Request no.

Put here an order number, the patron's last name, or other information to aid in retrieving the patron request form for further processing when the material arrives.

Date

Put here the date of submission.

Need before

Put here the last possible date the patron can use the material.

Notes

This space can be used for special instructions, circumstances, or explanations, for example, "Our copy missing," "Publisher out of stock," "Please send airmail, special delivery," "Send via fax," "We will reimburse," "Please rush," "Replacement pages, need wide margins," or "Will pay for loan." It may be necessary to use also the small space to the right of the Borrowing Library's address box.

Call No.

Leave blank for use of the lending library unless you are *positive* of the proper call number and copy it correctly, including any internal locations that might be given. The Library of Congress requests that their call number be added to requests sent to them.

Borrowing Library

Include your complete library name and full postal address with complete zip code in the top box on every form. This becomes the mailing address and can be used in a window envelope. Be careful not to reverse the borrowing and lending library addresses; preprinted forms prevent this problem.

Patron information

This space can be used for the patron's last name or other internal purposes. For subject requests within local networks, the status, such as high school student, adult, researcher, etc., may be helpful.

Book author; OR, Serial title, volume, issue, date, pages; OR, Audiovisual title

For books, give the author's name in full (see "Verify borrowing requests and find where

material is located," "Books and Pamphlets," in this chapter). For periodicals, put the periodical title using no abbreviations, the volume number, the issue number or issue date, the year, and the inclusive pages of the periodical article in this space (see "Verify borrowing requests and find where material is located," "Periodical Articles"). If the last page of the article is not known, use "eoa" for "end of article."

Book title, edition, imprint, series;
  OR, Article author, title

For books, put enough of the title so that the work can be identified easily. Include the edition (if there is one or if it is important), the place of publication, the publisher, the year of publication, and the complete series (if there is one). For periodicals, include the author and the title of the article.

☐ This edition only

Make a check mark here if no other edition is acceptable.

Verified in; AND/OR, Cited in

Here is where the verification or source of information goes. The source of location, if different from the verification, also goes here. See the OCLC Online Computer Library Center, "Appendix D," *Interlibrary Loan User Guide* (Dublin, Ohio: 1992), for abbreviations to be used. It is sufficient to cite an online union catalog record, such as "OCLC 2407606," as a source of verification and location if that is where the material was found. It is also sufficient to cite other online union catalogs or individual library catalogs as sources of verification and location. If there is no verification or source, briefly list where you looked and add "Cannot verify." Clearance of local, state, regional, and network libraries is given in this area if required.

ISBN, ISSN, LCCN, or other bibliographic
  number

This space is particularly useful for libraries organized into networks that use identifying numbers for machine-readable bibliographic data. The International Standard Book Number (ISBN), the International Standard Serials Number (ISSN), the Library of Congress Card Number (LCCN), unique codes for periodical titles (CODEN), and the Serial Item and Contribution Identifier (SICI, unique identification for articles) may be entered here.

Lending Library

Give full name and address of the lending library, including zip code. This becomes a mailing address, and a window envelope may be used to send the request. Address requests to the attention of the "Interlibrary Loan Service" or the "Photoduplication Service" as needed. Time will be saved if requests for materials in branch, departmental, or divisional libraries that do their own lending or photocopying are sent to that entity. For library addresses, see *American Library Directory* or *Directory of Special Libraries and Information Centers.*[20]

Request complies with

( ) 108(g)(2) Guidelines (CCG)

( ) other provisions of copyright law (CCL) For periodical article or other photoduplication requests, check the appropriate box (the Code, 4.7). See chapter 3, "Interlibrary Loan, Reproduction, and the Copyright Law," for an explanation of "CCG" and "CCL."

Authorization

The legible signature and the title of the librarian or staff member authorized to request loans *may* be included. The person who signs the request should check and revise the request to be sure the correct information has been included and the citation and verification are correct.

Telephone

The telephone number of the borrowing library goes here. Include a fax number or Ariel address, if asking for delivery by such modes. An e-mail address can also be useful.

TYPE OF REQUEST

( ) LOAN; WILL PAY FEE

( ) PHOTOCOPY; MAX. COST $ _____

( )

One of these three boxes should be checked.

If the borrowing library cannot pay for a loan, check the appropriate box, but cross off "WILL PAY FEE." If the request is for a photocopy, be certain to include the maximum cost that can be paid. Payment by coupon or voucher should be stated here. The third box is the place to request an estimate of charges for copying or any other special kind of request.

The other sections of the ALA Interlibrary Loan Request form include "LENDING LIBRARY REPORT," "NOT SENT BECAUSE," "BORROWING LIBRARY RECORD," and "RENEWALS." These sections will be used for response by the lending library and for tracking a request by the borrowing library.

Detach and retain the D form. Do not separate the A, B, and C forms and do not detach them from the stub. If there are carbons in your forms, do not remove the carbons. Send the A, B, and C forms in a standard business window envelope, together with a self-addressed, return, gummed shipping label (see appendix D). Include coupons for the libraries that charge for loans and require prepaid coupons. Retain the D form as your interim record of request. Some libraries attach the D form to the patron request form and place in an in-process file.

ALA Library Photoduplication Order Form

Approval of this form was given by the Reproduction of Library Materials Section, Association for Library Collections & Technical Services, American Library Association. Each form comes in four parts and can be used for periodical articles and other photoduplication orders. Remember to fill out the copyright law compliance section and to include authorization to charge. Follow instructions given for the ALA Interlibrary Loan Request form.

Telefacsimile, World Wide Web, and Electronic Mail Requests

The same information as that for the ALA Interlibrary Loan Request form must be included and in approximately the same order. Look above for a list

---

20. *American Library Directory,* 2 vols., 48th ed. (New Providence, N.J.: Bowker, 1995). *Directory of Special Libraries and Information Centers,* 1st ed.– (Detroit: Gale, 1963–).

and description of these data elements. Some libraries simply type an ALA Interlibrary Loan Request form and fax that. Abide by the instructions for such requests outlined in "Guidelines and Procedures for Telefacsimile and Electronic Delivery of Interlibrary Loan Requests and Materials" (see appendix S), and pay particular attention to the "Borrowing Guidelines." Be sure to follow directions for operation given by the manufacturer of your equipment and instructions given by your state library or network. Data entry should be accurate. Spacing the lines properly so that the form will be the same size as an ALA form helps the lending library. For fax numbers, see such reference tools as the *American Library Directory, Directory of Special Libraries and Information Centers, Library Fax/Ariel Directory,* etc.[21] Some requests can be sent to the World Wide Web home page of a particular interlibrary loan service. In that case, fill out the form and follow the directions that are given. More World Wide Web access for requests may be provided in the future. Be on the lookout for works that give e-mail and Internet addresses and protocol.

Computerized Circulation Systems Requests

Follow procedures established by the participating libraries where interlibrary loan can be done using computerized circulation systems.

Printout Requests from Online Public Access Catalogs, CD-ROM Catalogs, or Microform Catalogs

Printout requests from these catalogs may be sent only to libraries that agree to fill requests received in this form. One request should be made per printout. The printout should be legible and about the size of an ALA Interlibrary Loan Request form. Stamp, type, or use a photocopy overlay for the usual information, such as the request date, the "need before" date, the borrowing library's address, copyright compliance, authorization to charge, and other information required by agreement. Such requests can be submitted by telefacsimile, U.S. Postal Service, or by courier, where

appropriate. For an example of a printout request, see figure 10.

Special Forms

Special forms are required, usually for photoduplication, by a number of libraries, such as the Library of Congress Photoduplication Service. Request and use these forms as needed. (For information on the Library of Congress Photoduplication Service, see appendix L.)

Telephone Requests

Telephone requests should be made only where agreement exists to do them in this way or in case of dire emergency. Some commercial document delivery services accept telephone calls. Prepare the request carefully before calling. Have on hand the same information needed for the ALA Interlibrary Loan Request form. Spell out words as necessary. Be sure to include the "need before" date.

Receive, unwrap, and prepare material for patrons

Returnable Material

The borrowing library is responsible for returnable material from the time the item leaves the lending library until it has been returned and received by the lending library (the Code, 4.8). Unwrap interlibrary loan parcels, being careful not to damage the contents. Save any special packaging to be used when the item is returned. For example, videorecordings often come in special cases. It is imperative to return the material in the same case. See if there is a requirement to return the cost of postage, and note that on the forms. If the parcel was sent insured, note that also so you can return it insured. Acknowledge receipt of valuable shipments when requested to do so by the lending library. You may wish to pass incoming books by the desensitizing equipment, if you have a circulation security system. The lending library should take care of this before send-

21. *American Library Directory,* 2 vols., 48th ed. (New Providence, N.J.: Bowker, 1995). *Directory of Special Libraries and Information Centers,* 1st ed.– (Detroit: Gale, 1963–).

Library Fax/Ariel Directory, 1st ed.– (Kansas City, Mo.: CBR Consulting Services, 1989–).

EXAMPLE OF CARL/MARMOT SCREEN: FULL BIB RECORD

```
---------------------------Univ. of N. Colorado-------
AUTHOR(s):    Fedo, Michael.
TITLE(s):    The man from Lake Wobegon /by Michael Fedo.
               1st ed.

               New York : St. Martin's Press, c1987.
               xi, 234 p., [8] p. of plates: ill.; 22 cm.
               "A Thomas Dunne book."
               Includes index.
               Bibliography: p. 225-228.
               c.1


OTHER ENTRIES:  Keillor, Garrison  Biography.
               Authors, American  20th century  Biography.
               Radio broadcasters  United States  Biography.
LOCN:     MICHNR STACKS     STATUS: Not checked out
CALL #:    PS3561.E3755 Z65 1987


LOCN:     STATUS: Received (in process)
CALL #

---------------------------Univ. of N. Colorado-------
```

Request Date_____

Interlibrary Loan
(your library name)
(Street or P.O.Box)
(City, State Zip)

Courier Code:_____

(Contact Person)
(Phone Number)
(Fax Number)

__CCG __CCL __Max Cost

Needs before date_____

Notes:

FIGURE 10. Print Screen Interlibrary Loan Request Format (Note information on right, which has been added to the printout from an online public access catalog)

ing out the book, but this does not always happen. An interlibrary loan book that causes the alarm to sound is most embarrassing for the patron. Match the material with all your interlibrary loan forms to be certain the proper item has been received, including all volumes of a multivolume request.

For the ALA Interlibrary Loan Request form, you should have the D form and your patron request form. You should receive the B and C copies with the material. For electronic mail, you should have one or more copies of the interlibrary borrowing request, printed from the online request, and your patron request form. You should receive a copy of the form or other identifying information with the material. For OCLC requests, you should have the online computer record and your patron request form. If needed, this is a good time to print out the OCLC record because the information you need, such as the due date, is now there. OCLC loans often come with a copy of the request or a slip con-

taining the OCLC interlibrary loan transaction number. Keep the lending library's return-address shipping label with the forms for later use. This is particularly important for labels from the National Library of Canada (see chapter 6, "International Interlibrary Loan," "Canada").

Put appropriate information on the records (see figures 1–7 and appendix E). If it is not obvious, indicate which library supplied the material. Stamp the date received on the patron request forms and the interlibrary loan request forms. Update online records where appropriate. Record any charges that have been incurred, such as those for the loan of the material, for mailing, or for special delivery, so that they can be paid upon return or when an invoice is received (the Code, 4.3). These charges may be invoiced on the ALA Interlibrary Loan Request form or the OCLC online record, with the material, monthly, or at other intervals. Some libraries require advance payment or deposit accounts. Keep careful records of all charges for loans to ensure accurate financial transactions. Develop a method for passing these charges on to the patron, if that is the policy of your library.

Determine a due date for the patron. The most useful way for the lender to state a due date is "two weeks use" or "one month use." That way the date the patron brings the material back to interlibrary borrowing is two weeks or one month from the date of receipt. If the lender gives an actual date when the material is due back at the lending institution, transit time must be figured before setting a due date for the patron. Keep in mind that it is difficult for a patron to finish with borrowed materials in less than two weeks. One copy of the interlibrary loan form can be filed by date to form a date-due file. Some libraries enter interlibrary loans into the library's automated circulation system. This has the advantage of keeping track of all of a patron's library borrowing and producing timely overdue notices.

Note the conditions of loan and abide by them (the Code, 4.9). Photocopying is permitted if no damage to the material results and if the copyright law is observed, unless the lending library stipulates "Copying not permitted." Material designated "Library use only" must not leave the borrowing library. The condition of the material may prompt the borrowing library to restrict use to the library even though the lender has not so stipulated. "No renewals" means that the material must be returned by the specified time. Some universities that lend theses and dissertations require the patron to sign a statement of use of the manuscript: "Please sign signature sheet." The borrowing library is responsible for seeing that this is done. The patron must sign the statement. If the item is not used by the reader, the borrowing librarian should enclose a note when returning the volume explaining why no signature was added to the list. The names of all readers who wish to use a dissertation should be included in the original request; some major libraries lend for the exclusive use of the individual whose name appears on the request.

Notify the patron by mail, telephone, voicemail, e-mail, or fax that the material has arrived (see appendix I). Record the date of notification. Some academic institutions have campus delivery services that will deliver the book to the patron. If the supplier delivers directly to the patron, the borrowing library may have to get involved in the return of the material in a timely fashion. Let the patron know the conditions of loan, including the date the material must be returned. Many libraries use a book band or sleeve to convey this information. (For an example, see appendix H.) Do not use any paper with adhesives, such as Post-its, because damage to the book or paper might result. Collect money for charges, if these are passed on to the patron, before handing out the material.

Photocopy

Match the photocopy to the interlibrary loan forms to be certain the correct material has been received. For the ALA Interlibrary Loan Request form or the ALA Library Photoduplication Request form, you should have the D form and your patron request form. You should receive the B and C forms with the material. For electronic mail requests, you should have one or more copies of the interlibrary borrowing request, printed from the online request, and your patron request form. You should receive a copy of the form or other identifying information with the material. For OCLC requests, you should have the online computer record and your patron request form. If needed, this is a good time to print out the OCLC record because the information you need, including charges, should now be there. OCLC material often comes with a copy of the request or a slip containing the OCLC interlibrary loan transaction number. Check to be sure the photocopy is legible and the entire article has been included.

Put appropriate information on the records (see figures 1–7 and appendix E). If it is not obvious, indicate which library supplied the material. Stamp the date received on the patron request forms and the interlibrary loan request forms. Update online records where appropriate. Record any charges that have been incurred so they can be paid promptly (the Code, 4.3). These charges may be invoiced on the ALA Interlibrary Loan Request form or the OCLC online record, with the material, monthly, or at other intervals. Some libraries require advance payment or deposit accounts. Keep careful records of all photocopy requests to ensure accurate financial transactions.

Develop a method for passing photocopy charges on to the patron if that is the policy of your library. Estimate the charges using the lending library's interlibrary lending policy statement, if necessary. Notify the patron by mail, telephone, voice-mail, e-mail, or fax that the photocopy has arrived (see appendix I). Record the date of notification. Some libraries mail the photocopy to the patron or use campus mail or delivery. In other cases, although the library may do the ordering, the photocopy is sent directly from the supplier to the patron. Problems such as receiving the wrong item, not receiving the item, and updating of electronic records may have to be worked out for the patron by the borrowing library. Financial transactions must be worked out carefully in those instances. For patrons with fax machines, it is possible to fax the article. Collect money for charges before handing out the material, if that is your policy. Keep one copy of the interlibrary loan form for financial and statistical purposes and for copyright information (see chapter 3, "Interlibrary Loan, Reproduction, and the Copyright Law," "Retention of records"), or make sure the information is updated or entered into your electronic statistical package. Discard or recycle surplus forms.

Return borrowed materials

Interlibrary loan material should be returned promptly. The borrowing library must, of course, return the item within the time limit set by the lending library (the Code, 4.9 and 4.11). Timely return is particularly important for videorecordings because they are frequently in high demand. Return material recalled by the lending library quickly (the Code, 4.11). Notify the patron immediately of overdue material. Alert the lending library if an unusual circumstance prevents the timely return of the material. When returning a book, you may wish to pass it by the sensitizing equipment for the circulation security system if the book was received in a sensitized state. The book should always be returned to the lending library in the same condition in which it was received. Do not repair a book that was received in a damaged condition, but point out that repair is needed.

Prepare records and material for shipment, which may be by mail, courier, or package delivery service. The lending library should specify the shipping method and type of packaging to be used. Fol-

low these instructions. If no instructions are given, the item can be returned using the same method by which it was sent or your usual method of return. Match the records once again with the material. Pay charges for loans, mailing, and special delivery. Place a copy of the interlibrary loan request (D copy, photocopy, or printout), the order number, or other identifying information with the material to be shipped. Include postage or coupons, if required. Label all packages prominently "Interlibrary Loan." Stamp your return address on the shipping label supplied by the lending library or prepare a shipping label for the lending library (see appendix D). Update records on electronic interlibrary loan systems to show that the item is being returned. Neglecting this procedure causes difficulty for the lender in clearing records. In the case of valuable materials, notification that the item is being returned should be sent separately. Keep one copy of the request for financial and statistical purposes, or make sure the necessary information is entered into your statistical software. Discard or recycle surplus forms.

Wrap for mailing with care (the Code, 4.12). If the item was sent to you in a carton containing library markings, such as microfilm boxes or slipcases, be sure that this carton is returned to the lending library. The borrowing library is responsible for the safety of borrowed materials from the time they leave the lending library until they have been returned and received by the lending library (the Code, 4.8). See chapter 2, "Instructions for Lending Libraries," "Ship material," for instructions on packaging, insurance, and shipment.

Solve problems

Set aside time each day for working on problems. Typical problems occur when no response, the wrong or incomplete response, or a negative response requiring action is made to a borrowing request.

No Response

Request a status report from a potential lender when no response has been made to a borrowing request within a reasonable amount of time (shipment by mail should not exceed one month). Notify the lending library of nonreceipt of material that you have reason to expect.

Wrong or Incomplete Response

Return the book to the lending library if it is not what you requested. Request the material from another library, or try the original library again. Notify the library of incomplete photocopy orders and request the missing pages.

Negative Response

Pick a new location and send the request to another library when the lending library indicates the material is not available (see chapter 2, "Instructions for Lending Libraries," "Annotate interlibrary lending request forms"). If a negative response does not contain a reason for the request being unfilled and a number of libraries have been tried, assume that an item is noncirculating or inadequately cited.

Put the request aside to send again at a later date when the lending library indicates that it is possible to honor it and the patron has enough time, or pick a new location and send the request to another library or document delivery service. To avoid getting two copies of the material, cancel a "reserve" or "hold" or "recall" with the original lending library if another location is picked. Respond appropriately to requests for copyright compliance; clearing local, state, regional, or network sources; providing photocopy in lieu of loan; correct verification; and additional information.

Follow up on borrowed materials

Attend to follow-up procedures on borrowed materials. These procedures include payment of invoices, attention to renewal requests, retrieval of overdue material, and compensation or replacement for damaged materials.

Pay invoices for loan of material and for photocopy promptly (the Code, 4.3). Keep a record of the interlibrary loan requests (copy, photocopy, printout, or online) for which an invoice has not yet been received. Match interlibrary loan request forms to invoices carefully before authorizing payment. Group bills together, if possible, so the check can be issued for a reasonable amount. (It costs a significant amount of money for most organizations to issue a check.) Purchase and use coupons for payment where required by the lending library. Check coupon dates to be sure they are still current.

Set up deposit accounts where practical. Keep careful records of expenditures against these accounts. Credit cards for interlibrary loan can be used in some circumstances. OCLC (Online Computer Library Center) has developed an ILL Fee Management (IFM) system in which users can pay and be paid for interlibrary lending charges through their OCLC regular invoices.

Attend to renewals and overdue materials. Renewals should be requested only in unusual circumstances. If it is necessary to request a renewal, the request should be sent in time to reach the lending library before the date the material is due (the Code, 4.10). Send the renewal request online or by using a copy of the interlibrary loan request itself. No response to a renewal request means that the renewal has been granted for the same length of time as the original loan (the Code, 4.10). Send back overdue material or reply to overdue notices immediately. Send overdue audiovisual materials, carefully packaged, by the fastest method. For recalcitrant patrons a variety of actions can be taken: explain the importance of interlibrary borrowing and how one person can jeopardize the ability of the institution to borrow; suggest that a student assistant or secretary help keep track of when materials are due; block the use of interlibrary borrowing, circulation, and other library privileges; restrict further interlibrary borrowing materials to "Library use only"; charge fines; charge replacement plus processing costs; block the ability to register or obtain transcripts (academic libraries); or enlist the help of the person's supervisor, advisor, or employer. Try to deal individually with abuse of the system rather than set restrictive policies for all.

Lost or damaged materials require further action. It may be necessary to trace lost material. Respond to U.S. Postal Service claims promptly. Work with other kinds of suppliers to resolve problems. Meet all costs of repair or replacement for damaged or lost material in accordance with the preference of the lending library (the Code, 4.8).

Report interlibrary borrowing activities

Use an in-house interlibrary loan form or a statistical program for statistical purposes and for a permanent record of activity. See chapter 3, "Interlibrary Loan, Reproduction, and the Copyright Law," for information on retention of records for photocopy. See chapter 7, "Management of Interlibrary Loan," for suggestions on statistics, reports, and statistical software. Give an account of interlibrary borrowing activities to your administration at least once each year. Note any trends in borrowing that may have occurred, and include anecdotal information about successes you have had. Make suggestions based on borrowing activity for book, periodical, and other purchases that would enhance your library collection unless this has been adequately covered by other collection development activities. Recommend training for library users where appropriate.

Instructions
for Lending
Libraries

Lending libraries are often referred to as supplying libraries or suppliers. In this book the term *lending libraries* is used.

Interlibrary Lending Policies
    Which libraries will you serve?
    What will you lend?
    How will you assist the borrowing library?
Interlibrary Lending Procedures
    Supplies
    Receive and screen interlibrary lending requests
    Search for call numbers and internal locations
    Retrieve material
    Photocopy material
    Annotate interlibrary lending request forms
    Ship material
    Solve problems
    Follow up on loans
    Receive returned material
    Report interlibrary lending activities

INTERLIBRARY LENDING POLICIES

A policy statement for interlibrary lending should be developed and maintained so it can be consulted online and sent out on request (the Code, 5.1). Consider including answers to the following questions:

Which libraries will you serve?

What will you lend?

How will you assist the borrowing library?

For an example of an interlibrary lending policy, see appendix T.

Which libraries will you serve?

You may serve any library you wish. A lending library may serve other libraries within a library system, all the libraries within a state, a group of libraries in a consortium arrangement, libraries in a multistate area belonging to the same regional network, any library outside of all other arrangements with which traditional but less formal agreement exists, any library that complies with the National Interlibrary Loan Code for the United States, 1993 (see appendix A), and any foreign library that abides by International Lending: Principles and Guidelines for Procedure (1978) (revised 1987) (see appendix U).

In an ideal situation, all interlibrary lending requests are honored. The volume of lending requests today sometimes makes this impossible. Large libraries may find it necessary to establish priorities for lending. For instance, the borrowing libraries within a state might be served before libraries located in distant states, which presumably would have other possibilities for obtaining the needed material. Requests from libraries forming a consortium might be filled before requests from libraries not holding membership in the consortium. When the decision is made to prioritize lending requests, care must be taken to honor not only requests to fulfill existing agreements, but those for unique material as well.

Loans are generally not made to individuals (the Code, 1.1). The exception can be the provision of photocopy to an individual.

Borrowing libraries operating under the provisions of the National Interlibrary Loan Code for the United States, 1993, must abide by those provisions. Failure to do so gives the lending library the right to suspend service (the Code, 5.10).

What will you lend?

What is going to be lent is entirely the decision of the local lending library (the Code, 3.1 and 3.2). Be as generous as possible. Have a copy of your library's circulation policy on hand for guidance. Any item that circulates to local patrons should be available for interlibrary lending as well, provided it is not in constant use. Try to make exceptions if the readers in your library will not be inconvenienced. Provide photocopying or electronic transmission of articles in periodicals or unique items that cannot be loaned. Check your library's licensing agreements for the possibility of copying materials from electronic sources or lending material covered by such agreements. In the case of audiovisual materials, you may have to determine what use will be made of the item before consenting to lend. In addition to the kinds of materials listed in chapter 1, "Instructions for Borrowing Libraries," "Verify borrowing requests and find where material is located," special lending policies may be necessary for such categories as local history, maps, rare books, or special collections. Work with the librarians in charge of these materials, using the "Guidelines for the Loan of Rare and Unique Materials" (see appendix V).

How will you assist the borrowing library?

Interlibrary lending is best accomplished by publicizing your interlibrary lending policies, educating borrowing libraries, and processing requests promptly using efficient internal interlibrary lending procedures.

Make known your interlibrary lending policy so that those who borrow from you will know what to expect. If you use the OCLC (Online Computer Library Center) PRISM Interlibrary Loan system, enter your policy into the Name-Address Directory (NAD) and keep it up-to-date. It does no good to admonish a borrowing library to check your policy before requesting a loan if the policy is not accurate! You may want to enter your interlibrary lending policy on a World Wide Web home page. Have a copy of your regulations available to send to the libraries that request it (see appendix T; the Code, 5.1). Limit your interlibrary lending policy statement to important information, stated clearly and simply, following national and local codes. Information ordinarily should include

Date of the policy

Full address to which interlibrary lending requests should be sent

E-mail address, if requests are accepted that way

Fax number, if requests are accepted that way

Any other addresses or numbers used for receiving requests

Appropriate codes or location symbols used to designate your library

Departments or branches (if any) that do their own lending, to which requests should be sent directly, with address or numbers

Photocopy service address or numbers, if different from lending address

Policy concerning automatic substitution of photocopy in lieu of loan

Photocopy and transmission services available and fees charged

Loan or search fees charged, postage or insurance reimbursement, or other charges

Availability and cost of rush service (defined as processing within one working day, see appendix S, 5.3)

Lending policy for books, periodicals, newspapers, dissertations and masters' theses, government publications, technical reports, microforms, audiovisual materials, and any specially restricted materials

It is also helpful to include information about renewals and suspension of service during the Christmas holidays. You may want to require that a borrowing library abide by particular codes: state, network, regional, or the National Interlibrary Loan Code for the United States, 1993. You may also require a borrowing library to submit requests using procedures adopted by a particular state, network, or other organization.

Help to educate personnel in the borrowing libraries. Improvement can only come with awareness of what is adequate and accurate. The burden of bibliographic verification is on the borrowing library. For those libraries with inadequate bibliographic tools or lack of experience, suggestions from the lender can be a boon. It is especially important that borrowing libraries be encouraged to ascertain locations before sending requests. Many requests are regularly rejected because the borrowing library has not consulted available union lists or other location sources. Nevertheless, in the interests of cooperation and goodwill, if the first request you receive from a library is inadequate, try to make an exception to your usual requirements and fill the request, pointing out the inadequacies.

Process requests promptly (the Code, 5.2). Promptly means processing requests within the time frame established by the electronic network or using that same time frame to process requests coming by other means. Many libraries use 24 to 48 hours as the desirable time within which to fill a request or provide a negative reply. A performance standard is especially common where reimbursement for lending is provided. Use efficient interlibrary lending procedures and good management techniques (see chapter 7, "Management of Interlibrary Loan"). Such practice will ensure helpful interlibrary loan for the patron.

INTERLIBRARY LENDING PROCEDURES

Supplies

The supplies needed for the successful operation of interlibrary lending are listed below and followed

by the specific tasks needed to accomplish a loan. The minimum supplies needed are

Paper and ribbons or toner for the printer

Packing materials (see "Ship material," later in this chapter)

Shipping labels, self-addressed return, your library as receiver, gummed (see appendix D)

Your library's interlibrary lending policy, including photocopy and loan fees (see appendix T)

Additional supplies that would be helpful are:

Shipping labels, address section blank, your address as sender, gummed (see appendix D)

Window envelopes with return address

Form notices or letters (as necessary to indicate instructions, inadequacies, policies)

Interlibrary loan request forms with both address boxes blank for typing requests that are telephoned

Rubber stamps for commonly needed instructions or identification

Receive and screen interlibrary lending requests

Efficient completion of lending procedures depends on gathering all lending requests together at least once each day and proceeding through the necessary steps to make a loan or send a photocopy. Just how each task is accomplished depends upon the volume of requests, the size of the library, and the electronic capabilities. For a large interlibrary lending operation, requests may be received by a variety of means, such as mail (ordinary or electronic), fax, the Internet, courier, and telephone. By far the most common method of receipt today is by using the interlibrary loan system of a bibliographic utility, such as OCLC, RLIN, or WLN, or DOCLINE. Each of these interlibrary loan systems has carefully developed procedures with detailed manuals to help the person using the system. Familiarity with these procedures is essential for the smooth operation of lending.

Once the requests are gathered, proceed with preliminary preparations:

Be certain the borrowing library is identified

Date the lending request, if the electronic system has not already done so

Provide the proper number of copies of each form for processing, if multiple copies are necessary

Prepare "reverse" forms for telephone requests where needed

Screening requests is becoming very important in the efficient and effective provision of materials to other libraries. Screen by answering these questions:

Is this a library we serve? What priority is it? Are consortium agreements noted?

Is this material unique to our library?

Can we supply by the "need before" date?

Is copyright compliance indicated for photocopy requests?

Is a maximum cost indicated? (for those libraries that must pay charges)

Will an invoicing procedure be needed?

Are there any special instructions about delivery method?

Is a rush being requested, and can we comply?

Are there any other special handling requirements?

Those requests that do not meet the criteria for processing in your library, such as a photocopy request that lacks copyright representation, can be put aside for a negative response.

Search for call numbers and internal locations

Determine that the material is owned by your library. This is the most important step in lending, and it is one that can require a considerable amount of creative detective work. Learn how to use the online public access catalog and other catalogs for your collection. Try a variety of approaches, including a series approach, where appropriate. Ask someone else to help you find elusive materials until you become expert at searching. Learn how to use guides to any materials in your library not listed in your online public access catalog or card catalog. Be certain that you understand serials records. Pass on your expertise at finding materials to your successors.

Look to see if the material is checked out. (This is one of the real advantages of online public access catalogs.) If so, put the request aside for sending back with a negative response. Some libraries place "holds" for interlibrary lending. This is a questionable activity because the borrower may not wish to wait. Record the call number and internal location on the interlibrary lending request form. Sort requests for retrieval. Have a librarian check requests that are not found. This can present an opportunity to teach better searching techniques. Failure to find requests results when your library never owned the material in the first place or when the citation is such that it cannot be matched with anything in your records. Unscramble sloppy citations (when time permits), track down items supposedly published by your institution, and ferret out problematic materials. All such actions add to the pleasure of doing interlibrary lending.

Retrieve material

Teach staff how to read call numbers and how to look for slightly misshelved materials as well as for those in correct call number order. Show staff how to handle books carefully, keeping the preservation of each item in mind. Match basic information on the interlibrary lending request with the item on the shelf to be certain the correct material has been found. The call numbers should be the same. For books, a quick check of the author, edition (if one is specified), and the date will complete the match. Unless the borrowing library has checked or specified "This edition only," send the latest edition available, but explain any discrepancy on the request. For periodicals, find the correct volume and then the actual article needed. If necessary, make corrections on the interlibrary lending form in article pagination to ensure correct copying. Set the volume aside for photocopying or scanning. Make sure that audiovisual materials have all the parts present in the correct container and that these parts are not damaged. For materials not on the shelf, check the circulation records (if necessary), sorting shelves, oversize areas, and any other special places peculiar to your library.

Circulate materials to be loaned using your library's standard circulation routines. In setting a due date, allow enough time for adequate patron use and for transit both ways. Few patrons are speed readers, especially where difficult foreign-language material is concerned. An ample allowance for use will also decrease the requests for renewals. "Two weeks use" is a common minimum time for the item to stay in the borrowing library. Transit depends upon the method; the U.S. Postal Service may take two weeks in each direction while a commercial delivery service can often deliver an item in one to four days. Some libraries specify "one month use" and "no renewal" to avoid having to send frequent overdue notices or respond to renewal requests. Audiovisual materials, however, may have a shorter loan period because of intensive bookings. Whatever method is used for determining a due date, make certain that overdue notices are generated in a useful way—not too soon for the book to have been returned or not too late for adequate follow-up. If possible, avoid keeping a separate set of circulation records just for interlibrary lending. Make sure your library's property stamp appears on the material, particularly on microfilm cases and microfiche sleeves. If you have a circulation system that sensitizes material before it leaves the building, desensitize the item so that the borrowing library's security system will not be affected.

Photocopy material

The borrowing library must include a statement of copyright representation on photocopy requests. Note that the correct copyright representation for replacement pages is "CCL," complies with copyright law. Refer to chapter 3, "Interlibrary Loan, Reproduction, and the Copyright Law," "Copyright Representation." The lending library may reject the photocopy request that does not contain a statement of copyright compliance.

Make a quick estimate of costs to be sure the maximum amount the borrowing library is willing to pay is not exceeded. Reproduce legible photocopies with approximately the same size of image, with the image straight on the page, and with ample margins. Include all requested pages and illustrations. For replacement pages, leave wide margins (especially left margins), and reproduce back-to-back, when requested. The borrowing library usually does not want replacement pages copied from a microform. Refer to "Guidelines for Preservation Photocopying of Replacement Pages" (see appendix W). Notify the borrowing library of any long delay for microfilming or other service.

Keep invoicing as easy to comply with as possible. The best invoicing method for the borrowing library is to receive the bill with the material, or at least an indication of what the amount will be, so that charges can be passed on accurately to the patron when necessary. This method also means that there is no question about which bill goes with what material. Some libraries invoice on a copy of the interlibrary lending request form, using a rubber stamp to indicate that this is an invoice, and adding such information as the lending library address and telephone number, the cost incurred, the transaction number (if there is one), the invoice number, the date, to which entity a check should be issued, and the Federal Employer Identification Number (FEIN). (The FEIN is a number assigned to your organization for tax purposes. Your accounting or business office should be able to supply the number.) For other methods of invoicing, include the information mentioned above and a copy of the request or the request number so that the borrowing library will know for which item the payment is required. Abide by whatever accounting procedures are used by your institution. Cumulative billing, deposit accounts, or coupons are other ways to ease the burden of keeping track of invoices and payments. For payment information for international interlibrary loans see chapter 6, "International Interlibrary Loan," "International Interlibrary Borrowing." In the case of certain institutions that have elaborate accounting procedures, do everything in your power to see that the borrowing library has clear information about the transaction and adequate instructions about payment.

OCLC has developed an ILL Fee Management system (IFM) to help control the invoicing and payment problem. For participating libraries, the monthly network or OCLC bill has three additional line items:

- IFM library-to-library borrowing debit—charges your library incurred for borrowing items
- IFM library-to-library lending credit—credits your library receives for supplying items
- IFM administrative fee—a small fee OCLC applies to the borrowing library for a completed IFM transaction

Note: The degree to which your network or OCLC bill is affected depends on the extent to which your library uses the IFM service. If you are a large net-lender, your library could decrease its overall bill using IFM service.[1]

In addition, the IFM Monthly Detailed Report provides a request-by-request breakdown of library-to-library debits and credits. This includes a lender and borrower section and is arranged alphabetically by institution. The advantage of IFM is that the system avoids individual invoices and presents an invoice that the library already is used to paying.

Sometimes it is less expensive to provide photocopy without charging the borrowing library because of the cost of billing, receiving payment, and following up on delinquent accounts. Make reciprocal photocopy arrangements with libraries near you to avoid processing invoices. Libraries that process a large number of transactions for you might also be included in reciprocal agreements.

See "Ship material," below, for preparation and sending instructions for photocopy.

Deposit on-receipt payment for photocopies, and complete your records.

Annotate interlibrary lending request forms

Be as explicit as possible in replying to requests. Use codes, formats, and methods prescribed by an interlibrary loan system for replying electronically. Keep the interlibrary loan system procedure manual handy to refresh your memory and for unfamiliar routines. Indicate very clearly whether you are sending the item, sending a photocopy (including what the charge is), or not sending the item. State the type of packaging to be used and the shipping method by which any materials should be returned. Answer any questions asked by the borrowing library on the use of the material to save further communication.

ALA Interlibrary Loan Request forms have a section for the "LENDING LIBRARY REPORT." Use a ballpoint pen for multipart forms. Use space provided on the request where possible (see figure 11). The form should already be dated with the date of receipt, "Date" (see "Receive and screen inter-

---

1. OCLC, *ILL Fee Management . . . Handling Lending Charges through OCLC Invoices* (1995), 2.

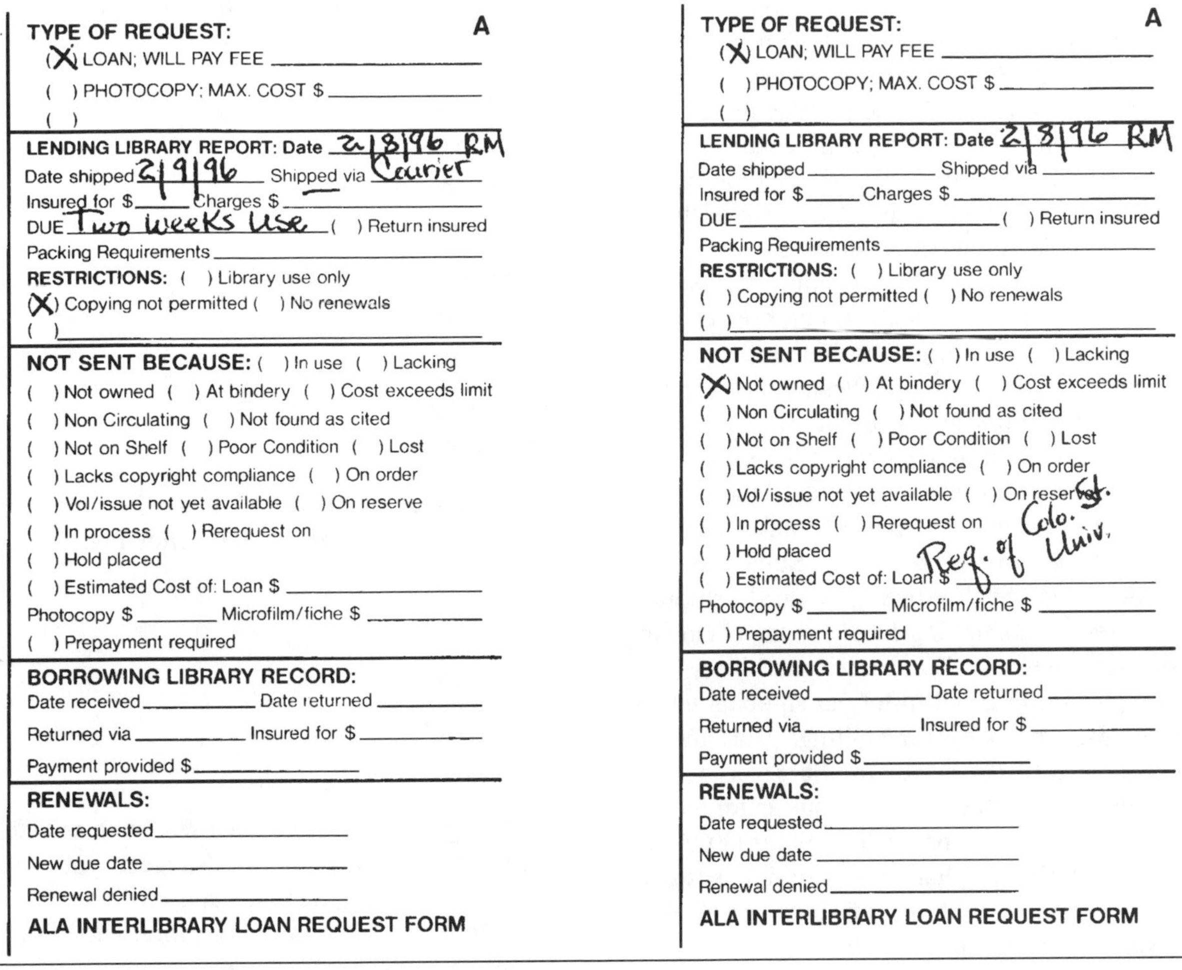

FIGURE 11. Lending Library Reports (Note "Restrictions" and "Not Sent Because")

library lending requests," above). Write in the "Date shipped" and the document delivery method, "Shipped via." Indicate whether or not the item was insured, "Insured for $." State the charges, if any, "Charges $." Remember that the best way may be for the lending library to pay the postage and insurance, if any, when sending the item and for the borrowing library to pay those charges when returning the item. Put the date due or the duration of loan in the blank marked "DUE" (the Code, 5.5). Check "Return insured," if that is appropriate. List any requirements for return packaging, "Packing Requirements." The packaging materials and shipping method by which the item should be returned can also be stated (the Code, 5.4).

Supply a clear statement on the conditions of the loan or restrictions on use (the Code, 5.4). A statement regarding the use that can be made of the material is particularly important for audiovisual materials.[2] Fill in the appropriate spaces or lender's notes when using electronic interlibrary loan systems. The ALA Interlibrary Loan Request form has a section for "RESTRICTIONS," with boxes to check for the most common ones. The lending library, for the protection of the material, may wish to stipulate that the item is "Library use only." The lending library may also wish to state "Copying not permitted" in order to protect the material from misuse. "No renewals" may be indicated. If a signature for the use of a dissertation or thesis is

---

2. The American Library Association Video Round Table is developing "Guidelines for the Loan of Video and Other Audiovisual Formats." Publication of the completed document was expected in 1996.

required, this should be specified. Some libraries like to indicate when an item is in high demand with a reminder to return it on time. Note any extraordinary conditions concerning the item on the request, including the number of physical volumes being sent, number of reels of microfilm, and the like. A request can be made for acknowledgment of the receipt of valuable shipments if desired.

For both books and photocopies, keep one copy of the request for statistical purposes or use a statistical software package for this purpose. Place the remaining copies of the request, the order number or other identifying information, and a self-addressed, return shipping label (for books) with the materials to be shipped (see appendix D; the Code, 5.3). Sending a shipment "naked" makes life very difficult for the borrowing library. Stamp your return address on the borrowing library's shipping label or prepare a shipping label for the borrowing library (see appendix D). Some interlibrary loan management systems will print out shipping labels. Address labels properly for mailing, using the address requested by the borrowing library as a "ship to" address. From time to time, requests for a batch of shipping labels must be made to libraries that use electronic interlibrary loan transmission systems. Notify the borrowing library of shipment of especially valuable materials.

Make negative replies quickly and clearly (the Code, 5.7). Correct inaccuracies when possible. Unfilled responses are listed and definitions given in *Interlibrary Loan Data Elements*.[3] This same terminology is used on the ALA Interlibrary Loan Request form.

For responses requiring an action by the borrowing library, use the following phrases:

Cost exceeds limit

Estimated cost of:	Loan	$ _____
	Photocopy	$ _____
	Microfilm/fiche	$ _____

Not found as cited

Lacks copyright compliance

Prepayment required

For material that might be available at a later date, use these phrases:

In use

At bindery

Not on shelf

On order

Vol/issue not yet available

On reserve

In process

Hold placed

Rerequest on (date)

For material that will never be available for loan, use such phrases as the following:

Lacking

Not owned

Noncirculating

Poor condition

Lost

Other negative replies can be used, such as "Cannot supply before deadline," "Suggest you request from _____ library," and the like.

Reply by electronic interlibrary loan system, e-mail, fax, or the Internet, as appropriate, using the transmission method by which the request was received as a guide (see appendix S, 5.6). A negative response to a rush request should be sent via fax, electronically, or by telephone within one working day (see appendix S, 5.3). Make sure that your negative response can be matched with the borrowing library's request.

A few suggestions are in order for responses that must be mailed. Envelopes that are automation compatible will be processed through the postal system in the fastest, most accurate, and most efficient manner available. Automation-compatible mail helps to keep the cost of mail processing from rising faster. Here are some pointers for preparing letter mail for OCR (optical character recognition) processing:

---

3. National Information Standards Organization, *Interlibrary Loan Data Elements: American National Standard for Interlibrary Loan Data Elements*, National Information Standard Series ANSI/NISO Z39.63–1989 (New Brunswick, N.J.: Transaction Publishers, 1990). (Revised edition in press)

- Machine printed (can be typewritten)
- Uniform left margin
- Formatted to allow equipment to "recognize" the information and "match" it in its files
- Complete as possible (important to include address directions such as NE and suite or room numbers)
- Uppercase letters preferred
- Punctuation is all right

The address format should be as follows (starting from the bottom):

Post Office, State, Zip Code Line: must be ⅝″ from bottom of envelope; use two-letter abbreviation for state; if necessary, the zip code can be on a lower line, aligned left and still ⅝″ from the bottom

Delivery Address Line: street address, post office box, suite, room number, or unit designation

Name of Recipient Line: name of institution and library go here

Information Attention Line: interlibrary loan goes here

The entire address must appear within an imaginary rectangle that extends from ⅝″ to 2¾″ from the bottom of the envelope, with ½″ margins on each side. It should be clear of the return address area. An "OCR Readable Type Styles" table is found in *Designing Business Letter Mail.*[4] Both Elite and Pica styles are included as well as those used by many computer printers. Dot-matrix characters are all right if the dots touch each other. Italic, highly stylized, scriptlike styles should be avoided.

Many libraries return the remaining copies of the ALA Interlibrary Loan Request form and the borrowing library's shipping label in a window envelope. Careful folding of the request is required. The U.S. Postal Service has a suggestion:

> For OCR processing, at least ⅛″ clearance (¼″ is preferred) should be maintained between the address and edges of the window, when the insert is moved to its full limits inside the envelope.[5]

Keep one copy of the request for statistical purposes or use a statistical software package for this purpose. Unless agreed on as suitable, routing a paper request to another library is discouraged because of the inconvenience for the lending library in processing an already used form.

Ship material

Note the method of transmission for the materials. Then separate the requested items by the way in which they will be sent. Send photocopied material by fax, Ariel, or the Internet when requested. The material should include not only the photocopied pages but a cover sheet with the sender, the receiver, the number of pages being transmitted, and the sender's voice telephone number, fax number, and/or electronic address. The cover sheet may be omitted providing all identifying information is included on a transmitted interlibrary loan request form (see appendix S, 3.2). Remember that a copy of the request or request identifier must accompany the photocopy (the Code, 5.3). Negative responses to fax requests (see appendix S, 5.6 and 5.7) can be sent at this time, including responses to rush fax requests, which must be made within one working day (see appendix S, 5.3). Some fax machines allow materials to be sent in a batch mode at night when long-distance telephone rates are lower. Make sure that you receive a confirmation for receipt of the transmission. You may want to keep the photocopy for several days in order to retransmit the pages if the first transmission was not readable or was incomplete. Discard the photocopy after the transmission is successful (see appendix S, 5.5).

Scan the pages of information that are to be sent by electronic document delivery over the Internet. Ariel, the document transmission system from the Research Libraries Group that delivers documents over the Internet, is gaining in popularity. It allows scanning directly from a book or periodical without having to photocopy first. The same procedures apply to the Internet delivery as to fax (see appendix S and the paragraph immediately above).

---

4. U.S. Postal Service, *Designing Business Letter Mail,* Publication 25 (Washington, D.C.: U.S. Government Printing Office, 1992), 19.

5. Ibid., 10.

Remind libraries that expect documents to come by fax or the Internet to keep their equipment turned on and maintained. Having to resend requests is very time consuming.

Send other photocopies by the U.S. Postal Service. "First-class mail" can be used for copies weighing less than eleven ounces. "Third-class mail" can be used for all photocopies, including those that weigh more than eleven ounces. "Third-class mail" is slower and cheaper. "Express mail," which is more expensive, will provide for next-day delivery or as soon as it arrives at the target city. "Priority mail" allows for two to three days for delivery with no special provisions when it reaches the target city. Include a copy of the interlibrary lending request or request identifier (the Code, 5.3) and an invoice or indication of the amount to be charged, if there is one.

Wrapping and packaging guidelines are of increasing importance to the library community. The Research Libraries Group has included wrapping and packaging guidelines in an appendix to the *RLG Shared Resources Manual.*[6] The American Library Association Reference and Adult Services Division's Interlibrary Loan Committee is working on guidelines, "Interlibrary Loan Packaging and Wrapping Guidelines," but at this writing they have not yet been approved. Look for them to be published in *RQ* when final approval is given.

Prepare library materials that are to be sent by the U.S. Postal Service. Packaging these materials carefully is very important because the borrowing library is responsible for the safety of the material once it leaves your premises and until you receive it again (the Code, 4.8). Items should be packaged to prevent damage in shipping (the Code, 5.6). The two major sources of potential damage to books in transit, caused by postal workers and equipment, are twisting of the package and the impact of heavier packages tossed onto lighter packages. The corners of books are particularly vulnerable to damage.

The best way to ship books is to wrap the volume in bubble wrap or brown paper and put it in a sturdy cardboard carton or cardboard book mailer.

Not every library can afford to do this. Padded envelopes are often used and reused when they are in good condition. Remember to mark out old addresses and postal marks when reusing envelopes. Those no longer serviceable should be discarded. It is best to wrap the volume in bubble wrap or custom-cut binder's board for protection when using padded envelopes. Packaging materials appropriate to the size of the material should be used. Using very heavy staples to close a padded envelope makes it difficult for the borrower to open the package without damaging the materials or oneself. Tape is the recommended closure material. Do not use polystyrene plastic bits ("peanuts") because they can allow movement within a carton. Be certain there are "to" and "from" addresses on the package. Microfilm should be packed in a sturdy box padded with crumpled paper or bubble wrap. Do not tape, glue, or otherwise mar the original microfilm container. Microfiche should be wrapped between two pieces of cardboard before placing in a padded mailing envelope. Read the "Guidelines for Packaging and Shipping Microforms" (see appendix X). Audiovisual materials require special packaging. Sometimes audiovisual material arrives in a special case; in that event be sure to return the material in the case in which it came.[7] Firmness in packaging is particularly important for audiovisual materials. Particular care should be taken to keep the wrapping material, such as dust from padded mailers, from getting onto the media. Bubble wrap is preferred to other packaging material. The "Guidelines for the Loan of Rare and Unique Materials" (see appendix V) should be consulted before packaging such materials. Be sure to let the borrowing library know what shipping method and type of packaging should be used to return the loaned material.

Money can be saved by understanding the U.S. Postal Service regulations regarding the mailing of library materials. These change with some frequency. For libraries with separate mail rooms, it may be necessary to make sure the mail-room personnel are knowledgeable about the mailing of books. The U.S. Government Printing Office pub-

---

6. "Appendix 5: Wrapping and Packaging Guidelines," in *RLG Shared Resources Manual,* 5th ed., rev. (Mountain View, Calif.: Research Libraries Group), in press.

7. The American Library Association Video Round Table

is developing "Guidelines for the Loan of Video and Other Audiovisual Formats." Publication of the completed document was expected in 1996.

lishes the quarterly *Domestic Mail Manual,* which gives all the requirements. This is available (for perusal but not for sale) at your local post office. Shipments of books weighing one pound or more fall into one of the categories of "Fourth-class mail" that all travel at the same rate of speed. The choice of category depends upon the weight of the package, where the package is going, and whether or not it is permanently bound printed matter. "Bound printed matter" can be used for permanently bound books weighing more than one pound and no more than ten pounds. This method of shipment is cheaper than "Library rate" for packages to be delivered within about 1,300 miles. (Sending books from San Francisco to New York using this rate would not be cost effective.) Some postal employees are reluctant to accept parcels of library materials for the "Bound printed matter" rate, but there have been official rulings stating that library materials *can* be mailed using this rate. For packages going further, "Library rate" is less expensive and may also be used for packages weighing more than ten pounds and those containing materials that are not permanently bound. The U.S. Postal Service appears to be phasing out "Library rate" in favor of "Bound printed matter." "Parcel post" is generally not used to mail books domestically because of the cost. "Book rate," generally used by individuals, is not a cost-effective way for libraries to mail books. If it is necessary to budget for the cost of shipping books, figure that the average book weighs two pounds; the cost per book will be the charge for the first pound, the cost for one additional pound, and the packaging material.

Label all packages prominently "Interlibrary Loan." This simple precaution should prevent the borrowing library from shelving or cataloging the book by mistake. Comply with requests for expedited delivery methods such as "Express mail," "Priority mail," "Airmail," and special delivery service. The borrowing library should expect to reimburse you for this. A shipping label should already have been prepared (see "Annotate interlibrary lending request forms," above). Be certain the right shipping label is affixed to the right parcel; mix-ups do happen.

Insure valuable library materials with the U.S. Postal Service or send by a package delivery service that includes insurance in its base rate. The ability to track the item is assured by these methods. It is especially important to insure dissertations and theses and other unique material. Audiovisual material is generally insured for the replacement value. Ask the borrowing library to insure the materials when returning them.

Package delivery services are also to be considered when sending library material to another library. Many libraries in reciprocal groups are changing to these services or a special courier for shipment. Compare the rates, insurance possibilities, packaging requirements, and delivery time to help make a decision as to which method is best. Sometimes it is possible for a group of libraries to negotiate a contract with reduced rates for delivery.

Libraries fortunate enough to use a courier service usually have less elaborate shipping preparations. It is still necessary to take care in affixing the right code or label to the package so that it does not go to the wrong library.

For sending packages out of the United States, see chapter 6, "International Interlibrary Loan," "International Interlibrary Lending."

Solve problems

Find time each day to deal with requests posing problems. Checking your lending policies and finding that you hold the needed item in your collection are the responsibilities of the borrowing library (the Code, 4.3). Yet a common reason for not filling a request is because it cannot be found in the online public access catalog, card catalog, or other library records. If the request does not show a verification source or original source of reference and does not have correct bibliographic data, the request may be returned unfilled, without special effort to identify the reference. A form letter, note, or electronic response can be sent to the borrowing library pointing out the lack of an adequate citation.

Even though verification on the part of the lending library is not required, the proportion of filled interlibrary loan requests increases when the lending library verifies. A quick deciphering of acronyms and abbreviations, for instance, often results in a filled request. Most libraries are much more willing to help verify citations if there is clear indication on the request that the borrowing library has exhausted its own resources. Help as much as time and staff permit. Make a concerted attempt to locate items published in your institution; no one else can help if you do not supply the item. Search carefully for missing items. Misshelved materials and inaccurate circulation records are often at fault. Bringing problems such as these to the attention of the library staff will help to provide better service to your own patrons. Take time to telephone, fax, or correspond about difficult problems.

Follow up on loans

Attend to follow-up procedures on loans. Recall books needed by your patrons (the Code, 4.11 and 5.9). Renew books promptly when possible. No response to a renewal request means that the borrowing library may assume that the renewal has been granted for the same length as the original loan period (the Code, 4.10 and 5.8). Send overdue notices when ample time for return transit has elapsed. Some libraries have instituted overdue fines for interlibrary lending. Persevere in collection of lending payments. Deal with problems on an individual basis. If all else fails, suspend service to a requesting library that fails to comply with the existing codes, agreements, or the National Interlibrary Loan Code for the United States, 1993 (the Code, 5.10).

Occasionally, you will have to arrange for repair of damage or replacement of lost material. Collection development or preservation librarians may need to be consulted. All costs of repair or replacement must be met by the borrowing library (the Code, 4.8). In addition to the cost of the material, a processing fee may be assessed. It is also possible to ask the borrowing library to purchase a copy of the lost item and forward it to you along with a processing fee. Respond to U.S. Postal Service claims promptly if a search process is initiated, or initiate a search procedure yourself if that is indicated. Searches can often be made through package delivery services as well.

Receive returned material

Unwrap and inspect material upon return. Notify the borrowing library of failure to return items in adequate packaging and of damage to the material. Discharge from the circulation records and sensitize the items if necessary. Reshelve the material.

Report interlibrary lending activities

Use a copy of the interlibrary loan form or use a statistical software package for statistical purposes and for a record of activity. See chapter 7, "Management of Interlibrary Loan," "Operations," for suggestions on statistics and reports. Give an account of interlibrary lending activities to your administration at least once each year.

3

Interlibrary Loan, Reproduction, and the Copyright Law

Interlibrary loan began with the lending and return of books. Only after reproduction equipment was plentiful in libraries did interlibrary loan include reproductions of works that could not be spared from the lending library's collection. The demand for reproductions, chiefly from periodicals though now increasingly from online sources, has continued to rise until some interlibrary loan offices now fill two reproduction requests for every book loan. Lending a book is a right that a library may exercise or not, as it chooses. Reproducing from copyrighted works may be done only in accordance with the copyright law as amended and its accompanying guidelines.

Librarians are more comfortable with the copyright law now than in 1978 when it went into effect, yet there are many unresolved issues that are continually being discussed and negotiated. Whether the intended balance between the rights of creators and the needs of users of copyrighted works has been reached is a matter of dispute between librarians and publishers. The largest issue for discussion at present is that of digitized information: When is it in fixed form? How does the fact that digitized information may not be a facsimile of a print source effect libraries? What digitized information can be copied by a library or archive? What rights under the copyright law are given up when a license is negotiated for an electronic database? These and many more questions remain to be resolved.

For the present, interlibrary loan librarians must work under the provisions of the copyright law as amended, the guidelines that have been developed, and the wisdom court cases bring. The discussion that follows has to do with interlibrary loan services in not-for-profit institutions—not with cost-recovery document delivery or for-profit document delivery. For an international copyright discussion, see chapter 6, "International Interlibrary Loan," "International Interlibrary Borrowing."

THE COPYRIGHT LAW

On January 1, 1978, the Copyright Act of October 19, 1976, went into effect. This is the most recent copyright law and the one we use today. A thorough understanding of the provisions of the copyright law and the accompanying documents is essential for the competent operation of interlibrary borrowing and lending. Indeed, the full exercise of rights under the copyright law cannot be realized unless the basic provisions of the law are mastered.

The first step is to acquire up-to-date copyright law information. Several works are a great help in understanding the copyright law (all prices subject to change):

Bruwelheide, Janis H. *The Copyright Primer for Librarians and Educators.* 2nd ed. Chicago: American Library Association; Washington, D.C.: National Education Association, 1995.

Purchase from the following source:
American Library Association
Book Order Fulfillment

155 N. Wacker Drive
Chicago, IL 60606-1719
ALA Order # 0642-7-2045
Telephone: (800) 545-2433, press 7
Fax: (312) 836-9958
$25 paperback, ALA members
$22.50
Shipping: $6

U.S. Copyright Office. *Reproduction of Copyrighted Works by Educators and Librarians.* Circular 21. Washington, D.C.: U.S. Government Printing Office, 1992.

Order from the following source:
Copyright Office
Publications Section, LM-455
Library of Congress
Washington, DC 20559-6000
Free from the Copyright Office
Telephone: (202) 707-9100

(Frequently requested Copyright Office circulars, announcements, copyright catalog entries, and regulations are available over the Internet. Access: telnet marvel.loc.gov and log in as "marvel" to access the system, then select the "Copyright" menu. The World Wide Web address can also be checked: URL: <http://lcweb.loc.gov/copyright>.)

Gasaway, Laura N., and Sarah K. Wiant. *Libraries and Copyright: A Guide to Copyright Law in the 1990s.* Washington, D.C.: Special Libraries Association, 1994.

> Purchase from the following source:
> Special Libraries Association
> Book Orders Department
> 1700 18th Street, NW
> Washington, DC 20009-2508
> Order number is ISBN: 0-87111-407-0
> Telephone: (202) 234-4700, ext. 643
> Fax: (202) 265-5317
> $50, SLA members $40
> Shipping: 5% of subtotal plus $5

All of these publications contain the following guidelines, which help explain the doctrine of fair use (§107):

Agreement on Guidelines for Classroom Copying in Not-for-Profit Educational Institutions with Respect to Books and Periodicals.[1]

Guidelines for Educational Use of Music.[2]

Guidelines for Off-Air Recording of Broadcast Programming for Educational Purposes.[3]

The most important sections of the copyright law for interlibrary loan purposes are as follows:

§106 Exclusive rights in copyrighted works

§107 Limitations on exclusive rights: Fair use

§108 Limitations on exclusive rights: Reproduction by libraries and archives

§504 Remedies for infringement: Damages and profits

Two works cited above contain significant sections of the copyright law. The *Copyright Primer for Librarians and Educators* contains a reprint of §106–110 of the copyright law. The *Reproduction of Copyrighted Works by Educators and Librarians* contains a reprint of §106–108 and 504 of the copyright law.

Much of the U.S. National Commission on New Technological Uses of Copyrighted Works "CONTU Guidelines on Photocopying under Interlibrary Loan Agreements" is reproduced later in this chapter. These guidelines, which contain "Guidelines for the Proviso of Subsection 108 (g)(2)," are of particular interest to interlibrary loan librarians because systematic reproduction, copyright representation for requests, and record maintenance for photocopy requests are all discussed.

Later in the chapter, §201.14, "Warnings of copyright for use by certain libraries and archives," is reprinted from the *U.S. Code of Federal Regulations.*

The law itself can be obtained:

U.S. Copyright Office. *Copyright Law of the United States of America, Contained in Title 17 of the United States Code . . . Revised to September 30, 1994 . . . .* Circular 92. Washington, D.C.: U.S. Government Printing Office, 1995.

> Purchase from the following source:
> Superintendent of Documents
> P.O. Box 371954
> Pittsburgh, PA 15250-7954
> Order # 030-002-00179-9
> Telephone: (202) 512-1800
> Fax: (202) 512-2250
> $4.75 paperback. Can pay by check, GPO deposit account, VISA, or MasterCard

Other free circulars of interest from the U.S. Copyright Office can be found in the bibliography at the end of this chapter (see "Bibliography: Further Reading").

---

1. U.S. House Committee on the Judiciary, *Copyright Law Revision; Report Together with Additional Views to Accompany Senate Bill 22,* 94th Cong., 2nd sess., 1976, H. Rept. 1476, §107, 67–70.

2. Ibid., 70–72.

3. *Congressional Record,* 1979, 97th Cong., 1st sess., vol. 127, pt. 18: 24,048–49.

UNDERSTANDING THE COPYRIGHT LAW

Copyright is a form of protection provided by the laws of the United States (title 17, U.S. Code) to the authors of "original works of authorship" including literary, dramatic, musical, artistic, and certain other intellectual works. This protection is available to both published and unpublished works.[4]

The copyright law also states in §102 that the works must be

> fixed in any tangible medium of expression, now known or later developed, from which they can be perceived, reproduced, or otherwise communicated, either directly or with the aid of a machine or device.[5]

Until such time as guidelines are developed or the law is amended, it appears that digitized materials are covered by the copyright law.

Exclusive rights in copyrighted works

The owner of a copyright has the right to do the following (§106):

(1) reproduce the copyrighted work . . . ;

(2) prepare derivative works based upon the copyrighted work;

(3) distribute copies . . . of the copyrighted work . . . ;

(4) perform the copyrighted work publicly; and

(5) display the copyrighted work publicly.[6]

Fair use

These rights are tempered by the fair use section of the copyright law (§107). The fair use section states that it is not an infringement of copyright to use copyrighted material for the purposes of "criticism, comment, news reporting, teaching, scholarship, or research." These factors must be considered in determining fair use:

(1) the purpose and character of the use, including whether such use is of a commercial nature or is for nonprofit educational purposes;

(2) the nature of the copyrighted work;

(3) the amount and substantiality of the portion used in relation to the copyrighted work as a whole; and

(4) the effect of the use upon the potential market for or value of the copyrighted work.[7]

The economic impact on the copyright owner is generally the most important one.

Because fair use is a difficult concept to understand in terms of libraries and reproduction, consulting other sources is recommended:

Bruwelheide, Janis H. *The Copyright Primer for Librarians and Educators.* 2nd ed. Chicago: American Library Association; Washington, D.C.: National Education Association, 1995, 11–15.

Gasaway, Laura N., and Sarah K. Wiant. *Libraries and Copyright: A Guide to Copyright Law in the 1990s.* Washington, D.C.: Special Libraries Association, 1994, 26–31.

When deciding whether any particular instance of copying is fair use, the criteria listed above must be considered. Guidelines have been developed by educators, publishers, and authors to help determine fair use. These are the "Agreement on Guidelines for Classroom Copying in Not-for-Profit Educational Institutions with Respect to Books and Periodicals," "Guidelines for Educational Use of Music," and "Guidelines for Off-Air Recording of Broadcast Programming for Educational Purposes."

---

4. U.S. Copyright Office, *Copyright Basics,* Circular 1 (Washington, D.C.: U.S. Government Printing Office, 1995), 2.

5. U.S. Copyright Office, *Copyright Law of the United States of America . . . ,* Circular 92 (Washington, D.C.: U.S. Government Printing Office, 1995), 9.

6. Ibid., 12–13.

7. Ibid., 15.

These guidelines are cited above, under "The Copyright Law."

Reproduction by libraries and archives

Knowledge of "§108. Limitations on exclusive rights: Reproduction by libraries and archives" is extremely important for the interlibrary loan librarian because it is here that the most explicit right for libraries to copy is given. It states the following:

(a) Notwithstanding the provisions of section 106, it is not an infringement of copyright for a library or archives, or any of its employees acting within the scope of their employment, to reproduce no more than one copy . . . of a work, or to distribute such copy . . . , under the conditions specified by the section, if—

   (1) the reproduction or distribution is made without any purpose of direct or indirect commercial advantage;

   (2) the collections of the library or archives are (i) open to the public, or (ii) available not only to researchers affiliated with the library or archives or with the institution of which it is a part, but also to other persons doing research in a specialized field; and

   (3) the reproduction or distribution of the work includes a notice of copyright.[8]

Section 108(b) has to do with the rights of reproduction and distribution in facsimile form of a copy of an unpublished work. This copy may be for preservation and security or for deposit for research use in another library, provided the copy reproduced is currently in the collections of the library.

Section 108(c) covers the right of reproduction in facsimile form of a copy for the purpose of replacement of a copy that is damaged, deteriorating, lost, or stolen, if an unused replacement cannot be obtained at a fair price. This section allows for the copying of replacement pages for articles torn out of periodicals. Some guidelines have been developed to give aid in deciding whether or not a replacement can be obtained at a fair price. "Guidelines for Seeking or Making a Copy of an Entire Copyrighted

Work for a Library, Archives, or User" can be found in appendix Y.

The first part of §108(d) reads as follows:

(d) The rights of reproduction and distribution under this section apply to a copy, made from the collection of a library or archives where the user makes his or her request or from that of another library or archives, of no more than one article or other contribution to a copyrighted collection or periodical issue, or to a copy or phonorecord of a small part of any other copyrighted work, if—

   (1) the copy or phonorecord becomes the property of the user, and the library or archives has had no notice that the copy or phonorecord would be used for any purpose other than private study, scholarship, or research; and

   (2) the library or archives displays prominently . . . a warning of copyright . . .[9]

This section allows a library to copy materials for a library patron, even if the library has to get that material from another library. The "CONTU Guidelines" and §108(g) should be used when sending the request to another library.

Section 108(e) allows for the reproduction and distribution of a copy of an entire work or a large part of a work copied from a library or archive if the library determines that a copy cannot be obtained at a fair price. The conditions listed under §108(d)(1) and (2) apply here. See also "Guidelines for Seeking or Making a Copy of an Entire Copyrighted Work for a Library, Archives, or User," appendix Y.

Section 108(f) has to do with unsupervised photocopying equipment located in the library.

Section 108(g) talks of isolated and unrelated reproduction of a single copy and systematic reproduction. For a discussion on how systematic reproduction is defined and what libraries must do, see the "CONTU Guidelines," later in this chapter.

Section 108(h) says that the rights of reproduction and distribution do not apply to a musical work; a pictorial, graphic, or sculptural work; or a motion picture or other audiovisual work other than

---

8. Ibid., 15–16.

9. Ibid., 16.

an audiovisual work dealing with news. It lists the exceptions granted under §108(b), (c), (d), and (e) as applying here.

Section 108(i), having to do with five-year reports from the Register of Copyrights, was repealed in June 1992.[10]

Infringement

Interlibrary loan librarians should be aware that there are penalties for not complying with the copyright law. The copyright owner would have to sue and win the case in order to collect damages. The remedies for infringement affecting librarians and educators follow:

> §504(c)(2) In a case where the copyright owner sustains the burden of proving, and the court finds, that infringement was committed willfully, the court in

its discretion may increase the award of statutory damages to a sum of not more than $100,000. In a case where the infringer sustains the burden of proving, and the court finds, that such infringer was not aware and had no reason to believe that his or her acts constituted an infringement of copyright, the court in its discretion may reduce the award of statutory damages to a sum of not less than $200. The court shall remit statutory damages in any case where an infringer believed and had reasonable grounds for believing that his or her use of the copyrighted work was a fair use under section 107, if the infringer was: (i) an employee or agent of a nonprofit educational institution, library, or archives acting within the scope of his or her employment who, or such institution, library, or archives itself, which infringed by reproducing the work in copies or phonorecords . . .[11]

BORROWING AND THE COPYRIGHT LAW

Someone in interlibrary loan or in your organization should be responsible for knowing the provisions of the copyright law so that questions can be answered. Many institutions, particularly universities and colleges, have in place or are now developing copyright policies as an aid in dealing with the copyright law.

For borrowing activities, attention must be paid to displaying copyright warnings, complying with the law when making requests, and retaining records as prescribed (the Code, 4.7).

Copyright warnings

There are two instances where copyright warnings *are required* by federal regulations. A Display Warning of Copyright using the prescribed wording should be posted where interlibrary loan and document delivery requests are accepted. An Order Warning of Copyright must be included on the printed forms supplied by libraries and used by their

patrons for ordering copies. Both the Display Warning of Copyright and Order Warning of Copyright must consist of the following notice:

NOTICE: WARNING CONCERNING COPYRIGHT RESTRICTIONS

The copyright law of the United States (title 17, United States Code) governs the making of photocopies or other reproductions of copyrighted material.

Under certain conditions specified in the law, libraries and archives are authorized to furnish a photocopy or other reproduction. One of these specific conditions is that the photocopy or reproduction is not to be "used for any purpose other than private study, scholarship, or research." If a user makes a request for, or later uses, a photocopy or reproduction for purposes in excess of "fair use," that user may be liable for copyright infringement.

This institution reserves the right to refuse to accept a copying order if, in its judgment, fulfillment

---

10. Ibid., 15, footnote 2.

11. Ibid., 90–91.

of the order would involve violation of copyright law.[12]

The federal regulations contain the following instructions:

> (c) FORM AND MANNER OF USE
>
> > (1) A Display Warning of Copyright shall be printed on heavy paper or other durable material in type at least 18 points in size, and shall be displayed prominently, in such manner and location as to be clearly visible, legible, and comprehensible to a casual observer within the immediate vicinity of the place where orders are accepted.
> >
> > (2) An Order Warning of Copyright shall be printed within a box located prominently on the order form itself either on the front side of the form or immediately adjacent to the space calling for the name or signature of the person using the form. The notice shall be printed in type size no smaller than that used predominantly throughout the form, and in no case shall the type size be smaller than 8 points. The notice shall be printed in such manner as to be clearly legible, comprehensible, and readily apparent to a casual reader of the form.[13]

The federal regulations relate to the library patron and not library-to-library transactions. It is true that the regulations do not take into account electronic patron request forms. Suggestions for using the proper wording and appending it to a reasonable place on electronic patron request forms are these: (1) include the Display Warning of Copyright before an electronic form for requesting a copy of a periodical article appears and (2) include the Order Warning of Copyright adjacent to the space for the name of the person using the form. For telephone requests, the Order Warning of Copyright can be read over the telephone. Responses to fax requests can contain the Order Warning of Copyright.

Copyright compliance

When requesting photocopies of library materials, a determination of copyright compliance must be made for each request. (This does not apply to library materials that are borrowed and returned, but only to those that are reproduced.) The first step is to decide whether or not the work to be copied is covered by copyright. The general description of works covered by copyright is contained in §102 of the copyright law and is discussed in "Understanding the Copyright Law," above. Other considerations follow.

Duration of Copyright

The duration of copyright (§ 302–304) is not easy to understand or remember. What follows is a short summary of the law:

> *Works created on or after January 1, 1978:* Works by an individual: life of author plus 50 years. Joint works: life of surviving author plus 50 years. Anonymous works, pseudonymous works, works made for hire, "corporate" authors: 75 years from date of first publication or 100 years from year of its creation, whichever expires first. Works in these categories will not begin to pass into the public domain until January 1, 2053 (1978 + 75).
>
> *Works created but not published or copyrighted on or before January 1, 1978* (not previously declared to be in the public domain): The duration is the same as in the preceding paragraph except that no term of copyright shall expire before December 31, 2002. If the work is published on or before December 31, 2002, the term will not expire before December 31, 2027 (minimum term of 25 years).
>
> *Copyrights in effect as of January 1, 1978,* Section 304: Copyrights on these works were extended to 75 years from first date of copyright.[14]

For further clarification, see the chart prepared by Laura N. Gasaway, "When Works Pass into the Public Domain," figure 12.

---

12. *U.S. Code of Federal Regulations,* vol. 37, sec. 201.14(b) (1995).

13. Ibid., sec. 201.14(c).

14. Janis H. Bruwelheide, *The Copyright Primer for Librarians and Educators,* 2nd ed. (Chicago: American Library Association; Washington, D.C.: National Education Association, 1995), 5.

When Works Pass into the Public Domain

Date of Work	Protected From	Term
Created 1–1–78 or after	When work is fixed in tangible medium of expression	Life + 50 years (or, if work of corporate authorship, 75 years from publication, or 100 years from creation, whichever is first)
Published between 1964–77	When published with notice	28 years for first term; now automatic extension of 47 years for second term
Published between 75 years ago and 1963	When published with notice	28 years + could be renewed for 47 years; if not so renewed, now in public domain
Published more than 75 years ago	Now in public domain	None
Created before 1–1–78 but not published	1–1–78, the effective date of the 1976 Act, which eliminated common law copyright	Life + 50 years. All works that remain unpublished as of 12–31–2002 will pass into public domain on that date.
Created before 1–1–78 but published between then and 12–31–2002	1–1–78, the effective date of the Act, which eliminated common law copyright	Passes into public domain 12–31–2027

FIGURE 12. When Works Pass into the Public Domain

Notice of Copyright

The notice of copyright was mandatory on all works published before March 1, 1989. Any work first published before that date must bear a notice of copyright or it may risk loss of copyright protection. For works first published on or after March 1, 1989, use of the copyright notice is optional.[15]

The notice of copyright should contain the symbol ©, the word "Copyright," or the abbreviation "Copr."; the year of first publication; and the name of the owner of copyright.[16]

Works Not Covered by Copyright

Several categories of works are not protected by copyright. They are as follows:

- Works that have *not* been fixed in a tangible form of expression . . .
- Titles, names, short phrases, and slogans; familiar symbols or designs; mere variations of typographic ornamentation, lettering, or coloring; mere listings of ingredients or contents.
- Ideas, procedures, methods, systems, processes, concepts, principles, discoveries, or devices, as distinguished from a description, explanation, or illustration.
- Works consisting *entirely* of information that is common property and containing no original authorship . . .[17]

Some works are not protected by a valid copyright and are in the public domain. These works can be copied at will. These are generally works that were published more than 75 years ago. For works that were created but not published or copyrighted before January 1, 1978, the term is life of the author plus 50 years, and the law provides that in no case will the term of copyright for works in this category expire before December 31, 2002. For such works published on or before December 31, 2002, the term of copyright will not expire before December 31, 2027.

United States government works are not covered by the copyright law (§105), but copyrights can be transferred to the government. Works produced under federal contract might be copyrighted by the author. State and municipal governments are not dealt with in the copyright law. There is some controversy as to whether they can claim copyright protection or not.[18]

Some periodicals are covered by copyright, but a release is given in the masthead that might allow library reproduction, such as in *American Libraries:*

> Materials in this journal subject to ALA copyright may be photocopied for noncommercial educational purposes.

CONTU Guidelines

Once a decision is reached that a needed work is copyrighted, a determination must be made whether or not the intended interlibrary loan copying is permissible under provisions of the copyright law and the "CONTU Guidelines." Refer to the section "Understanding the Copyright Law," earlier in this chapter, for information on fair use and reproduction by libraries. A library essentially forfeits legal copying rights by sending *all* copying requests to a commercial document supplier that includes royalty payments in the price of the document. Five copies provided for under the "CONTU Guidelines" can be requested from another library before permission is sought or royalties paid.

The U.S. National Commission on New Technological Uses of Copyrighted Works (CONTU) was created by Congress as part of the effort to revise the copyright laws. It was created to provide the president and Congress with recommendations on copyright law or procedure to assure that both public access and the rights of owners of copyrights were addressed. CONTU's recommendations are not law, but they were incorporated into the Conference Committee Report on Senate Bill 22 written while the copyright law was under consideration.[19]

15. U.S. Copyright Office, *Copyright Basics,* Circular 1 (Washington, D.C.: U.S. Government Printing Office, 1995), 4.

16. Ibid., 5.

17. Ibid., 3.

18. Laura N. Gasaway and Sarah K. Wiant, *Libraries and Copyright: A Guide to Copyright Law in the 1990s* (Washington, D.C.: Special Libraries Association, 1994), 19.

19. U.S. House Conference Committee on Senate Bill 22, *General Revision of the Copyright Law, Title 17 of the United States Code; Conference Report to Accompany Senate Bill 22,* 94th Cong., 2nd sess., 1976, H. Rept. 1733.

The section of the copyright law the guidelines address, §108(g)(2), is as follows:

(g) The rights of reproduction and distribution under this section extend to the isolated and unrelated reproduction or distribution of a single copy or phonorecord of the same material on separate occasions, but do not extend to cases where the library or archives, or its employee—

(2) engages in the systematic reproduction or distribution of single or multiple copies or phonorecords of material described in subsection (d): *Provided,* That nothing in this clause prevents a library or archives from participating in interlibrary arrangements that do not have, as their purpose or effect, that the library or archives receiving such copies or phonorecords for distribution does so in such aggregate quantities as to substitute for a subscription to or purchase of such work.[20]

The "CONTU Guidelines," "Guidelines for the Proviso of Subsection 108(g)(2)," were written to clarify what was meant by "systematic reproduction." Libraries, in general, follow these guidelines:

Guidelines for the Proviso of Subsection 108(g)(2)

1. As used in the proviso of subsection 108 (g)(2), the words "such aggregate quantities as to substitute for a subscription to or purchase of such work" shall mean:

(a) with respect to any given periodical (as opposed to any given issue of a periodical), filled requests of a library or archives (a "requesting entity") within any calendar year for a total of six or more copies of an article or articles published in such periodical within five years prior to the date of the request. These guidelines specifically shall not apply, directly or indirectly, to any request of a requesting entity for a copy or copies of an article or articles published in any issue of a periodical, the publication date of which is more than five years prior to the date when the request is made. These guidelines do not define the meaning, with respect to such a request, of "such aggregate quantities as to substitute for a subscription to [such periodical]."

(b) With respect to any other material described in subsection 108(d) (including fiction and poetry), filled requests of a requesting entity within any calendar year for a total of six or more copies or phonorecords of or from any given work (including a collective work) during the entire period when such material shall be protected by copyright.

2. In the event that a requesting entity:

(a) shall have in force or shall have entered an order for a subscription to a periodical, or

(b) has within its collection, or shall have entered an order for, a copy or phonorecord of any other copyrighted work, material from either category of which it desires to obtain by copy from another library or archives (the "supplying entity"), because the material to be copied is not reasonably available for use by the requesting entity itself, then the fulfillment of such request shall be treated as though the requesting entity made such copy from its own collection. A library or archives may request a copy or phonorecord from a supplying entity only under those circumstances where the requesting entity would have been able, under the other provisions of section 108, to supply such copy from materials in its own collection.

3. No request for a copy or phonorecord of any material to which these guidelines apply may be fulfilled by the supplying entity unless such request is accompanied by a representation

---

20. U.S. Copyright Office, *Copyright Law of the United States of America . . . ,* Circular 92 (Washington, D.C.: U.S. Government Printing Office, 1995), 17–18.

by the requesting entity that the request was made in conformity with these guidelines.

4. The requesting entity shall maintain records of all requests made by it for copies or phonorecords of any materials to which these guidelines apply and shall maintain records of the fulfillment of such requests, which records shall be retained until the end of the third complete calendar year after the end of the calendar year in which the respective request shall have been made.

5. As part of the review provided for in subsection 108(i), these guidelines shall be reviewed not later than five years from the effective date of this bill.[21]

It helps to think of number 1 of the "CONTU Guidelines" as a guideline of 1–1–5–5: during one calendar year, for one periodical title, five articles can be copied from a title published within the last five years. The "CONTU Guidelines" suggest that the sixth copy would represent systematic copying. This applies to reproduction of articles made from copyrighted collective works as well as to periodicals.

Alternatives to Library Copying

Libraries that find their photocopy needs exceed the limits of the copyright law and the guidelines may consider using alternatives to securing the needed material. Here are some suggestions:

1. Borrow the periodical or other item from another library. Checking the policy of the lending library is a prerequisite because many libraries will loan periodicals only under unusual circumstances.

2. Request a reprint of the article directly from the author of the publication.

3. Ask for permission of the copyright owner (often the publisher) to copy beyond the provisions of §107 and §108. A request to copy should include a complete citation for the material to be copied, the number and kind of copies to be made, the expected use to be made of the copies, the form of distribution, and whether or not the material is to be sold. The request should be sent to the permissions department of the publisher in question, along with a self-addressed return envelope. Sometimes payment of a fee is required for such permission to photocopy.

4. Direct patrons to libraries nearby that hold the material.

5. Print out the article from a full-text database that includes payment of royalties in its print charge.

6. Print out the article from a licensed database that includes permission in the license to copy under certain circumstances.

7. Purchase individual periodical issues from the publisher or a periodicals jobber.

8. Purchase a copy from a commercial document supplier whose fee includes payment of royalties.

9. Obtain a copy through interlibrary loan and pay royalties to the copyright owner or the Copyright Clearance Center (CCC). The CCC is a not-for-profit service through which libraries and other organizations may conveniently pay for much of their photocopying that exceed exemptions in the copyright law. The center distributes royalties to the appropriate publishers. The center itself does not provide documents. Contact the following for more information:

    Copyright Clearance Center
    222 Rosewood Drive
    Danvers, MA 01923
    Telephone: (508) 750-8400
    Fax: (508) 750-4470
    World Wide Web:
    <http://www.copyright.com/>
    <http://www.directory.net/copyright/>

10. Enter a subscription or purchase order for the title.

11. Wait until the next calendar year to place the copying request.

---

21. U.S. National Commission on New Technological Uses of Copyrighted Works, *Final Report . . .*, July 31, 1978 (Washington, D.C.: Library of Congress, 1979), 55.

Copyright Representation

If the copying is permissible, an interlibrary loan request may be transmitted to another library. The request for copying must contain a representation concerning copyright (see number 3 of the "CONTU Guidelines" above). Chapter 1 describes the way conformity is represented by the borrower. A discussion of the representation is given below and is reprinted from *American Libraries* by permission of the American Library Association.

COPYRIGHT REPRESENTATION ON THE NATIONAL INTERLIBRARY LOAN OR PHOTOCOPY REQUEST FORM*

*This is the form which transmits a request from *one library to another,* not the form which the *user* fills out to request materials. . . .

The form used to request a loan or photocopy of an item from another library has been modified to facilitate conformity with the Copyright Revision Act of 1976 (PL 94–553) and the guidelines which are intended to provide assistance in the application of the law. The sections of the law which relate to copies that may be requested by using the interlibrary loan or photocopy request form are sections 107 and 108. . . .

The guidelines which relate directly to interlibrary loan are the "Guidelines for the Proviso of Subsection 108(g)(2)" which were developed by the National Commission on New Technological Uses of Copyrighted Works (CONTU).

The requesting entity (borrowing library) is responsible for making sure that the request conforms to the copyright law and the accompanying guidelines. To assure the supply entity (lending library) that the request does so conform, the requesting library must check one of the two boxes provided in the lower left corner of the paper form or include one of the corresponding codes, CCG (Conforms to Copyright Guidelines) or CCL (Conforms to Copyright Law), in the electronic transmission of the request. Unless one of these boxes is checked or one of the codes is included, the supplying entity may refuse to fill the request.

A check in the first box or transmission of the code "CCG" means that the request is in conformity with the CONTU "Guidelines." Request-

ing libraries should bear in mind that the "Guidelines" apply *only* to materials described in Subsection 108(d) of the law, i.e., an article or other contribution to a copyrighted collection or periodical issue or a small part of any other copyrighted work. A check in the second box or transmission of the code "CCL" means that the request is legitimate because it is authorized elsewhere in the copyright law.

108(g)(2) GUIDELINES (CCG)

The first box should be checked by the requesting entity, or the code "CCG" included in transmission of the request, under the following circumstances:

1) When the requesting entity has observed the quantitative restrictions set forth in guideline #1, or

2) When the requesting entity has in force or has entered an order for a subscription to a periodical (See "Guidelines" #2a) or has entered an order for a copy of any other copyrighted work (See "Guidelines" #2b), or

3) When the requesting entity owns the material to be copied and would have been able, under the provisions of Section 108 of the law, to supply the requested copy from materials in its own collection had such materials been reasonably available (See "Guidelines" #2b).

OTHER PROVISIONS OF COPYRIGHT LAW (CCL)

This box should be checked by the requesting entity, or the code "CCL" included in transmission of the request, whenever a copy of material in the public domain is requested or the request for a copy is sanctioned under parts of the law other than Subsection 108(d) as qualified by 108(g)(2) and its interpretive guidelines. This box should be checked under the following circumstances:

A. When the requested copy becomes the property of the user:

1) If the request is for an entire work or substantial part of a work where the requesting library has determined that a copy cannot be obtained at a fair price (See Subsection 108(e));

2) If the request is for a copy of book or periodical material made for a teacher in conformity with the "Agreement on Guidelines for Classroom Copying in Not-for-Profit Educational Institutions" or for copying of music under the "Guidelines for Educational Uses of Music";

3) When the requesting library believes, because of the circumstances of the request, that the reproduction and distribution of the copy is a "fair use" (See Section 107 for four statutory tests to determine whether a given reproduction is or is not a "fair use");

4) When the requested photocopy is a copy of the kind of material described in 108(d) but published earlier than five years prior to the date of the request and, therefore, not covered by the "Guidelines";

5) When the requested material is not subject to the reproduction rights granted by Section 108 (i.e., is a musical work, a pictorial, graphic or sculptural work, or a motion picture or other audiovisual work dealing with news), but the requesting library believes that, because of the circumstances of the request, the reproduction and distribution of the copy would be a "fair use" (See Subsection 108(d) for limitation of Section 108. See Section 107 for four statutory tests to determine whether a given reproduction is or is not a "fair use").

B. When the requested copy becomes a part of the collection of the requesting library:

1) If the request is for a facsimile copy of a published work requested solely for replacement of a damaged, deteriorating, lost, or stolen copy of a work and the requesting library has determined, after reasonable investigation, that an unused

replacement is unavailable at a fair price (See Section 108(c));

2) Where, because of the circumstances of the request, the requesting library believes that the reproduction and distribution of the copy would be a "fair use" (See Section 107 for four statutory tests to determine whether a given reproduction is or is not a "fair use").[22]

If a library states that royalties are being paid, the lending library should supply the request. It is not necessary to check either "CCG" or "CCL" when such a statement is made. See chapter 1, figures 2, 3, and 9, for examples of copyright representation.

Retention of records

Some sort of records are usually kept for all interlibrary loans, if only until statistical compilations are created (see chapter 7, "Management of Interlibrary Loan," "Operations"). The "CONTU Guidelines," number 4, state that records for requests for copies shall be kept until the end of the third complete calendar year. This means that filled requests for copies must be kept for three years plus the current year. Throw away records that are older. They are no longer required and might prove a detriment in case of litigation. Automated interlibrary loan management systems often keep track of this information for interlibrary loan. Because the "CONTU Guidelines" do not specify how to keep track of filled requests for copy, you may devise a system, or you may make use of the suggestions offered by the American Library Association Reference and Adult Services Division, Interlibrary Loan Committee, "Guidelines: Records of Interlibrary Photocopying Requests" (see appendix Z). Many libraries have found that an annual review of interlibrary loan photocopy records is helpful for making a decision to purchase a new periodical subscription. Such records can show demonstrated rather than estimated use by a number of patrons for a particular title.

---

22. Reprinted from "Copyright Law Prompts New ILL Form," *American Libraries* 8 (Oct. 1977): 492B-C.

LENDING AND COPYRIGHT

A thorough knowledge of the copyright law is as necessary for lending as for borrowing. It is in lending activities that a lack of understanding of the law shows up and an opportunity for gentle instruction presents itself.

The borrowing library is responsible for making certain that the request conforms to the copyright law and the accompanying guidelines. A lending library may choose not to process a photocopy request if a representation is not made as to copyright conformity. This representation must be made on both paper and electronic forms: "CCG" (Conforms to Copyright Guidelines) or "CCL" (Conforms to Copyright Law). Lacking this representation, the request for copying should be returned to the borrowing library stating the reason for refusal. Do fill requests for periodical replacement pages that are marked "CCL" because those requests fall under §108(c), not §108(g)(2) and the "CONTU Guidelines." Occasionally, it is necessary to return a request to the borrowing library, even though representation has been made, because it is obvious that the borrowing library does not understand the law. The licensing contract will have to be checked if the request for copying must be done from a licensed database.

The other responsibility for the lending library is stated in the copyright law §108(a)(3):

> The reproduction or distribution of the work includes a notice of copyright.[23]

The language for this notice has been suggested by the American Library Association:

> Notice: This material may be protected by copyright law (Title 17 U.S. Code).[24]

There is some discussion of this form of the notice because it does not convey any information about the copyright. A formal notice—which contains the ©, the word "copyright," or the abbreviation "copr."; the year of first publication; and the name of the copyright owner (not necessarily the author)—does convey the necessary information. A rubber stamp could be developed to make the recording of this information on copies simple and straightforward. A copyright notice cannot be found in some copyrighted works. Laura N. Gasaway and Sarah K. Wiant suggest this alternative wording:

> This material is subject to the U.S. Copyright Law; further reproduction in violation of that law is prohibited.[25]

The recommendation here is to copy the formal notice of copyright or the Gasaway-Wiant wording when there is no discernable notice of copyright.

Though records may well be kept for statistical purposes, there is no requirement in the copyright law or "CONTU Guidelines" that specific lending records be kept.

23. U.S. Copyright Office, *Copyright Law of the United States of America . . . ,* Circular 92 (Washington, D.C.: U.S. Government Printing Office, 1995), 16.

24. "Language Suggested for the Notices Required by the Copyright Revision Act of 1976" (n.p.: American Library As-

sociation, Reference and Adult Services Division, Interlibrary Loan Committee, 1977).

25. Laura N. Gasaway and Sarah K. Wiant, *Libraries and Copyright: A Guide to Copyright Law in the 1990s* (Washington, D.C.: Special Libraries Association, 1994), 45.

KEEPING UP WITH COPYRIGHT DEVELOPMENTS

Training new staff, consulting additional information (particularly guidelines), and noting news items in the professional literature are all essential for keeping up with the copyright law.

Training new staff requires patience and perseverance. Each new employee should read the pertinent section of the law, the accompanying guidelines, and the information in this chapter. Then the work performed should be reviewed and revised until you are certain that the employee has a basic understanding of this matter. Encourage the employee to ask copyright questions as he or she proceeds with the work.

Constant vigilance is required for keeping up with copyright developments. Many journals covering professional library concerns carry news and information about the copyright law and copyright cases that are before the courts. There may well be more guidelines developed to help librarians cope. There is a copyright listserv, CNI-COPYRIGHT; and information on how to subscribe is found in "Keeping Up with Interlibrary Loan and Document Delivery Developments," appendix GG, p. 3.

What will happen in the future? The prevalence of digitized information has brought a new way of information access and retrieval to libraries and patrons. Questions abound concerning the efficacy of the copyright law in protecting intellectual property on the one hand and ensuring the rights of users on the other. Concerned about future developments, the Association of Research Libraries has promulgated a "Statement of Principles," which includes these points:

1. Copyright exists for the public good.
2. Fair use, the library, and other relevant provisions of the Copyright Act of 1976 must be preserved in the development of the emerging information infrastructure.
3. As trustees of the rapidly growing record of human knowledge, libraries and archives must have full use of technology in order to preserve our heritage of scholarship and research.
4. Licensing agreements should not be allowed to abrogate the fair use and library provision authorized in the copyright statute.
5. Librarians and educators have an obligation to educate information users about their rights and responsibilities under intellectual property law.
6. Copyright should not be applied to U.S. government information.
7. The information infrastructure must permit authors to be compensated for the success of their creative works, and copyright owners must have an opportunity for a fair return on their investment.[26]

The Clinton Administration Working Group on Intellectual Property Rights has looked at the application and effectiveness of copyright law and the National Information Infrastructure (NII). The report of the Working Group was published in September 1995.[27] The debate about the report's contents continues, with the parts about extending the length of a copyright, licensing digitized information, and needing library guidelines being of most interest to interlibrary loan librarians. New guidelines could be developed, the copyright law might be amended, or court cases may change how librarians serve their patrons. For the present, the best advice is to know the law and to exercise full rights granted in all its various sections.

---

26. "Intellectual Property: An Association of Research Libraries Statement of Principles" (Washington, D.C.: Association of Research Libraries, 1994), 4.

27. *Intellectual Property and the National Information Infrastructure: The Report of the Working Group on Intellectual Property Rights.* Bruce A. Lehman, Assistant Secretary of Commerce and Commissioner of Patents and Trademarks, Chair. Information Infrastructure Task Force, Ronald H. Brown, Secretary of Commerce, Chair. September 1995. Available on World Wide Web: <http://iitf.doc.gov>.

BIBLIOGRAPHY: FURTHER READING

See "The Copyright Law," at the beginning of this chapter, for a basic bibliography.

Bennett, Scott. "The Management of Intellectual Property." *Computers in Libraries* 14 (May 1994): 18–22, 24.

Crews, Kenneth D. *Copyright, Fair Use and the Challenge for Universities: Promoting the Progress of Higher Education.* Chicago: University of Chicago Press, 1993.

Dukelow, Ruth H. *Library Copyright Guide.* Washington, D.C.: Association for Educational Communications and Technology, 1992.

"Fair Use in the Electronic Age: Serving the Public Interest, a Working Document from the Library Community (Jan. 1995)." In *The Copyright Primer for Librarians and Educators,* by Janis H. Bruwelheide, 118–20. 2nd ed. Chicago: American Library Association; Washington, D.C.: National Education Association, 1995.

Gasaway, Laura N. "Document Delivery." *Computers in Libraries* 14 (May 1994): 25–28, 30–32.

Hemnes, Thomas M. S., Alexander H. Pyle, and Laurie M. McTeague. *A Guide to Copyright Issues in Higher Education.* 3rd ed. Washington, D.C.: National Association of Colleges and University Attorneys, 1994.

LeClercq, Angie Whaley. *Unpublished Materials: Libraries and Fair Use.* SPEC Kit 192. Washington, D.C.: Association of Research Libraries, Office of Management Services, 1993.

"Model Policy Concerning College and University Photocopying for Classroom, Research and Library Reserve Use." *College & Research Library News* 43 (April 1982): 127–31.

Patterson, L. Ray, and Stanley W. Lindberg. *The Nature of Copyright: A Law of Users' Rights.* Athens, Ga.: University of Georgia Press, 1991.

Reed, Mary Hutchings, and Deborah Stanek. "Library and Classroom Use of Copyrighted Videotapes and Computer Software." *American Libraries* 17 (Feb. 1986): 120A-D.

Risher, Carol A., and Laura N. Gasaway. "The Great Copyright Debate; Two Experts Face Off on How to Deal with Intellectual Property in the Digital Age." *Library Journal* 119 (Sept. 15, 1994): 34–37.

U.S. Copyright Office. *Copyright Notice.* Circular 3. Washington, D.C.: U.S. Government Printing Office, 1994.

———. *Duration of Copyright.* Circular 15a. Washington, D.C.: U.S. Government Printing Office, 1994.

———. *Extension of Copyright Terms.* Circular 15t. Washington, D.C.: U.S. Government Printing Office, 1994.

———. *How to Investigate the Copyright Status of a Work.* Circular 22. Washington, D.C.: U.S. Government Printing Office, 1995.

———. *Publications on Copyright.* Circular 2. Washington, D.C.: U.S. Government Printing Office, 1994.

"Using Software: A Guide to the Ethical and Legal Use of Software for Members of the Academic Community" (EDUCOM Brochure, 1992 ed.). In *Copyright, Fair Use and the Challenge for Universities,* by Kenneth D. Crews, 214–20. Chicago: University of Chicago Press, 1993.

Valauskas, Edward J. "Copyright: Know Your Electronic Rights!" *Library Journal* 117 (Aug. 1992): 40–43.

Vlcek, Charles W. *Adoptable Copyright Policy: Copyright Policy and Manuals Designed for Adoption by Schools, Colleges and Universities.* Washington, D.C.: Copyright Information Services, Association for Educational Communications and Technology, 1992.

Dissertations
and
Masters' Theses

Dissertations and masters' theses represent a category of library material that is vital to research but not always readily accessible. Sources of bibliographic information and sugges-tions for obtaining dissertations and masters' theses will be outlined in this chapter. The bibliographic references are generally listed in the order in which they should be used.

GENERAL BIBLIOGRAPHIC SOURCES

Bibliographies of dissertations or masters' theses may be found in a number of reference works, such as the following:

Bibliographic Index: A Cumulative Bibliography of Bibliographies. Vol. 1– , 1937/42– . New York: Wilson, 1945– . Available on CD-ROM. Available online: WILSONLINE, OCLC EPIC, OCLC FirstSearch.

Guide to Reference Books. 11th ed. Edited by Robert Balay. Chicago: American Library Association, 1996.

Reynolds, Michael M. *Guide to Theses and Dissertations: An International Bibliography of Bibliographies.* Rev. and enl. ed. Phoenix, Ariz.: Oryx Press, 1985.

Robitaille, Denis, and Joan Waiser. *Theses in Canada: A Bibliographic Guide=Thèses au Canada: Guide bibliographique.* Ottawa: National Library of Canada, 1986.

Look in the online public access catalog or the card catalog to locate references for verifying dissertations and masters' theses in your library. The Library of Congress subject headings to use are "Bibliography-Bibliography-Dissertations, Academic" and "Dissertations, Academic" (which encompasses both doctoral dissertations and masters' theses). The latter heading may be subdivided by "-Abstracts" and "-Bibliography." For those lists confined to one country, look under the main heading followed by the name of the country, such as "Dissertations, Academic-United States." For a bibliography confined to a particular university or college look under the name of the institution followed by "-Dissertations," such as "Harvard University-Dissertations." Dissertations on a particular subject are not distinguished by special headings but are found under the subject headings mentioned in this paragraph.

Another bibliographic source is provided by UMI (University Microfilms International). It publishes and distributes a number of free special subject bibliographies and catalogs to assist researchers in locating relevant dissertations and masters' theses. For information on subject catalogs, call (800) 521-0600, ext. 3736.

CORRECT CITATION

The correct citation for dissertations and masters' theses includes the author, title, institution, degree, and year.

Author

The full name, correctly spelled, is especially helpful for authors with common names.

Title

A complete title will prevent receipt of the wrong item when both a master's thesis and doctoral dissertation have been done at the same institution.

Institution

The name of the institution (and location) must be carefully determined when the request is sent directly. The issuing department can be helpful in some instances.

Degree

The lending library will have an easier time determining the circulation policy if the degree is stated (e.g., M.A., Ph.D., etc.).

Year

The date is always important because it can be an aid to searching and often determines whether or not the item will be loaned.

VERIFYING U.S. DISSERTATIONS AND MASTERS' THESES

Suggested reference tools for verifying and locating U.S. dissertations and masters' theses are

■ **Online union catalogs (a first choice for verification and location)**

OCLC (Online Computer Library Center)
RLIN (Research Libraries Information Network)
WLN

■ **UMI sources (for verification and purchase)**

Dissertation Abstracts Online [database online]. Ann Arbor, Mich.: UMI. Contains bibliographic citations to more than 1.3 million North American doctoral dissertations dating back to 1861 and more than 85,000 masters' theses. Full text of dissertation abstracts are available since July 1980. Masters' abstracts are available from 1988 on. Available on CD-ROM as *Dissertation Abstracts Ondisc*. Available online: CDP Online, Data-Star, DIALOG, OCLC EPIC, OCLC FirstSearch, and STN International.

Comprehensive Dissertation Index, 1861–1972. 37 vols. Ann Arbor, Mich.: Xerox University Microfilms, 1973.

Comprehensive Dissertation Index, 1973–1982. 38 vols. Ann Arbor, Mich.: UMI, 1984.

Comprehensive Dissertation Index: Five-Year Cumulation 1983–1987. 22 vols. Ann Arbor, Mich.: UMI, 1989.

Comprehensive Dissertation Index. 1988– . Ann Arbor, Mich.: UMI, 1989– .

Dissertation Abstracts International. Vol. 1– . Ann Arbor, Mich.: UMI, 1938– . Beginning July 1966 (vol. 27), issued in two sections: A, *Humanities and Social Sciences,* and B, *Sciences and Engineering*. Section C, *Worldwide* (formerly *European Abstracts*), began with 1976 (vol. 37).

Masters Abstracts International. Vol. 1– . Ann Arbor, Mich.: UMI, 1962– . *Masters Abstracts* until vol. 24, spring 1986, when the title changed to *Masters Abstracts International*. Only a portion of the masters' theses produced each year are recorded here.

■ **Other sources (for verification and location)**

U.S. Library of Congress. Catalog Division. *A List of American Doctoral Dissertations Printed in [1912]–1938*. 26 vols. Washington, D.C.: U.S. Government Printing Office, 1913–40.

Doctoral Dissertations Accepted by American Universities. 22 vols. New York: Wilson, 1934–56. Compiled for the Association of Research Libraries.

American Doctoral Dissertations. 1955/56– . Ann Arbor, Mich.: UMI, 1957– . Continuation of *Doctoral Dissertations Accepted by American Universities*.

National Union Catalog and *National Union Catalog: Register of Additional Locations* may be consulted for verification and location. See chapter 1, "Instructions for Borrowing Libraries," "Suggested Reference Tools for Books and Pamphlets," " United States national catalogs," for complete bibliographic information.

OBTAINING U.S. DISSERTATIONS AND MASTERS' THESES

Dissertations and masters' theses completed in the United States can be obtained by borrowing a copy or purchasing a reproduction.

Borrowing a copy is often the easiest way to see the dissertation or master's thesis. Many libraries today know the importance of the material contained in dissertations. These are often added to the collection in academic institutions other than the one granting the degree. The best way to find out who holds such material is to search for it on OCLC, RLIN, or WLN. The *National Union Catalog* and the *National Union Catalog: Register of Additional Locations* also give locations. The material is often in microform. These copies are frequently, but not always, available for loan.

If no one but the granting institution holds the dissertation or master's thesis, then it is necessary to check the lending policies to see if the doctoral dissertation or master's thesis can be borrowed. These policies change with more frequency than one might expect. Many institutions will loan all their masters' theses and dissertations while others will loan only those produced before participation was begun in the UMI program for publishing dissertations and masters' theses. UMI does not require participating institutions to discontinue lending typescripts, computer printouts, or microform copies of these dissertations. The decision is solely within the province of the individual library to lend copies, or not, as it wishes. Masters' theses are generally available from the degree-granting institution.

Lending policies for dissertations and masters' theses can be found in several places. The Name Address Directory (NAD), part of the OCLC online system, should give some information about lending these materials. A dissertations lending policy may be mounted on a World Wide Web home page. Another place to look for policies is in the *Interlibrary Loan Policies Directory*.[1] You may wish to collect dissertation and thesis lending policies from individual libraries you go to frequently because such

policies do not always lend themselves to a brief statement.

Sending an ALA Interlibrary Loan Request form is recommended when the borrowing library's patron must know the reason the item was not lent. For an example of a complete dissertation citation correctly typed on an ALA Interlibrary Loan Request form, see figure 13.

The easiest way to purchase a reproduction is through UMI. In cooperation with the Association of Research Libraries, UMI started a micropublishing program for doctoral dissertations in 1938. From that modest beginning, the program has grown so that more than 1.3 million dissertations and 85,000 masters' theses are listed, and many of these are available for purchase. A comprehensive list of participating institutions is located in *Dissertation Abstracts International* and other UMI reference sources. The dates when institutions first began using the service are given. Some institutions do not send all of their dissertations; others have decided to publish earlier dissertations. The entries containing an order number are available for purchase from UMI. Without an order number, the institution granting the degree must be contacted for purchasing information for dissertations and masters' theses.

Ordering dissertations from UMI is not difficult. Dissertation and master's thesis copies are available in the following formats:

Softcover paper copies

Hardcover paper copies

35mm positive microfilm

98-page positive microfiche (for all titles published from 1976 forward)

United States and Canadian institutions will be billed when orders are shipped. Orders can be placed using special UMI forms, "Dissertation and Thesis Order Form D," shown in figure 14. Orders can be made

---

1. Leslie R. Morris, *Interlibrary Loan Policies Directory*, 5th ed. (New York: Neal-Schuman, 1995).

TYPE OF REQUEST:
(X) LOAN; WILL PAY FEE __Any Fee__
( ) PHOTOCOPY; MAX. COST $_____
( ) _____

LENDING LIBRARY REPORT: Date _____
Date shipped _____ Shipped via _____
Insured for $_____ Charges $_____
DUE _____ ( ) Return insured
Packing Requirements _____

RESTRICTIONS: ( ) Library use only
( ) Copying not permitted ( ) No renewals
( ) _____

NOT SENT BECAUSE: ( ) In use ( ) Lacking
( ) Not owned ( ) At bindery ( ) Cost exceeds limit
( ) Non Circulating ( ) Not found as cited
( ) Not on Shelf ( ) Poor Condition ( ) Lost
( ) Lacks copyright compliance ( ) On order
( ) Vol/issue not yet available ( ) On reserve
( ) In process ( ) Rerequest on _____
( ) Hold placed
( ) Estimated Cost of: Loan $_____
Photocopy $_____ Microfilm/fiche $_____
( ) Prepayment required

BORROWING LIBRARY RECORD:
Date received _____ Date returned _____
Returned via _____ Insured for $_____
Payment provided $_____

RENEWALS:
Date requested _____
New due date _____
Renewal denied _____

ALA INTERLIBRARY LOAN REQUEST FORM

DEMCO
Madison, Wis
Fresno, Calif.
NO. 165-270

BORROWING LIBRARY

FILL IN LEFT HALF OF FORM INCLUDING BOTH LIBRARY ADDRESSES IN FULL

FOLD HERE

recycled paper

SEND SHEETS A, B AND C TO LENDING LIBRARY, AND ENCLOSE SHIPPING LABEL

LENDING LIBRARY

FILL IN PERTINENT ITEMS UNDER REPORTS, RETURN SHEETS B AND C TO BORROWING LIBRARY

REV 11/88

Request no.: _____ Date: 2/26/96 Need before: 5/15/96 Notes:

Call No. _____

INTERLIBRARY LOAN SERVICE
UNIVERSITY LIBRARIES, CAMPUS BOX 184
UNIVERSITY OF COLORADO
BOULDER, CO 80309

Patron information: __Lightfoot, Ellen__
Book author; OR, Serial title, volume, issue, date, pages; OR, Audiovisual title:

Mitchell, Richard Gilchrist

Book title, edition, imprint, series; OR, Article author, title: □ This edition only

Mountaineering: A Sociologist's Perspective. Ph.D.
Univ. of Southern California, 1981.

Verified in; AND/OR, Cited in: FirstSearch: Diss. Abs.; DAI:41-11A, p. 4844
ISBN, ISSN, LCCN, or other bibliographic number:

Interlibrary Loan
University of Southern California
P.O. Box 77916
Los Angeles, CA   90007

Request complies with
( ) 108(g) (2) Guidelines (CCG)
( ) other provisions of copyright law (CCL)

Authorization: __V. Boucher__
Telephone: __(303) 492-6176__

FIGURE 13. ALA Interlibrary Loan Request Form: Dissertation

DISSERTATION AND THESIS ORDER FORM

ORDER FORM D
Effective January 1, 1995
Prices subject to change
without notice.

	MICROFILM/FICHE	SOFTCOVER PAPER			HARDCOVER PAPER
		REGULAR	RUSH**	BLITZ***	
Academic	$32.50 each	$36.00 each	$25.00 extra per copy	$100 extra per copy	$43.50 each
Non-Academic	$46.00 each	$57.50 each	$25.00 extra per copy	$100 extra per copy	$69.50 each

*Academic prices apply to U.S. and Canada university, college, and school libraries, departments, faculty, staff, and students. Shipping costs are included in price. For prices outside the U.S. and Canada, call or write UMI. Allow up to three weeks for delivery for regular orders.

**RUSH (softcover only): American and Canadian titles from 1980 forward only. (University of Chicago titles temporarily excluded.) Delivery within 5 working days of receipt of order at UMI; 6 working days if order received after 3:00 p.m. EST.

***BLITZ (softcover only): American and Canadian titles from 1980 forward only. (University of Chicago titles temporarily excluded.) Delivery within 2 working days of receipt of order at UMI; 3 working days if order received after 3:00 p.m. EST.

ORDER NUMBER	AUTHOR'S FULL NAME OR TITLE	FORMAT†	RUSH/BLITZ (IF SO, MARK "R" FOR RUSH, "B" FOR BLITZ)	QUANTITY	PRICE (INCLUDE RUSH/BLITZ CHARGES)	TOTAL

†Indicate in **Format** column:
Film for 35mm Roll Microfilm
Fiche for 98-frame Microfiche
(for titles with a 76+ prefix)

PS for Softcover Paper Copy
PH for Hardcover Paper Copy

(NEED MORE ROOM? SEE OTHER SIDE.)

SUBTOTAL ____
YOUR STATE SALES TAX ____
TOTAL ____

The UMI Guarantee

Each dissertation and master's thesis you order will be individually reproduced from the microfilm negative of the original manuscript. With the exception of photographic material, UMI guarantees the quality of the reproduction, whether you order paper or microform copies. If you are not completely satisfied with the quality of the reproduction, you may return any undamaged copies to UMI within 15 days of receipt for a full refund.

UMI
A Bell & Howell Company
300 North Zeeb Road
PO Box 1346
Ann Arbor MI 48106-1346

D-685 110M 11/94

Individuals

Please prepay by check or money order or use:
Visa ☐   Mastercard ☐   American Express ☐
Account Number_____ Expiration Date_____
Telephone Number (____)_____

☐ I am enclosing a check ☐   money order ☐   in the amount of $_____

Libraries and Institutions

P.O. No._____
Telephone No. (____)_____
Librarians: If you use an institutional purchase order, please attach it to our order form.

Ship to:

Name_____
Title_____
Institution_____
Address_____
City_____ State or Province_____
Zip or Postal Code_____ Country_____

Bill to:

Name_____
Title_____
Institution_____
Address_____
City_____ State or Province_____
Zip or Postal Code_____ Country_____

CALL TOLL FREE
FOR FAST
SERVICE!
1-800-521-3042
or
fax your order to
313-973-2682

**Thank You
for Your
Order**

Need more forms? Call UMI toll free at 1-800-521-0600, ext. 3736, and request Order Form D.

84

FIGURE 14. (UMI) Dissertation and Thesis Order Form

also on institutional or library purchase order forms and should include purchase order number and tax exemption number (if applicable). Orders may be placed through the OCLC PRISM Interlibrary Loan system. For a patron who wishes to purchase a copy, a check, money order, or complete credit card information (American Express, MasterCard, or VISA number; expiration date; signature; and telephone number) must be included. Prices are based on the form of reproduction rather than the length of the dissertation. Customers in the United States and Canada may call UMI toll free at (800) 521-0600 to place an order. Ask for a UMI Dissertations Order Representative. For more information, inquire at the telephone number above or write to

> UMI Dissertation Services
> 300 North Zeeb Road
> Ann Arbor, MI 48106-1346

Dissertations and masters' theses are usually on deposit in the library of the degree-granting institution. Purchasing a copy from the institution that granted the degree can be a time-consuming process. Check the institution's lending policy to see if a copy can be purchased from it or if the purchasing request must be sent to UMI. A common practice is to sell only copies of dissertations produced before participation was begun in the UMI program. In some cases the author's permission must be obtained (also a time-consuming process), and frequently the reproduction process itself may take a matter of weeks or months. The cost is often high, particularly for photocopies, because of the length of these works. For dealing with institutions that do not deposit with UMI and generally do not loan, ordering a copy from the institution is the only recourse. Normal interlibrary borrowing procedures can be used for ordering.

If neither borrowing nor purchasing is successful, the patron has the option of visiting the institution granting the degree for a personal view of the dissertation or master's thesis. It is wise to inquire first to make sure there are no restrictions on the material or on access to the library.

VERIFYING CANADIAN DISSERTATIONS AND MASTERS' THESES

Canadian reference works use the word *theses* to mean both doctoral dissertations and masters' theses.

- **Canadian reference sources (for verification and location)**

Canadiana. Jan. 15, 1951– . Ottawa: National Library of Canada, 1951– . All theses listed here have been microfilmed and deposited at the National Library of Canada. Dissertations and masters' theses are included in vol. 1, 1951 through 1966. "Theses in Microform/Microcopies de thèses" began as a separate part in 1967: part 2 or 3, depending on which year is consulted. In 1981 a new format put theses in part 1 with other Canadian imprints. The last printed issue of *Canadiana* was December 1991. The microfiche edition of *Canadiana* has been available since 1978 and continues to be available. Available online: AMICUS (the Canadian Online Library System operated by the National Library of Canada, Information Technology Services, primarily for Canadian libraries).

Canadian Theses=Thèses canadiennes, 1947–1960. 2 vols. Ottawa: National Library of Canada, 1973. Lists all theses including those *not* available at the National Library of Canada.

Canadian Theses=Thèses canadiennes. 1960/61– . Ottawa: National Library of Canada, 1962– . Lists all theses including those *not* available at the National Library of Canada. The last printed issue of *Canadian Theses=Thèses canadiennes* was 1979/80, published in 1983. The microfiche edition of *Canadian Theses =Thèses canadiennes* has been available since the 1980/81 listing published in 1984. It continues to be available.

- **UMI sources (for verification and purchase)**

Dissertation Abstracts Online, Dissertation Abstracts Ondisc, Comprehensive Dissertation

Index, Dissertation Abstracts International, and *Masters Abstracts International,* see above for complete bibliographic details. The abstracts listed in these reference works are important for learning about Canadian dissertations and masters' theses.

- **Online union catalogs (for verification and location)**

OCLC (Online Computer Library Center)

RLIN (Research Libraries Information Network)

WLN

OBTAINING CANADIAN DISSERTATIONS AND MASTERS' THESES

Canadian dissertations and masters' theses can be obtained by purchasing a reproduction or borrowing a copy. The following publication gives information about reproduction and lending policies of the various institutions:

Symbols and Interlibrary Loan Policies in Canada =Sigles et politiques de prêt entre bibliothèques au Canada. Ottawa: National Library of Canada, 1995– . This alphabetic listing of Canadian library symbols with the corresponding names of the institutions to which the symbols have been assigned is issued along with a diskette containing the English and French text of interlibrary loan policies in Canada.

This work is updated annually and can be ordered from the following publisher:

    Canada Communication
        Group—Publishing
    Ottawa, Ontario K1A 0S9 Canada
    Telephone: (819) 956-4802
    Fax: (819) 994-1498
    Cat. No. SN13-2/2-1995; ISBN
      0-660-59788-8
    Price: $49.95 (Canada) and $64.95
      (elsewhere including U.S.)

The National Library of Canada (NLC) plays a major role in making Canadian dissertations and masters' theses available. In 1965 NLC and four participating universities began a microfilming project. Today nearly 50 institutions of higher education submit doctoral dissertations and masters' theses for filming. NLC works with Micromedia Limited and UMI to provide copies of these materials. While many Canadian dissertations and masters' theses are abstracted in the reference works listed in "UMI sources," above, UMI sells reproductions of them only if their citation includes an order number.

A microform copy of a dissertation or master's thesis held by the National Library of Canada can be borrowed. Requests can be sent by the OCLC PRISM Interlibrary Loan system (enter NLD twice), or fax (613) 996-4424, for libraries that do not have access to an electronic system capable of sending interlibrary borrowing requests. Internet can be used for interlibrary borrowing requests only with interlibrary loan protocol-based software (Internet: oonlpebill@nlc-bnc.ca). For mailing ALA Interlibrary Loan Request forms, the address is

    Interlibrary Loan
    National Library of Canada
    395 Wellington Street
    Ottawa, Ontario K1A 0N4 Canada

Theses filmed after 1974 are usually available on microfiche while those filmed earlier are available on microfilm. As of 1995 there was no charge for the loan.

See chapter 6, "International Interlibrary Loan," "Canada," for directions on dealing with the National Library of Canada and other Canadian libraries. The mailing instructions discussed there are particularly important.

To purchase a reproduction of a dissertation or master's thesis, do the following:

- Ascertain where a reproduction can be purchased by consulting the reference sources listed above
- For theses completed and copied by NLC between 1965 and 1989, for paper or microfiche copies, contact

    Micromedia Limited
    Technical Information Centre
    240 Catherine Street, Suite 305
    Ottawa, Ontario K2P 2G8 Canada

Telephone: (800) 567-1914
(Canada toll free)
(613) 237-4250
Fax: (613) 237-4251

- For theses completed and copied by NLC from 1990 on (ISBN numbers greater than ISBN 0-315-58857-8), for microfiche or paper copies, contact

UMI (American and other non-Canadian libraries)

See discussion of UMI ordering under "Obtaining U.S. Dissertations and Masters' Theses," above.

Micromedia Limited (Canadian libraries only)

See address and telephone numbers, above.

For more information about Canadian dissertations and masters' theses, contact

The National Library of Canada
Canadian Theses Service
395 Wellington Street
Ottawa, Ontario K1A 0N4 Canada
E-mail: theses@nlc-bnc.ca

For those masters' theses and dissertations not available for loan or purchase in the manner described above, borrowing or purchasing a copy from the institution granting the degree is much the same in Canada as it is in the United States. Bibliographic verification must be done, lending policies must be checked, and requests must be submitted following common interlibrary loan procedure. Libraries in the United States occasionally add Canadian dissertations and masters' theses to their collections. The online union catalogs (OCLC, RLIN, WLN), the *National Union Catalog,* and *National Union Catalog: Register of Additional Locations* will show which libraries have Canadian thesis holdings.

VERIFYING OTHER FOREIGN DISSERTATIONS

A collection of information about foreign dissertations, *World Guide to Doctoral Dissertations in Science and Technology,* has been prepared by the International Federation of Library Associations and Institutions (IFLA). Basic information can be found at the following World Wide Web site:

URL: <http://www.nlc-bnc. ca/ifla/V/wgddst/wgddst.htm>

For a description of individual countries (24 in 1995) containing general dissertation information, bibliographic control, and access, use the following gopher address:

gopher.konbib.nl
Directory: IFLA, Directory: Reports from IFLA Headquarters
File: World Guide to Doctoral Dissertations in Science and Technology

Information about the United Kingdom, France, Germany, and Russia is included in this report.

Some foreign dissertations have been acquired and cataloged by U.S. libraries. Therefore, starting

with U.S. bibliographic sources is advised. Should these sources fail, there are many foreign bibliographic tools for individual countries or institutions. In addition, a beginning list of reference tools for verifying foreign dissertations is as follows:

- **Online union catalogs (a first choice for verification and location)**

OCLC (Online Computer Library Center)

RLIN (Research Libraries Information Network)

WLN

- **Other sources (for verification and location)**

Dissertation Abstracts International: Section C, Worldwide. Vol. 37– . Ann Arbor, Mich.: UMI, 1976– . Before 1976 some foreign dissertations were listed in the A and B sections. From listing a majority of European institutions, *DAI-C* was expanded to include institutions worldwide with volume 50, spring 1989. It includes institutions that send abstracts on a regular basis, between 15 and 30 each from France and Germany.

National Union Catalogs. See chapter 1, "Instructions for Borrowing Libraries," "Suggested Reference Tools for Books and Pamphlets," "United States national catalogs," for complete bibliographic information.

United Kingdom

- **United Kingdom sources (for verification and location)**

Index to Theses Accepted for Higher Degrees by the Universities of Great Britain and Ireland and the Council for National Academic Awards. Vol. 1– , 1950/51– . London: Aslib, 1953– . Title varies. Latest title given. Abstracts from vol. 36– . Available on CD-ROM: *Aslib Index to Theses on CD-ROM,* Edition 2, 1970–92.

British Reports, Translations and Theses Received by the British Library Document Supply Centre. Boston Spa, Wetherby, West Yorkshire, U.K.: British Library Document Supply Centre, 1981– . Preceded by *BLLD Announcement Bulletin* and *BLL Announcement Bulletin.*

The BRITS Index: An Index to the British Theses Collections, 1971–1987 Held at the British Document Supply Centre and London University. 3 vols. Godstone, Surrey: British Theses Service, 1989.

The BRITS Index: Supplement. 2 vols. Godstone, Surrey: British Theses Service, 1989–90.

Retrospective Index to Theses of Great Britain and Ireland, 1716–1950. 5 vols. Edited by Roger R. Bilboul. Santa Monica, Calif.: ABC-Clio, 1975–77. *Addenda* published in 1977.

France

- **French sources (for verification and location)**

Available in France, there are online and CD-ROM products listing dissertations. Refer to the *World Guide to Doctoral Dissertations in Science and Technology,* listed at the beginning of the "Verifying Other Foreign Dissertations" section in this chapter. Print sources follow:

Inventaire des thèses de doctorat soutenues devant les universités françaises. 1981– . Paris: Univ. de Paris I, Bibliothèque de la Sorbonne, Direction des Bibliothèques, des Musées et de l'Information Scientifique et Technique, 1982– . Issued in three sections each year: *Droit, sciences économiques, sciences de gestion, lettres, sciences humaines, théologies; Médecine, médecine vétérinaire odontostomatologie, pharmacie; Sciences.*

Catalogue des thèses de doctorat soutenues devant les universités françaises. 1959–78. Paris: Cercle de la Librairie, 1960–85.

Catalogue des thèses de doctorat soutenues devant les universités françaises. 1884/89–1972. Paris: 1885–1973.

Bibliographie de la France. Vols. 1–160. Paris: Cercle de la Librairie, 1811–1971. From 1930 on, there is an alphabetical list of dissertations. This appeared as Supplement D, "Theses," from 1947–73. The last year covered is 1970.

Marie, Albert. *Répertoire alphabétique des thèses de doctorat ès lettres des universités françaises, 1820–1900.* Paris: Picard, 1903.

Germany

- **German sources (for verification and location)**

Deutsche Nationalbibliographie und Bibliographie der im Ausland erschienenen deutschsprachigen Veröffentlichungen. Reihe H: Hochschulschriften. Frankfurt am Main: Buchhändler-Vereinigung, 1991– . Formed by the union of *Deutsche Bibliographie, Hochschulschriften-Verzeichnis* and *Deutsche Nationalbibliographie und Bibliographie der im Ausland erschienenen deutschsprachigen Schrifttums. Reihe C: Dissertationen und Habilitationsschriften.* Available on CD-ROM. Available online: STN International, "BIBLIODATA."

Jahresverzeichnis der Hochschulschriften. Vol. 78– , 1962– . Leipzig: VEB Verlag für Buch- und Bibliothekswesen, 1963– . Title and publisher vary.

Jahresverzeichnis der deutschen Hochschulschriften. Vols. 1–77, 1885/86–1961. Nendeln/Liechtenstein: Kraus Reprint, 1965–75.

Gesamtverzeichnis deutschsprachiger Hochschulschriften (GVH), 1966–1980. 24 vols. Munich, New York: K. G. Saur, 1984–87.

Gesamtverzeichnis des deutschsprachigen Schrifttums (GV), 1911–1965. 150 vols. Munich: Verlag Dokumentation, 1976–81.

Gesamtverzeichnis des deutschsprachigen Schrifttums (GV), 1700–1910. Munich and New York: K. G. Saur, 1979–87, microfiche.

Russia

- **Russian and Union of Soviet Socialist Republics sources (for verification)**

Katalog kandidatskikh i doktorskikh dissertatsiĭ postupivshikh v Biblioteku imeni V.I. Lenina i

Gosudarstvennuĭu tsentral'nuĭu nauchnuĭu meditsinskuĭu biblioteku. Moscow: Publichnaia Biblioteka, 1957– .

Knizhnaĭa letopis', Dopolnitel'nyĭ vypusk. Avtoreferaty dissertatsiĭ. Moscow: Kniga, 1981–92.

Knizhnaĭa letopis', Dopolnitel'nyĭ vypusk. 19 vols. Moscow: Palata, 1962–80.

OBTAINING OTHER FOREIGN DISSERTATIONS

Some foreign dissertations can be located in the United States. Members of the Center for Research Libraries can find a great number of foreign dissertations readily available there. The center's dissertations are not necessarily cataloged and so may not be listed in online union catalogs, OCLC, RLIN, or WLN, or the *National Union Catalog.* In fact, the center holds more than 640,000 doctoral dissertations from universities outside of the United States and Canada. Most dissertations held are from countries in western Europe. There are also dissertations from Latin America, South America, and Africa. In January 1990, the center began receiving abstracts of dissertations written at institutions in the USSR. The Institute for Scientific Information in Social Sciences (INION) of the Academy of Sciences of the USSR sends to the center microfiche copies of all dissertations listed in *Knizhnaĭa letopis', Dopolnitel'nyĭ vypusk, Avtoreferaty dissertatsiĭ* under the subject headings "Philosophy" (which includes political science), "History," and "Economics." The center also acquires dissertations on a title-by-title basis when patrons from member libraries request items not in the center's collection.

The Center for Research Libraries will loan to nonmembers in North America for $20 per prepaid filled request. Nonmembers are limited to ten filled requests per year (loans and copies). For further information, see chapter 5, "Interlibrary Coopera-

tion," "Center for Research Libraries (national/North America)," and contact the center directly:

Access Services Department
Center for Research Libraries
6050 South Kenwood Avenue
Chicago, IL 60637-2804
Telephone: (312) 955-4545,
    ext. 313 or 314

To find dissertations located in other American libraries, the usual online union catalogs should be consulted—OCLC, RLIN, and WLN—as well as the *National Union Catalog* and *National Union Catalog: Register of Additional Locations.* Another approach is to search for the foreign dissertation as a published work (book or periodical article) because some European countries require that dissertations be published. Failing these approaches, a request must be sent abroad.

Discovering the availability of foreign dissertations not located in U.S. libraries requires patience and perseverance. See the beginning of the "Verifying Other Foreign Dissertations" section in this chapter for information on *World Guide to Doctoral Dissertations in Science and Technology.* Another good place to start is the following publication:

Dissertation Abstracts International: Section C, Worldwide. Vol. 37– . Ann Arbor, Mich.: UMI, 1976– .

Before 1976 some foreign dissertations were listed in the A and B sections. From listing a majority of European institutions, *DAI-C* was expanded to include institutions worldwide with volume 50, spring 1989. It includes institutions that send abstracts on a regular basis. Between 15 and 30 institutions each from France and Germany are found. A list of participating institutions is included. When full-text copies of dissertations are available from UMI, the order number appears in bold type at the end of the bibliographic description. Check "Obtaining U.S. Dissertations and Masters' Theses," above, for information on ordering from UMI. If full-text copies of the dissertations are not available from UMI, information on location or availability is provided. If the dissertation is published, the International Standard Book Number (ISBN) is given, if assigned, and the publisher's name and city, if known. If the dissertation is unpublished, a location where a reference copy may be found is listed if other than the library of the degree-granting institution.

Should a request to borrow from the institution granting the degree seem feasible and an address for the institution's library is needed, consult these two references:

The World of Learning. 1st– . London: Europa Publications, 1947– .

World Guide to Libraries=Internationales Bibliotheks-Handbuch. Ed. 1– . Handbook of International Documentation and Information, vol. 8. Munich and New York: K. G. Saur, 1966– .

Further information about international loan services, as well as international loan procedures, can be found in chapter 6, "International Interlibrary Loan."

A brief presentation of additional information on dissertations in the United Kingdom, France, Germany, and Russia may be helpful when copies cannot be located using the methods described above.

United Kingdom

Pre-1971 British dissertations are difficult to obtain either as a loan or a reproduction. Copyright regulations or the necessity of getting the author's permission may restrict access that is often only at the degree-granting institution. In 1954 the Standing Conference on National and University Libraries (SCONUL) proposed a fourfold standard of availability for dissertations, which are often referred to simply as "theses":

At least one copy of every thesis should be deposited in the university library.

Subject to the author's consent, every thesis should be available for interlibrary loan.

Subject to the author's consent, every thesis should be available for photocopying.

Authors of theses should be asked at the time of deposit to give their consent in writing for interlibrary loan and photocopying, and this consent should be inserted in the deposit copy of the thesis.

In 1971 the British Library Document Supply Centre (BLDSC), supported and encouraged by SCONUL, initiated a scheme to make British doctoral dissertations more widely and easily accessible. Universities participating in the scheme lend copies of their dissertations to be microfilmed by BLDSC; as of 1996 more than 120,000 British doctoral dissertations are now available. The dissertations themselves are acquired as soon as they are released by the institution awarding the doctorate. Duplicates of microfilm, or microfiche if held, are made available for loan. Copies of most dissertations can be purchased as bound photocopies or microfilm. Requests for British dissertations identified by a "D" prefix must be accompanied by a completed BLDSC Thesis Declaration Form (see figure 15), signed by the person wishing to consult the dissertation. For $30 each search, BLDSC will list all British doctoral dissertations on a chosen topic from 1980 to date. A copy of each dissertation is available from BLDSC. Theses accepted for masters' degrees are, in general, excluded from the scheme. For further information on ordering from BLDSC, see chapter 6, "International Interlibrary Loan," "British Library Document Supply Centre."

France

Before World War II, France required publication of all dissertations; one copy was given to the University of Paris, one to the Bibliothèque Nationale, one to each French university, and many were saved for

THE BRITISH LIBRARY

DOCUMENT SUPPLY CENTRE
Thesis Orders (RMS)
Boston Spa, Wetherby
West Yorkshire LS23 7BQ

Telephone: +44 937 546229   Fax no: +44 937 546286

BRITISH THESES

The thesis you require is held as D

Please indicate which format you require:

Cash orders:

Paper:	£70.00/US$126.00
Microfilm:	£40.00/US$72.00
Microfiche:	£40.00/US$72.00
Courier Service	£20.00/US$36.00

Payment must be sent with order to the above address.
Cheques should be made payable to 'The British Library'

Deposit Account customers only:

User code:

registered loan customer? Y/N

I authorise DSC to debit our account

Credit card: Access ☐ Mastercard ☐ Visa ☐ Eurocard ☐ Am Ex ☐

card number

expiry date

commencement date   card batch no.

Contact Name / Address

Name

Address

Telephone no .... FAX no ....

DSC Request form order:

Paper:	14 coupons
Microfilm:	8 coupons
Microfiche:	8 coupons
Courier Service +	4 coupons

International Photocopy Service customers may apply through the normal request system, using a photocopy request form with coupons attached as above.

LOAN

Format	unit cost
Microfilm	2 units
Microfiche (if available)	2 units

PURCHASE

Format	
Paper:	14 units
Microfilm:	8 units
Microfiche:	8 units
Courier Service +	4 units

THESIS DECLARATION FORM (TDF)

A complete TDF signed by the person wishing to consult the thesis must accompany request for BRITISH THESES with a D prefix (Theses with DX prefix do not need a TDF.)

Title of thesis

Name of Author

University

I recognise that the copyright of the above-described thesis rests with the author or the university to which it was submitted, and that no quotation from it or information derived from it may be published without the prior written consent of the author or university (as may be appropriate).

Signed .... Date ....
(to be signed by the person wishing to consult thesis)

Address

FOR DSC USE: Code No .... Req No ....
L

date received $ date returned

VALID UNTIL FURTHER NOTICE

T3-9
OS-D

FIGURE 15. British Library Document Supply Centre, British Theses; Thesis Declaration Form

exchange. The practice was discontinued in 1948. At present, two copies of a dissertation are kept by the degree-granting institution, where they are available for interlibrary loan. If a U.S. location is not found using the usual verifying and locating sources, request the loan of a dissertation from the degree-granting university. *The World of Learning* and *World Guide to Libraries=Internationales Bibliotheks-Handbuch,* mentioned above, can be used to find the university library's address. For dissertations before 1948, request from the library listed below:

> Bibliothèque Nationale de France
> Centre du Prêt
> 58 rue de Richelieu
> 75084 Paris Cedex 02
> France

Since 1986 ANRT (National Dissertation Reproduction Service) has been producing microfiche of French dissertations. These are deposited at an appropriate institution from which a microfiche copy can be purchased. The document delivery service for science is Institut de l'Information Scientifique et Technique (INIST-CNRS):

> INIST Diffusion/Customer Services
> 2, allée du Parc de Brabois
> 54514 Vandoeuvre-les-Nancy Cedex
> France
> Telephone: +33 83.50.46.00
> Fax: +33 85.50.46.50
> E-mail: infoclient@inist.fr

The document delivery service for law, economics, business, letters (literature), humanities, and theology is

> Fichier Central des Thèses
> Université de Paris-X-Nanterre
> 200 avenue de la République
> 92001 Nanterre
> France

The document delivery service for medicine, veterinary medicine, odontology, and pharmacy is

> Bibliothèque Interuniversitaire de
>   Clermont-Ferrand
> Section Médicine
> 28 place Henri-Dunant
> 63033 Clermont-Ferrand Cedex
> France

Germany

Borrowing German dissertations from an American library may be possible because German universities used to require that dissertations be published. These earlier dissertations are frequently listed in the *National Union Catalog,* the *National Union Catalog: Register of Additional Locations,* and the online union catalogs: OCLC, RLIN, and WLN, which give locations for libraries in the United States. Since World War II, copies of dissertations have been required to be deposited in two locations, depending upon whether they were done in West or East Germany:

> *West Germany*
> Deutsche Bibliothek
> Zeppelinalle 4-8
> 60325 Frankfurt am Main
> Germany

> *East Germany*
> Deutsch Bücherei
> Deutscher Platz 1
> 7010 Leipzig
> Germany

Following the reunification, the German national library is now Deutsche Bibliothek. Dissertations deposited at these locations are not available for lending.

At present, all scientific and technical dissertations are sent to the Technische Informationsbibliothek, which acts as a document supply center:

> Technische Informationsbibliothek
>   Hannover
> Postfach 6080
> 30060 Hannover
> Germany
> Telephone: +49 (511) 762-2531
> Fax: +49 (511) 71 59 36
> E-mail: rosemann@tib.uni-hannover.
>   d400.de

If the dissertation is not in the field of science and technology and a location cannot be found in the United States, try the degree-granting university library. *The World of Learning* and *World Guide to Libraries=Internationales Bibliotheks-Handbuch,* mentioned above, can be used to find the university library's address.

Russia

Scientific and technical dissertations are frequently published and can be found by searching common bibliographic sources for books and periodical articles, such as *Chemical Abstracts* and similar sources. Abstracts of 15 to 60 pages and more are written for dissertations. These are fairly well covered in the three Russian verification sources listed above.

Russian libraries, especially major special libraries, may have copies of dissertations or abstracts for loan or purchase. For photocopies or microfiche of abstracts of dissertations in science and technology, try the following:

Russian National Public Library for
    Science and Technology
12, Kuznetsky most
103031 Moscow
Russia
Telephone: +7 (095) 921-1750
Fax: +7 (095) 921-9862

The most complete collection of dissertations is located at the Russian State Library. Try there especially for humanities and social science dissertations or dissertation abstracts:

Russian State Library
Loan Department
3, Vozdvizhenka Street
101000 Moscow, Russia
Telephone: +7 (095) 202-3565
              +7 (095) 202-7404
Fax: +7 (095) 200-2255
E-mail: main@irgp.msk.su

With the dissolution of the Union of Soviet Socialist Republics, each new country is now responsible for its own higher education degrees and the resulting dissertations.

HINTS FOR HANDLING DISSERTATIONS AND MASTERS' THESES

Borrowing

Special care should be taken of dissertations and masters' theses because of the uniqueness and format. Watch for special instructions given by the lending library. For the protection of the material, make sure the "Library use only" instruction is carried out. Have the patron sign the signature sheet indicating use when there is one. Permission should be requested of the lending library for copying an entire dissertation or thesis. When returning the material, be certain it is insured for an amount that would cover replacement costs.

Lending

A detailed lending policy is particularly important for dissertations and masters' theses, because many libraries handle them differently from general materials. Have copies of the lending policy available to send to borrowing libraries (see appendix T). If you are an OCLC PRISM Interlibrary Loan system user, make certain your Name Address Directory (NAD) information is current.

In replying to libraries, it is helpful to include information about purchasing from UMI if that is part of your policy. Such information as the UMI order number, UMI address, and cost are useful. Be sure to indicate such instructions as "Library use only" and "Patron signature required" if these are necessary.

Package a loaned dissertation or master's thesis very carefully, and insure it (see chapter 2, "Instructions for Lending Libraries," "Ship material").

5

Interlibrary Cooperation

INTRODUCTION: COOPERATIVE STRUCTURES

The very character of interlibrary loan dictates involvement in interlibrary cooperation. In fact, interlibrary loan is one of the oldest examples of such cooperation. The milieu in which an individual interlibrary loan and document delivery service finds itself is rather like the coiled shell of a chambered nautilus. The first coil of the shell is small and may be compared to arrangements with libraries in a single community or small geographical area. The next coil of the shell is often a government-sponsored system of libraries or consortium covering a wider geographical area. A larger coil is usually the state structure or network for interlibrary loan, while the largest band of all might represent developments in a multistate region, the whole country, or even abroad. All of these layers and configurations of interlibrary cooperation, like the complete nautilus shell, form the structure surrounding the life of the organism. Understanding the structures and learning to operate within them become the task facing the interlibrary loan and document delivery librarian.

The task is not always simple. Some kind of structure or set of external arrangements to facilitate interlibrary loan is essential, no matter what size or type of library is involved. Many kinds of such arrangements are possible. They can vary from a simple agreement to give priority treatment to requests from a particular library, to informal or formal networks between individual libraries or organizations, to a national (and international) organization such as OCLC (Online Computer Library Center) in which thousands of individual libraries are linked by a common computer system. The fascination with cooperation comes from the variety of people involved, the spirit of mutual helpfulness, and the give and take of the operations. The success comes from developing workable ways of proceeding, comprehending those ways, and following them to a logical conclusion. The importance comes with extracting from other libraries and document suppliers needed materials quickly and inexpensively. And the excitement comes with making meaningful contributions to the cooperative venture.

When such a cooperative structure involves interlibrary loan, it almost always has these basic characteristics:

The structure operates in a specific geographical area: local, regional, state, multistate, or national.

The types of activity include some or all of these possibilities: bibliographic verification, location of materials, transmission of interlibrary loan requests, document delivery, and management of interlibrary loan operations.

There are usually policies, procedures, and specific processes that regulate the activity.

And the underlying mission for this kind of interlibrary cooperation—no matter how complex—is to augment for the patron the local library's supply of available materials.

A CASE STUDY OF INTERLIBRARY COOPERATION: THE UNIVERSITY OF COLORADO AT BOULDER LIBRARIES

Interlibrary loan by its very nature is a cooperative venture. It is a part of the library that looks outward to the state, the region, the nation, and the world to fulfill its mission.

Rather than a general discussion of interlibrary cooperation, some examples—shown from the viewpoint of a single institution, the University of Colorado at Boulder—will be given to help illustrate the complexity of interlibrary cooperation today. Some aspects will be idiosyncratic to that library and the array of cooperative efforts it uses. But much will be analogous to the situation faced by most libraries today as both economic and technological breakthroughs generate a demand for new and more efficient ways to share scarce resources.

The University of Colorado at Boulder (UCB), founded in 1876, is located at the foot of the Rocky Mountains, some 30 miles from Denver. Enrollment runs about 24,500 students. Full-time faculty number 1,100. Ten colleges and schools offer more than 2,500 courses. Programs offered include 59 bachelor's degree programs, 48 master's degree programs, and 40 doctoral programs. The University of Colorado system ranks eleventh among U.S. public universities and nineteenth among all U.S. universities in federal research support.[1]

Interlibrary loan at the University of Colorado at Boulder Libraries must take into account, among other cooperative ventures, the following diverse organizations:

Colorado Alliance of Research Libraries (CARL)—local

Central Colorado Library System (CCLS)—state

Bibliographical Center for Research (BCR)—multistate

Greater Midwest Research Library Consortium (GMRLC)—multistate

OCLC (Online Computer Library Center)—national/international

National Network of Libraries of Medicine (NN/LM)—multistate/national

Center for Research Libraries (CRL)—national/North America

These organizations all have an important part to play in providing interlibrary loan service. A brief look at each one will help to show relationships.

Colorado Alliance of Research Libraries (local)

The Colorado Alliance of Research Libraries (CARL) began in 1974 as a group of the seven largest libraries in Colorado that banded together to develop mutually beneficial cooperative library programs. The voluntary alliance was composed of four state universities, one private university, a state mining school, and the Denver Public Library. The University of Colorado at Boulder is one of the original members. More recently, other libraries have been added to the alliance, notably the Health Sciences Center of the University of Colorado and the University of Wyoming. Resource-sharing activities, collection development, and cooperative purchasing of databases are among the activities of the organization. The guiding premise of the alliance is to use geographically close collections as if they were one.

Fostered by the alliance, CARL Corporation (recently acquired by Knight-Ridder) maintains an online public access catalog, as well as circulation, acquisitions, serials control, and bibliographic maintenance services. Another service originating in CARL Corporation is UnCover, the citation access and document delivery service.

Interlibrary loan has been a key function of this alliance from the beginning. There is a CARL interlibrary loan agreement, which specifies such things as the amount of verification that will be done, turnaround time, and no charges for photocopies or loans. Materials that have been cooperatively purchased are available on interlibrary loan. Requests are generally transmitted by using the OCLC PRISM Interlibrary Loan system. Delivery of library materials in a timely manner is still an important part of interlibrary loan for the CARL libraries. The courier service, which is managed by the Central Colorado Library System at present, was originally operated by CARL. Along with use of the courier, fax and Ariel are also possibilities for speeding up document delivery.[2]

Central Colorado Library System (state)

In Colorado, seven regional library service systems were legally established by the legislature and funded primarily with state money. These systems permit participation by all types of publicly supported libraries within a broad geographical area. The major purpose is to improve services for patrons through interlibrary cooperation.

The Central Colorado Library System (CCLS), one of the seven, is a library cooperative whose purpose is to assist member libraries and

1. University of Colorado at Boulder, *1995–1996 Directory* (Boulder, Colo., 1995), i.

2. James F. Williams II, telephone conversation with the author, August 9, 1995.

media agencies in providing improved services to their users through systematic interlibrary cooperation. CCLS serves Denver and the surrounding counties, including Boulder County, wherein the University of Colorado at Boulder is found. CCLS serves 190 academic, public, school, and special libraries. It is a major provider of continuing education and training for librarians and library staff. Courier service for participating libraries is offered through a contract with a commercial carrier. System staff consult in the areas of strategic planning and space planning, meeting facilitation and problem solving, and public relations. A newsletter is published eight times a year. CCLS works closely with the other six regional systems in Colorado and the Colorado State Library.

The Interlibrary Loan Service at the University of Colorado at Boulder uses the courier service contracted for by CCLS to receive and return borrowed materials. The University of Colorado Health Sciences Center Library and the Denver campus Auraria Library are served by this courier. Connections to other couriers in the state link the Colorado Springs campus and such other university libraries as Colorado State University to the University of Colorado at Boulder. Lending materials to other Colorado libraries is facilitated by couriers in Colorado. The principal value of this service for interlibrary loan is its capacity for dependable daily delivery and return of library materials.

Continuing education is a constant need for a large and changing library staff. Interlibrary Loan Service personnel participate in CCLS continuing education, when appropriate. A recent offering in Internet training was particularly appreciated.[3]

Bibliographical Center for Research (multistate)

The Bibliographical Center for Research (BCR) is a nonprofit, multistate library cooperative that serves all libraries in its six member states, as well as numerous libraries throughout the rest of the nation. Libraries, whether academic, public, school, research, medical or corporate, in the member states of Colorado, Iowa, Kansas, Nevada, Utah and Wyo-

ming automatically are considered to be BCR member libraries. BCR helps member libraries acquire, implement and manage automated information services by providing access to automated library systems, automated cataloging including current cataloging and retrospective conversion, Internet services, microcomputer products and online- and CD-ROM-based databases.[4]

The University of Colorado at Boulder (UCB) procures its OCLC services through BCR. In addition to the OCLC PRISM Interlibrary Loan system and other pertinent OCLC services, the UCB Interlibrary Loan Service participates in the BCR Group Access Library Project. This project began with the intent to help medical libraries borrow from non-medical libraries in their group without actually having to do their cataloging on OCLC. This group, which includes UCB, was based originally in Colorado. It has been expanded to Iowa, Utah, and some document delivery suppliers.

BCR sponsors a reciprocal interlibrary loan code for the six member states. One of the provisions of the code is that the libraries will not charge one another for filling photocopy requests. An additional interlibrary loan agreement was arranged with AMIGOS, the network to the south. A similar provision for free photocopy for member libraries is part of that agreement. UCB signed both the BCR and the AMIGOS/BCR interlibrary loan codes, but later was forced to withdraw from the latter agreement because of the inability to supply such a large volume of free photocopy over and above the free photocopy that was received from libraries in the AMIGOS region.

A major breakthrough for library resource sharing in Colorado was the agreement that allowed Colorado libraries access to the basic databases on OCLC's FirstSearch reference system. BCR purchased a subscription for access to fifty FirstSearch ports for the Colorado library community. Participating Colorado libraries were assessed an annual fee for using the FirstSearch system based on their levels of use during the five-month, free pilot project in early 1995. The group subscription purchase resulted in savings for Colorado's libraries.

3. Gordon Barhydt, letter to the author, July 26, 1995. Central Colorado Library System, *By-laws and Articles of Organization* (Wheat Ridge, Colo., 1992).

4. BCR Bibliographical Center for Research, press release, August 17, 1995.

UCB, as a larger library paying larger fees, helps smaller institutions gain inexpensive access to First-Search. The quality of interlibrary loan requests is expected to improve as a result of FirstSearch use.[5]

UCB takes advantage of continuing education opportunities provided by BCR. Of particular interest are those in the areas of database searching, the use of microcomputers in libraries, and the OCLC PRISM Interlibrary Loan system.

The Greater Midwest Research Library Consortium (multistate)

The Greater Midwest Research Library Consortium (GMRLC) is composed of those libraries whose parent university belongs to the Association of Big-Eight Universities (ABEU-Plus), including the University of Colorado at Boulder. Other libraries have been accepted into the membership of GMRLC by a three-fourths vote of ABEU-Plus members. GMRLC is a regional consortium of medium-size research libraries (17 in 1995) located in the greater Midwest, with common interests in programs related to the following:

a. Information access/document delivery

b. Outreach and distance learning

c. New information technologies

d. Cost containment/reallocation of resources

e. Methods of measurement and accountability

f. Staff development

g. Cooperative collection development

h. Diversity/multiculturalism

i. Information exchange

Specific objectives are (1) to seek funding and mount projects or studies of interest to two or more members that can serve as prototypes for the membership and to report on those projects, and (2) to institute programs that cannot be done by individual institutions but can be done cooperatively.[6]

Though decisions for action must be approved by the directors of their libraries, the interlibrary loan and document delivery librarians meet separately, have their own purpose and structure (including committees), and work on developing cooperative projects to further their aim of enhanced resource sharing.

The consortium agreement includes the following provisions:

- Reciprocal lending
- Reciprocal copying of articles, with no limit to the number of pages
- Priority service
- Reciprocal Ariel transmissions, telefacsimile service, and first-class mailing for copies
- Ariel will be used for transmission of articles when possible, with telefacsimile or first-class mail when use of Ariel is not possible

For the Interlibrary Loan Service at UCB, there are additional initiatives of importance:

Federal Express delivery for photocopy and books (a model being studied by the Association of Research Libraries for all their members is a project to see if better service results)

User-satisfaction survey administered and analyzed by all member libraries

Other projects under consideration are guidelines for Ariel requests, guidelines for rush requests, and serving as Beta test sites for the Association of Research Libraries new cost study.[7]

The participation of UCB in these cooperative ventures is of great benefit to the users of the Interlibrary Loan Service.

OCLC (Online Computer Library Center) (national/international)

OCLC Online Computer Library Center, Inc., is a nonprofit, membership organization that helps libraries increase access to the world's information and reduce the rate at which their operating costs rise. OCLC provides computer-based services to help libraries improve every part of their operations, including cataloging, interlibrary loan, collection

---

5. Sandra Sternfield, letter to the author, 1995.

6. Greater Midwest Research Library Consortium, "Bylaws" (n.p., 1993).

7. Greater Midwest Research Library Consortium, "Agreement and Interlibrary Lending" (n.p., 1992). "Greater Midwest Interlibrary Loan Group (GIG)" (n.p., n.d.).

development, bibliographic verification, and reference searching. The international connections include libraries (many of them national libraries) in Europe and the Asia Pacific region. OCLC maintains an Office of Research, one of the largest centers of research in library and information science. The data processing center, along with the central offices, is located in Dublin, Ohio:

OCLC Online Computer Library
    Center, Inc.
6565 Frantz Road
Dublin, OH 43017-3395

For the national sales division:
    Telephone: (800) 848-5878
        (U.S. and Canada)
    Telephone: (800) 848-8286
        (Ohio only)

For products and services:
    Internet: URL: <http://www.oclc.org>
        URL: <http://www.oclc.org/
            oclc/new/list.htm>

OCLC-affiliated regional networks contract to provide OCLC services and support to libraries in the United States and Canada.

Recent OCLC statistics (as of May 22, 1995) are as follows:

Participating libraries—20,926

Total interlibrary loan requests—58,964,663

Highest OCLC record number—32,514,772

Location listings (holdings)—557,214,766

EPIC sessions (since January 1990)—857,172

FirstSearch searches (since October 1991)—
    22,792,446[8]

Interlibrary loan librarians use a variety of OCLC services. The OCLC online union catalog provides bibliographic verification and location of an enormous variety of library materials. The OCLC PRISM Interlibrary Loan system, which allows the user to create, send, and track interlibrary loan requests, is the most-used electronic interlibrary loan system in the United States. The EPIC service and FirstSearch catalogs are of particular interest. EPIC service offers trained professionals online searching of more than 40 databases. FirstSearch catalogs give patrons an interface and access to databases including WorldCat (the OCLC online union catalog), ERIC, MEDLINE, and many others. There is an ILL link available that will transfer a FirstSearch document request to the OCLC PRISM Interlibrary Loan system for review and processing. OCLC also accepts requests from other systems. Libraries are sending interlibrary loan requests to the OCLC PRISM Interlibrary Loan system electronically through ILL PRISM transfer, eliminating the need for handwritten, paper forms. Union Listing and the Name Address Directory (NAD) are two other OCLC programs of help to interlibrary loan librarians. The OCLC ILL Fee Management system is designed to decrease the burden of financial transactions between institutions. New statistical management tools are being investigated for OCLC PRISM Interlibrary Loan system users.[9]

UCB uses many of the OCLC services. The OCLC online union catalog is consulted for bibliographic and library holdings information. The OCLC PRISM Interlibrary Loan system is the primary method for processing both borrowing and lending requests. There is also participation in the newly developing programs, such as the FirstSearch ILL link and the ILL Fee Management system. The OCLC services are used to accomplish more without increasing the staff.

National Network of Libraries of Medicine (multistate/national)

The purpose of the National Network of Libraries of Medicine (NN/LM) is to provide health science practitioners, investigators, educators, and administrators in the United States with timely, convenient access to biomedical and health care information resources.

The Network is administered by the National Library of Medicine. It consists of eight Regional Medical Libraries (major institutions under contract with the National Library of Medicine), 140 Resource Libraries (primarily at medical schools), and some 4,500 Primary Access Libraries (primar-

8. "OCLC Statistics," OCLC Newsletter 215 (May/June 1995): 10.

9. "OCLC PRISM Interlibrary Loan Service" (Dublin, Ohio: OCLC Online Computer Library Center, 1993).

ily at hospitals). The Regional Medical Libraries administer and coordinate services in the Network's eight geographical regions.

New programs focus on reaching health professionals in rural, inner city, and other areas who do not have access to medical library resources. The goal is to make them aware of the services that Network libraries can provide. Other important Network programs include the interlibrary lending of more than two million journal articles, books and other published materials each year; reference services; training and consultation; and online access to MEDLINE and other databases made available by the National Library of Medicine.

Three of the Regional Medical Libraries have been designated Online Centers, to conduct National Library of Medicine online training classes and coordinate online services in several regions.[10]

There is a list of Regional Medical Libraries in appendix AA.

Any interlibrary loan librarian who has need for medical information should contact the proper Regional Medical Library for policies and procedures used in obtaining medical interlibrary loans. The toll-free telephone number of all Regional Medical Libraries is (800) 338-7657. There are usually charges associated with all loans from medical libraries.

The Midcontinental Region of NN/LM serves Colorado, Kansas, Missouri, Nebraska, Utah, and Wyoming. There are resource libraries in each state. For Colorado, the resource library is the Denison Memorial Library of the University of Colorado Health Sciences Center in Denver. The Interlibrary Loan Service of the University of Colorado at Boulder sends many medical requests to the Health Sciences Center, because both are part of the University of Colorado. Other Colorado medical libraries are also a first choice for borrowing, as are resource libraries in the Midcontinental Region. The OCLC PRISM Interlibrary Loan system is often used as a method of request transmission. DOCLINE, the National Library of Medicine's automated interlibrary loan request and referral system, also can be used for rapid routing of interlibrary loan requests throughout the NN/LM system. The courier, fax, Ariel, and U.S. Postal Service all deliver documents.

Center for Research Libraries (national/ North America)

The Center for Research Libraries is a not-for-profit corporation established and operated by scholarly and research institutions to strengthen the library and information resources for research and to enhance the accessibility of those resources.

Founded in 1949, the Center functions as a cooperative, membership-based research library dedicated to acquiring, storing, preserving, providing bibliographic access to, and lending/delivery from a collection that complements and supplements the collections of the major research libraries of North America. Through its programs, the Center supports individual member libraries in meeting their local users' needs for research materials.[11]

The collections include archival materials in microform, microform and reprint sets, foreign doctoral dissertations, serials, newspapers, U.S. state documents, monographs, foreign documents, and area studies microform projects. Some of these collections are not cataloged, such as the foreign doctoral dissertations. *CRLCATALOG*, the online public access catalog, covers virtually all titles in the center's *cataloged* collections, including newspapers, serials, and the like.

The Center for Research Libraries is a membership organization of more than 130 universities, colleges, and research libraries. The important thing is that those who are *not* members can still use the interlibrary loan and document delivery services for a cost-recovery fee. As of 1994 nonmembers were limited to ten filled requests per year. The transaction fee is $20 for each such request, and it must be prepaid. For more information contact the center:

Center for Research Libraries
6050 South Kenwood Avenue
Chicago, IL 60637-2804
Telephone: (312) 955-4545
Fax: (312) 955-9732
Center's home page:
    URL: <http://www.crl.uchicago.edu/
    crlhp.html>

The University of Colorado at Boulder, a member, has found the collections at the center to

---

10. "National Network of Libraries of Medicine," *National Library of Medicine Fact Sheet* (April 1995), 1.

11. "Center for Research Libraries" (Chicago: CRL, 1994).

contain valuable research material for both graduate students and faculty. An example of such materials would be the Chinese newspapers borrowed for a history graduate student studying Chinese opinion of their students who study abroad.

OTHER EXAMPLES OF INTERLIBRARY COOPERATION

There are many examples of interlibrary loan processing centers that facilitate interlibrary loans for member libraries. These are usually part of a library system that offers a number of services. What follows is a brief description of one such center.

Traverse des Sioux Library System, Mankato, Minnesota

The Traverse des Sioux Library System (TdS) was formed in 1975 as one of 12 regional public library systems in Minnesota. City, county, and multi-county public libraries comprise the membership. Its mission is to encourage cooperation through the development of a union catalog of the holdings of public libraries in the nine-county region of south central Minnesota, to create an interlibrary loan system for sharing these resources, to establish a backup reference service for the region, and to provide a means for delivering both information and materials to member libraries. In addition to these mandated services, TdS offers its members discounts on materials ordered through its Technical Services Department and provides centralized cataloging through OCLC. An integrated public access catalog and online circulation system (TdS/PALS) with several additional modules, including interlibrary loan, was chosen for use by members of TdS in 1990. These services are supported by Minnesota tax dollars with supplementary funds from the Federal Library Services and Construction Act and independent grants.

Additional academic, school, and special libraries, which make up the South-Central Minnesota Inter-Library Exchange, are served by TdS.

Contracts pay for interlibrary loan, delivery, and call-in reference service to all libraries in the region.

A regional interlibrary loan service is offered by TdS to help libraries obtain materials not listed in the TdS/PALS online catalog or the Sioux Line microfiche. TdS checks the OCLC online union catalog and forwards interlibrary loan requests to other interlibrary loan referral centers and then to out-of-state locations found on OCLC. Follow-up work is done until the request is filled, there are no holdings left to contact, or the deadline for the request is past. The backup reference service can also be of help in delineating interlibrary loan requests. A very high interlibrary loan fill rate is achieved. By facilitating interlibrary loan requests not easily located within the region, TdS provides a valuable service to its member libraries.[12]

The reader should know about two other bibliographic utilities of significance in the United States: Research Libraries Group and WLN.

Research Libraries Group

The Research Libraries Group (RLG) is a not-for-profit membership corporation of universities, archives, historical societies, museums, and other institutions devoted to improving access to information that supports research and learning. Founded in 1974 by Harvard, Yale, and Columbia universities and the New York Public Library, RLG became a pioneer in developing cooperative solutions to the problems these and many other organizations faced in the acquisition, delivery, and preservation of research information.

Today, RLG is an international alliance of nearly 150 members, for whom RLG is a catalyst

---

12. Traverse des Sioux Library System, *Reference and Interlibrary Loan Manual* (Mankato, Minn.: Traverse des Sioux Library System, 1994), 1–6.

for collaborative efforts in pursuit of their scholarly mission. RLG provides a highly skilled staff, sophisticated technical resources, and a long, successful track record in managing and supporting interactions among its members.[13]

The Shared Resources Service (SHARes), operated by RLG for its members, is a resource-sharing program that centers on reciprocal resource sharing, priority lending, expedited delivery, access to noncirculating materials, equitable interlibrary loan costs (net lender/net borrower payments), and on-site access. An electronic interlibrary loan system can be used to make requests and send messages concerning those requests. Borrowing and lending statistics reports are available online. A set of policies and procedures have been developed to facilitate resource sharing.

A number of services are available to those who are *not* members. The RLIN bibliographical files contain records for books, serials, maps, computer files, visual materials, recordings, and scores. These files can be searched for reference, cataloging, acquisitions, and interlibrary loan purposes. There is an Archival and Manuscripts Control system. CitaDel is a database for citation access and document delivery. Eureka provides access to RLIN and CitaDel files. Zephyr uses Z39.50 protocol to allow patrons to search these files using their local system's interface. Ariel uses a standard personal computer, scanner, and a laser printer to produce high-resolution copies over the Internet. There is no need to photocopy first. For more information about RLG's products and services contact

> Research Libraries Group
> 1200 Villa Street
> Mountain View, CA 94041-1100
> Telephone: (800) 537-7546
> (ask for a sales associate)
> Fax: (415) 964-0943
> E-mail: bl.sal@rlg.stanford.edu

WLN

WLN was formerly known as the Western Library Network and, before that, the Washington Library Network.

WLN provides a broad range of innovative, high quality products and services to libraries of all types and sizes throughout North America, including a full-service online MARC bibliographic database, online interlibrary loan (ILL) communications, Internet services, *LaserCat* and *LaserPac* CD-ROM catalogs, database preparation and authority control services, collection assessment software and products . . .

WLN's customers include the full range of libraries from large academic institutions and public libraries to very small school and special libraries. WLN products and services are tailored to fit the needs of each library, regardless of size and budget. With WLN, you pay no membership fees, but only for the products and services you actually need . . .[14]

WLN's online Interlibrary Loan system serves a number of subscribers. The WLN Interlibrary Loan system generates interlibrary loan requests from bibliographic records and automatically transfers library symbols and local call numbers to the request. Requests can be routed to as many as eight libraries, and there is an interlibrary loan policy file available online and in printed format. For more information contact

> WLN
> P.O. Box 3888
> Lacey, WA 98503-0888
> Telephone: (800) 342-5956
> (360) 923-4000
> Fax: (360) 923-4009
> E-mail: info@wln.com

---

13. "What Is RLG?" (Mountain View, Calif.: Research Libraries Group, 1995), 1.

14. "WLN Systems and Services" (Lacey, Wash.: WLN, 1994), 1.

CONCLUSION

Here are some suggestions that might prove useful for becoming acquainted and keeping up with the interlibrary cooperation in which your interlibrary loan office should be involved. One good way to learn is to ask someone who knows. State library agencies, the largest medical library in the state, or another library of the same type are all good places to start. Know the policies of each interlibrary cooperative organization with which your library is involved and learn the particular procedures required. Collect and read the documentation pertinent to a particular system. OCLC, for example, has training materials and user's manuals for each of its systems. Take advantage of any training that is offered. When a new system is introduced, there are usually workshops to show how the system works. Above all, keep up with new developments, for interlibrary cooperation alters and changes in the most surprising ways. Many states have annual interlibrary loan workshops on topics of current interest. Conferences of state library associations and the American Library Association frequently provide interlibrary loan programs and an opportunity to learn about new developments. Technical bulletins, library system newsletters, state publications, and library journals can also be good vehicles for learning of new developments. Articles in annuals provide updated information (e.g., JoAn S. Segal's "Library Cooperation and Networking, 1994").[15]

Variations in interlibrary cooperation will continue to alter the interlibrary loan landscape. Technology is developing so fast that it takes effort and concentration to keep up with the latest innovations. Bibliographic and location information are now readily available. So too are effective request transmission systems. Document delivery can be done more rapidly today than in the past. What the future holds is uncertain. Publishing itself is headed in new directions. Copyright has not yet been defined for electronic documents. Patrons are more demanding and wanting, in some cases, to do everything for themselves. Funding for cooperative ventures can be problematic. Changes are coming in interlibrary cooperation, and interlibrary loan librarians are among those who should be involved in helping to make them.

15. JoAn S. Segal, "Library Cooperation and Networking, 1994," in the *Bowker Annual: Library and Book Trade Almanac,* 40th ed. (New Providence, N.J.: Bowker, 1995).

6

International
Interlibrary Loan

INTERNATIONAL DEVELOPMENTS

An international program has enhanced the possibility of satisfying the demand for publications not found in the United States. The Universal Availability of Publications (UAP), initiated by the International Federation of Library Associations and Institutions (IFLA) and supported by Unesco, has been gaining increased attention from countries around the world. UAP is involved with collecting the materials published within a country and describing them using accepted bibliographic practice. It helps to organize interlibrary lending on a national basis so that collections can be made available easily to others wherever they may be. It helps to develop rapid transmission of requests using common formats, procedures, and routines. Maurice B. Line emphasized the need for UAP when he wrote that "it is abundantly clear that not even the most highly developed country can ever hope to satisfy all the document needs of all its own population."[1]

Meetings attended by participants from many nations have been held, studies have been conducted, problems have been identified, and possible solutions to some of them have been recommended. The International Lending: Principles and Guidelines for Procedure (1978) (revised 1987) and the IFLA International Loan/Photocopy Request form are two of the achievements that have resulted from this concern. Work on UAP continues and is focused in the International Programme for UAP, which was established and located at the British Library Document Supply Centre. The program officer at this writing is Graham P. Cornish. The work of the office will continue to be of interest to interlibrary loan librarians in the years to come.

An important part of IFLA for interlibrary loan librarians is the IFLA Office for International Lending, which was created at the British Library Document Supply Centre in 1975. Recently this office has been combined administratively with the UAP program. The Office for International Lending has a number of activities, among them being the sales point for the IFLA International Loan/Photocopy Request form and a publishing program for information on interlibrary loan topics. The *Model Handbook for Interlending and Copying* is an example of a general interlibrary loan publication that contains a very useful section on "International Requests."[2] The IFLA Section (committee) on Document Delivery and Interlending acts as an advisory committee to the IFLA Office for International Lending. The section's main objective is to promote interlibrary lending and document delivery both nationally and internationally in support of the UAP program, using rapidly developing technology as well as traditional methods to extend and accelerate the availability of documents. The section meets annually during the IFLA General Conference. Membership in the section frequently includes librarians from the United States. For more information, contact the IFLA International Programme for UAP and the Office for International Lending at the following address:

IFLA Offices for UAP and
    International Lending
c/o The British Library
    Document Supply Centre
Boston Spa, Wetherby
West Yorkshire LS23 7BQ
United Kingdom
Telephone: +44 1937 546255
E-mail: IFLA@bl.uk
URL: <http://www.nlc-bnc.ca/
    ifla/VI/2/uap.htm>

Another part of IFLA is the Universal Dataflow and Telecommunications (UDT) core program, currently directed by Leigh Swain and based at the National Library of Canada. Among the concerns of this program are international interlibrary loan communications and protocol and the application of international standards to interlibrary loan activities. UDT publishes reports of interest in a series, "UDT Series on Data Communication Technologies and Standards for Libraries" (ISSN: 1018–0311). Other information of interest, *UDT Occasional Papers,* is published in paper and in electronic form at the following World Wide Web site:

URL: <http://www.nlc-bnc.
    ca/ifla/VI/5/op/index.htm>

UDT also published the informative *UDT Newsletter,* which contained such news as a short article about a project to improve interlibrary loan communications and document delivery in Africa. The "Focus on Technology" part of each issue included such information as an excellent introduction to the World Wide Web. The final printed issue of the *UDT Newsletter* was number 18, summer 1995. The *UDT Newsletter* is to be replaced with the electronic *UDT Digest,* which will be distributed through electronic mail and the IFLANET World Wide Web service, which can be reached at the following address:

URL: <http://www.nlc-bnc.ca/ifla/>

For more information about the work of the UDT program, write to the following address:

---

1. Maurice B. Line, "Universal Availability of Publications," *Unesco Bulletin for Libraries* 31 (May 1977): 143.

2. Graham P. Cornish, *Model Handbook for Interlending and Copying* (Boston Spa, Wetherby, West Yorkshire, U.K.: IFLA Office for International Lending, British Library Document Supply Centre, 1988).

IFLA International Office for UDT
c/o National Library of Canada
395 Wellington Street
Ottawa, Ontario K1A 0N4 Canada
Telephone: (819) 994-6833
Fax: (819) 994-6835
E-mail: ifla@nlc-bnc.ca

A World Wide Web page for Interlibrary Loan Protocol Resources has been created by IFLA:

URL: <http://www.nlc-bnc.ca/II/illprot.htm>

Among other items are found such topics as where to purchase International Standards Organization interlibrary loan protocol documents; profiles; and articles, tutorials, overheads, etc.

The basis for conduct of international interlibrary loan is contained in International Lending: Principles and Guidelines for Procedure (1978) (revised 1987) (see appendix U), which was approved by the IFLA Section on Document Delivery and Interlending. Because the American Library Association is a member of IFLA, these principles and guidelines should be followed when dealing with libraries outside North America.

International interlibrary loan is growing due to the use of the Internet and other electronic sources. Good common sense and reasonable interlibrary loan practice are needed when dealing with libraries outside the United States as well as those within. Refer to the procedures recommended in chapter 1, "Instructions for Borrowing Libraries," when they apply. Keep in mind the time required to complete an international loan transaction.

CANADA

Loans between Canada and the United States are conducted on much the same basis as domestic loans, with the exception of the mailing procedure, which is outlined below. The latest version of the *CLA/ASTED Interlibrary Loan Code* was officially adopted by the Canadian Library Association and the Association pour l'avancement des sciences et des techniques de la documentation in 1995 and is similar to the National Interlibrary Loan Code for the United States, 1993.[3]

Canadian procedures are outlined in the *CLA/ASTED Interlibrary Loan Procedures Manual,* which cautions Canadian libraries that requests for photocopy from U.S. libraries are apt to be returned unless U.S. copyright law compliance is indicated.[4] The four-part forms used in both countries are similar. As in the United States, Canadian libraries are transmitting more requests electronically, by a variety of systems, not all found in American libraries.

Symbols and Interlibrary Loan Policies in Canada gives information useful to American libraries on Canadian library symbols and interlibrary loan policies.[5] *National Guidelines for Document Delivery* offers many suggestions for sound borrowing and lending practice.[6] Of interest in understanding resource-sharing projects in Canada is *Canadian Inventory of Resource Sharing.*[7]

A request may be sent directly to a Canadian library known to have what is needed. Some Canadian libraries use the OCLC (Online Computer Library Center) PRISM Interlibrary Loan system. Other libraries can be reached by using fax or the

3. *CLA/ASTED Interlibrary Loan Code/Code canadien 1995 CLA/ASTED de prêt entre bibliothèques,* rev. ed. prepared by the CLA Resource Sharing Committee (Ottawa: Canadian Library Association, 1995).

4. *CLA/ASTED Interlibrary Loan Procedures Manual* (Ottawa: Canadian Library Association, 1989).

5. *Symbols and Interlibrary Loan Policies in Canada/ Sigles et politiques de prêt entre bibliothèques au Canada* (Ottawa: National Library of Canada, 1995–).

6. Carol Smale, *National Guidelines for Document Delivery* (Ottawa: National Library of Canada, 1994).

7. *Canadian Inventory of Resource Sharing/Répertoire canadien de la mise en commun des ressources,* compiled by Carrol D. Lunau and Holly Yu, rev. ed. (Ottawa: National Library of Canada, 1995).

Internet. For some requests, the latest edition of the following publication can be consulted for addresses of Canadian libraries:

American Library Directory. 2 vols. 48th ed. New Providence, N.J.: Bowker, 1995.

When locations for Canadian materials cannot be found, interlibrary loan and photoduplication requests may be sent to the National Library of Canada for materials in the humanities and social sciences. The interlibrary loan period is four weeks. As of 1995, there are no charges for photocopies, loans, or locations, although limited funding could alter this situation. If an item is not available from the National Library of Canada's collections, locations for other Canadian libraries are provided. Requests can be sent by the OCLC PRISM Interlibrary Loan system (enter NLD twice) for libraries that do not have access to another electronic system capable of sending interlibrary borrowing requests. It is helpful to learn just how the National Library of Canada uses the OCLC PRISM Interlibrary Loan system before sending a request. Fax can be used (613) 996-4424, and a fax form is available from the National Library of Canada Interlibrary Loan Division. Internet can be used for interlibrary loan requests only with interlibrary loan protocol-based software (Internet: oonlpebill@nlc-bnc.ca). For mailing ALA Interlibrary Loan Request forms, the address is

> Interlibrary Loan Division
> National Library of Canada
> 395 Wellington Street
> Ottawa, Ontario K1A 0N4 Canada

For general information about interlibrary loan, contact the following:

> Client Services Coordinator
> Interlibrary Loan Division
> National Library of Canada
> 395 Wellington Street
> Ottawa, Ontario K1A 0N4 Canada
> Telephone: (613) 996-7527
> Fax: (613) 996-4424
> E-mail: illser@nlc-bnc.ca

For materials in science and technology, requests should be sent to the Canada Institute for Scientific and Technical Information (CISTI). This organization offers a fee-based, copyright-cleared service for customers, including those in the United States. CISTI supplies articles, technical reports, and loans. Documents are delivered by electronic options through the Internet (including Ariel) using a new Intelligent Document Delivery Scanning (IntelliDoc) system. Materials can also be delivered by fax or a parcel delivery service.

Finding out what CISTI owns and placing orders can be achieved in a number of ways. CISTI is a document supplier on the OCLC PRISM Interlibrary Loan system (OCLC symbol CAI). DOCLINE, the National Library of Medicine's document ordering system, can also be used. Printed and diskette versions of a selective list of 16,000 currently received serials are available without charge. Similar information can be found by using the World Wide Web, although complete holdings are not included there:

> URL: <http://www.cisti.nrc.ca/cisti.html>

Requests can also be placed using this system. There are many holdings for CISTI in *Chemical Abstracts Service Source Index (CASSI).*[8] Romulus is a union list CD-ROM that contains all of CISTI's serial holdings, those of the National Library of Canada, and those of 400 other Canadian libraries. Romulus can be searched for holdings, an interlibrary loan order form can be called up, and the form can be saved in a microcomputer for sending in a batch to CISTI or the National Library of Canada via the Internet. Documents can be ordered using the World Wide Web:

> URL: <http://www.cisti.nrc.ca/cisti/docdel/order.html>

The Internet address for making requests to CISTI is

doccisti@info.cisti.nrc.ca

The fax numbers for making requests are

> (613) 941-0177
> (613) 952-8243 (for urgent requests)

The telephone can also be used for placing orders for documents:

---

8. *Chemical Abstracts Service Source Index, 1907–1989,* 3 vols. (Columbus, Ohio: Chemical Abstracts Service, 1990).

Chemical Abstracts Service Source Index, Annual Cumulation, 1990– (Columbus, Ohio: Chemical Abstracts Service, 1990–).

(613) 993-1585

(613) 993-1412 (for urgent requests)

For mail requests and more information about document search service, document obtain service, and urgent service, contact CISTI at the following address:

Document Delivery
CISTI
National Research Council of Canada
Montreal Road, Bldg. M-55

Ottawa, Ontario K1A 0S2 Canada
Telephone: (800) 668-1222 or
(613) 993-9251
Fax: (613) 993-7619
E-mail: cisti.docdel@nrc.ca

Mail must be handled very carefully so that Canadian libraries do not have to pay a Goods and Services Tax when the books go through Canadian customs. The National Library of Canada includes special return mailing labels (see figure 16) when

★★ ATTENTION LIBRARIES ★★
★★ AVIS AUX BIBLIOTHÈQUES ★★

Please use this label when returning items borrowed on Interlibrary Loan to the National Library of Canada. This will alert Revenue Canada **NOT** to charge duty and taxes. We prefer items to be returned <u>by mail</u>. If you use a courier, please ensure that you use one which <u>includes</u> the services of a licenced customs broker in your fees.

Veuillez utiliser cette étiquette quand vous retournez des documents empruntés par prêt entre bibliothèques à la Bibliothèque nationale du Canada. Ainsi Revenue Canada n'imposera **PAS** d'impôt ou de frais de douane. Nous préférons que les documents nous soient retournés <u>par la poste</u>. Si vous utilisez un service de courrier, veuillez vous assurer que les frais <u>incluent</u> aussi les services d'un agent en douane agréé.

NL/BN 731 (94-06)

Sender / Expéditeur

_____

_____

_____ Postal Code _____
                                  Code postal

*** ATTENTION REVENUE CANADA ***
TARIFF / TARIF: 9813.00.00 or 9814.00.00
GST/TPS Code: 66
Property of the National Library of Canada returned on Interlibrary Loan / Propriété de la Bibliothèque nationale du Canada, retour de prêt entre bibliothèques

INTERLIBRARY LOAN DIVISION	DIVISION DU PRÊT ENTRE BIBLIOTHÈQUES
NATIONAL LIBRARY OF CANADA	BIBLIOTHÈQUE NATIONALE DU CANADA
395 WELLINGTON ST	395, RUE WELLINGTON
OTTAWA ON K1A 0N4	OTTAWA ON K1A 0N4
CANADA	CANADA

FIGURE 16.   National Library of Canada, Return Mailing Label

sending materials out on loan. These labels, which have information designed to smooth passage of interlibrary loans through customs, must be used to return items to Canada. Do not use a parcel delivery service to return borrowed material to Canada unless the service includes the use of a registered customs broker. Loans from the United States to Canada must also contain specific customs information. See "Facilitating the Entry of Interlibrary Loan Material into Canada," figure 17, for the correct information and format for both kinds of labels. The Association of Research Libraries' "Transborder Interlibrary Loan: Shipping Interlibrary Loan Materials from the U.S. to Canada" fact sheet covers rate classification, package markings, weight limit of packages, costs, and insurance (see appendix BB). All of this information should be passed along to whoever does the wrapping and mailing to Canada.

MEXICO

Interlibrary loan between the United States and Mexico can be attempted, but the results are somewhat unpredictable. Elda Monica Guerrero reports that the mail is slow and unsafe and that there is a lack of qualified staff for loan operations in some libraries.[9] S. Carolyn Kahl cites budget cuts and economic crises as contributing factors to difficult interlibrary loan.[10] Another factor is often the lack of online or CD-ROM public access catalogs, making verification and location of materials difficult. Only a few Mexican libraries have the OCLC PRISM Interlibrary Loan system.

In 1988 work was begun on a cooperative project, the U.S.-Mexico Interlibrary Loan Project, designed to exchange library resources among higher education and research institutions in Mexico and the United States. A. Robert Seal, then director of the University of Texas at El Paso Library, worked with the Instituto Technológico Autónomo de México (ITAM) and the Biblioteca Benjamin Franklin in Mexico City to develop an agreement and get the project started.[11] Twenty-one American universities (now twenty-eight) and seven Mexican institutions (now ten) participated. Beginning with materials on social sciences and humanities, the project at present includes the subject areas of science and technology as well. The traffic has not been heavy, with much of the lending going from the United States to Mexico.

Progress has been made in the area of online public access catalogs. The following libraries should have such catalogs available now or in the near future:

Fundación Universidad de las Américas

Instituto Technológico de Estudios Superiores de Monterrey

El Colegio de México

Universidad Iberoamericana

Instituto Technológico Autónomo de México

Instituto Mora

Centro de Investigación y Docencia Económicas[12]

Under the sponsorship of the U.S.-Mexico Fund for Culture, there is a project (ABIMEX) in Mexico to catalog books published by Mexican or Latin American publishers between 1521 and 1910. About 10,000 titles have been cataloged. This research database is available online, and a CD-ROM product is expected in the future.

The U.S.-Mexico Interlibrary Loan Project has been watched with great interest by research

---

9. Elda Monica Guerrero, "Mexico Interlibrary Loan Project: A Five Year Overview" (paper presented to the Fourth Interlending and Document Supply International Conference, Calgary, Canada, June 11, 1995), 1.

10. S. Carolyn Kahl, "A First Step: The U.S.-Mexico Interlibrary Loan Project," *Journal of Interlibrary Loan, Document Delivery & Information Supply* 4, no. 1 (1993): 19.

11. A. Robert Seal, "The U.S.-Mexico Interlibrary Loan Project," in *Advances in Library Resource Sharing*, vol. 2 (Westport, Conn., and London: Meckler, 1991), 165–75.

12. Guerrero, op. cit., 3.

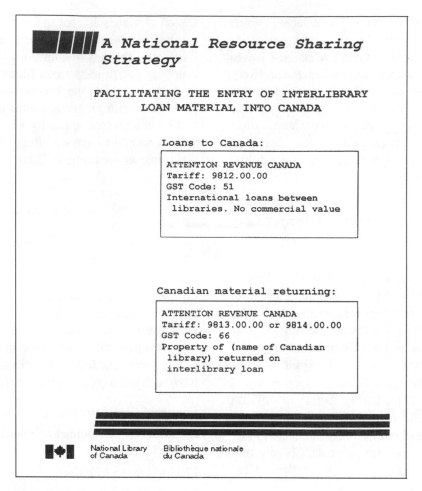

FIGURE 17.   National Library of Canada, Facilitating the Entry of Interlibrary Loan Material into Canada

libraries in the United States. It "may be considered as the first step toward providing for educational need through cooperation and communication between the U.S. and Mexico." [13]

Some information to keep in mind when approaching Mexican libraries follows:

There is no referral center for interlibrary loans in Mexico.

Each library has its own policy, including payment requirements.

ALA Interlibrary Loan Request forms are acceptable in Mexican libraries. (The Mexican form is modeled on the ALA one.)

The majority of research and academic libraries have e-mail and access to the Internet.

Verifying and locating a bibliographic citation increases the chances of having a lending request filled. [14]

One key thing to remember is to include "interlibrary loan," which is "Prestamo Interbibliotecario," as part of the address when sending a request to a Mexican library.

Sources for addresses and other information about Mexican libraries follow:

American Library Directory. 2 vols. 48th ed. New Providence, N.J.: Bowker, 1995.

---

13. Kahl, op. cit., 22.

14. Letter from Estela Morales Campos to the author, May 22, 1995.

Añorve Guillén, Martha Alicia. *Directorio de Bibliotecas de Universidades Oficiales de la República Mexicana.* 1st ed. México: Universidad Nacional Autónoma de México and Secretaria de Educación Pública, 1987.

Vazquez Melchor, Alvaro. *Directorio de Bibliotecas en Ciencias de la Salud en la República Mexicana.* México: Universidad Nacional Autónoma de México, Instituto de Investigaciónes Biomédicas, 1982.

Directorio de Bibliotecas de la República Mexicana. 6th ed. 2 vols. México: Dirección General de Publicaciónes y Bibliotecas, Secretaria de Educación Pública, 1979.

Directorio de Bibliotecas [computer disk]. México: Universidad Nacional Autónoma de México, Secretaria de Servicios Académicos, Dirección General de Bibliotecas, Subdirección de Planeacion y Desarrolo, Departamento de Planeacion, 1995.

A suggestion for a library suitable for filling *public library* requests is

> Dirección General de Bibliotecas
> Consejo Nacional para la Cultura y las Artes

Av. Revolución 1877 - 9o.piso
Barrio Loreto, San Angel, D.F.
México 01090
Fax: (525) 550 70 98
    (525) 550 00 03
At'n Dra. Ana Maria Magaloni

A suggestion for a library suitable for filling *academic library* requests is

> Dirección General de Bibliotecas
> Universidad Nacional Autónoma de
>   México
> Edificio Biblioteca Central
> Cuidad Universitaria
> Coyoacan, D.F.
> México 04520
> At'n Mtro. Adolfo Rodriquez

Because the mail is problematic in Mexico, it might be wise to use a parcel delivery service when sending materials to Mexico. The service is more reliable than mail, and the parcel can be tracked. Inquiry should be made about customs processing and possible payments.

BRITISH LIBRARY DOCUMENT SUPPLY CENTRE

A first choice for obtaining materials from overseas is the British Library Document Supply Centre (BLDSC). This is the largest literature collection in the world dedicated solely to document delivery. The collection contains 247,000 journal titles (about 45,000 titles currently received), 500,000 theses, 335,000 conference proceedings, and 3 million books. Report literature, official central or national government publications, translations into English, Cyrillic/Slavonic language books, and music scores round out this remarkable collection. Identify exactly what is needed before ordering. Specific reference tools for verification can be found in chapter 1, "Instructions for Borrowing Libraries," "Verify borrowing requests and find where material is located," under the headings for the specific kinds of

material. In addition, the OCLC online union catalog lists 34,000 current journal titles for BLDSC (OCLC symbol BRI). The contents data of the 10,000 most frequently used journal titles are currently available on Research Libraries Information Network (RLIN) via CitaDel and on EBSCO via EBSCONet. The addition of 4,500 BLDSC titles augments journal coverage in OCLC's Contents-First and ArticleFirst. If it is not possible to verify what is needed, BLDSC does accept unverified requests. Requests may be sent by the OCLC PRISM Interlibrary Loan system, online from a personal computer via the Internet, through database hosts, by e-mail, or via fax. Mail using special BLDSC forms can also be used. Contact BLDSC before sending a request for the first time because applications must be signed, the method of payment determined, and the like.

A number of important services are offered. Copyright clearance is automatically built into all of the photocopy services offered. That means a fee is collected, which is then paid to the Copyright Licensing Agency in the United Kingdom. With reciprocal agreements worldwide, the payments are then distributed to the appropriate agencies and publishers. Journal Contents Page Service provides photocopies of the contents page of journals currently received on a regular subscription basis. Ordering a photocopy of a particular article is then made very easy. The Copyright Fee Paid Photocopy Service is the basic service for account customers. Upon receipt of a completed request, the collection is searched, documents are located, and copy is sent via airmail. The account is debited if the request is sent by automated means; otherwise, payment is by prepaid forms and coupons. Of all the orders, 90 percent are dispatched within 48 hours. Urgent Action Service can be requested for immediate attention to a request. Most such requests can be processed within two hours. All documents will be sent via fax, courier, or airmail. LEXICON allows account customers to send a list of bibliographic citations. Photocopies of the requested documents are dispatched in a single package within a few days. Nonregistered customers can order via LEXICON. An invoice will be sent with the documents. Payments can then be made by check, bank transfer, or credit card. The Loan Service, for books and the like, requires an additional registration form and is available only to institutions and universities—not to individuals. If the item is not at BLDSC, a notice is sent immediately by e-mail or mail. A backup search will be made only for United Kingdom publications. If the requested item is located, it is then forwarded to a library to fill.

There are a number of payment options. Account requestors can establish a deposit account or a billing account or use prepaid coupons and request forms. OCLC network members can use a network billing account, which is a convenient way to save time and money.

For information, contact the British Library Document Supply Centre office in the *United States* at the following address:

> The British Library
>   Document Supply Centre
>   In America
> One Appleton Street
> Boston, MA 02116
> Telephone: (800) 932-3575
> Fax: (617) 451-1193

BLDSC can also be reached in the *United Kingdom:*

> The British Library
>   Document Supply Centre
> Enquiries and Registration Section
> Boston Spa
> Wetherby
> West Yorkshire LS23 7BQ
> United Kingdom
> Telephone for customer services:
>   +44 1937 546060
> Fax: +44 1937 546333
> E-mail: dsc-customer-services@bl.uk

Information about the whole range of services the British Library provides can be found by using the World Wide Web:

> URL: <http://portico.bl.uk>

INTERNATIONAL INTERLIBRARY BORROWING

Procedures for borrowing internationally are similar to those used for the United States. Be sure the patron's "need before" date allows sufficient time for transmittal of the request and receipt of the material. If surface mail is used, a request can easily take six weeks or more to arrive, depending on the country and the individual library. Verification of the bibliographic citation is just as important when borrowing from overseas as it is in the United States. For verification procedures, refer to chapter 1, "Instructions for Borrowing Libraries," "Verify borrowing requests and find where material is located." Remember that photocopies are generally easier to obtain than the actual loan of library materials.

Copyright laws can be different in other countries. The United States is a party to a number of agreements that set forth its copyright relations with independent nations of the world.[15] Of particular importance is the Berne Convention:

On March 1, 1989, the United States became a member of the Berne Convention for the Protection of Literary and Artistic Works. On the same day, amendments to the U.S. copyright law went into effect that bring U.S. law into conformance with this convention. In adhering to the Berne Convention the United States joins the Berne Union, a prestigious association of 79 member countries linked together in a single unit. Thus the United States makes available to its nationals copyright protection in foreign countries under the laws of member nations of the Union, and in the same manner, foreign works covered by the Berne Convention became eligible for copyright protection in the United States under the amended copyright law.[16]

This means that "protection against unauthorized use in a particular country basically depends on the national laws of that country."[17] Because the United States is a party to the Berne Convention and the Universal Copyright Convention, among others, abiding by the U.S. copyright law will go a long way toward acceptable international copyright transactions.[18] Chapter 3, "Interlibrary Loan, Reproduction, and the Copyright Law," gives some basic information about the U.S. copyright law. The authority for an organization "operated for scholarly, educational, or religious purposes and not for gain" to import reproductions for libraries, §602(a)(3), also mentions that reproduction should not exceed the provisions of §108(g)(2).[19] A discussion of §108(g)(2) is found in chapter 3. In addition, be sure to comply with any particular instructions concerning copyright made by foreign libraries. *Interlending and Document Supply in Europe* contains comments about copyright laws for the countries covered by that publication.[20] IFLA maintains a "Copyright and Intellectual Property Resources Page" at the following World Wide Web address:

URL: <http://www.nlc-bnc.ca/ifla/II/cpyright.htm>

Make certain that no location can be found for books in the United States. Photocopy, of course, may be purchased wherever it is more convenient and the price is agreeable. A foreign library or document supply center known to have the material may be addressed directly. If no location is known, find out if the country from which you wish to borrow has a center for international interlibrary loans and what procedures must be followed by using the following:

A Guide to Centres of International Lending. Compiled and edited by Margaret M. Barwick and Pauline A. Connolly. 5th ed. Boston Spa, Wetherby, West Yorkshire, U.K.: IFLA Office for International Lending, 1995.

Should an address be required for a library not listed in the above work, consult one of the following:

The World of Learning. 1st– . London: Europa Publications, 1947– .

World Guide to Libraries=Internationales Bibliotheks-Handbuch. Ed. 1– . Handbook of International Documentation and Information, vol. 8. Munich and New York: K. G. Saur, 1966– .

World Guide to Special Libraries. 3rd ed. 2 vols. Handbook of International Documentation and Information, vol. 17. Munich and New York: K. G. Saur, 1995.

15. U.S. Copyright Office, *International Copyright Relations of the United States,* Circular 38a (Washington, D.C.: U.S. Government Printing Office, 1994).

16. U.S. Copyright Office, *The United States Joins the Berne Union,* Circular 93a (Washington, D.C.: U.S. Government Printing Office, 1989), 2.

17. U.S. Copyright Office, *International Copyright Relations of the United States,* Circular 38a (Washington, D.C.: U.S. Government Printing Office, 1994), 7.

18. U.S. Copyright Law (Title 17 U.S. Code) and U.S. legislation implementing the Berne Convention (P.L. 100-568, 702 stat. 2853, October 31, 1988).

19. U.S. Copyright Office, *Copyright Law of the United States of America Contained in Title 17 of the United States Code,* Circular 92 (Washington, D.C.: U.S. Government Printing Office, 1995), 98–99.

20. Graham P. Cornish, *Interlending and Document Supply in Europe,* for the General Information Programme and UNISIST, PGI-90/WS/13 (Paris: Unesco, 1990).

Directory of Special Collections in Western Europe. Edited by Alison Gallico. London and New York: Bowker/K. G. Saur, 1993.

Guide to Libraries in Central and Eastern Europe. Compiled by Maria Hughes. London: The British Library, 1992.

National Libraries of the World: An Address List. Boston Spa, England: IFLA Office for International Lending, 1988. Constantly updated, this address list can be obtained free from the IFLA Offices for UAP and International Lending. The IFLA address is above. The list is also available on the World Wide Web at the following address: URL: <http://www.nlc-bnc.ca/ifla/VI/2/p2/natlibs.htm>

The IFLA International Loan/Photocopy Request form approved by IFLA (see figure 18) should be used for requests sent beyond North America unless the individual library stipulates otherwise. The instructions (dated 1992) for using these forms are below. The form itself is put together B, C, D, A, with the customer copy A (borrowing library copy), which is yellow, on the bottom. You will notice that the practice for filling out and routing interlibrary loan requests differs from common American practice.

IFLA Office for International Lending

INTERNATIONAL LOAN/PHOTOCOPY REQUEST FORM

The IFLA Loan/Photocopy Request Form has been in use since 1975, following the approval of the IFLA Committee on International Lending and Union Catalogues in 1974. Recently redesigned, it is a multipart self-carboned form, designed for use in both requesting and supplying libraries. The bottom copy is kept by the requesting library and the top three copies are sent to the supplying library.

INSTRUCTIONS FOR LIBRARIES SENDING REQUESTS

1. Where possible, forms should be typed; otherwise, use a ball-point pen. Ensure that all four copies are legible.

2. If you wish to assign a reference number to your requests, use the box marked "Request Ref. No" in the top right-hand corner.

3. Fill in the bibliographic details of the required item, giving all the information you have and quoting your source of reference in full.

4. If a loan, photocopy or microfilm is specifically required, mark the appropriate box. Enter the date by which the item is needed and any cost limit in the appropriate boxes.

5. A responsible officer within the requesting library must sign the copyright statement (bottom right), so that photocopies supplied instead of loans conform to international regulations.

6. Fill in your address in the box provided (top left) and supply a self-addressed sticky label for the library to which you wish the item to be sent. This may differ from that on the form. If, for example, you are a national co-ordinating centre and the requested item is to be sent direct to the requesting library, the address to which the requested item is to be sent should be on the label and that for any other correspondence on the form.

7. Bend the stub of the forms and tear it off to separate the copies. Retain the yellow copy A as your own record of the request. Send copies B, C and D to the library of your choice.
Note: Loans received in response to the requests should be returned by the fastest postal service available (airmail or equivalent).

INSTRUCTIONS FOR LIBRARIES RECEIVING REQUESTS

You should receive copies B, C and D of the form. Working space is provided on the back of copy D and this can be used as your file copy. Copy C can be used at the shelf as a loan record and discarded when the item is returned.

If you can satisfy the request

1. Enter your address in the box marked "Lending library's address" and the return date of a loan in the "Lent until" box. Mark the "Use in library only" box if the loan is to be used for reference only. Enclose copy B with the requested item and despatch using the address label supplied by the requesting library. If none is supplied, the address will have to be written or typed on the envelope or parcel.

2. Include notification of any charges for the supply of loans or photocopies which you wish to make.

I.F.L.A. INTERNATIONAL LOAN/PHOTOCOPY REQUEST FORM
FORMULAIRE DE DEMANDE DE PRET/PHOTOCOPIE INTERNATIONAL

COPY B   EXEMPLAIRE B

Request ref. no/Patron identifier
No. de Commande/identité de lecteur

Borrowing library's address
Adresse de la bibliothèque emprunteuse

Needed by
Demande avant

Shelfmark
Cot de placement

Request for:
Commande de :

☐ Loan
Pret

☐ Photocopy
Photocopie

☐ Microform

Quote if cost exceeds
Prix si plus que

Report/Reponse

☐ Part not held/Volume/fasciscule non detenu

☐ Title not held/nous n'avons pas ce titre

☐ Not traced/Ne figure pas dans cette bibl.

☐ Not for loan/Exclu de prêt

☐ Copyright restrictions

☐ Not immediately available. Reapply in ....weeks
Non disponible actuellement. Renouvelez la
demande dans.........semaines

☐ Lent until/Prête jusqu'au.........

☐ Use in library only/A consulter sur place uniquement

I declare that this publication is required only for the
purpose of research or private study.
Je declare que cette publication n'est demande qu'à des
fins de recherche ou d'étude privée

Signature.........

Date.........

Books: Author, title - **Livres:** Auteur, titre / **Serials:** Title, article title, author - **Périodiques:** Titre, titre de l' article, auteur

Place of Publication
Lieu de publication

Publisher
Editeur

Year-Annee | Volume-Tome | Part-No. | Pages | ISBN/ISSN

Edition

Source of verification/reference
Reference bibliographique/Verification

Lending library's address/adresse de la bibliothèque prêteuse

SNAP APART   BRING TOGETHER   GRASP ENDS   BEND STUB

This is a
Multipart Set
Please use a
Ball Point Pen

Send copies B,C and D to the supplying library keep the Yellow A copy for
your own records.

FIGURE 18.   IFLA International Loan/Photocopy Request Form

3. Retain copy D as your record of the return date of a loan copy.

If there will be a delay in satisfying the request

If the delay is likely to exceed three weeks (e.g., the requested item is on a waiting list), either send the request (copies B, C and D) immediately to the next location on the rota (on the back of copy D) or, if there are no more locations, complete the "not immediately available" box and return copies B and C to the requesting library. You may wish to retain copy D in your records.

If you cannot satisfy the request

1. A rota may be drawn up by a national or union catalogue centre, or libraries that are unable to satisfy the request may suggest other possible locations. Minimize delay by listing only positive union catalogue locations or, failing this, by limiting speculative locations to the most likely ones only.

2. If there are further locations listed on the rota (on the back of copy D), fill in the report response on the back of copy D and send the request (copies B, C and D) to the next location.

3. If you are the only, or last, location, complete the final report stating the reason for non-supply and return copies B and C to the requesting library. You may wish to retain copy D in your records.

ORDERING IFLA INTERNATIONAL LOAN/PHOTOCOPY FORMS

1. Forms may be ordered from:

   Customer Services (PRF)
   British Library Document
     Supply Centre
   Boston Spa, Wetherby
   West Yorkshire, LS23 7BQ
   United Kingdom
   Switchboard: +44 1937 546000
   Direct Dial: +44 1937 546250
   Fax: +44 1937 546333
   Telex: 557381

2. The cost of the forms is £8 (eight pounds) or US$15.00 for Western Europe, North America, South Africa, Australia, New Zealand and Japan; £6 (six pounds) elsewhere, per hundred. (This covers the printing and distribution costs of the forms, and does not include any payment to supplying libraries.)

3. PAYMENT IS REQUIRED IN ADVANCE (the form is sold on a non-profit basis and pre-payment minimizes administration costs); pro-forma invoices will be supplied if required.

4. Cheques should be drawn in sterling or American dollars. Cheques drawn in other currencies are subject to a surcharge. Cheques should be made payable to "The British Library" and sent to the Finance Department at the above address. Payment may be made from BLDSC deposit accounts or by credit card.

5. If payment by credit or bank transfer is unavoidable, payment should be made to:

   The National Westminster Bank
   High Street, Wetherby
   West Yorkshire, LS22 4LS
   United Kingdom
   Sort code 55 81 11
     Account Number 03525988

   The transfer voucher should show the name and address of the payer, the invoice number (where applicable) and the reference 'IFLA/IL/1'.

6. All orders will be despatched by fast postal services (airmail or equivalent).

The OCLC PRISM Interlibrary Loan system serves a number of foreign libraries and is a first choice for transmission of a request. Faster delivery can be achieved today by using fax or the Internet where these methods of communication and document delivery are available. In fact, the use of fax and such systems as Ariel are to be preferred for photocopy requests because of the quickness of delivery. The *IFLA Fax Guidelines* should be consulted when using fax overseas (see appendix CC). Paying for airmail both directions cuts down considerably on time. Be certain that "U.S.A." is added to any address label that might be sent with the request.

Returning library materials takes special care. Be certain to abide by any directions the lending library gives. Mark all packages "International loan between libraries." This may help to avoid customs payments, although a custom declaration may be required when using some types of mail. Read the discussion below concerning international mail. Using a parcel delivery service may cause the lending library to have to pay customs charges. Investigate this possibility before attempting to use a parcel delivery service. Insurance policies covering the loss in the mail of books within the United States usually do not apply to overseas shipments.

Payment for photocopy or postage can be a problem. Choosing a method of payment, the currency required, and the ease of the transaction are among the considerations for payment of an international nature. Methods of payment are outlined below:

The IFLA voucher scheme: The most interesting development in recent years is the IFLA voucher scheme, the new payment system for international interlibrary transactions that began a two-year trial in January 1995. The scheme is based on a reusable plastic voucher, which represents a standard payment for one transaction. Vouchers can be purchased from the IFLA Offices for UAP and International Lending for U.S.$8 each at this writing. Half-vouchers can be purchased for U.S.$4. The voucher can be sent to the lending library as payment for the transaction. They can be reused any number of times. Libraries that lend more than they borrow can receive a refund for vouchers they will not use. This promises to be an effective way to pay for international loans and photocopy. Contact the IFLA Offices for UAP and International Lending for information and participation details:

Sara Gould
IFLA Offices for UAP and
International Lending
The British Library
Boston Spa, Wetherby
West Yorkshire LS23 7BQ
United Kingdom
Telephone: +44 1937 546254
Fax: +44 1937 546478
E-mail: sara.gould@bl.uk

Deposit accounts: Depositing a specific amount of money with a foreign lender can be helpful in that payment of individual invoices can then be avoided. Some foreign suppliers strongly recommend or even require this method of payment.

International reply coupons: Some libraries accept the Universal Postal Union's international reply coupons, which must be purchased and redeemed for postage stamps at the post offices in member countries of the Universal Postal Union. In 1995, these coupons sold for U.S.$1.05 each. This is a good method of payment when only the return of postage is required.

Bank drafts and bank transfers: This method of payment is sometimes specified by the lending library. Remember that making such a transfer incurs charges. Electronic transfer of funds can be effective, but whoever handles your finances may find this method of payment a burden because it does not conform to customary internal routine.

Prepaid forms: Some libraries require the borrower to purchase specific forms for borrowing, the cost of which pays for the transaction.

Coupons from a specific library: Just as in the United States, some foreign libraries issue their own coupons that must be purchased in advance and sent with each request.

International postal money orders: These are not accepted in all countries. The post office issues these, but the method of payment renders them complicated and unwieldy.

Unesco coupons: Unesco coupons can be used by developing foreign countries. These coupons are for educational, scientific, and cultural purposes. Sometimes they are sent as payment for an interlibrary lending transaction. Redeeming these coupons may not be worth the hassle, but they can be redeemed at the following place:

Banker's Trust Company
P.O. Box 2579, Church Street Station
New York, NY 10008
Attention: Unesco Coupon Paying
Department

Personal checks: Occasionally an overseas library will accept a personal check drawn on an American bank. Bank charges do reduce the value of the check.

OCLC Fee Management Service (IFM): This service can be used by foreign libraries that use the OCLC PRISM Interlibrary Loan system and participate in this program.

Credit cards: Some libraries will accept payments using credit cards.

The important thing to remember in international borrowing is that a month or two might elapse before a response to a request is received. When using a source for the first time, it is best to allow plenty of time, to be patient, and eventually to follow up on lack of response.

USEFUL FOREIGN LIBRARIES AND DOCUMENT SUPPLIERS

Listed below are some other foreign libraries that may be especially useful:

Australia
National library

National Library of Australia
Document Supply Service
Canberra
ACT 2600
Australia
Telephone: +616 262 1421 or
            +616 262 1269
Fax: +616 273 2719
E-mail: docss@nla.gov.au

France
Institut de l'information scientifique et technique (Institute of Scientific and Technical Information) for photocopy only

INIST Diffusion
Information Service
2, allée du Parc de Brabois
54514 Vandoeuvre-les-Nancy Cedex
France
Telephone: +33 83.50.46.64
Fax: +33 83.50.46.66
E-mail: infoclient@inist.fr

National Library

Service de Prêt de la
    Bibliothèque National de France
Réf. post 1101
78011 Versailles Cedex
France
Telephone: +33 39.51.67.98
Fax: +33 39.51.36.85

Germany
Technische Informationsbibliothek (with the University of Hannover it forms Germany's central library for technology and related sciences)

Technische Informationsbibliothek
    Hannover
Postfach 6080
30060 Hannover
Germany

Telephone: +49 (511) 762-2531
Fax: +49 (511) 71 59 36
E-mail: rosemann@tib.
            uni-hannover.d400.de

Japan
Japan Information Center of Science and Technology
United States

Japan Information Center of Science
    and Technology (JICTS)
1550 M Street NW, Suite 1050
Washington, DC 20005
Telephone: (202) 872-6370
Fax: (202) 872-6372
E-mail: jicstdc@tigger.jvnc.net

Japan

Japan Information Center of Science
    and Technology (JICST)
International Programs
5-3 Yonbancho
Chiyoda-ku
Tokyo 102
Japan
Telephone: +81 3-5214-8403
Fax: +81 3-5214-8430

National library

International Cooperation Division
Library Cooperation Department
National Diet Library
1-10-1, Nagata-cho
Chiyoda-ku
Tokyo 100
Japan
Telephone: +81 3-3581-2331
Fax: +81 3-3597-9104

Russia
Science and technology

Russian National Public Library for
    Science and Technology
12, Kuznetsky most
Moscow 103031
Russia
Telephone: +7 (095) 921-1750
Fax: +7 (095) 921-9862

National library
    Russian State Library
    Loan Department
    3, Vozdvizhenka Street
    Moscow 101000
    Russia

Telephone: +7 (095) 202-3565 or
    +7 (095) 202-7404
Fax: +7 (095) 200-2255
E-mail: main@irgb.msk.su

INTERNATIONAL INTERLIBRARY LENDING

Libraries that borrow abroad should be prepared to lend abroad as well. The United States does not have an official national loan center. Foreign libraries may address directly a library known to have a title and known to engage in international loan. The lending library should accept IFLA International Loan/Photocopy Request forms. The lending library should not keep incoming requests more than one week. Airmail, fax, Ariel, or the Internet should be employed whenever possible. If surface mail has to be used for books, the library material may be gone as long as four to six months. Payment for charges can be very slow, and it may be necessary to require payment in U.S. dollars. Refer to payment information in the preceding section.

You may want to have some information ready for foreign libraries that come to you for loans or photocopy. Some ideas are contained in "Interlibrary Lending Suggestions for Foreign Libraries That Request Books and Photocopies from Libraries in the United States" (see appendix DD).

Most international mail falls into two categories: postal union mail and parcel post. The United States is a member of the Universal Postal Union Convention and the Postal Union of the Americas and Spain, which establish the rules and regulations for postal union mail. The classification includes books with eight or more pages, consisting of reading matter, which contain only incidental advertising. Photocopy also comes under this classification. Important facts follow:

Weight limit
    22 pounds to many South American countries for both photocopy and books
    11 pounds to most other countries; for parcels over 11 pounds, consult the post office

Registration
    usually available and especially recommended for Mexico and South American countries

Return receipt
    consult the post office for availability

Package
    must be labeled "printed matter" for photocopy and "printed matter—books" for books; may be sealed only under certain circumstances; check with the post office

Airmail
    usually possible for photocopy and books; must be marked "Par Avion"; usually takes 10 to 14 days

Customs declaration
    label packages "International loan between libraries"; even though this is not a requirement, it may help to avoid customs payment

There is a classification of postal union mail called "printed matter," which cannot weigh more than four pounds except for catalogs and directories.

Postal union mail also includes a classification known as "small packets," which must weigh no more than one to four pounds, depending on the country.

Parcel post, though more expensive than postal union mail, does allow for insurance to many countries. Insuring the parcel means, among other things, that it can be traced. Air parcel post is also available for many countries. Such parcels must be marked "Par Avion" and contain a customs declaration.

Checking the regulations for international mail for a particular country is necessary. The U.S. Postal Service's *International Postal Rates and Fees* can be obtained free at the post office. Also at the post office, the U.S. Postal Service's *International Mail Manual* can be consulted.[21]

A parcel delivery service may be used for many countries. Inquire about procedures, delivery time, and customs requirements. Care should be taken so that the borrowing library does not have to pay customs charges.

MORE INFORMATION ON INTERNATIONAL INTERLIBRARY LOANS

IFLA maintains a World Wide Web home page that includes "What's New on IFLANET" and a table of contents. The home page can be found at the following address:

URL: <http://www.nlc-bnc.ca/ifla/home.htm>

This service is a help in keeping up with new developments and recent publications.

A total of four Interlending and Document Supply International Conferences have been held, the fourth in Calgary, Alberta, Canada, June 11–14, 1995. The sponsors were the IFLA Office for International Lending, the National Library of Canada, and the Canadian Library Association. Another conference is scheduled for 1997 in Denmark. The papers presented at these conferences make for informative reading on topics of international interest. Here are the ones that have been published as of 1995:

Interlending and Document Supply: Proceedings of the First International Conference Held in London, November 1988. Edited by Graham P. Cornish. Boston Spa, Wetherby, West Yorkshire, U.K.: The British Library and IFLA Office for International Lending, 1989.

Interlending and Document Supply: Proceedings of the Second International Conference Held in London, November 1990. Edited by Alison Gallico. Boston Spa, Wetherby, West Yorkshire, U.K.: IFLA Office for International Lending, 1991.

Interlending and Document Supply: Proceedings of the Third International Conference Held in Budapest, March 1993. Edited by Andrew J. Swires. Boston Spa, Wetherby, West Yorkshire, U.K.: IFLA Office for International Lending, 1994.

Interlending and Document Supply: Proceedings of the Fourth International Conference. Papers from the Conference Held in Calgary, June 1995. Edited by Judy Watkins. Boston Spa, Wetherby, West Yorkshire, U.K.: International Federation of Library Associations and Institutions, Programme for Universal Availability of Publications and Office for International Lending, 1996?

Several articles of interest follow:

Bleek, Wilhelm, and Lothar Mertens. "Secret Dissertations in the German Democratic Republic." *College & Research Libraries* 56 (Sept. 1995): 381–93.

Bradbury, David, and Graham P. Cornish. "Worldwide View of Information: Availability of Publications and International Interlibrary Loan." *RQ* 32 (Winter 1992): 185–92.

Gregory, Gwen. "NAFTA Spurs Cooperation at Trinational Forum in Mexico City." *American Libraries* 26 (June 1995): 507–508.

Mitchell, Eleanor, and Sheila A. Walters. "International Document Delivery: Regional and Worldwide Systems." In *Document Delivery Services: Issues and Answers.* Medford, N.J.: Learned Information, 1995.

Swain, Leigh, and Paula Tallim. "The Interlibrary Loan (ILL) Protocol: Progress and Projects." *IFLA Journal* 18, no. 4 (1992): 325–32.

---

21. U.S. Postal Service, *International Mail Manual,* Issue 14 (Washington, D.C.: U.S. Government Printing Office, 1994).

Current periodicals give additional information on international loan:

IFLA Journal. Vol. 1– . Munich: Verlag Dokumentation, 1975– .

Information Development. Vol. 1– . London: Mansell, 1985– .

Interlending and Document Supply. Vol. 11, no. 1– . Boston Spa, Wetherby, West Yorkshire, U.K.: British Library Document Supply Centre, 1983– . Preceded by *Interlending Review* and *BLL Review.*

International Information and Library Review. Vol. 24, no. 1– . London and San Diego: Academic Press, 1992– . Preceded by *International Library Review.*

Bibliographies of interlending and document supply are published periodically in *Interlending and Document Supply.* A collected bibliography is listed below:

Cornish, Graham P. *Cumulative Bibliography on Interlending and Document Supply.* Boston Spa, Wetherby, West Yorkshire, U.K.: IFLA Office for International Lending, 1989.

7

Management of Interlibrary Loan

Interlibrary loan is an open system in which there is little control over much that impinges from the outside. The unexpected is routine. One never knows when requests for materials in Tibetan, information on the pedagogy of the tuba, all of the books of Ellis Peters, facts on underwater archaeology, the annual report of a company, or treatises on windmills as a source of energy will be made. One never knows when the "heavy user" will descend with armloads of requests. One never knows when the whole communication system will be changed and mastery of new software required in record time. One never knows when the use of a new online database or the lack of acquisitions money will increase demand for interlibrary loan. One never knows when a much-used library will suddenly raise its fees for lending. The gathering of routine statistics, while necessary as an indication of normal interlibrary loan activity, will not provide enough information to foresee or even track the changes that come along.

The literature of management, even specifically of library management, abounds. Volumes and articles have been written on each aspect of what managers do: plan, organize, staff, direct, and control. Rather than espousing one theory of personnel management, describing in detail alternative methods of budgeting, or discoursing on how to chart the flow of

work, what follows are practical suggestions gleaned from 25 years of managing an academic interlibrary loan service. Not all of these suggestions will be applicable to every situation. The size of what is to be managed can range from devoting two hours to interlibrary loan on Fridays to shepherding 150,000 requests through an office each year.

The comments here apply primarily to larger libraries, although some information, such as that on records and files, applies to libraries of all sizes. Small libraries should adapt the suggestions to fit their situation, making sure to maintain consistency and regularity in whatever they do. For the person who needs to expand knowledge or to learn techniques not discussed here, the selected bibliography at the end of this chapter may be consulted as a starting place.

The term *interlibrary loan* is used here to mean interlibrary borrowing, interlibrary lending, and document delivery.

ORGANIZATIONAL CLIMATE AND PLANNING

Each interlibrary loan service finds itself within an organizational climate. Thus a thorough knowledge of the milieu surrounding interlibrary loan is essential.

There are a number of principles to which most libraries subscribe. The American Library Association has promulgated a statement on "Professional Ethics," which many libraries have adopted.[1] Concern for intellectual freedom has caused libraries to include the American Library Association's "Library Bill of Rights" and subsequent interpretations as part of their official policies.[2] Many states have passed legislation concerning the confidentiality of library records.[3] In records, there are implications for interlibrary loan where the patron's name and the material requested appear together.[4] Interlibrary loan staff must know and understand all

of the policies and statements that are part of the organizational climate.

Most interlibrary loan offices are part of a well-established library or of a library network that offers interlibrary loan service. Hence, the mission statement, goals, and objectives these larger structures have already adopted will usually sanction the goal of interlibrary loan, which is to borrow or obtain for the library clientele materials not in the local collection and to lend materials to other libraries in turn. One must be alert to the changes made by the library or network that will have an effect on interlibrary loan. A network might decide to change its pricing structure or to enlarge its service area. The library itself might change its collection development policy or decide to conduct circulation using

1. American Library Association, *ALA Handbook of Organization and Membership Directory 1994/1995* (Chicago: American Library Association, 1994), 146.

2. Ibid., 143–44.

3. Shirley A. Wiegand, *Library Records: A Retention and Confidentiality Guide* (Westport, Conn.: Greenwood Press, 1994).

4. Christopher W. Nolan, "The Confidentiality of Interlibrary Loan Records," *Journal of Academic Librarianship* 19 (May 1993): 81–86.

a new system. In an even larger context, electronic publishing might become a widespread reality. All of these outside decisions can push interlibrary loan into a new environment.

Policies

General policies adopted by the library itself may have sections that have to do with interlibrary loan. For instance, the Association of College and Research Libraries has prepared a document called "ACRL Guidelines for the Preparation of Policies on Library Access."[5] Listed under "Public Services," the following section is found:

IV. Interlibrary and other delivery services

  A. Availability of telefacsimile, document delivery, interlibrary loan and other such services.

  B. Categories and formats of materials that can be loaned or borrowed.

  C. Patron categories and borrowing privileges for each service.

  D. Special services available through resource-sharing agreements.

  E. Borrowing period and turn-around time for these services.

  F. Existence of charges for use of interlibrary loan and document delivery services.

  G. Impact of interlibrary services on local access to the collection.

  H. Collection of data for collection management staff on items requested and departmental use of service.

  I. Policies and procedures for copyright compliance.[6]

While many of these things will already be in the interlibrary borrowing and lending policies, thought might have to be given to "G" and "H." Discussion

with colleagues will help to clarify how these ideas affect interlibrary loan.

Another document that might receive attention in your library is the "Information Services Policy Manual: An Outline."[7] This outline was developed by the Management of Reference Services Committee of the Reference and Adult Services Division of ALA. Under the "Organizational Structure for Reference Services," the following section can be found:

L. Document Delivery

  1. Describe the department's role in providing document delivery service, including the following parameters:

     a. Overall goals.

     b. Personnel providing the service.

  2. Identify the types of materials that are available via document delivery services. These types could include:

     a. Books.

     b. Journal articles.

     c. Print-outs from electronic media.

  3. Specify the document delivery options that are available. These options could include:

     a. Interlibrary loan.

     b. Fax.

     c. Full text online.

     d. UnCover.

  4. Specify the availability of each type of document delivery service.

     a. Type of inquiries warranting the service.

     b. Categories of users eligible for the service.

     c. Timeliness.

  5. Explain the library's policy regarding charging fees, if any, for each type of document delivery service, including the clientele for whom these charges apply, and the schedule of fees.

---

5. "ACRL Guidelines for the Preparation of Policies on Library Access," *College & Research Libraries* 51 (June 1990): 548–56.

6. Ibid., 553, 556.

7. "Information Services Policy Manual: An Outline," *RQ* 34 (Winter 1994): 165–72.

6. Specify the statistics kept regarding this service.

7. Describe the manner in which this service is evaluated. Specify who or what is evaluated, who is responsible for conducting the evaluation, the criteria for evaluation, the schedule for evaluation, and the methods and instruments to be used. Specify also how the results of the evaluation are to be applied.[8]

This document illustrates the viewpoint of library managers in looking at interlibrary loan. Negotiations may have to take place to align the everyday policies and practices of interlibrary loan with what is expected by the overall management of the organization.

The development of an interlibrary borrowing policy, for example, can make you think about what you are doing and why you are doing it. It can be used to gain emphasis and agreement on borrowing from the director and the entire library staff. It can provide official sanction for actions. It is also good public relations in that it emphasizes a service-minded part of your library's program. The borrowing policy can be developed using the following outline:

I. Definition.

II. Purpose.

III. Conditions of service.

IV. Interlibrary borrowing.
   A. Who can use the service?
   B. When can the service be used?
   C. What kinds and numbers of materials can be borrowed?
   D. Will there be any fees?
   E. How long will it take? Can the request be rushed?
   F. How will notification of arrival be given?
   G. Other considerations.

V. Library patron's responsibilities.

VI. Library's responsibilities.

VII. Policy review and change.

See also chapter 1, "Instructions for Borrowing Libraries," "Interlibrary Borrowing Policies."

An interlibrary lending policy defines the relationship between your library and other libraries concerning interlibrary lending. A full discussion of the contents of such a document can be found in chapter 2, "Instructions for Lending Libraries," "Interlibrary Lending Policies."

Place, location, and name for interlibrary loan

Interlibrary loan has a place in the organizational structure of the library. The library may be small and fairly informal in organizational pattern, with interlibrary loan being a tiny part of the reference function. Interlibrary loan in a larger library fits into the organizational structure in a variety of ways. Some libraries have separate units that report to a head of public services. Some are combined with circulation and other services to form access services, which in turn reports to the head of public services. Some are part of reference or of circulation, and there have even been units lodged in government publications or special collections. Some libraries split interlibrary borrowing and interlibrary lending, giving them different reporting structures. This makes for difficulty in keeping track of reciprocal agreements and giving special help to someone who has given special help. It precludes the chance of moving staff from one part to another when crises occur and makes the reference role in verification difficult. Some libraries also split interlibrary loan and document delivery into two different offices, while others see them as all part of one service.

The location of interlibrary loan in the organizational structure is largely a matter of the size of the library, the number of requests processed by interlibrary loan, and tradition. Where there is enough volume, a separate unit is the most efficient. Close ties with reference are most helpful when engaging in verification. Circulation is especially important for lending. Wherever the work of interlibrary loan

8. Ibid., 169–70.

can be most effective and most easily accomplished is where it belongs. There should be no doubt, however, to whom interlibrary loan reports and just what its importance is in the scheme of things. With increasing emphasis on interlibrary loan, it is necessary to understand the total organizational structure of the library, who influences decisions, and how to have a voice in changes that might be made.

There has been much discussion of what interlibrary loan should be named in order to show the expanded service offered by many libraries. It is true that not all documents today are obtained from libraries nor are they necessarily loaned. It is also true that library patrons can be confused easily by such names as "resource retrieval service" or "document supply service," which may mean the delivery of the document from the library's collection to the patron, not what is generally thought of as interlibrary loan. The only advice offered here is to *ask* the patrons what they would recognize as a good name for interlibrary loan and document delivery services or just call it interlibrary loan and document delivery.

Important general aspects of the library

In addition to the mission statement, goals, objectives, policies, and organizational structure, at least five other aspects of the library as a whole need continuing attention by the interlibrary loan librarian:

1. The clientele the library serves is generally specified in the library's published statements (and sometimes may change as overall policies adjust to shifting political and fiscal realities). However such clientele is defined, ideally all should have the right to interlibrary loan service. However, distinctions will sometimes have to be made between primary and secondary clientele, and interlibrary loan must clearly ascertain what groups it must serve and what priorities may be necessary.

2. Knowledge of sources of overall funding and how funds are allotted is important. It may be unwise, for example, to ask for a new staff person just as the library is experiencing a cut in funds.

3. Understanding of the physical plant can be most helpful when extended quarters are

needed, something must be stored, or the service is located in an inconvenient place.

4. Because interlibrary loan's horizons are limitless in terms of what library materials might be requested, a thorough acquaintance with the special abilities and talents of all library staff is invaluable.

5. A thorough knowledge of the library's collections and where each part is housed is helpful and takes constant work.

Planning

Planning is the process of identifying desirable change and making it desired. And evaluation and leadership go hand-in-hand with planning. These three aspects of management can be used to confront the problems that arise, from trying to maintain an efficient and effective interlibrary loan service, to dealing with complaints or "squeaky wheels," to developing new aspects of service, including new and more efficient ways of doing interlibrary loan. Often, key people, such as staff, patrons, and librarians in other libraries, must be involved if change is to be effective. With their help or sanction, the process for problem solving can proceed along these lines:

1. Describe the problem or situation, including the need for making a change.

2. Gather data pertinent to the problem and its solution.

3. Analyze the data.

4. Recommend change, including the fiscal and human resources necessary to accomplish it.

5. Work with appropriate people to implement the change.

6. Evaluate the effectiveness of the new service.

An example may help to illustrate this process. Complaints have been received that photocopy requests from the health sciences library 30 miles distant do not arrive in time for the patron to use. (This is the squeaky wheel.) A goal of interlibrary loan is effective service, which includes timely delivery of materials.

1. (Describe the problem.) Medical materials are not being delivered in a timely fashion. Informa-

tion on how long it actually takes a medical request to be filled is vague and undocumented.

2. (Gather data.) Data are gathered by looking at 700 medical interlibrary loan request forms completed during a period of six months to calculate the turnaround time from request transmission to check-in of material. Seven working days is the average time it takes.

3. (Analyze the data.) Seven days is indeed unreasonably long.

4. (Recommend change.) More data gathering and brainstorming among the staff bring to light a number of possibilities for speeding up the turnaround time. These data include restructuring courier routes to put the two libraries on the same route, using fax for "rush" requests, and giving priority to medical requests by processing them first, both as the requests come into the office and as the photocopy arrives. These steps seem feasible. On the other hand, more staff for interlibrary loan or for the health sciences library is deemed not to be a current possibility.

5. (Implement change.) The next step is to convince the library administration, the health sciences library, and the courier manager to restructure courier routes. Changes can be made immediately in the processing of medical requests to speed them up.

6. (Evaluate effectiveness.) Data are gathered on the turnaround time from request transmission to check-in of material for medical requests for a four-month period following implementation of changes. A log is kept of patron comments about medical requests. A determination can then be made about the effectiveness of the service.

This way, a body of complaints has been addressed by planning, evaluating, and exerting leadership to provide new ways to meet a goal.

A refinement of the general planning process outlined above can be called *containment*. Many interlibrary loan offices are experiencing rapidly increasing workloads with no increase in staff, space, or equipment. There comes a time when all the incoming requests simply cannot be done. Making decisions to limit the number of requests to an amount that can be processed is difficult. What follows are some suggestions on how to contain the amount of work interlibrary loan must do. It is useful to think of borrowing and lending parts of interlibrary loan separately because of the difference of the tasks involved with each operation.

1. Assemble the appropriate staff.

2. State the purpose of the activity.

3. Formulate assumptions that must be considered.

4. Think of all possible containment measures—practical or way out—without judgment.

5. Discuss and rate the containment measures using these questions as a guide:

   Is the measure feasible or likely? Can it actually be done?
   How desirable is this measure? For the patrons? For the interlibrary loan staff?
   How does this measure fit into the library's goals, objectives, and practices?
   What needs to be done to implement this measure?

6. Divide the measures into groups using these headings:

   a. Feasible and desirable, no authorization needed, do now. (*Borrowing example:* Cross-train staff and schedule to clear up backlogs. *Lending example:* Look at the shelf only once for requested material.)

   b. Feasible and desirable, authorization needed, get approval to proceed. (*Borrowing example:* Close office two hours each day for uninterrupted processing time. *Lending example:* Raise charges to cover the cost of billing.)

   c. Feasible, not desirable, do not do, reconsider in future if necessary. (*Borrowing example:* Do not process "rush" requests. *Lending example:* Do not supply current year imprints.)

   d. Not feasible, desirable, do not do, reconsider in future if necessary. (*Borrowing example:* Refuse to serve visiting faculty and visiting scholars. *Lending example:* Set up deposit accounts for lending charges.)

7. Make adjustments in policy and procedures to accomplish measures listed in 6.a.

8. Request authorization for changes in policy and procedures to accomplish measures listed in 6.b.

9. Report to supervisor and library director what has been considered, what is being done, what can be done with authorization, and what was rejected.

10. Evaluate the effectiveness of the containment measures.

Budgeting

Budgeting for interlibrary loan depends largely on the budgeting procedures of the library itself. It is important to know if interlibrary loan has a budget of its own or from which part of the overall library budget interlibrary loan funds come. Do personnel funds pay for the interlibrary loan staff? Do operations funds pay for supplies, electronic services, and the like? Do collection development funds pay for charges against interlibrary loan so they do not have to be passed on to the patron? Does the library require cost recovery for parts of interlibrary loan? Does interlibrary loan receive money by passing charges on to the patron or by charging for lending activities? Is the library reimbursed for lending by another agency, such as a state library? If so, what happens to that money?

The important two interlibrary loan budget categories are personnel (the largest single cost in interlibrary loan service, coming to between 75 percent and 90 percent of the total cost of the service) and operations. Supplies, communications, and the purchase of such services as OCLC, RLIN, and WLN constitute a large portion of the operations part of the budget. Equipment, for some libraries, is a separate category. Interlibrary loan usually does not have to concern itself with such budgetary categories as capital investment, depreciation, or the acquisition of library materials. Both personnel and operations budgeting are simple when little change from the preceding year is anticipated. What can be difficult is planning for future change; help in this area should be sought from those in the library knowledgeable about the budgetary process.

Determining costs and fees

Determining the cost of interlibrary borrowing and interlibrary lending can be a valuable exercise for a number of reasons. The cost of borrowing an item can be compared to the cost of acquiring an item, cataloging it, and maintaining it in the collection. Borrowing costs can help in the decision-making process for canceling periodicals. Borrowing costs also show the importance of interlibrary borrowing to the library clientele. Lending costs are valuable for libraries involved in a reimbursement scheme for lending. An accurate cost for lending materials can be computed upon which to base the reimbursement amount. A lending cost can also give an amount that might be charged for cost recovery, if that is something the library must do. Figuring interlibrary loan costs has even been known to get a raise in pay for the interlibrary loan librarian because of the amount of money actually involved in the operation.

At present, two methods can be used for determining costs. The easiest to use is "A Methodology for Determining Costs of Interlibrary Lending" and "A Methodology for Determining Costs of Interlibrary Borrowing," by Stephen P. Dickson and Virginia Boucher (see appendix EE). The other methodology, somewhat based on Dickson and Boucher, has been developed by the Association of Research Libraries (ARL) and the Research Libraries Group (RLG) and is particularly applicable to large research libraries. The ARL/RLG study involved a number of libraries, which, taken together, provided some interesting data:

> Analysis of the data provided custom *benchmark data* for each participating institution and shows that a research library spends an average of $18.62 to borrow a research document/article or to purchase a photocopy of the item for a patron, and $10.93 to lend a document to another library. Therefore, the cost for a completed ILL transaction (combining borrowing and lending components) averages $29.55.[9]

While this amount may be high for smaller libraries or libraries of a different type, it does show that

---

9. Marilyn M. Roche, *ARL/RLG Interlibrary Loan Cost Study* (Washington, D.C.: Association of Research Libraries, 1993), iv.

costs for interlibrary borrowing and lending are something to be considered in total library planning and budgeting.

Some libraries take into account this cost when determining whether to charge the library patron for borrowing services. A few libraries demand full cost recovery, some charge flat fees to cover part of the cost, others charge a processing fee, a few charge a fee for value-added service (fax, Ariel, etc.), and some charge a fee after a certain number of requests have been supplied. The trend, however, seems to be toward not charging the patron at all.

For lending services, fees are often charged. Some libraries charge for filling photocopy requests but not for filling book requests. Some charge a cost-recovery fee, while others charge a partial cost-recovery fee. Some use a uniform fee, while others charge a fee depending on the number of pages supplied, cost of postage, and the like. Some libraries only want to recover postage money.

In settling the question of whether to charge or not, the library needs to think about the service it wishes to provide to the patron. Other factors have to do with the cost of collecting money, accounting for it, depositing it, disbursing it, and the like. For lending, the time and money involved in computing costs, issuing invoices, receiving payment, accounting for it, and depositing it should be considered. Cooperative agreements can be important in decreasing the amount of money collected and disbursed. The OCLC ILL Fee Management (IFM) system can be a help in this regard. (See chapter 2, "Instructions for Lending Libraries," "Photocopy material.") A decision about charging should only be made after careful consideration by the library management and interlibrary loan.

PHYSICAL ORGANIZATION AND OPERATIONS

Physical organization

The physical location, equipment, supplies, and safety of employees concern the interlibrary loan supervisor.

The physical location of interlibrary loan is important to both the patron and the staff. In years past, the interlibrary loan office was found, only after diligent searching, tucked away in a remote corner of the library. Today, it is more apt to be in full view of the library patron. The patron should know upon entering a library where to ask a question. The patron should also know upon discovering that the desired item is not in the library where to make an interlibrary loan request, whether it be at the interlibrary loan office, the reference desk, or at some other point in the library. Many libraries that do not have large interlibrary loan operations point out to patrons that materials not found in their libraries can be obtained through their membership in a library cooperative. A sign with such information can be placed near the entrance to the library. Because interlibrary loan is a service offered to the library's clientele, this fact should be made known to all, particularly in flyers, brochures, and other publicity about library service. Interlibrary loan should be located with convenient access for staff to the reference collection and to circulation. Time lost in long trips to these areas means fewer requests processed in a speedy manner.

Equipment, such as microcomputers, should be kept clean and in good repair. Nothing is more uncomfortable for the worker than to try to make sticky keys move or to see a computer screen through a haze of institutional dust. Find out about any service contracts that your library has to facilitate prompt repair. Such a contract may provide pre-paid service. Security should be provided for equipment by putting library identifying marks on it, alerting security personnel about it, and locking it up when not in use. The matter of insurance for expensive equipment should be investigated.

Two other imperatives should be kept in mind when considering equipment. The first is that new equipment will come along at an alarming rate, which means that the librarian must keep up with developments in document transmission, new microcomputers, and, of course, new software to help with operations. The speed in accomplishing tasks is certainly a consideration here. The other imperative is that new equipment brings new problems for employees in terms of their well-being. Keyboards must be at a comfortable height, computer screens should be adjusted so that there is no neck strain, and lighting should be enough but not so much as to cause glare. Andrea Michaels and David Michaels offer some help in designing today's workstations.[10]

Supplies need to be ordered in a timely fashion. Library supply firms are listed annually in *Library Journal.* Those supplies on which the library's address is printed usually take longer to acquire. There is nothing more deflating than to have a bunch of rush requests submitted and ready to go only to discover there is no paper for the printer or no four-part forms.

Safety of employees is, of course, of paramount importance. There must be no cords lying on the floor where someone is apt to trip, and there needs to be enough room to move around without colliding with equipment or people. The whereabouts of the nearest fire extinguisher should be noted. Plans should be made for the evacuation of the area and whom to call in emergencies.

Operations

Operations have to do with accomplishing the work of interlibrary loan. Thinking about these questions can be helpful in gaining a good idea of the total operation.

1. What tasks must be accomplished to borrow materials? (See chapter 1, "Instructions for Borrowing Libraries.")
2. What tasks must be accomplished to lend materials? (See chapter 2, "Instructions for Lending Libraries.")
3. What person does each task?
4. Are people scheduled effectively?
5. How does a request move through the office or library?

6. How long does the request take before it is transmitted or supplied? Where do backlogs occur throughout the operations?
7. How are problems handled?

Keeping the work flowing requires, besides a logical progression of chores, smooth-running peripheral tasks and careful scheduling. For large offices, routines can be developed for quickly opening and sorting the mail, answering the telephone properly, filing correctly, and opening and closing the office with security in mind. Deciding when to do a particular task, however, is often dictated by external circumstances, such as mail-delivery time and availability of computers. (The ideal of a computer on each worker's desk is not yet common practice for all libraries.) Scheduling of part-time employees is a challenge. Negotiating shared use of automated systems requires effective lobbying in presenting the case for use by interlibrary loan staff. Finally, time must be scheduled to work on those hard-to-solve operational problems.

Records and files, statistics, and reports all contribute to a smooth-running interlibrary loan service. Records and files provide a means of keeping track of the progress of an interlibrary loan request from the moment it is submitted until it is completed. Statistics can be generated from these records and, subsequently, reports can be written using them. Because creation of records, filing, and searching all take appreciable time, *as few records and as little duplication as possible* should be a goal. Another goal should be simplicity of records to facilitate quick retrieval of information.

Whatever is done by an automated interlibrary loan management system need not be done "by hand." Fortunately, there are interlibrary loan management systems available today that help to keep track of all the necessary information surrounding an interlibrary loan transaction. A useful discussion of "The Automation of ILL Statistics" can be found in Barbra Buckner Higginbotham and Sally Bowdoin's book, *Access versus Assets.*[11] The automated systems vary; they often do not accomplish everything that is wanted. They may do any or all of the following:

---

10. Andrea Michaels and David Michaels, "Designing for Technology in Today's Libraries," *Computers in Libraries* 12 (Nov. 1992): 8–15.

11. Barbra Buckner Higginbotham and Sally Bowdoin, *Access versus Assets,* Frontiers of Access to Library Materials, no. 1 (Chicago: American Library Association, 1993), 121–28.

Track interlibrary loan requests and activities

Download bibliographic and location information

Manage and transmit requests electronically

Provide copyright compliance tracking

Generate statistical reports

Careful study is needed to find the system best suited to an individual interlibrary loan operation. Virginia A. Lingle and Dorothy L. Malcom list the following criteria when considering a software system for interlibrary loan:

Ease of use	Upgrades
Equipment specifications	User support
Adaptability	Cost
Report generation	Record retrieval
Data security	Comprehensiveness[12]
Availability	

The names and addresses of the most commonly used interlibrary loan management systems follow:

Aviso

Developed in Canada and modified for the United States, this is a comprehensive interlibrary loan management system. For information:

> ISM Library Information Services
> 3300 Bloor Street West
> 16th Floor, West Tower
> Etobicoke, Ontario M8X 2X2 Canada
> Telephone: (416) 236-7171
>   (800) 684-8184 (U.S.)
>   (800) 268-0982 (Canada)
> Fax: (416) 236-7541
> URL: <http://www.ism.ca/lis/
>   aviso.htm>
> E-mail: AVISO@lismail.ism.ca

PRS/Interlibrary Loan Patron Request System

An interlibrary loan management system that works with borrowing data. For information:

> PRS (Patron Request System)
> Interlibrary Loan Service

> Harold B. Lee Library
> Brigham Young University
> P.O. Box 26800
> Provo, UT 84602
> Telephone: (801) 378-6344
> Fax: (801) 378-6347

QuickDOC

Interlibrary loan management program designed to manage activity on the National Library of Medicine's DOCLINE system. For information:

> Jay Daly
> QuickDOC
> 45A Mason Terrace
> Brookline, MA 02146
> Telephone: (617) 734-0918
> Fax: (617) 734-3154
> E-mail: jay@bih.harvard.edu

SAVEIT

An interlibrary loan record-keeping and reports/statistics software package that can capture ILL records from online systems and also allows users to enter records manually for production of ALA and fax requests. For information:

> Patrick Brumbaugh
> Interlibrary Software and Services, Inc.
> P.O. Box 12237
> Research Triangle Park, NC 27709-2237
> Telephone: (800) 572-4252
> Fax: (919) 929-0881
> E-mail: SAVEIT@ILSS.com

The bibliographic utilities, OCLC, RLIN, and WLN, provide some statistical information to their users. Internal tabulating of some kinds of data can be avoided by using the information in these reports. They do not, however, supply all the information needed for interlibrary loan management.

It is possible, of course, to develop your own automated method for dealing with interlibrary loan management data. The *Directory of Library Automation Software, Systems, and Services* is beginning to list interlibrary loan software found with larger systems such as those managing online public

---

12. Virginia A. Lingle and Dorothy L. Malcom, "Interlibrary Loan Management with Microcomputers: A Descriptive Comparison of Software," *Medical Reference Services Quarterly* 8 (Summer 1989): 41–64.

access catalogs, circulation, and the like.[13] Word-Perfect and dBase III Plus can also be used for interlibrary loan data. Amy Chang describes in detail her implementation of a dBase III Plus system.[14]

The following list of data elements, records, and files constitutes the information needed for interlibrary loan management that can be collected manually or electronically.

DATA ELEMENTS FOR BORROWING

Patron Information
> Need-before date
> Name
> Address
> Telephone number
> Fax number (optional)
> E-mail address (optional)
> Maximum cost patron willing to pay
> Signature showing reading of "Order Warning of Copyright"
> Identification number (optional)
> Department affiliation (optional)
> Status (optional)
> Age group (optional)

Bibliographic Information
> Book: author, title, edition (if any), place of publication, publisher, date of publication, and series (if any)
> Periodical: title of periodical, volume and issue number or issue date, year, author of article, title of article, pages to be copied
> Dissertation or thesis: author, title, university, degree, date
> Newspaper: title, edition (if known), section (if known), place of publication and state, date of publication; author of article, title of article, pages to be copied (if any)
> Government publication: same as for book or periodical plus corporate author, issuing agency, Superintendent of Documents classification number (federal publications), and contract number (if any)

Other information: ISBN, ISSN, LCCN, and the like
Reference source: where the information was found by the patron

Subject Information
> Nature of the subject
> Type of material needed
> Purpose of the request (optional)
> Degree of reading difficulty (optional)
> Degree of generality
> Currency of information
> Amount of material needed
> Photocopy okay
> Material already used
> Where information has already been sought

Processing Information
> Date request submitted
> Verification and location
> Borrower notes
> Lending libraries or document suppliers (where sent)
> Type of request: loan, photocopy, cost estimate, etc.
> Reciprocal agreement
> Copyright compliance
> Cost conditions
> Transmission system
> Request number
> Date of transmission
> Date received
> Date due
> Format of material (if not obvious)
> Date of patron notification
> Financial information
> Date returned
> Returned via
> Insured for
> Payment provided
> Date not filled
> Unfilled response
> Other: renewals, overdues, etc.

---

13. *Directory of Library Automation Software, Systems, and Services* (Medford, N.J.: Learned Information, 1993–).

14. Amy Chang, "Interlibrary Loan Automation: An Implementation Guide," *Library Software Review* 8 (March-April 1989): 58–63.

RECORDS FOR BORROWING

Patron Request Form

Purpose: work form for collecting patron, bibliographic, subject, and processing information; and may be used to compile statistics

Form: can be designed and duplicated to suit needs or can exist electronically (see appendixes E and F)

Note: A complete record of the interlibrary loan transaction can go on this form.

Interlibrary Loan Request Form

Purpose: form created to transmit request to lending library

Form: depends on method of transmittal

Bibliographic utilities requests (OCLC, RLIN, WLN)

ALA Interlibrary Loan Request form

ALA Library Photoduplication Order form

Telefacsimile request

E-mail request

Computerized circulation system request

Printout request from online public access catalog, CD-ROM catalog, or microform catalog

Special form

Telephone request

Note: See chapter 1, "Instructions for Borrowing Libraries," "Prepare and transmit borrowing requests."

FILES FOR BORROWING

Process File

Purpose: for requests transmitted to the lending library that have not been received

Record: patron request form or patron request form and a copy of the interlibrary loan request form stapled together

Filed: by patron's name (most common for best service), main entry, lending library, or whatever is most useful

Note: Reactivated forms resulting from rejection by a lending library go back into this file.

Use File

Purpose: to keep track of what the patron has in his or her possession

Record: patron request form or patron request form and a copy of the interlibrary loan request form stapled together, pulled from the Process File

Filed: by patron's name (most common for best service), lending library, or whatever is most useful

Note: Some libraries combine the Process File and the Use File into one.

Date-Due File

Purpose: for retrieving overdue materials, renewals, etc.

Record: a copy of the interlibrary loan request form

Filed: by due date

Note: This is a temporary file for use in conjunction with the Use File. For small numbers of requests, this file may not be necessary.

Completed File

Purpose: for completed transactions (e.g., photocopy that has arrived and has been processed for use or originals that have been returned to the lending library)

Record: a copy of the patron request form (where all transaction information is recorded) or the interlibrary loan request form

Filed: by lending library for originals and by periodical title for periodicals from which photocopy has been received (keeping each *calendar* year separate for periodicals)

Note: Keep the file for originals only as long as it is needed to solve any problems arising from borrowed and returned items. One year to 18 months is usually sufficient. Keep the photocopy records for three years plus the current year (see appendix Z).

DATA ELEMENTS FOR LENDING

The borrowing library submits the necessary bibliographic and processing information from its perspective on an interlibrary loan request form. The lending library adds to this information on whatever form arrives, whether it be online or manual.

Lending Processing Information

Date of response

Date shipped

Date due
Shipped via
Insured for
Return insurance required
Packing requirements
Use restrictions
Charges
Reason for unfilled response
Lender notes
Other: renewal response, overdue notification, etc.

FILES FOR LENDING

Process File

Purpose: to keep track of what is being processed

Record: whatever interlibrary loan request forms are submitted

Filed: by call number, requesting library, or whatever is most useful

Note: If the turnaround time is fast, there is no need for this file.

Date-Due File

Purpose: for keeping track of material checked out, for sending overdues, and for billing

Record: whatever interlibrary loan request forms are submitted

Filed: by borrowing library or by date due

Note: Many electronic circulation systems take care of checking out material and producing overdue notices, in which case this file is not needed, except perhaps for billing purposes.

Completed File

Purpose: for completed transactions, both originals or returnables and photocopy or nonreturnables

Record: whatever interlibrary loan request forms are submitted

Filed: by the borrowing library

Note: Keep the file for statistical purposes and to solve problems. There is no requirement to keep it for a specific length of time.

Statistics show a summary of interlibrary loan activity. They provide information about what is happening in interlibrary loan and management data for planning. Automated interlibrary loan management systems provide a wealth of valuable statistics that can be used for a variety of purposes. Keeping statistics manually can be a time-consuming burden, so keep regularly only what is required or absolutely necessary. Routine measures should fit in with the statistics of the library as a whole and should fit whatever external standards and guidelines are available.

Some state library agencies set forth a methodology for the collection of interlibrary loan statistics so that they can be grouped together in a meaningful way. They usually adhere to national standards promoted by the federal government: (1) Federal/State Cooperative System for Public Library Data and (2) the Integrated Post Secondary Education Data System. The latter now has a section designated "Interlibrary Loan/Document Delivery." Other organizations, such as the Association of Research Libraries, request that interlibrary loan statistics be submitted in standard format so that one library can be compared with another.

Plan time to work on statistics so that they can be presented in a prompt way. Routine statistics are generally kept on a monthly basis with annual cumulations. What follows are suggestions for keeping statistics for both borrowing and lending, beginning with the absolute minimum and continuing on to more complex presentations. "Original" or "returnable" means all material borrowed and returned, regardless of format. "Photocopy" or "nonreturnable" means all material that is retained—usually copies.

Level One

Borrowing
    Total requests processed

Lending
    Total requests processed

          Grand total requests processed

Level Two

Borrowing	*Lending*
Filled requests	Filled requests
Unfilled requests (processed but not supplied)	Unfilled requests (processed but not supplied)
Found in library (processed, even if found)	
Total requests processed	Total requests processed

Grand total requests processed

Level Three

Borrowing	*Lending*
Filled by originals or returnables	Filled by originals or returnables
Filled by photocopy or nonreturnables	Filled by photocopy or nonreturnables
Unfilled	Unfilled
Found in library	
Total requests processed	Total requests processed

Grand total requests processed

Level Four

Borrowing	*Lending*
Found in library	
Unfilled	
Filled by originals or returnables, in state	Filled by originals or returnables, in state
Filled by photocopy or nonreturnables, in state	Filled by photocopy or nonreturnables, in state
Subtotal, filled in state	Subtotal, filled in state
	Unfilled, in state
	Requests processed, in state
Filled by originals or returnables, out of state	Filled by originals or returnables, out of state
Filled by photocopy or nonreturnables, out of state	Filled by photocopy or nonreturnables, out of state
Subtotal, filled out of state	Subtotal, filled out of state
	Unfilled, out of state
	Requests processed, out of state
	Total filled, in and out of state
	Total unfilled, in and out of state
Total requests processed (sum of found in library, unfilled; and total filled, in and out of state)	Total requests processed (sum of total filled, in and out of state; and total unfilled, in and out of state)

Grand total requests processed

Reports—monthly, quarterly, or annually—can document the successes (filled requests), the failures (unfilled requests), and significant happenings, as well as indicate a workload for interlibrary loan. These reports, concise in nature, should go to the supervisor and to the library director. Statistics should be presented in a readable form with three-year comparisons, charts, graphs, explanations, and examples. Percentages and trend lines can be used to advantage. Sampling, rather than keeping the statistics for everything, can be used for showing why requests are unfilled, who the borrowers are, from which part of the library the loans come, turnaround time for various activities, what type of library is borrowing, which states borrow the most, what type of material is most frequently requested, which methods of transmission are used, and many other facts. Automated interlibrary loan management systems often produce these statistics routinely.

A narrative report should accompany the statistics. It need not be long. It could contain such items as new developments, special work with library patrons, transactions compared to the same month for previous years, staff matters, expenditures compared to the budget, concerns about equip-

ment and space, and outstanding needs. It is particularly important to include interesting success stories to make the operation of interlibrary loan vivid for administrators.

Annual reports submitted to supervisors are an excellent opportunity to restate the goal and objectives of interlibrary loan and to show what happened during the year, including ordinary activity, new developments, special contributions, and financial considerations. Trends for the future and recommendations for improvement and change can also be part of the report. Every interlibrary loan office should not miss an opportunity to keep library management and the rest of the library staff informed about the important contribution interlibrary loan makes to library service.

STAFF

Hiring

A thorough knowledge of the personnel structure of the institution is necessary. Are civil service systems or unions part of the scene? What steps must be taken to comply with equal employment opportunity and affirmative action? What levels of positions are there? What promotion opportunities exist? What pay and benefits are available? What methods of performance appraisal are used? Is there a grievance procedure? Are there educational opportunities? For specific help with hiring employees, including questions that should *not* be asked in an interview, see Richard E. Rubin's *Hiring Library Employees: A How-to-Do-It Manual.*[15]

For a particular job there should be a clear statement of the education, knowledge, and skills required as well as a careful description of what the job entails. A job description should include the purpose of the job, who supervises the employee, whom the employee supervises, the specific tasks to be accomplished, the equipment to be used, and any unusual aspects of the work. Individual tasks, which are de-

scribed in chapter 1, "Instructions for Borrowing Libraries," and chapter 2, "Instructions for Lending Libraries," can be grouped into jobs. For instance, one employee might be in charge of all the lending activities from receiving interlibrary lending requests to reporting on interlibrary lending accomplishments. This employee might have several part-time assistants to pick up materials. The job will vary according to the number of requests processed, the complexity of the library as a whole, and the importance of interlibrary cooperation commitments.

Care should be given to assigning tasks to the level of staff where the work can be done most efficiently for the least cost. Having a professional librarian retrieve books from the stacks when a beginning paraprofessional or a student assistant could do it makes no sense. In an operation of any size, it does make sense, however, to have a professional librarian in charge of all interlibrary loan because of the expertise needed for policy making, planning, solving complex problems, dealing with other librarians on an equal basis, nurturing special

---

15. Richard E. Rubin, *Hiring Library Employees: A How-to-Do-It Manual,* How-to-Do-It Manuals for Librarians, no. 37 (New York: Neal-Schuman, 1993).

relationships with other institutions, stressing needs with the library administration, and keeping up with new developments in the field.

After posting a job notice, reading applications comes next. The major indicators to look for in an application are accomplishments, formal education, consistency, and commitment. Handwriting and the care with which the application was completed indicates something about accuracy and the ability to handle detail. There may also be particular skills needed for a given job, such as experience with OCLC or specific bibliographic searching experience. A certain amount of information can be gleaned from the application, but that is only a start.

Finding out from previous supervisors about the applicant's work experience, whether ordinary employment or volunteer work, can add to the knowledge base about the prospective employee. It is wise to telephone more than one reference for a rounded picture. Here are some questions that might be used with persons giving recommendations:

How long have you known the applicant?

What was your relationship to the applicant?

Can you describe the applicant's work experience?

How does the applicant get along with the public? Fellow workers? Supervisors?

Can you describe the applicant's communication skills?

How does the applicant respond to changes in routine?

How does the applicant respond to criticism?

How does the applicant perform in high-stress situations?

What do you consider the strong points of the applicant to be?

What do you consider the weak points of the applicant to be?

Would you rehire this person?

Is there anything else you could tell us that would be helpful?

Asking appropriate questions and listening thoughtfully to the answers during a job interview is a good way to gain information about an applicant. Those doing a lot of interviewing can find additional help in Susan Carol Curzon's *Managing the Interview: A How-to-Do-It Manual for Hiring Staff*.[16] Be sure to give the applicant a chance to be heard and ask questions that help the applicant to reveal strengths and weaknesses; explain what the job, benefits, and performance appraisal are; and inform the applicant of what further action is to be expected. The answers to several general questions need to be assessed:

Can the applicant do detailed and accurate work? (Examples of what detailed and accurate work is and probing previous work experience for samples of what the applicant has done is one way to go about this.)

Can the applicant understand and manipulate bibliographic data? (Writing term or research papers complete with footnotes and bibliography give experience in this area.)

Can the applicant interact with other people in a nonthreatening, pleasant way? (Explaining how a previous job was done can give some insight into how the applicant deals with other people.)

Can the applicant handle the physical demands of the job? (Someone with sore feet or back problems might have to compensate somehow to work as a book retriever.)

Questions of the candidate tend to center around library skills, including computer skills, work with library users, and supervisory skills. In addition, questions should be asked relating to the major parts of the job description. For a job managing interlibrary lending, for example, a question might be "What kinds of materials might not be listed in the online public access catalog?" or "Will you explain how to go about finding where a given call number can be found in this library?" To get an idea of how the applicant might handle a particular situation, there are always the "What are . . . " and "What would you do if . . . " questions.

---

16. Susan Carol Curzon, *Managing the Interview: A How-to-Do-It Manual for Hiring Staff*, How-to-Do-It Manuals for Librarians, no. 47 (New York: Neal-Schuman, 1995).

What would you do if you needed to verify a reference not found in the online access provided in the library?

What are the elements of a bibliographic citation for a book?

What is the purpose of a circulation record?

What would you do if a patron became irate because the requested materials had not yet arrived?

What would you do if someone asked where circulation was located?

How would you go about explaining the need for filling out an interlibrary loan patron request form?

What would you do if your student employee spent twenty minutes talking to a friend during each two-hour work stint?

How would you go about supervising someone who is doing a task with which you are not familiar?

How would you go about implementing a new computer application?

And there are the usual questions generally asked:

What do you think a supervisor should expect of you?

What expectations do you have of the supervisor?

Why should we hire you?

Pulling together the information and impressions gained from the job application, recommendations, and the interview, a decision for hiring can be reached. Where little or no choice of applicant is available, look for someone with any library experience at all, a lively curiosity, a wide range of interests, and a willingness to learn new things. A good memory, flexibility, and a modicum of patience are also a boon.

Training and continuing education

Training and continuing education for interlibrary loan personnel have long concerned library managers. A core body of skills, knowledge, and objectives for training was developed by the American Library Association Reference and Adult Services Division, Interlibrary Loan Committee, Subcommittee on Continuing Education and Training. This document, "Interlibrary Loan Training and Continuing Education Model Statement of Objectives," can be found in appendix FF. The bibliography at the end of the chapter includes some additional references on training and continuing education.

Most of the comments in this section have to do with support staff, although librarians can benefit from the information as well. One of the best ways to learn, when only one person is doing interlibrary loan and document delivery, is to find an experienced practitioner in another library who can serve as a mentor. Visiting the mentor's library and asking the mentor questions as they arise is certainly preferable to the trial-and-error method.

For an individual to feel comfortable in a new work situation and to understand the organization well enough to make a contribution to it, orientation on many levels is needed. Orientation takes place best over a period of time so that the person is not overwhelmed by too many new facts all at once. It can well be interspersed with learning specific tasks.

Orientation to the interlibrary loan office environment is of immediate concern. H. Scott Davis offers help with orientation in *New Employee Orientation: A How-to-Do-It Manual for Librarians*.[17] Information about the office environment should include such things as the whereabouts of coatracks, drinking water, restrooms, bulletin boards, mailboxes, calendars, supplies, and the staff room. The employee's desk, work space, and the equipment to be used need to be made known. Policies concerning food and smoking must be made clear. This is also the time for describing the plans for evacuation of the building and other emergency procedures.

Personnel matters need some attention. Keys, parking stickers, and filling out various personnel forms are among the items that must be addressed. Annual leave, sick leave, holidays, breaks, lunch hours, pay periods, and the pay itself are all important to the employee. Benefits of various kinds need to be explained in detail. If there are policies con-

---

17. H. Scott Davis, *New Employee Orientation: A How-to-Do-It Manual for Librarians,* How-to-Do-It Manuals for Librarians, no. 38 (New York: Neal-Schuman, 1994).

cerning personal telephone calls and personal use of computers, these need to be mentioned. Personnel manuals or other written personnel statements must be identified. The performance appraisal system should be explained.

Introduce the new employee to the staff. Giving a brief description of what the other employees do as well as their names helps the learning process. Make certain the new employee knows who his or her supervisor is and who is directing the library. Make a special effort to introduce outside staff, such as mail-room personnel, who contribute to the smooth running of interlibrary loan.

The library itself must be discussed. The mission statement, goals, and objectives need to be understood. The organizational structure, lines of authority, and where the real power lies should be explained. Where funding comes from is of importance as well as whom the library serves. The major functions of the library, where they are located, and the nature of the collections are all vital pieces of information. Also of interest are policies adopted by the library, such as those for collection development, circulation, reference services, the Library Bill of Rights, and the confidentiality of library records. Noting important, recent library history can be helpful.

Training begins with basic instruction on how to find and retrieve library materials, including learning what information is contained in the online public access catalog or card catalog, how information is retrieved or what the filing rules are, the importance of serial records, and the function of call numbers and location devices. Show the new employee how to check out a book and how to find a periodical article and photocopy it. Let the employee know the hours of service and the service points in the library, including where to ask questions. The two books listed below may be of assistance in explaining what libraries do:

Bloomberg, Marty. *Introduction to Public Services for Library Technicians*. 4th ed. Library Science Text Series. Littleton, Colo.: Libraries Unlimited, 1985.

Evans, G. Edward, and Sandra M. Heft. *Introduction to Technical Services*. Library Science

Text Series. 6th ed. Englewood, Colo.: Libraries Unlimited, 1994.

The structure of interlibrary loan service needs to be described. The National Interlibrary Loan Code for the United States, 1993; a state interlibrary loan code; and any other interlibrary loan codes that are used form a part of the framework. Policies of lending libraries, policies of interlibrary borrowing, and the copyright law add to the structure. Specific procedures are outlined in this manual, state interlibrary loan manuals, and internal manuals. Online systems in use can be put into perspective. To get an overall view it sometimes helps to give the employee an annual report to read and to "walk through" an interlibrary borrowing request and an interlibrary lending request.

As the general knowledge is imparted, an assessment of what the new employee already knows and what he or she needs to know, who is going to do the specific training, and how the training will be done should be considered. Reviewing information about how adults learn can be useful before beginning intensive training. Susan Jurow's article in *Staff Development: A Practical Guide* discusses how people learn.[18] The method generally employed is to have someone who knows how to do the task proceed in the following manner. First, verbal instructions are given containing an orienting statement, specific instructions are given in segments, perception is checked to see if the information is understood, and a description is given of the expected results. Next, accomplishing the task is demonstrated. Following that, the employee does the task while the tutor answers questions and offers encouragement. Finally, the task is done independently by the employee with the supervisor checking the work upon completion. Feedback from employee to tutor on what the employee is doing is of immense help. Feedback from the tutor to the employee on how he or she is doing speeds up learning. When training for a specific task is considered complete, there may well be only spot checking, or none at all, as the employee assumes complete responsibility for doing the task correctly.

There may be a number of aids to help with the teaching process. A well-written, step-by-step

18. Susan Jurow, "How People Learn: Applying the Adult Learning Model to Training Sessions," in *Staff Develop-* *ment: A Practical Guide,* 2nd ed. (Chicago: American Library Association, 1992), 1–2.

procedure manual can be of assistance to the tutor when explaining the work and to the employee in reviewing the necessary steps. Upon completion of training, a "quick check" listing of steps for a particular task can be an easy memory refresher. Such a manual can be of double service when someone unfamiliar with the task is forced to do it because of staff illness or vacation. Having the person who does the task write the procedures in the first place serves as a powerful learning device in itself. Actual training manuals exist for some activities, such as the OCLC PRISM Interlibrary Loan system. Some libraries have online help for learning about automated systems. Role playing can be used for teaching employees how to manage an interlibrary loan interview.

Train staff to deal with electronic modes of accomplishing tasks. It is particularly important to explain why automation is used and why it is necessary to learn complicated protocol for accomplishing tasks. The answer to that question is often "speed." *All* of the electronic methods for accomplishing interlibrary loan and document delivery tasks used at your institution need to be learned. There may be an electronic system for the library user to request a loan. There will likely be electronic methods for searching bibliographic records: online union catalogs, online databases, CD-ROMs, World Wide Web sites, and the like. Electronic transmission of requests is common, as is the use of fax or the Internet. The document itself may come electronically either to the interlibrary loan and document delivery office or to the library user. Communication with the library user is faster using an electronic means. A management system for interlibrary loan and document supply may be locally controlled on a computer.

Training for these sorts of systems requires patience and practice. The usual methods of training apply here. Coaching the beginner is particularly helpful. When the initial training has been accomplished, there is still a need for continuing education. There must be "free" time working with a computer to allow the staff to increase knowledge and discover things. Being able to find needed information on the Internet does not come with one training session. It comes with experimentation and repetition. Though it is hard to convince administrators that "free" time is important, it is essential for continued growth.

Another requisite to continued learning about electronic ways of doing things is to find a person who is an expert in these matters. Very often a quick telephone call to such a person will produce an answer to a vexing question and make the work much easier. Though there may be no formal relationship between you and the expert, such a person is often very glad to impart a bit of his or her expertise.

Taking advantage of continuing education opportunities contributes to perfecting ways of doing business and to increasing knowledge about the changing world in which we live. Refer to "Keeping Up with Interlibrary Loan and Document Delivery Developments," appendix GG, for suggestions in this area.

Supervision

Two questions plague the mind of the interlibrary loan supervisor:

Now that the trained employee is doing his or her job each day, how do I know the job is being done efficiently and effectively?

Are the day-to-day employee questions being answered so that work continues to flow through the system without the creation of needless backlogs?

First let us look at how well the job is being done. A supervisor cannot check all the minutiae involved in the performance of each task, but there are some good stages in the total operation for taking a look at what is happening. For interlibrary lending, it is wise to look at what is not being found in the online public access catalog or card catalog, or the serial records. Inability to search these records properly, as well as difficult verification problems that only the supervisor can solve, come to light. It is a good idea to check the shelves occasionally to be certain that something marked "Not on shelf" is indeed not there. For interlibrary borrowing, the information prepared for transmission can be checked before a request is sent to see if the verification and location information appears to be appropriate and correct. Another area for checking is those requests that have been returned unfilled to see if mistakes have been made or further work is necessary. Those methods for feeling the pulse of the interlibrary loan operations allow filled requests to go through unchallenged while bringing potential problems to light.

The creation of backlogs is an albatross weighing on many interlibrary loan services. The usual methods of batching work, handling an individual request as little as possible, and working in a logical manner do not always prevent backlogs. As much as possible, supervisors must be available to answer questions involving difficult requests as they arise. This prevents the request from being put aside to be worked on "later." And when problems of a more lengthy nature occur, time needs to be allotted specifically for solving the difficulties of nonroutine requests. Sometimes it is necessary to allot a specific time for a staff person to bring up problems.

Deciding which member of the staff should do what is not always an easy job. With adequate intelligence and manual dexterity, many people can do the tasks, some taking longer to learn than others; but the exceptional person develops a real knack for making bibliographic connections, solving tricky problems, or forging ahead with automation changes. In general, the least complicated tasks should be reserved for those with no experience or a minimum of ability. In a large office, there can be a progression from easier tasks to harder ones as vacancies occur. In an academic setting, for example, the newest student might return books to the lending library. When a vacancy occurs, that student might move on to checking the online public access catalog or card catalog. Next the student could learn to search an online union catalog such ac OCLC, RLIN, or WLN.

Learning new tasks can keep an employee interested as well as provide a backup for illness, vacations, or vacancies. Those libraries with electronic systems are fortunate in that giving the employee experience with such systems enhances his or her value as an applicant for future jobs. Any kind of experience in interlibrary loan also enables the employee to use a library more effectively.

Special care must be taken with those who work with computers. In addition to the correct and comfortable placement of equipment and light, the time spent in front of computer screens needs to be noted. A frequent "walkabout" may need to be part of the daily routine in order to give eyes and straining muscles a chance to relax.

The professional librarian in interlibrary loan must show unusual flexibility to respond to constant change. This librarian must have a detailed knowledge of how each task is accomplished, even though he or she does not actually do the job, so that wise decisions are made. In libraries where interlibrary loan is largely staffed by support personnel, there should be a professional librarian assigned to back up interlibrary loan in the areas of difficult bibliographic problem solving and negotiation with peers and supervisors concerning availability of materials for loan, adequate staffing, and other matters.

The good employee wants to know more than once a year how he or she measures up to the task. Let the employee know when something is done well, that the solution to a vexing problem is indeed remarkable, that faithful attendance at work is appreciated, and that the enthusiasm for a particular task is well placed. Let the employee know, too, about mistakes, without assigning blame, and make suggestions for improving the situation. Acknowledge that interlibrary loan is hard, demanding work. Emphasize the importance of delivering information to those who need it. Encourage participation in decision making.

Creativity in interlibrary loan can be a boon or a bugaboo. When confronted with the necessity to write a new routine or solve a new problem, the creative employee can be of immense value in coming up with a workable scheme. On the other hand, the person who decides to file in a highly individual manner or does a routine task in a unique way can cause havoc. A nice balance of "Can you see a better way to do that?" and "Do not change procedures without approval!" can sometimes be achieved. With interlibrary loan operations in such a fluid state of change, the spark of creativity should be nurtured but also controlled.

Performance appraisal

To augment the comments given throughout the year concerning an employee's performance, most institutions require an annual performance appraisal. For help with this process, consult the bibliography at the end of the chapter. The first thing to do is to become thoroughly familiar with your institution's system. Performance appraisal systems can vary from a simple statement that a salary increase should or should not be given to an elaborate plan in a final written document. Do the best you can within whatever system there is, but be sure to keep it simple and to involve the employee in the process as much as possible.

The evaluated areas should have some relation to the job description, the work that is actually done, or the work that needs to be done. When deciding whether the work was done well, consider such elements as turnaround time for completing requests, accuracy of bibliographic descriptions, quantity of work accomplished, responses received from other libraries, and praise or complaints coming into the office from library patrons. Whatever standards have been established for interlibrary loan, such as a three-day turnaround time for lending requests, should play a part in the performance appraisal. This is a good time to express gratitude for a job well done and to plan for improving those areas that need it.

Appropriate monetary reward is always acceptable, but it is not always possible. There are other ways to show appreciation for a job well done.

Sometimes flexible scheduling or job rotation can be managed. Celebrating accomplishments, listening, advising, and providing general support and encouragement can be rewards for good performance. Special assignments, such as attending a meeting in place of the supervisor or serving on a committee, can sometimes be arranged. The opportunity to learn new skills, develop increased abilities, or take an academic course can be beneficial. Keeping the employee aware of developments outside the library can spark interest.

Should disciplinary action or dismissal be warranted, a thorough knowledge of the institution's policies is necessary. Go ahead when there is backing from your supervisor. Extreme care in proceeding should be exercised to protect the employee and yourself.

EVALUATION

Measurement and evaluation of interlibrary loan and document delivery are done in order to answer questions about the service. Some measurements, such as fill rate and turnaround time, can be computed without too much trouble. Other measurements can only be done by using a variety of techniques. Two useful techniques are sampling to produce special statistics and conducting a survey.

Producing statistics from a sample for many areas of interlibrary loan is highly desirable as opposed to keeping track on an individual basis. There are measures for interlibrary loan that lend themselves to this technique, especially for data that already exist but are not generally tabulated. For instance, a sample of interlibrary borrowing requests can be drawn and a determination made as to who is using the service: faculty, graduate students, undergraduate students, or staff. One need not count each request. Peter Hernon has given information on how to select a meaningful sample.[19] Any of the data elements present on the various interlibrary loan forms can be sampled to produce management information.

Surveys for which no data already exist are more difficult. Designing a good survey is not as easy as one might think, so it is always a good idea to get advice and to test it before actually conducting the survey. For instance, there is a growing interest in just what the library patron needs and wants and what he or she thinks about the service. A user survey is a tempting way to try to find out about the library patron. Anna H. Perrault and Marjo Arseneau have designed a survey, which is printed in the fall 1995 issue of *RQ*.[20] This survey could be adapted for use by any interlibrary loan service.

Information collected in these ways can be used to contemplate three important questions:

What can be left undone and not affect the service?

What changes should be made to facilitate service?

What issues need further attention and analysis?

19. Peter Hernon, "Research Notes: Determination of Sample Size and Selection of the Sample: Concepts, General Sources, and Software," *College & Research Libraries* 55 (March 1994): 171–79.

20. Anna H. Perrault and Marjo Arseneau, "User Satisfaction and Interlibrary Loan Service: A Study at Louisiana State University," *RQ* 35 (Fall 1995): 90–100.

OPPORTUNITIES

The management of interlibrary loan and document delivery offers satisfying opportunities to those who engage in it. First of all, the work itself brings the practitioner in contact with all parts of the library, resulting in a broad understanding of library functions. How the circulation system works, where reference electronic sources and books are located and how they are used, and what various cataloging tags mean are only some of the facets of library work that are encountered. Interlibrary loan offers a unique chance to work with patrons on a one-to-one basis to help solve their more difficult information needs. The public relations aspect of this contact is important.

The focus of interlibrary loan is outward and brings the librarian in contact with other libraries and librarians as well as commercial document delivery services. A personal network of those knowledgeable in interlibrary loan can be established. With the development of cooperatives, consortia, and networks, the interlibrary loan librarian is given a chance to play a role in establishing standards, finding more effective ways for accomplishing new tasks, and contributing to problem-solving techniques using new kinds of technology. Finally, interlibrary loan offers an arena in which to conduct research about what library users do and how tasks can be better accomplished. Meaningful data can be provided to the profession by this means.

Interlibrary loan never stands still. What is done today may very well not be done or be done in a different way tomorrow. Among those looking to the future is OCLC (Online Computer Library Center). OCLC's strategy for resource sharing through the remainder of the decade is characterized thus:

> OCLC's strategy in the 1994–2000 timeframe is to combine searching, interlibrary loan, and document delivery into a single, fast, low-cost service. Resource sharing will move beyond interlibrary loan to include electronic and physical document delivery and electronic publishing. The strategy will: 1) integrate PRISM ILL, FirstSearch and document delivery; 2) be consistent with OCLC's chartered objectives of furthering access to the world's information and reducing information costs; and 3) build on and strengthen existing library relationships. . . . Cooperation is one of the enduring watchwords of librarianship. The next stage of the electronic library will see greatly expanded opportunities for library cooperation as electronic resource sharing fulfills the promise of providing information to users when and where they need it.[21]

Another organization thinking about the future is the Association of Research Libraries (ARL). Work on interlibrary loan and document delivery intensified in 1992 with the publication of a paper by Shirley K. Baker and Mary E. Jackson.[22] Subsequently ARL initiated the North American Interlibrary Loan and Document Delivery (NAILDD) Project, the goal of which is to promote developments that will improve the delivery of library materials to users at costs that are sustainable for libraries. The project has focused on system design priorities accomplishing the following:

- identified priority improvements for online systems that support ILL and document delivery services (a management system, a financial/accounting system, and essential linkages between and among local and national systems),
- set in place a forum to encourage and promote these developments in the private sector,
- secured the agreement of the National Information Standards Organization to work with ARL and private sector partners to speed the development of standards necessary to improve ILL and document delivery services, and

21. "OCLC's Resource Sharing Strategy" (Dublin, Ohio: OCLC Online Computer Library Center, 1994), 3–4.

22. Shirley K. Baker and Mary E. Jackson, *Maximizing Access, Minimizing Cost: A First Step toward the Information Access Future* (Washington, D.C.: Association of Research Libraries, 1992).

■ designed a strategy to assist a library to redesign ILL/DD services and develop the policies and new organizational and management structures needed to support these services.[23]

The NAILDD project has developed educational materials on two policy issues associated with interlibrary loan and document delivery service: fees and copyright compliance. ARL has also received a grant from the Andrew W. Mellon Foundation to measure the performance of interlibrary loan and document delivery. Measures include turnaround time, fill rate, user satisfaction, and cost. Benefits for libraries of all types and sizes should accrue from these activities.

All the experience, talent, and creativity of interlibrary loan and document delivery librarians can be brought to bear on the problems that must be solved in the future:

Truly putting the patron first when considering organization and operations,

Learning to be an excellent teacher for patrons and employees, especially on how to use electronic resources,

Defending the patron's right to confidentiality, free speech, and equal access to information,

Working with evolving technology to create and operate a better interlibrary loan and document delivery service, moving from a paper to a technological environment,

Knowing the copyright law, now and as it changes, and abiding by it, and

Keeping up with a rapidly changing field.

The material requested on interlibrary loan never ceases to amaze and confound. The opportunity to acquire new bits of information is endless. The practice of interlibrary loan and document delivery is what you make of it, but it can be the most challenging, satisfying, and exciting part of librarianship.

BIBLIOGRAPHY

This bibliography is not comprehensive. It does suggest sources for information to get one started on additional reading.

General

Bremer, Suzanne W. *Long Range Planning: A How-to-Do-It Manual for Public Libraries.* How-to-Do-It Manuals for Librarians, no. 40. New York: Neal-Schuman, 1994.

Christianson, Elin B., David E. King, and Janet L. Ahrensfeld. *Special Libraries: A Guide for Management.* 3rd ed. Washington, D.C.: Special Libraries Association, 1991.

Costa, Betty, and Marie Costa with Larry Costa. *A Micro Handbook for Small Libraries and Media Centers.* 3rd ed. Englewood, Colo.: Libraries Unlimited, 1991.

Coughlin, Caroline M., and Alice Gertzog. *Lyle's Administration of the College Library.* 5th ed. Metuchen, N.J.: Scarecrow, 1992.

Curzon, Susan Carol. *Managing Change: A How-to-Do-It Manual for Planning, Implementing, and Evaluating Change in Libraries.* How-to-Do-It Manuals for Librarians, no. 2. New York: Neal-Schuman, 1989.

DuBrin, Andrew J. *Contemporary Applied Management: Behavioral Science Techniques for Managers and Professionals.* 3rd ed. Homewood, Ill.: BPI/Irwin, 1989.

Gertzog, Alice, and Edwin Beckerman. *Administration of the Public Library.* Metuchen, N.J.: Scarecrow, 1994.

Katz, William A. *Introduction to Reference Work.* 2 vols. 6th ed. New York: McGraw-Hill, 1992.

23. "North American Interlibrary Loan and Document Delivery (NAILDD) Project: Overview and Vision" (Washington, D.C.: Association of Research Libraries, 1995), 2.

Morris, Betty J. *Administering the School Library Media Center.* 3rd ed. New Providence, N.J.: Bowker, 1992.

Mount, Ellis. *Special Libraries and Information Centers: An Introductory Text.* 2nd ed. Washington, D.C.: Special Libraries Association, 1991.

Saffady, William. *Introduction to Automation for Librarians.* 3rd ed. Chicago: American Library Association, 1994.

Stein, Barbara L., and Risa W. Brown. *Running a School Library Media Center: A How-to-Do-It Manual for Librarians.* How-to-Do-It Manuals for School and Public Librarians, no. 1. New York: Neal-Schuman, 1992.

Stueart, Robert D., and Barbara B. Moran. *Library and Information Center Management.* 4th ed. Englewood, Colo.: Libraries Unlimited, 1993.

Weingand, Darlene E. *Administration of the Small Public Library.* 3rd ed. Chicago: American Library Association, 1992.

Audiovisual Materials

Brancolini, Kristine, and Rick E. Provine. *Video Collections and Multimedia in ARL Libraries.* SPEC Kit, no. 199. Washington, D.C.: Association of Research Libraries, Office of Management Services, 1993.

Massis, Bruce E., and Winnie Vitzansky, eds. "Interlibrary Loan of Alternative Format Materials: A Balanced Source Book." *Journal of Interlibrary Loan & Information Supply* 3, no. 1/2 (1992): 1–196.

Evaluation

Baker, Sharon L., and F. Wilfrid Lancaster. *The Measurement and Evaluation of Library Services.* 2nd ed. Arlington, Va.: Information Resources Press, 1991.

Waldhart, Thomas J. "Patterns of Interlibrary Loan in the United States: A Review of Research." *Library & Information Science Research* 7 (1985): 209–29.

———. "Performance Evaluation of Interlibrary Loan in the United States: A Review of Research." *Library & Information Science Research* 7 (1985): 313–31.

Some Recent Studies

Adams, Judith A., and Sharon C. Bonk. "Electronic Information Technologies and Resources: Use by University Faculty and Faculty Preferences for Related Library Services." *College & Research Libraries* 56 (March 1995): 119–31.

Allen, Mary Beth. "International Students in Academic Libraries: A User Survey." *College & Research Libraries* 54 (July 1993): 323–33.

Dalrymple, Prudence Ward, and others. "Measuring Statewide Interlibrary Loan among Multitype Libraries: A Testing of Data Collection Approaches." *RQ* 30 (Summer 1991): 534–47.

Jardine, Carolyn W. "Maybe the 55 Percent Rule Doesn't Tell the Whole Story: A User-Satisfaction Survey." *College & Research Libraries* 56 (Nov. 1995): 477–85.

Kimmel, Janice L. "ILL Staffing: A Survey of Michigan Academic Libraries." *RQ* 35 (Winter 1995): 205–16.

Perrault, Anna H., and Marjo Arseneau. "User Satisfaction and Interlibrary Loan Service: A Study at Louisiana State University." *RQ* 35 (Fall 1995): 90–100.

Fax

Dewey, Patrick R. *FAX for Libraries.* Westport, Conn.: Meckler, 1990.

Fishman, Daniel, and Elliot King. *The Book of Fax: An Impartial Guide to Buying and Using Facsimile Machines.* 2nd ed. Chapel Hill, N.C.: Ventana Press, 1990.

Higginbotham, Barbra Buckner. "Telefacsimile: The Issues and the Answers." *Journal of Interlibrary Loan & Information Supply* 1, no. 1 (1990): 67–86.

Higginbotham, Barbra Buckner, and Sally Bowdoin. "Telefacsimile Transmission." In *Access versus Assets,* 217–39. Chicago: American Library Association, 1993.

Smith, Lorre. "Facsimile Transmission: Progress in Resource Sharing." *RQ* 33 (Winter 1993): 254–62.

Interlibrary Loan and Document Delivery

Baker, Shirley K., and Mary E. Jackson. "The Future of Resource Sharing." *Journal of Library Administration* 21, no. 1/2 (1995): 1–202.

Bustos, Roxann. *Interlibrary Loan in College Libraries.* CLIP Note, no. 16. Chicago: Association of College and Research Libraries, American Library Association, 1993.

Dearie, Tammie Nickelson, and Virginia Steel. *Interlibrary Loan Trends: Making Access a Reality.* SPEC Kit, no. 184. Washington, D.C.: Association of Research Libraries, Office of Management Services, 1992.

———. *Interlibrary Loan Trends: Staffing and Organization.* SPEC Kit, no. 187. Washington, D.C.: Association of Research Libraries, Office of Management Services, 1992.

Higginbotham, Barbra Buckner, and Sally Bowdoin. *Access versus Assets.* Frontiers of Access to Library Materials, no. 1. Chicago: American Library Association, 1993.

Jackson, Mary E. "The Ideal ILL Service Model." *Wilson Library Bulletin* 69 (Jan. 1995): 68–69, 125.

———. "Redesigning Access and Delivery Services." *Wilson Library Bulletin* 69 (Nov. 1994): 73–74.

———. "Redesigning Interlibrary Loan and Document Delivery Services." *Wilson Library Bulletin* 69 (May 1995): 68–69, 113.

Jackson, Mary E., and Karen Croneis. *Uses of Document Delivery Services.* SPEC Kit, no. 204. Washington, D.C.: Association of Research Libraries, Office of Management Services, 1994.

Khalil, Mounir A., and Suzanne R. Katz. "Document Delivery: An Annotated Selective Bibliography." *Computers in Libraries* 12 (Dec. 1992): 25–33.

LaGuardia, Cheryl M., and Connie V. Dowell. "The Structure of Resource Sharing in Academic Research Libraries." *RQ* 30 (Spring 1991): 370–76.

Mancini, Alice Duhon. "Evaluating Commercial Document Suppliers: Improving Access to Current Journal Literature." *College & Research Libraries* 57 (March 1996): 123–31.

Mitchell, Eleanor, and Sheila A. Walters. *Document Delivery Services: Issues and Answers.* Medford, N.J.: Learned Information, 1995.

Weaver-Meyers, Pat, Shelly Clement, and Carolyn Mahin. *Interlibrary Loan in Academic and Research Libraries: Workload and Staffing.* Occasional Paper, no. 15. Washington, D.C.: Association of Research Libraries, Office of Management Services, 1989.

The Internet

Benson, Allen C. *The Complete Internet Companion for Librarians.* New York: Neal-Schuman, 1995.

Farley, Laine, ed. *Library Resources on the Internet: Strategies for Selection and Use.* RASD Occasional Papers, no. 12. Chicago: American Library Association, Reference and Adult Services Division, 1992.

Johnson, Peggy, and Lee English. *The Searchable Internet Bibliography: An On-Disk Annotated Guide to Timely Materials about the Internet* [three disks]. Chicago: American Library Association, 1996.

Krol, Ed. *The Whole Internet User's Guide and Catalog.* 2nd ed. Sebastopol, Calif.: O'Reilly & Associates, 1994. A new edition is expected in 1996.

Levine, John R. *Internet for Dummies.* 3rd ed. Foster City, Calif.: IDG Books Worldwide, 1995.

Machovec, George S. *Telecommunications, Networking and Internet Glossary.* LITA Monographs, no. 4. Chicago: Library and Information Technology Association, American Library Association, 1993.

Schankman, Larry. "How to Become an Internet Power User." *College & Research Libraries News* 55 (Dec. 1994): 718–21.

Shindler, Adrian. *Internet: A Literature Guide.* London: British Library Information Sciences Service, 1994.

Wiggins, Richard W. *The Internet for Everyone: A Guide for Users and Providers.* New York: McGraw-Hill, 1995.

Performance Appraisal

Kathman, Jane McGurn, and Michael D. Kathman. "Performance Measures for Student Assistants." *College & Research Libraries* 53 (July 1992): 299–304.

Stueart, Robert D., and Maureen Sullivan. *Performance Analysis and Appraisal: A How-to-Do-It Manual for Librarians.* How-to-Do-It Manuals for Librarians, no. 14. New York: Neal-Schuman, 1991.

Procedure Manuals

Blake, Gary, and Robert W. Bly. "Ten Tips for Better User Manuals." *Computer Decisions* 16 (Sept. 1984): 68, 70.

Cubberly, Carol W. "Write Procedures That Work." *Library Journal* 116 (Sept. 15, 1991): 42–45.

Page, Stephen Butler. *Business Policies and Procedures Handbook.* Englewood Cliffs, N.J.: Prentice-Hall, 1984.

Supervision

Practical Help for New Supervisors. Prepared by the Supervisory Skills Committee, Personnel Administration Section, Library Administration and Management Association; edited by Joan Giesecke. Chicago: American Library Association, 1992.

Rooks, Dana C. *Motivating Today's Library Staff: A Management Guide.* Phoenix, Ariz.: Oryx Press, 1988.

Training

Beaton, Barbara. "Interlibrary Loan Training and Continuing Education Model Statement of Objectives." *RQ* 31 (Winter 1991): 177–84. See appendix FF.

Bessler, Joanne M. *Putting Service into Library Staff Training.* LAMA Occasional Papers series. Chicago: American Library Association, 1994.

Boone, Morell D., Sandra G. Yee, and Rita Bullard. *Training Student Library Assistants.* Chicago: American Library Association, 1991.

Cornish, Graham P. *Training Modules for Interlibrary Lending and Document Supply.* PGI-91/WS/7. Paris: General Information Programme and UNISIST, Unesco, 1991.

———. "Training Opportunities for Interlibrary Loan and Document Supply Staff." *Journal of Education for Library & Information Science* 35 (Spring 1994): 138–46.

Ercegovac, Zorana. "Information Access Instruction (IAI^4): Design Principles." *College & Research Libraries* 56 (May 1995): 249–57.

Jackson, Mary E. "Training for ILL Practitioners." *Wilson Library Bulletin* 68 (Jan. 1994): 75–76.

Learning to Teach: Workshops on Instruction. A Project of the Learning to Teach Task Force, Bibliographic Instruction Section, Association of College and Research Libraries. Chicago: American Library Association, 1993.

Staff Development: A Practical Guide. Prepared by the Staff Development Committee, Personnel Administration Section, Library Administration and Management Association; coordinating editors Anne Grodzins Lipow and Deborah A. Carver. 2nd ed. Chicago: American Library Association, 1992.

Weissinger, Nancy J., and John P. Edwards. "Online Resources for Internet Trainers." *College & Research Libraries News* 56 (Sept. 1995): 535–39, 572.

APPENDIXES

National Interlibrary Loan Code for the United States, 1993

Prepared by the Interlibrary Loan Committee, Management and Operation of Public Services Section, Reference and Adult Services Division, American Library Association. Approved by the RASD Board of Directors, February 8, 1994.

INTRODUCTION

The Reference and Adult Services Division, acting for the American Library Association in its adoption of this code, recognizes that the exchange of material between libraries in the United States is an important element in the provision of library service and believes it to be in the public interest to encourage such an exchange.

Interlibrary loan is essential to the vitality of libraries of all types and sizes and is a means by which a wider range of materials can be made available to users. In the interests of providing quality service, libraries have an obligation to obtain materials to meet the informational needs of users when local resources do not meet those needs.

Interlibrary loan has been described as an adjunct to, not a substitute for, collection development in individual libraries. Changes in the last decade have brought increasing availability of materials in alternative formats, an abundance of verification and location information, and a shift in the very nature of interlibrary cooperation. Interlibrary borrowing is an integral element of collection development for all libraries, not an ancillary option.

The effectiveness of a national resource sharing system depends upon the responsible distribution of borrowing and lending. Libraries of all types and sizes should be willing to share their resources liberally so that a relatively few libraries are not overburdened. Libraries must be willing to lend if they wish to borrow.

This code is designed to regulate lending and borrowing relations between libraries. It is not the intent of this code to prescribe the nature of interlibrary cooperation within formally established networks and consortia, or to regulate the purchase of materials from document suppliers. However, this code may be used as a model for development of state, regional, or local interlibrary loan codes.

This code provides general guidelines for the requesting and supplying of materials between libraries. Specific guidelines and procedures are found in such sources as those listed in the bibliography.

CODE

1.0 Definition
1.1 Interlibrary loan is the process by which a library requests materials from, or supplies materials to, another library.

2.0 Purpose
2.1 The purpose of interlibrary loan as defined by this code is to obtain, upon request of a library user, materials not available in the user's local library.

3.0 Scope
3.1 Interlibrary loan is a mutual relationship and libraries should be willing to supply materials as freely as they request materials.
3.2 Any materials, regardless of format, may be requested from another library. The supplying library determines whether the material can be provided.

4.0 Responsibilities of the Requesting Library
4.1 The requesting library should establish and maintain an interlibrary loan policy for its borrowers and make it available.
4.2 The requesting library should process requests in a timely fashion.
4.3 The requesting library should identify libraries that own and might provide the requested materials. The requesting library should check

RQ 33, no.4, Summer 1994, p.477–79

the policies of potential suppliers for special instructions, restrictions, and information on charges prior to sending a request. The requesting library is responsible for all authorized charges imposed by the supplying library.

4.4 Requests for materials for which locations cannot be identified, should be sent to libraries that might provide the requested materials and be accompanied by the statement "cannot locate." The original source of the reference should be cited or a copy of the citation provided.

4.5 The requesting library should avoid sending the burden of its requests to a few libraries. Major resource libraries should be used as a last resort.

4.6 The requesting library should transmit all interlibrary loan requests in standard bibliographic format in accordance with the protocols of the electronic network or transmission system used. In the absence of an electronically generated form, the American Library Association interlibrary loan request form should be used.

4.7 The requesting library must ensure compliance with the U.S. copyright law and its accompanying guidelines. Copyright compliance must be determined for each copy request before it is transmitted, and a copyright compliance statement must be included on each copy request. Copyright files should be maintained as directed in the CONTU Guidelines. (See bibliography for full citations to these documents.)

4.8 The requesting library is responsible for borrowed materials from the time they leave the supplying library until they have been returned and received by the supplying library. If damage or loss occurs, the requesting library is responsible for compensation or replacement, in accordance with the preference of the supplying library.

4.9 The requesting library is responsible for honoring due dates and enforcing all use restrictions specified by the supplying library.

4.10 The requesting library should request a renewal before the item is due. If the supplying library does not respond, the requesting library may assume that the renewal has been granted for the same length of time as the original loan.

4.11 The requesting library should return materials by the due date and respond immediately if the item has been recalled by the supplying library.

4.12 The requesting library should package materials to prevent damage in shipping, and comply with special instructions stated by the supplying library.

4.13 The requesting library is responsible for following the provisions of this code. Continued disregard for any provision may be reason for suspension of borrowing privileges by a supplying library.

5.0 Responsibilities of the Supplying Library

5.1 The supplying library should establish and maintain an interlibrary loan policy, make it available in paper and/or electronic format, and provide it upon request.

5.2 The supplying library should process requests within the timeline established by the electronic network. Requests not transmitted electronically should be handled in a similar time frame.

5.3 The supplying library should include a copy of the original request, or information sufficient to identify the request, with each item.

5.4 The supplying library should state any conditions and/or restrictions on use of the materials lent and specify any special return packaging or shipping requirements.

5.5 The supplying library should state the due date or duration of the loan on the request form or on the material.

5.6 The supplying library should package the items to prevent damage in shipping.

5.7 The supplying library should notify the requesting library promptly when unable to fill a request and, if possible, state the reason the request cannot be filled.

5.8 The supplying library should respond promptly to requests for renewals. If the supplying library does not respond, the borrowing library may assume that the renewal has been granted for the same length as the original loan period.

5.9 The supplying library may recall materials at any time.

5.10 The supplying library may suspend service to any requesting library which fails to comply with the provisions of this code. ■■

BIBLIOGRAPHY

Interlibrary loan personnel should be familiar with and use current editions of relevant documents and aids, including:

Boucher, Virginia. *Interlibrary Loan Practices Handbook.* Chicago: ALA, 1984.

"Confidentiality of Library Records, Section 52.4, ALA Policy Manual." In *ALA Handbook of Organization 1993/1994,* H146–H147. Chicago: ALA, 1993.

Copyrights, Pub. L. No. 94-533, 90 Stat. 2541 (codified as amended in scattered sections of 17 U.S.C.).

"Guidelines and Procedures for Telefacsimile and Electronic Delivery of Interlibrary Loan Requests." Chicago: Reference and Adult Services Division, 1993. (Available from ALA Headquarters Library.)

Guidelines for Packaging and Shipping Microforms. Chicago: Association for Library Collections and Technical Services, ALA, 1989. (Available from ALA Headquarters Library.)

Guidelines for Preservation Photocopying of Replacement Pages. Chicago: Association for Library Collections and Technical Services, ALA, 1989. (Available from ALA Headquarters Library.)

Guidelines for the Loan of Rare and Unique Materials. Chicago: Ad Hoc Committee on the Interlibrary Loan of Rare and Unique Materials, Rare Books and Manuscripts Section, Association of College and Research Libraries, ALA, *College & Research Libraries News* 54, no. 5 (May 1993): 267–69.

Intellectual Freedom Manual. 4th ed. Comp. ALA Office of Intellectual Freedom. Chicago: ALA, 1992.

Interlibrary Loan Training and Continuing Education Model Statement of Objectives. Chicago: Interlibrary Loan Committee, Reference and Adult Services Division, ALA, 1990.

"International Lending: Principles and Guidelines for Procedure (1987)." *International Lending and Document Supply* 16 (Jan. 1988): 28–32.

"Library Bill of Rights, Section 53.1, ALA Policy Manual." In *ALA Handbook of Organization 1993/1994,* H147. Chicago: ALA, 1993.

Morris, Leslie, and Sandra Chass Morris. *Interlibrary Loan Policies Directory.* 4th ed. New York: Neal-Schuman, 1991.

National Commission on New Technological Uses of Copyrighted Work. "Guidelines for the Proviso of Subsection 108(g)(2)" (Called "CONTU Guidelines"). In H.R. Conf. Rep. No. 1773, 94th Cong., 2d sess., 1976.

National Information Standards Organization. *Interlibrary Loan Data Elements.* New Brunswick, N.J.: Transaction, 1990.

In addition, the following are necessary:

- Procedure manuals for online interlibrary loan systems
- Lending policies of all libraries to which requests are sent
- All consortium, state, or regional codes that apply
- The standard bibliographic tools and services necessary for verification and location of requested materials

I.   Introduction

Interlibrary loan is a primary service that supports the mission of the University Libraries by providing enhanced access to and delivery of research and instructional materials. The purpose of interlibrary loan is to obtain material not available in the Libraries and to provide material from the Libraries collection to other libraries.

II.   Definition

The term "interlibrary loan" encompasses a range of activities beyond the traditionally defined library to library transaction. Interlibrary loan service includes the use of commercial and fee-based document suppliers to obtain requested materials; the use of electronic technologies to transmit requests and documents; and may involve the delivery of items from libraries directly to patrons.

III. Conditions of Service

The Libraries adheres to the Colorado Interlibrary Loan Code, 1986, Colorado Interlibrary Loan Guidelines, 1991, Colorado Statewide Telefacsimile Guidelines for Interlibrary Loan Applications, 1990; the National Interlibrary Loan Code for the United States, 1993; International Lending: Principles and Guidelines for Procedure, 1987; special consortial arrangements and reciprocal agreements with other libraries; copyright laws and CONTU guidelines; and laws, rules and procedures pertaining to interlibrary loan activity and confidentiality of records as promulgated by the State of Colorado.

Statistics will be kept in accordance with internal, state, federal and Association of Research Libraries guidelines and requirements.

IV.   Interlibrary Borrowing

This service is offered to University of Colorado at Boulder faculty, faculty spouses, emeritus faculty, visiting scholars, staff, and students; and faculty of other University of Colorado campuses. The Libraries assumes most of the cost of this service and does not charge patrons, except in extraordinary circumstances.

Interlibrary borrowing is an integral element of collection development as stated in the national code. Accordingly, the Interlibrary Loan unit will obtain materials not owned by the University Libraries. This includes borrowing items that are loanable, obtaining photocopies, and purchasing documents as needed from document suppliers. This service may be used when items are designated as missing from the Libraries' collections, or when items are at the bindery and temporarily unavailable.

Materials which will not be obtained include: books owned by the Libraries and temporarily in use; recent newspapers not microfilmed; materials assigned for class texts or reserve;

reference books; rare or valuable materials; most audiovisual materials. Exceptions will be made on a case by case basis.

Requests must be submitted in writing on interlibrary loan paper forms or electronic formats with complete bibliographic information. Requests for photocopies must include an indication of compliance with the Copyright Law, Title 17 U.S. Code.

Service will be provided as quickly as possible. Turnaround time varies depending upon the lending library. Patrons will be notified via phone, mail or electronically. Photocopies may be sent via campus mail. In some instances conditions of use on loanable materials may be imposed by a lending library and must be strictly observed.

Requests for rush service are considered on a case by case basis and generally not available for undergraduates.

V.   Interlibrary Lending

This service is offered to other publicly supported or not-for-profit libraries which abide by the conditions set forth in the documents described in III. above. The Colorado Technical Reference Center (CTRC) primarily serves businesses and individuals who are not affiliated with the University of Colorado at Boulder. CTRC will also serve university offices and individuals who may wish to pay for expedited service.

Materials which ordinarily circulate to library users may be sent out on interlibrary loan. These include books, dissertations, master's theses and government documents. Holds are not placed on items in use. Most items are loaned for three weeks use. Exceptions include Colorado newspapers on microfilm and juvenile books which are loaned for one week. Fiche-to-fiche copies and photocopies are provided free of charge to Colorado libraries and at a small fee to libraries outside of the state.

Materials not loaned include periodicals, tapes, records, disks, and items in non-circulating collections.

Requests for items from the Libraries are accepted via OCLC, ARIEL or other electronic system; via fax as set forth in the Colorado Telefacsimile Guidelines; and via courier or mail on ALA Interlibrary loan forms. Rush requests are accommodated as time and staffing permit. Lending priorities may be designated based on the Libraries' consortial arrangements and reciprocal agreements.

Interlibrary lending will provide speedy turnaround on most items, usually responding within two days.

UNIVERSITY
LIBRARIES

INFORMATION DELIVERY SERVICES

MAKING
CONNECTIONS

INTERLIBRARY LOAN

Purpose
A wide variety of materials can be obtained through Interlibrary Loan (ILL). This service broadens your research scope by allowing you to use materials that are not owned by the University Libraries.

Eligibility
Currently enrolled students, faculty and spouses and staff of the University of Colorado, Boulder may use the services of Interlibrary Loan by presenting a valid UCB ID.

Materials Offered
Books, theses and dissertations, musical scores and some materials reproduced in microform, such as newspapers, can be borrowed. Photocopy of non-circulating materials, primarily periodical articles, can be requested in accordance with the copy-right law. Items missing from the University Libraries can also be obtained.

Materials Not Offered
Unfortunately, we are unable to obtain the following materials: books owned by this library and temporarily in use; periodical volumes; recent newspapers not microfilmed; materials intended for reserve; bulky or fragile items; audio tapes, video tapes and compact disks; reference books; and rare or valuable materials such as manuscripts.

Cost
The University Libraries pays for most interlibrary loan costs.

Location of the Office
Interlibrary Loan is located in Norlin Library-Room E156-inside the east entrance, to the right of the Security Office. The hours of service are 10 a.m. to 5 p.m., Monday through Friday. When our office is closed and the Reference desk is staffed, you may pick up your ILL materials by asking at the Reference Desk. The ILL telephone number is 492-6176.

How Interlibrary Loan Works
Make sure the material is not located in the University Libraries before submitting a request. Check the Public Access Catalog (PAC), the Reference Department, and other resources, such as the Catalog of Serials, and the Government Publications Department.

Please submit requests on forms available to the right of the ILL public window. There are specific forms for books, theses and dissertations, newspapers and photocopy of periodical articles. For faster service, accurate and complete bibliographic citations must be supplied, along with the source of the citation and full personal information. A copy of the original citation will expedite the process.

Plan Ahead
Typically, two to three weeks is needed to process in-state requests and receive them. Out-of-state requests take longer. When requesting materials, please be aware that the time taken for material to arrive depends upon the difficulty of the request, how near the lending library is to Boulder, and how long lending libraries spend on the request.

Notification
When material arrives, you'll be notified by mail. Photocopies may be sent to your campus box.

Loan Period

The loan period and renewal options are determined by the lending library. The loan period is usually two weeks. Photocopies can be kept by the requestor. Some lending libraries may specify special conditions regarding the use of their materials, such as "No Renewals" or "In Library Use Only."

Returning Materials

All materials borrowed through Interlibrary Loan must be returned to the Interlibrary Loan Office. Late return of materials jeopardizes the ability of the University Libraries to borrow from other libraries in the future. Please leave the yellow or orange book bands attached to the material. When the office is closed, use the book return to the right of the Interlibrary Loan door under the window.

COLORADO TECHNICAL REFERENCE CENTER

A Research and Information Delivery Service For Business and Industry

"Knowledge is of two kinds. We know a subject ourselves, or we know where we can find information upon it."

—Boswell

The Colorado Technical Reference Center (CTRC) offers document delivery and custom research services to businesses and professionals in Colorado and throughout the world. CTRC is an on demand, fee based information service of the University Libraries. Operating with over 25 years of experience, the Center accesses an international network of library catalogs, online resources and databases. CTRC specializes in knowing where to look for information and how to obtain it.

The center provides data and documents companies need to make informed business decisions. CTRC offers expertise in researching industry and market trends, competitive intelligence, emerging technologies, and patent and trademark searches.

For more information contact CTRC at:
Phone: (303) 492-8774
Fax: (303) 492-9775
Email: ctrc@spot.colorado.edu

CTRC SERVICES

Document Delivery

CTRC provides documents to companies from the University Libraries collection, and accesses an international network of suppliers to provide documents that are not available locally. This network includes national and international libraries such as the British Library Document Supply Centre, Library of Congress, and the National Technical Information Service.

Research Services

When businesses need information quickly, CTRC uses electronic resources to find what clients need when they need it. Whether it is a government statistic, current market trends, or an in-depth literature review, CTRC's information specialists can assist in finding the right information.

Online Research

CTRC accesses over 500 multidisciplinary databases, ranging from Dow Jones financial services to NASA research. Major services:

- DIALOG Information Services
- LEGI-SLATE: U.S. legislation and federal regulations
- NASA/RECON: NASA sponsored, scientific and technical research
- DATATIMES: newspapers and financial services
- STN International: scientific and technical
- Internet resources

A computer literature search scans thousands of journal articles and technical reports in minutes. Using keywords, a database search replaces long hours in a library with an efficient, cost-effective retrieval process.

Custom Research

When companies need to solve a problem and the information is not in databases, CTRC will use traditional library resources, innovative problem solving and nontraditional research to find answers.

157

SELF-ADDRESSED

TO:

University of Colorado at Boulder
INTERLIBRARY LOAN SERVICE
UNIVERSITY LIBRARIES
BOULDER, COLORADO 80309-0184

RETURN POSTAGE GUARANTEED—ADDRESS CORRECTION REQUESTED

MAY BE OPENED FOR POSTAL INSPECTION IF NECESSARY

FROM:

BLANK

FROM: **University of Colorado at Boulder** INTERLIBRARY LOAN SERVICE UNIVERSITY LIBRARIES UNIVERSITY OF COLORADO AT BOULDER BOULDER, COLORADO 80309-0184

TO:

RETURN POSTAGE GUARANTEED—ADDRESS CORRECTION REQUESTED

MAY BE OPENED FOR POSTAL INSPECTION IF NECESSARY

UNIVERSITY OF COLORADO AT BOULDER LIBRARIES

INTERLIBRARY LOAN SERVICE : REQUEST

BOOK

PLEASE PRINT CLEARLY. ABSENCE OF INFORMATION WILL DELAY FILLING YOUR REQUEST.

NAME	
TODAY'S DATE	
NEED BEFORE	
ADDRESS	
ADDRESS	
TELEPHONE	
DEPARTMENT	
CAMPUS BOX	
CAMPUS PHONE	
CU ID NUMBER	

AUTHOR

TITLE

SERIES

PLACE OF PUBLICATION

PUBLISHER

DATE OF PUBLICATION

EDITION   THIS EDITION ONLY ☐

STATUS	☐ FACULTY ☐ STAFF ☐ STUDENT
DEGREE IN PROGRESS	☐ DOCTORAL ☐ MASTERS ☐ BACHELORS ☐ OTHER:

SOURCE OF CITATION: AUTHOR, TITLE, DATE, VOLUME, PAGE, CALL NUMBER, ETC.

PLEASE DO NOT WRITE BELOW THIS LINE. OFFICE USE ONLY.

SOURCES CHECKED:

PAC [A,T,S,C]

PUB CAT [A,T,S]

SBC

GOV PUBS

OCLC

RLIN

MELVYL

ULS

NST

NUC

BLC

BIP

CBI

PROC

REQUEST OF:

VERIFIED IN:

SUPPLIED BY:

ACCEPTED BY

DATE OF TRANSACTIONS

RECEIVED

DUE

RENEWAL REQ

NEW DUE

RETURNED

COST

MESSAGES:

PERIODICAL

INTERLIBRARY LOAN SERVICE : REQUEST

PLEASE PRINT CLEARLY. ABSENCE OF INFORMATION WILL DELAY FILLING YOUR REQUEST.

PERIODICAL TITLE

ARTICLE AUTHOR

ARTICLE TITLE

	SOURCE OF CITATION. PLEASE GIVE SPECIFICS: AUTHOR, TITLE, DATE, VOLUME, PAGE, CALL NUMBER, ISSN, ETC.
VOLUME	
NUMBER	
DATE	
PAGES	

PLEASE SIGN REVERSE SIDE TO INDICATE YOU HAVE READ THE COPYRIGHT RESTRICTIONS WARNING. THANK YOU.

NAME

TODAY'S DATE

NEED BEFORE

ADDRESS

ADDRESS

TELEPHONE

DEPARTMENT

CAMPUS BOX

CAMPUS PHONE

CU ID NUMBER

STATUS
- ☐ FACULTY
- ☐ STAFF
- ☐ STUDENT

DEGREE
IN
PROGRESS
- ☐ DOCTORAL
- ☐ MASTERS
- ☐ BACHELORS
- ☐ OTHER:

PLEASE DO NOT WRITE BELOW THIS LINE. OFFICE USE ONLY.

REQUEST OF:

ACCEPTED BY

DATE OF TRANSACTIONS

RECEIVED

DUE

RENEWAL REQ

NEW DUE

RETURNED

MESSAGES:

VERIFIED IN:

SUPPLIED BY:

SOURCES CHECKED:

PAC [A,T,S,C]

UNCOVER

SBC

CARL

CCMLJLoc

OCLC

ULS

NST

BLDSC

KIST

CASSI

FAXON

NUC

ULRICH

RLIN

MELVYL

☐ CCG

☐ CCL

160

UNIVERSITY OF COLORADO AT BOULDER LIBRARIES

NEWSPAPER

INTERLIBRARY LOAN SERVICE : REQUEST

PLEASE PRINT CLEARLY. ABSENCE OF INFORMATION WILL DELAY FILLING YOUR REQUEST.

TITLE OF NEWSPAPER

PLACE OF PUBLICATION [PLEASE INCLUDE CITY AND STATE/COUNTRY]

DAY/MONTH/YEAR

SPECIFIC ARTICLE NEEDED

PAGES

SOURCE OF CITATION. PLEASE GIVE SPECIFICS: AUTHOR, TITLE, DATE, VOLUME, PAGE, CALL NUMBER, ETC.

PLEASE SIGN REVERSE SIDE TO INDICATE YOU HAVE READ THE COPYRIGHT RESTRICTIONS WARNING. THANK YOU.

NAME	
TODAY'S DATE	
LAST USE DATE	
ADDRESS	
ADDRESS	
TELEPHONE	
DEPARTMENT	
CAMPUS BOX	
CAMPUS PHONE	
CU ID NUMBER	
STATUS	☐ FACULTY ☐ STAFF ☐ STUDENT
DEGREE IN PROGRESS	☐ DOCTORAL ☐ MASTERS ☐ BACHELORIATE ☐ OTHER:

PLEASE DO NOT WRITE BELOW THIS LINE. OFFICE USE ONLY.

ACCEPTED BY	
DATE OF TRANSACTIONS	
RECEIVED	
DUE	
RENEWAL REQ	
NEW DUE	
RETURNED	
COST	
MESSAGES:	

REQUEST OF:

SOURCES CHECKED:

PAC [A,T,S,C]

PUB CAT

SBC

CARL

NIM [US] 1948-83

NIM [FOR] 1948-

VERIFIED IN:

☐ CCG

☐ CCL

OCLC

ULS

NST

NUC

SUPPLIED BY:

UNIVERSITY OF COLORADO AT BOULDER LIBRARIES

DISSERTATION & THESIS

INTERLIBRARY LOAN SERVICE : REQUEST

PLEASE PRINT CLEARLY. ABSENCE OF INFORMATION WILL DELAY FILLING YOUR REQUEST.

NAME	
TODAY'S DATE	
NEED BEFORE	
ADDRESS	
ADDRESS	
TELEPHONE	
DEPARTMENT	
CAMPUS BOX	
CAMPUS PHONE	
CU ID NUMBER	
STATUS	☐ FACULTY ☐ STAFF ☐ STUDENT
DEGREE IN PROGRESS	☐ DOCTORAL ☐ MASTERS ☐ BACHELORS ☐ OTHER:

AUTHOR

TITLE

UNIVERSITY

ABSTRACT READ?
PURCHASE?

DEGREE	
MASTERS	
PhD	
DATE	

SOURCE OF CITATION. PLEASE GIVE SPECIFICS: AUTHOR, TITLE, DATE, VOLUME, PAGE, CALL NUMBER, ETC.

PLEASE DO NOT WRITE BELOW THIS LINE. OFFICE USE ONLY.

ACCEPTED BY		DATE OF TRANSACTIONS
RECEIVED		
DUE		
RENEWAL REQ		
NEW DUE		
RETURNED		
COST		
MESSAGES:		

REQUEST OF:

VERIFIED IN:

SUPPLIED BY:

SOURCES CHECKED:

PAC [A,T,S,C]

PUB CAT [A,T,S]

OCLC

NUC

CDI

DAI

UMI-DISC

MA

ASLIB

CANADIANA

POLICY:

163

```
                            Welcome to
        Colorado State University's Electronic Access to Interlibrary Loan

        You will be prompted for your name, University identification number,
        and current Colorado State University affiliation.  After completing
        this information you may enter as many Interlibrary Loan requests
        as you want.

        Lending libraries vary in their response time, but the average time
        is 10 working days.


                        To begin, press <enter>

                Type "//EXIT" at any time to exit the program.

 lamar                                                              09.57
```

```
First Name:        Greg
Last Name:         Eslick
Id number:         478787214
Dept/Major:        CS
Status:            undergrad
Extension:         491-1867
Home phone:        484-8467
Fax number:
E-mail address:    eslick@cs.colostate.edu
Surge Student:     n

Campus address
---------------

  Department:      ILL
  Room No./Bldg:   Morgan Library

Is this all correct (Y or N)?
 lamar                                                              09:58
```

Colorado State University's Electronic Access to Interlibrary Loan

(M)ake a request
(R)equest a renewal
(A)sk for a status check
(H)elp

Enter choice:

Type "//EXIT" at any time to end program

09:58

lamar

Colorado State University's Electronic Access to Interlibrary Loan

Make a Request:

(A)rticle
(B)ook
(D)issertation/Thesis
(G)overnment Document/Technical Report
(M)ain menu

Enter Choice:

Type "//EXIT" at any time to exit

09:59

lamar

```
Title:  Old Doniphan Station
Author:  Miller, Mary Buck
Publisher:
Publishing date:  1945
Publishing place:  Atchison, KS
Edition:
This edition only:  yes
Citation found:  unverified
LCCN:
ISBN:
Not needed after: 930604
Notes:  Rush this in a hurry please!

Is this all correct (y or n)?
# lamar
                                                    10 03
```

```
Name of periodical:  Rheol. Acta
Place of publication:
Volume:  17
Number:  2
Pages:  201-3
Date of publication:  1978
Author of article:  Tormala,P.
Title of article:  Viscoeleasticity of polyethylene oxide melts.
Citation found:
ISSN:  0035-4511
Not needed after:  asap
Notes:

Is this all correct (y or n)?
# lamar
                                                    HB 26
```

Report or Document Number: EPA 68-03-6304
Title: Enhanced Methods for characterizing uncertainties in computational inten
sive models
Date: 1988.h
Author(s): WoodWard - Clyde consultants.
Issuing Agency or Institution and Location: EPA, Oakland, CA
Citation found:
Not needed after:
Notes:

Is this all correct (y or n)?
■ lamar
                                                                        AR 39

Author: Byron, Lorene Sandra
Title: A Comparative Evaluation of Two Indexing Languages
Location: Univ. of Wisconsin - Madison
Degree: PHD
Date: 1974
Citation found:
Not needed after: 5/15/94
Notes:

Is this all correct (y or n)?
■ lamar
                                                                        08 37

```
                    INTERLIBRARY LOAN (ILL) HELP
                         - 20 Questions -

            If you don't find the information you need,
                    please call ILL at 491-1868


1.      Who can use ILL?
2.      How long does ILL take?
3.      What does ILL cost?
4.      What are ILL's hours?
5.      Where is ILL?

6.      What items can I get through ILL?
7.      How much information do I need?
8.      Do I need to give ILL a call number?
9.      How many items can I request at a time?
10.     Can my book be renewed?




            Choice (0 to quit) or <enter> to continue):
 lamar
                                                          10:01
```

```
                    INTERLIBRARY LOAN (ILL) HELP
                         - 20 Questions -

            If you don't find the information you need,
                    please call ILL at 491-1868


11.     What libraries participate in ILL?
12.     How does ILL decide who to borrow items from?
13.     Will I know if my request isn't filled?
14.     What is a status check?
15.     What is a last usable date?

16.     What do I do if I need a rush?
17.     What are my options if ILL cannot get my material fast
        enough?
18.     What is an LCCN, and where can I find it?
19.     What is an ISSN, and where can I find it?
20.     What is an ISBN, and where can I find it?

                         Choice:
 lamar
                                                          10:39
```

Patron Response Form

REPORT

UNIVERSITY OF COLORADO AT BOULDER LIBRARIES

INTERLIBRARY LOAN SERVICE

WE ARE RETURNING YOUR INTERLIBRARY LOAN REQUEST FORM FOR THE REASON INDICATED BELOW. IF YOU WISH TO SPEAK WITH US CONCERNING THIS REQUEST, PLEASE BRING THE ORIGINAL REQUEST FORM AND THIS REPORT WITH YOU. WE HAVE NOT KEPT A COPY. THANK YOU.

MATERIAL IS IN OUR LIBRARIES

☐ AND IS BEING HELD FOR YOU
  ☐ UNTIL: _____
  ☐ CIRC DESK: _____

☐ BUT IS CHECKED-OUT
  ☐ YOU MAY PLACE A RECALL/HOLD
  ☐ CIRC DESK: _____

☐ BUT IS NON-CIRCULATING
  ☐ LOCATED BY TITLE ON THE CURRENT PERIODICALS SHELF
  ☐ LOCATION: _____

☐ CALL NUMBER: _____

MISCELLANEOUS

☐ AVAILABLE ONLY AS PHOTOCOPY OR MICROFILM. CAN YOU USE IN THIS FORMAT?

☐ MATERIAL TOO NEW TO BE AVAILABLE FOR LOAN FROM OTHER LIBRARIES. PLEASE TRY AGAIN IN THREE TO TWELEVE MONTHS.

☐ UNABLE TO LOCATE IN U.S. LIBRARIES.

☐ SORRY, UNABLE TO SUPPLY BEFORE YOUR DEADLINE EXPIRED. PLEASE RESUBMIT THIS REQUEST IF YOU ARE STILL INTERESTED IN OBTAINING THE MATERIAL.

☐ CANNOT IDENTIFY FROM ABBREVIATION(S). PLEASE SUPPLY COMPLETE INFORMATION.

☐ LENDING LIBRARY INFORMS US THIS CANNOT BE LOCATED AS CITED.

☐ OTHER: _____

☐ COPYRIGHT LAW PROHIBITS COPYING THIS MATERIAL.

☐ PLEASE SIGN THE COPYRIGHT STATEMENT ON THE BACK OF THE REQUEST FORM. YOUR SIGNATURE IS REQUIRED BEFORE WE CAN PROCEED.

☐ UNABLE TO VERIFY FROM INFORMATION YOU SUPPLIED. PLEASE BRING IN MORE INFORMATION OR YOUR WRITTEN SOURCE OF REFERENCE. WE WILL AGAIN ATTEMPT TO VERIFY THE REQUEST.

☐ REQUEST WAS RETURNED UNFILLED BY: _____

THIS PROBABLY MEANS THE MATERIAL IS NON-CIRCULATING.

DATE OF THIS REPORT: _____

INITIALS: _____

Book Sleeve

INTERLIBRARY LOAN SERVICE, CAMPUS BOX 184, UNIVERSITY OF COLORADO LIBRARIES, BOULDER, COLORADO 80309

FOR _____

DUE AT INTERLIBRARY LOAN OFFICE. Open 8-5, Monday-Friday*

Under the National Interlibrary Loan Code we are obliged to honor any conditions set by the lending library. Please note the special conditions of this loan checked below:

☐ **FOR USE IN LIBRARY ONLY**

☐ **NO RENEWAL**

☐ **PHOTOCOPYING NOT PERMITTED**

☐ **SIGN SIGNATURE SHEET**

If book is renewable, a request for renewal may be made when there is a special need. Please ask for this privilege at least FOUR DAYS PRIOR TO DUE DATE indicated above.

Failure to return books on time may jeopardize future borrowing privileges for you and for this library.

DATE OF NOTICE _____

Please do not remove this slip.

_____

*Use book drop next to the Interlibrary Loan door when office is closed.

_____

University of Colorado at Boulder

UNIVERSITY OF COLORADO AT BOULDER LIBRARIES

INTERLIBRARY LOAN SERVICE

IT'S HERE!

DATE:

The item you requested is waiting for you to pick up at the Interlibrary Loan Office.
Please bring this letter with you. Thank you.

AUTHOR/TITLE:

☐ Article to keep.

☐ Book to be returned:

☐ Microform to be returned:

☐ In library use only.

☐ Overdue. Please return at once.

Interlibrary Loan Office
Room E156
Norlin Library
CB 184
University of Colorado
Boulder, CO 80309

303-492-6176

Hours
Monday - Friday
8 AM - 5 PM

J

Patents

Margaret M. (Peggy) Jobe

A patent grants to inventors exclusive rights to their inventions for a limited period of time. In return for this protection, the governments of the United States of America and other countries, disclose details of the patent to the public to promote the usefulness of inventions. Patent research is a very specialized area of law and librarianship. Consult *Patent Searching for Librarians and Inventors*[1] for information on patent research.

The following bibliographic elements are commonly used to describe patents:
- Country or Agency of Issue (An example of an agency would be the European Patent Office which can obtain patent protection for the 17 member states of the European Patent Organization)
- Patent number
- Title
- Name of the Inventor
- Year of Issue
- Date of application
- Assignee (if any)

At a bare minimum, interlibrary loan departments need to know the country or agency of issue and patent number to obtain copies of patents. Since numbers can easily be transposed at any stage of the interlibrary loan or document delivery process, it is recommended that requests include the country or agency of issue, patent number, title, inventor, and year of issue. All requests for patents should be clearly marked "patent"; for example, "United States Patent" should precede the patent number on a request.

United States Patent and Trademark Office

Copies of United States patents can be obtained from the United States Patent and Trademark Office and its depository libraries throughout the United States. The Patent Office supplies uncertified copies of patents for a small fee in one to two weeks. Patent depository libraries will also make copies, but the depth of historic patent collections available at depository libraries may vary widely as will fees and services of these libraries. The full text of United States patents is also available online for patents issued 1974 to the present from many online database vendors. In November of 1995 the United States Patent and Trademark Office made the *U.S. Patents Bibliographic Database* (below) freely available on the Internet.

Commissioner of Patents & Trademarks
Washington, DC 20231
Telephone: 703-305-4350 ($3.00 per copy for uncertified patents)
Telephone: 703-308-9726, 9727, 9728 ($25.00 per copy for certified patents)
WWW: http://www.uspto.gov/
- U.S. Patents, Patent number required to fill orders.

U.S. Patents Bibliographic Database
WWW: http://patents.cnidr.org:4242/
- Online bibliographic database of U.S. patents 1976–1995, patent numbers 3,930,271–5,446,924 as of Jan. 12, 1996. Abstracts of patents available for patents granted 1994– . This database is a good verification tool for U.S. patents issued after 1975.

Reprinted with the permission of Margaret M. Jobe, Government Publications Librarian for International Documents, University of Colorado at Boulder

Patent and Trademark Depository Libraries

Directory of Patent Depository Libraries. Washington, DC: Department of Commerce, Patent and Trademark Office, 1986.

- Phone numbers and addresses including detailed information about collections, but dated.

Patent and Trademark Depository Libraries.
WWW: http://www.uspto.gov/web/ptdl/ptdl.html

- Online phone/address list of U.S. Patent and Trademark Libraries. Holdings and interlibrary loan policies vary by library. Contact libraries individually for information about collections and services.

Document Delivery Vendors with Patent Services

Numerous document delivery services offer patent copies. Many of the document delivery services rely on depository library collections, collections in major universities, and other vendors to fill orders. The following document delivery vendors have captive paper, microprint, or electronic collections of United States and international patents and offer various patent services. Several vendors offer translation services for international patent documents. Many vendors have product and price information on the World Wide Web (WWW) which may be more current than printed literature. Since document delivery prices are subject to constant change, contact the vendors by phone, mail, e-mail or via the World Wide Web for current price and delivery options.

CAS Document Delivery Service
2540 Olentangy River Rd.
P.O. Box 3012
Columbus, OH 43210-1112
USA
Telephone: 800-678-4337
Telephone: 614-447-3670
Fax: 614-447-3648
E-mail: ds@cas.org
Telex: 6842086 via WUI
WWW: http://www.cas.org/Support/dds.html

- U.S. Patents 1971– , and most international chemical patents published since 1978.

Derwent International
Patents Copy Service
PO Box 243
14 Great Queen Street
London WC2B 5DE
United Kingdom
Telephone: 44 171 344 2859
Fax: 44 171 344 2971
E-mail: patents@derwent.co.uk
WWW: http://www.derwent.co.uk/

- U.S. and International Patents, translation services, current awareness, patent status.

KR Source One
429 Union Avenue
Westbury, NY 11590-3202
USA
Telephone: 800-238-3458
Fax: 516-997-0891
WWW: http://www.dialog.com/dialog/krinfo/source-one/home.html

- U.S. and International Patents.

Patent Express
The British Library
Science Reference and Information Service
25 Southampton Buildings
London WC2A 1AW
United Kingdom
Telephone: 44 171 412 7926, 7927, 7928, 7929
Fax: 44 171 412 7930
Fax (US toll-free number): 800-325-2221
E-mail: patent-express@bl.uk
Telex: 266959 SCIREF G
WWW: http://icarus.bl.uk/sris/pexpress.html
- U.S. and International Patents, translation services.

Rapid Patent Service
1725 Duke Street, Suite 250
Arlington, VA 22313
USA
Telephone: 800-336-5010
Fax: 800-457-0850
E-mail: rpinfo@rapidpat.com
- U.S. and International Patents, patent searches, translations.

Online Patent Database and Full-Text Vendors

The online database industry has gone through an active period of consolidation and change in the 1990's. Many vendors publish or produce information in a variety of formats including paper, CD-ROM databases, and online interactive databases. The following vendors offer access to online fee-based databases to search and retrieve United States and international patent bibliographic data and full text patent documents. In many cases the database producer (as distinguished from the vendor) is also a document supplier. Derwent produces many of the databases available from online vendors and supplies copies of the patents through its document delivery services. The following online vendors were chosen because they offer access to a variety of United States and international bibliographic and full-text patent databases. CD-ROM databases were excluded from this list because of the ongoing purchase commitment.

Dialog
Knight-Ridder Information, Inc.
2440 El Camino Real
Mountain View, CA 94040
USA
Telephone: 415-254-8800
Fax: 415-254-8123
E-mail: customer@www.dialog.com
WWW: http://www.dialog.com/
- U.S. and International Patent databases.

Questel/Orbit
France Telecom Group
8000 Westpark Drive
McLean, VA 22102
USA
Telephone: 703-442-0900
Telephone: 800-456-7248

Fax: 703-893-4632
WWW: http://www.bedrock.com:80/patents/
- U.S. and International Patent databases, document delivery through its Questal/Orbit PATService.

STN International
Chemical Abstracts Service
2540 Olentangy River Road
Columbus, OH 43210
USA
Telephone: 800-848-6533
Fax: 614-447-3798
E-mail: help@cas.org
WWW: http://www.cas.org/stn.html
- U.S. and International Patent databases.

Intellectual Property Offices on the World Wide Web (WWW)

Additional information about United States and international patents can be obtained on the Internet at the following World Wide Web addresses:

Austrian Patent Office
WWW: http://www.ping.at/patent/index.htm

Brazilian Patent Office
WWW: http://www.bdt.org.br/inpi/

Canadian Intellectual Property Office
WWW: http://info.ic.gc.ca/opengov/cipo/

European Patent Office
WWW: http://www.austria.eu.net/epo/

Intellectual Property (IP) Department Hong Kong Government
WWW: http://pluto.houston.com.hk:80/hkgipd/

Swedish Patent and Registration Office
WWW: http://www.prv.se/

United Kingdom Patent Office
WWW: http://www.netwales.co.uk/ptoffice/

United States Patent and Trademark Office
WWW: http://www.uspto.gov/

World Intellectual Property Organization
WWW: http://www.uspto.gov/wipo.html

Note
1. Timothy Lee Wherry, *Patent Searching for Librarians and Inventors* (Chicago: American Library Association, 1995).

Acknowledgments
The author wishes to thank John R. Wheeler for his assistance in compiling this information.

 **Library of Congress Loan Division
Interlibrary Loan Policy**

ADDRESS: Library of Congress
Loan Division
Washington, DC 20540-5560
Telephone: (202) 707-5444
Fax   : (202) 707-5986

NUC   : DLC
OCLC : LCL (5 times in lender field)
RLIN : DCLW

GENERAL POLICIES:
Last resort requests only
No charge for Loan Division services
Loan period 30 days
Use in borrowing library only

BOOKS:
Lend most material in general collection
Do not lend material
- available from publisher
- published pre-1801
- genealogy, heraldry, most music
- local history (F below 1000)
- audio-visual material

PERIODICALS:
Do not lend original
Complimentary photocopies (maximum of 25 exposures)
  when possible and not elsewhere available

NEWSPAPERS:
Lend microfilm only

MICROFORMS:
Lend - if filmed by LC
  - others selectively

DISSERTATIONS:
Do not lend if film available from other sources

LAST RESORT

The Library of Congress is a source for material not available through local, state or regional libraries. Requests are accepted from recognized libraries that are listed in standard directories or are affiliated with networks and that make their own material available on interlibrary loan. School libraries below the college level should seek assistance with a local academic or public library system. Our policies are complementary to the U. S. National Interlibrary Loan Code, 1980. No charges are levied for interlibrary loan and we assume reciprocity.

REQUESTING PROCEDURES

Each request must be verified through electronic databases or other bibliographic tools, and submitted electronically, or on a separate ALA form. An LC call or card number, or ISSN/ISBN must be included whenever possible. If no bibliographic verification is available, a copy of the citation, footnote, CASSI printout, ULS record, or other published verification that would indicate the existence of an actual publication should be provided. If the requested material is not in our collection, we will try to provide another location using relevant non-standard sources. If a request is resubmitted, clearly indicate that it is a second request.

PHOTODUPLICATION

Complimentary photocopies of non-circulating material, up to 25 exposures, are provided by the Loan Division if the item is not available elsewhere. Requests over 25 exposures, multiple requests for the same material, and extensive photocopying and photoreproduction should be sent directly to the Library of Congress, Photoduplication Service, Washington, DC 20540-5234. The Photoduplication Service, a fee-for-service operation, can be contacted at Tel: (202) 707-5640, FAX: (202) 707-1771.

76-93 (rev 10/93)

COPY AND INFORMATION SERVICES

The Photoduplication Service provides expanded access to the collections of the Library of Congress through a wide range of reprographic services, from a single-page photocopy to color slides and microfilm. These services are designed to assist scholars, publishers, and members of the public unable to visit the Library and use the Library's collections in the reading rooms. Material is copied in accordance with U.S. copyright law and certain items cannot be copied, however, every effort will be made to respond to inquiries and fill requests in a timely manner. The service receives no appropriated funds and must recover all of its costs, including the cost of identifying and retrieving material, through service fees. Other information on products, services, and prices can be obtained by contacting:

> Library of Congress
> Photoduplication Service
> Washington, DC 20540-5230
>
> Tel: (202) 707-5640
> Fax: (202) 707-1771
>
> Hours: 8:30 AM - 4:45 PM
> Monday - Friday (except holidays)

Before we can proceed with an order, the Photoduplication Service requires an **advance payment** of $10.00 *per item* to cover the cost of identifying and assembling the material to be copied. We will apply the payment to the cost of photocopying short articles and to the final cost of all orders exceeding $10.00. Because a search is required even if an article is not located or cannot be properly identified from your citation, *the advance payment is non-refundable.*

This $10.00 prepayment covers the following services:

- Verification, search, and retrieval of items
- Photocopies of journal articles and short excerpts (up to 25 exposures)
- Subsequent searches for items temporarily unavailable
- Price quotations and partial payment for longer photocopy and microfilm orders
- Estimates for photographic reproductions
- Copyright clearance fee or copyright compliance requirements
- Alternative sources for material

Many regular patrons prefer to establish deposit accounts with the Photoduplication Service. Prepayment is not required for deposit account patrons.

Payment can be made by cash, check, credit card (Visa or Mastercard), or money order drawn on a U.S. bank. International money orders and UNESCO coupons are also accepted. Please make checks and money orders payable to the Library of Congress Photoduplication Service and include a daytime phone number with your order. Customers paying by credit card or having a deposit account may order by fax.

An Alternative - Free Interlibrary Loan Service

Individuals seeking material from the general book collections of the Library of Congress may consider requesting items on interlibrary loan through a local public library. The Library of Congress provides free assistance through its Loan Division to libraries worldwide. In some cases, these loan and copying services are equivalent to those provided by the Photoduplication Service.

25-71c (rev 10/94)

PRICE LIST FOR SELECTED SERVICES
Effective October 1, 1994

The prices listed below apply to basic copying of routine material. Additional charges may be necessary to cover unusual variations in size, format, or density, to provide customized service, or for extensive reference work. Quality is dependent on the condition of the materials being reproduced. For specific estimates or descriptions of numerous additional products and services, write the Library of Congress, Photoduplication Service, Washington, DC 20540-5230, or telephone 202-707-5640, Fax 202-707-1771.

PHOTOCOPY SERVICE

The prices listed below are for general copying of textual material, including journal articles, books, microfilmed newspapers, maps, or any other material that can be copied satisfactorily using an office photocopier or equivalent technology. **Prices for photocopying including postage and handling.**

Photocopy (including journal articles)

Each article, not to exceed 25 exposures (approximately 50 pages) $10.00
Other photocopying beyond 25 exposures, per exposure .... .50
Minimum charge per volume/item handled 3.00
Minimum charge per order 10.00
Foldout charts or other variations in material format
    that require reduction and/or filming in parts, per exposure 2.00

Color Photocopy

Text/color material overall size not exceeding:
8″ × 11″, per exposure .... $ 2.50
11″ × 17″, per exposure 5.00
Minimum charge per order 10.00

Reader Print from Microfilm (frame-by-frame enlargement from microfilm reader printer)

Enlargement up to 11″× 17″ per exposure .... $ 1.00
Minimum charge per citation 3.00
Minimum charge per order 10.00

Note: This process is recommended for printing microfilm of standard size newspapers although they may be reduced in size and/or may require two exposures per page.

Copyflo Print from Microfilm (automatic 14x enlargement from roll of negative microfilm)

Rate per foot (generally 8 exposures per foot of microfilm) .... $ 2.00
Minimum charge per order 20.00

Note: Newspapers and other large format material may not be legible if printed by this process.

National Agricultural Library
Interlibrary Loan Policy

The National Agricultural Library (NAL) makes its collections available to on-site users and to others worldwide through document delivery services and interlibrary loan. NAL offers a variety of delivery formats and methods. Document Delivery services include photocopy and microform duplication. Circulating materials from the collection are loaned to U.S. and Canadian libraries. Delivery methods include telefacsimile, Ariel, express mail and standard U.S. Postal Service.

The National Agricultural Library (NAL) expects individuals who are not employees of the U.S. Department of Agriculture to submit requests first to their local and state libraries before submitting requests to NAL. Document delivery is available to individuals through their local libraries. NAL loans items and provides photocopies from its collection only to other libraries, media centers, and information centers. As an AGLINET participant, NAL provides free document delivery service for materials published in the United States to AGLINET libraries. Requests are accepted by mail, telefacsimile, electronic mail, Ariel, OCLC, and DOCLINE.

Information on NAL holdings and details about policies may be requested by telephone at 301-504-5755, by telefacsimile at 301-504-5675, or by electronic mail at circinfo@nal.usda.gov.

Submit requests for audiovisual materials at least 4 weeks before intended show date, indicating show date and an alternate if possible. Specify format if more than one is given in the citation.

Requests by mail
Submit requests on the American Library Association (ALA) or the International Federation of Library Associations and Institutions (IFLA) interlibrary loan request forms. Submit one form for each request. Mail requests to:

> USDA, ARS, National Agricultural Library
> Document Delivery Services Branch, ILL, 4th floor
> 10301 Baltimore Avenue
> Beltsville, Maryland 20705-2351

Electronic mail and Ariel requests
Submit one document delivery request per electronic mail or Ariel message. Submit requests to lending@nal.usda.gov. NAL's Ariel address is 198.202.222.162. The following data elements are required in electronic requests:

1. Requestor's address in block format with at least two blank lines above and below.
2. Complete citation including verification.
3. Authorizing official's name.
4. Statement of copyright law compliance.
5. Indication of willingness to pay charges.
6. NAL call number if available.

OCLC and DOCLINE requests
NAL's OCLC symbol is AGL. NAL's DOCLINE libid is nal61.

Copyright Compliance
Copyright material will be copied in compliance with copyright law (Title 17, U.S. Code) and the CONTU Guidelines, therefore, with each request, NAL requires a statement indicating compliance with copyright regu-

lations and a signature of the individual responsible for copyright compliance. Monographs will not be copied in their entirety. Special arrangements must be made for microfilm of entire issues or long runs of a journal title.

Verification
The title of the reference tool that indicates that the requested item is owned by NAL must appear on the request. If this cannot be verified, indicate what tools have been searched. Include verification or the source of the citation on each request. If the citation is from one of NAL's bibliographic databases, AGRICOLA and ISIS, indicate the NAL call number on the request.

Interlibrary Loan
The National Agricultural Library loans monographs and other circulating materials such as audiovisual titles and computer software to other libraries in the U.S. and Canada. The standard loan period is 28 days, or less if indicated on the date due slip. One renewal for 28 days may be granted if the renewal request is received prior to the due date. The borrowing library is responsible for any loss or damage from the time the material is charged out until it is received by NAL. In case of loss or damage, the borrowing library is responsible for repair or replacement costs.

NAL does not loan the following materials: serials (except USDA serials), rare or reference books, reserve copies of materials, conference and symposia proceedings, titles in high demand for on-site use, and microforms. Photocopy or microform will be supplied automatically if the requesting organization indicates that this is acceptable on the interlibrary loan form.

Document Delivery Services
Photocopy or microforms of non-circulating materials and journal articles will be supplied if the requesting library indicates that this is acceptable. Submit a separate interlibrary loan form for each article required. Indicate willingness to pay and compliance with copyright law. NAL will deliver up to 30 pages by Ariel or telefacsimile if an Ariel address or fax number is provided on the request.

NAL fees for service
Photocopy or paper copy from microform:
- $5.00 for the first 10 pages or fraction copied from a single article or publication.
- $3.00 for each additional 10 pages or fraction.
Duplication of NAL-owned microfilm:
- $10.00 per reel
Duplication of NAL-owned microfiche:
- $5.00 for the first fiche and $0.50 for each additional fiche per title.

Fees include postage and handling, and are subject to change. Invoices are issued quarterly by the National Technical Information Service (NTIS), 5285 Port Royal Road, Springfield, Virginia, 22161. Do not send prepayment with your request.

Direct **comments or questions** about NAL programs and policies to:

Head, Document Delivery Services Branch
U.S. Department of Agriculture, Agricultural Research Service
National Agricultural Library
10301 Baltimore Avenue
Beltsville, Maryland 20705-2351

301-504-6503 (voice)
ddsbhead@.nal.usda.gov (electronic mail)
301-504-5675 (telefacsimile)

NATIONAL INSTITUTES OF HEALTH
NATIONAL LIBRARY OF MEDICINE
FACT SHEET

A World of Knowledge for the Nation's Health   May 1995

INTERLIBRARY LOAN POLICY

Most of the literature in the general and historical collections of the National Library of Medicine (NLM) is available for interlibrary loan to any library. NLM does not loan directly to individuals. Libraries should send requests via DOCLINE®, NLM's automated ILL request and referral system, through the National Network of Libraries of Medicine™ (NN/LM™). Requests should be sent directly to NLM only for those titles not held in NN/LM libraries. The statement "Not Available in Region" must appear on the interlibrary loan request. The Regional Medical Libraries (RMLs) have established lending procedures for their regions. To reach your RML, phone 1-800-338-RMLS. (See NLM Fact Sheet, National Network of Libraries of Medicine.) Loans requested from NLM must comply with the instructions in this policy and with the provisions of the National Interlibrary Loan Code of the American Library Association (ALA).

Methods of Borrowing

Requests will be accepted via the following methods:

1. DOCLINE, using the following Library Identification (LIBID) numbers:
   20209A-general collection
   20209C-general collection, Clinical Emergency
   20209B-historical collection
2. ALA or IFLA Interlibrary Loan Request Forms
3. Internet: ill@nlm.nih.gov
4. Telefacsimile: (301) 496-2809

Inquiries regarding ILL policy, practice and information pertaining to specific requests may be sent to the ILL internet address or the ILL fax number.

All requests for material to be photocopied must include the applicable statement of conformance to either the U.S. Copyright Act of 1976 (CCL) or Copyright Guidelines (CCG). Requests for loans of audiovisuals must include the CCL statement.

- Requests must include the authorizing person's name (if sent by electronic transmission) or the signature of the authorizing person at the borrowing library (if the form is sent by mail).

- NLM requires that a requesting library include its LIBID number and complete address on each request. The LIBID may be obtained by searching the DOCUSER® database on the MEDLARS® system or by contacting the appropriate Regional Medical Library.

- Each item or item segment (chapter, part of issue, etc.) must be requested separately.

- Citations verified in NLM publications or NLM databases should include NLM call numbers. The call number is identified by 02NLM in CATLINE® and recently printed catalogs and 04NLM or DNLM in catalogs printed before January 1983. NLM's CATLINE, SERLINE® and AVLINE® databases are accessible via the Locator system. To access Locator, set terminal emulation to VT100, telnet to *locator.nlm.nih.gov* and enter *locator* (in lower case letters) at the login: prompt.

- Give source of verification whenever possible, stating the specific NLM database containing the citation and the MEDLINE® or SERLINE unique identifier. Requests not verified or those which do not contain the summary of sources searched will not be processed.

- It is not possible for NLM to cancel a request once it is received.

Forms of Loans

Material will be provided in the original form, as a photocopy, or in microform. The form will be determined by NLM. Literature in the collection printed before 1914 is usually loaned in the form of microfilm or photocopy. These materials are available from the History of Medicine Division (HMD). Audiovisual titles are available for loan. Pre-1970 audiovisuals are available from the HMD.

U.S. DEPARTMENT OF HEALTH AND HUMAN SERVICES • Public Health Service • National Institutes of Health
Bethesda • Maryland • 20894

182

Computer-Assisted Instruction (CAI) materials are not loaned. (See NLM Fact Sheet, Access to Audiovisual Materials.) NLM will accept DOCLINE requests for transmission of materials via Ariel and fax. Ariel and fax requests must contain a complete citation, the Ariel address or facsimile phone number, an office telephone number, the complete address and LIBID number of the borrowing library.

Clinical Emergencies

To request fax transmission for emergency patient care requests, the CLINICAL EMERGENCY requirement must be indicated on the request. DOCLINE participants should prefix these requests to NLM at LIBID 20209C. During the hours the Library is open, these requests will be filled within 2 hours. If NLM is unable to fill the request, notification will be transmitted within 2 hours.

NLM will refer requests when *Refer On* is indicated as a comment on an electronically transmitted request or at the top of an ALA or IFLA form. Requests must be within the scope of the NLM collection, not available at NLM, carry complete citation information and be identified as held by another library.

The loan period for original material, microfilm and audiovisuals is one month, not including transit time. No renewals are granted.

Libraries with overdue items will be billed for lost materials after two overdue notices have been sent. Interlibrary loan service will not be provided to delinquent accounts.

Delivery and Returns

NLM will pay postage for outgoing loans. The borrowing library will pay postage for the return of borrowed materials; is responsible for material from time of receipt until returned and received at NLM; will replace materials lost or irreparably damaged, and meet repair cost for damaged materials. For the protection of the borrowing library, it is suggested that materials be insured or registered and that a return receipt be requested.

- Return post-1913 printed materials, post-1969 audiovisuals, and pre-1914 microfilm to the Collection Access Section. Return pre-1970 audiovisuals to the History of Medicine Division.

- Pack materials properly for return, and inspect all materials to ensure that all parts, including guides are returned. Protect corners and edges of books well and mail unbound materials flat. *Do not reuse NLM's jiffy bag.* Audiovisual materials should not be returned in fiber jiffy bags.

International Requests

Materials in the original form will not be loaned outside the U.S. International libraries may submit requests through their MEDLARS Center. If the item is not available from the MEDLARS Center and the Center does not have access to DOCLINE, international libraries may send requests to the ILL internet address, fax number, or by mail.

Charges

- U.S. libraries—$8.00 for each filled interlibrary loan in the form of a photocopy or loan of a book, audiovisual, or microfilm.

- There is a $3.00 surcharge for photocopies provided via telefacsimile.

- International libraries—$10.00 (U.S.) for each filled interlibrary loan in the form of a photocopy.

- Federal libraries - NLM will provide service free of charge to most federal libraries if the requesting library has complied with NN/LM policy for routing of interlibrary loan requests. Special arrangements will be made with high volume requestors.

- Do not send payment with the loan request. Invoices will be issued quarterly by the National Technical Information Service (NTIS), 5285 Port Royal Road, Springfield, Virginia 22161 and are payable to NTIS. Libraries are *expected* to establish a deposit account with NTIS to facilitate payment. Coupons are not accepted as payment for these charges. Interlibrary loan service will not be provided to libraries with delinquent accounts.

- Please keep a copy of each loan request form returned with each item. The loan request number appears on the summary page of the invoice and is needed to interpret the invoice charges. NLM is unable to provide a second copy at the end of each quarter.

Special Photographic Services

Photographs or slides of portraits, prints, charts, and other pictorial work require special procedures. Write to: Prints and Photographs Collection, History of Medicine Division (address below) for information and costs. Orders requiring copyright owner's permission will not be accepted unless accompanied by this permission in writing.

Interlibrary Loan Information

Address requests as follows:

1) For journal and monograph material published after 1913 and audiovisual material produced after 1969:

COLLECTION ACCESS SECTION

National Library of Medicine
LIBID: 20209A (Regular) or
20209C (Clinical Emergency)
8600 Rockville Pike
Bethesda, Maryland 20894
Telephone: (301) 496-5511
Fax: (301) 496-2809
Internet: ill@nlm.nih.gov

2) For journal and monograph material published before 1914 and audiovisual material produced before 1970:

HISTORY OF MEDICINE DIVISION

National Library of Medicine
LIBID: 20209B
8600 Rockville Pike
Bethesda, Maryland 20894
Telephone: (301) 496-5405
Fax: (301) 402-0872
Internet: ill@nlm.nih.gov

All NLM Fact Sheets are available via the NLM Gopher at *gopher://gopher.nlm.nih.gov:70/* and via anonymous ftp at *ftp://nlmpubs.nlm.nih.gov*

Federal Depository Library Program

The Federal Depository Libray Program was established by Congress to provide free public access to Government publications. Nearly 1400 public, academic, State, and law libraries serve as an information link with the Federal Government by maintaining collections of Government publications. These collections, which are tailored to local needs, are open to the public. Fifty-three of the libraries are designated as regional depository libraries. They have the responsibility of retaining material permanently and providing inter-library loan and reference services in their regions. They also assist the other depository libraries with the disposal of obsolete material.

Copies of documents no longer available through the GPO Sales Program can usually be found in regional depository collections. A complete listing of regional depositories follows. To obtain a complete listing of all depository libraries, write to:

Federal Depository Library Program
U.S. Government Printing Office
Superintendent of Documents
Stop: SM
Washington, DC 20402

ALABAMA
AUBURN UNIV. AT MONTGOMERY
   LIBRARY
7300 University Drive
Montgomery, AL 36117-3596
(205) 244-3650
FAX: (205) 244-0678

UNIVERSITY OF ALABAMA LIBRARIES
Documents Dept.—Box S
Tuscaloosa, AL 35487-9784
(205) 348-6046
FAX: (205) 348-8833

ALASKA
Served by Washington State Library

AMERICAN SAMOA
Served by the University of Hawaii

ARIZONA
DEPARTMENT OF LIBRARY, ARCHIVES
   AND PUBLIC RECORDS
Third Floor—State Capitol
1700 West Washington
Phoenix, AZ 85007
(602) 542-4417
FAX: (602) 542-4400 or 542-4500

ARKANSAS
Arkansas State Library
One Capital Mall
Little Rock, AR 72201
(501) 682-2326
FAX: (501) 682-1529

CALIFORNIA
CALIFORNIA STATE LIBRARY
Government Publications Section
P.O. Box 942837
Sacramento, CA 94237-0001
(916) 653-0085
FAX: (916) 654-0241

COLORADO
UNIV. OF COLORADO LIB.
Government Pub. Division
Campus Box 184
Boulder, CO 80309-0184
(303) 492-8834
FAX: (303) 492-8875

DENVER PUBLIC LIBRARY
Govt. Pub. Department
1357 Broadway
Denver, CO 80203
(303) 640-8874
FAX: (303) 640-8817

CONNECTICUT
CONNECTICUT STATE LIBRARY
Government Documents Unit
231 Capitol Avenue
Hartford, CT 06106
(203) 566-4971
FAX: (203) 566-3322

DELAWARE
Served by the University of Maryland

DISTRICT OF COLUMBIA
Served by the University of Maryland

FLORIDA
UNIVERSITY OF FLORIDA LIBRARIES
Library West
Documents Department
Gainesville, FL 32611
(904) 392-0367
FAX: (904) 392-7251

GEORGIA
UNIVERSITY OF GEORGIA LIBRARIES
Government Reference Dept.
Athens, GA 30602
(706) 542-8949
FAX: (706) 542-6522

GUAM
Served by the University of Hawaii

HAWAII
UNIVERSITY OF HAWAII LIBRARY
Govt. Documents Collections
2550 The Mall
Honolulu, HI 96822
(808) 956-8230
FAX: (808) 956-5968

IDAHO
UNIV. OF IDAHO LIBRARY
Documents Section
Moscow, ID 83843
(208) 885-6344
FAX: (208) 885-6817

ILLINOIS
ILLINOIS STATE LIBRARY
300 South Second Street
Springfield, IL 62701-1796
(217) 782-4887
FAX: (217) 782-6437

INDIANA
INDIANA STATE LIBRARY
Serials Documents Section
140 North Senate Avenue
Indianapolis, IN 46204
(317) 232-3686
FAX: (317) 232-3728

IOWA
UNIV. OF IOWA LIBRARIES
Govt. Documents Department
Iowa City, IA 52242
(319) 335-5925
FAX: (319) 335-5830

KANSAS
UNIVERSITY OF KANSAS
6001 Malott Hall
Lawrence, KS 66045-2800
(913) 864-4662
FAX: (913) 864-5380

KENTUCKY
UNIVERSITY OF KENTUCKY LIBRARIES
Govt. Pub. Department
Lexington, KY 40506-0039
(606) 257-8400
FAX: (606) 257-1563

LOUISIANA
LOUISIANA STATE UNIVERSITY
Middletown Library
Govt. Docs. Dept.
Baton Rouge, LA 70803
(504) 388-2570
FAX: (504) 388-6992

LOUISIANA TECHNICAL UNIV. LIBRARY
Prescott Memorial Library
Ruston, LA 71272-0046
(318) 257-4962
FAX: (318) 257-2447

MAINE
UNIVERSITY OF MAINE
Raymond H. Fogler Library
Tri-State Regional Documents Deposits
Orono, ME 04469
(207) 581-1681
FAX: (207) 581-1653

MARYLAND
UNIVERSITY OF MARYLAND
McKeldin Lib.—Doc. Div.
College Park, MD 20742
(301) 405-9165
FAX: (301) 403-4167

MASSACHUSETTS
BOSTON PUBLIC LIBRARY
Government Docs. Dept.
666 Boylston Street
Boston, MA 02117
(617) 536-5400 ext. 227
FAX: (617) 267-8273 or 267-8248

MICHIGAN
DETROIT PUBLIC LIBRARY
5201 Woodward Ave.
Detroit, MI 48202-4093
(313) 833-1025
FAX: (313) 832-5333

MICHIGAN STATE LIBRARY
Library of Michigan
717 West Allegan Street
P.O. Box 30007
Lansing, MI 48909
(517) 373-1307
FAX: (517) 373-3381 or 373-5700

MICRONESIA
Served by the University of Hawaii

MINNESOTA
UNIVERSITY OF MINNESOTA
Government Pubs. Division
409 Wilson Library
309 South 19th Street
Minneapolis, MN 55455
(612) 624-0241
FAX: (612) 626-9353

MISSISSIPPI
UNIVERSITY OF MISSISSIPPI LIB.
Williams Library
University, MS 38677
(601) 232-5857
FAX: (601) 232-5453

MISSOURI
UNIVERSITY OF MISSOURI AT
   COLUMBIA
Ellis Library-Government Documents
Columbia, MO 65201
(314) 882-6733
FAX: (314) 882-8044

MONTANA
UNIVERSITY OF MONTANA
Mansfield Library
Documents Division
Missoula, MT 59812
(406) 243-6700
FAX: (406) 243-6090

NEBRASKA
UNIVERSITY OF NEBRASKA-LINCOLN
Love Library
Documents Dept.
Lincoln, NE 68588-0410
(402) 472-2562
FAX: (402) 472-1531

NEVADA
UNIVERSITY OF NEVADA LIB.
Govt. Pub. Department
Reno, NV 89557-0044
(702) 784-6579
FAX: (702) 784-1751

NEW HAMPSHIRE
Served by the University of Maine

NEW JERSEY
NEWARK PUBLIC LIBRARY
5 Washington Street
Newark, NJ 07101-0630
(201) 733-7812
FAX: (201) 733-5648

NEW MEXICO
UNIVERSITY OF NEW MEXICO
General Library
Government Pub. Dept.
Albuquerque, NM 87131
(505) 277-5441
FAX: (505) 277-6019

NEW MEXICO STATE LIBRARY
Reference Department
325 Don Caspar Avenue
Santa Fe, NM 87503
(505) 827-3826
FAX: (505) 827-3820

NEW YORK
NEW YORK STATE LIBRARY
Cultural Education Center
Albany, NY 12230
(518) 474-3940
FAX: (518) 474-5163

NORTH CAROLINA
UNIVERSITY OF NORTH CAROLINA AT
   CHAPEL HILL
Davis Library
CB #3912, BA/SS Division
Chapel Hill, NC 27599
(919) 962-1151
FAX: (919) 962-0484

NORTH DAKOTA
NORTH DAKOTA STATE UNIVERSITY
   LIB.
P.O. Box 5599
Fargo, ND 58105
(701) 237-8863
FAX: (701) 237-7138

UNIVERSITY OF NORTH DAKOTA
Chester Fritz Library
Documents Department
Grand Forks, ND 58202
(701) 777-4630
FAX: (701) 777-3319

NORTHERN MARIANAS
Served by the University of Hawaii

OHIO
STATE LIBRARY OF OHIO
Documents Department
65 South Front Street
Columbus, Ohio 43266-0334
(614) 644-7061
FAX: (614) 644-7004

OKLAHOMA
OKLAHOMA DEPT. OF LIBRARIES
Government Documents
200 NE 18th Street
Oklahoma City, OK 73105
(405) 521-2502, ext. 252
FAX: (405) 525-7804

OKLAHOMA STATE UNIV. LIB.
Documents Department
Stillwater, OK 74078
(405) 744-6313
FAX: (405) 744-5183

OREGON
PORTLAND STATE UNIV. LIB.
Documents Department
P.O. Box 1151
Portland, OR 97207
(503) 725-4126
FAX: (503) 464-4524

PENNSYLVANIA
STATE LIBRARY OF PENN.
Government Pub. Section
P.O. Box 1601
Harrisburg, PA 17105
(717) 787-3752
FAX: (717) 783-2070

PUERTO RICO
Served by the University of Florida

RHODE ISLAND
Served by the Connecticut State Library

SOUTH CAROLINA
CLEMSON UNIVERSITY
Cooper Library
Documents Department
Clemson, SC 29634
(803) 656-5174
FAX: (803) 656-3025

UNIVERSITY OF SOUTH CAROLINA
Thomas Cooper Library
Documents/Microform Department
Green & Sumter Street
Columbia, SC 29208
(803) 777-4841
FAX: (803) 777-9405

SOUTH DAKOTA
Served by the University of Minnesota

TENNESSEE
MEMPHIS STATE UNIVERSITY LIB.
Government Documents Dept.
Memphis, TN 38152
(901) 678-2206
FAX: (901) 678-2511

TEXAS
TEXAS STATE LIBRARY
Public Services Department
P.O. Box 12927-Cap. Sta.
Austin, TX 78711
(512) 463-5455
FAX: (512) 463-5436

TEXAS TECH UNIV. LIBRARY
Govt. Documents Department
Lubbock, TX 79409
(806) 742-2268
FAX: (806) 742-1920

UTAH
UTAH STATE UNIVERSITY
Merrill Library, U.M.C. 30
Logan, UT 84322
(801) 750-1000 ext. 2683
FAX: (801) 750-2677

VERMONT
Served by the University of Maine

VIRGIN ISLANDS
Served by the University of Florida

VIRGINIA
UNIVERSITY OF VIRGINIA
Alderman Lib.-Public Doc.
Charlottesville, VA 22093-2498
(804) 924-3133
FAX: (804) 924-4337

WASHINGTON
WASHINGTON STATE LIBRARY
Documents Section
Olympia, WA 98504
(206) 753-4027
FAX: (206) 753-3546

WEST VIRGINIA
WEST VIRGINIA UNIV. LIB.
Documents Department
Morgantown, WV 26506-6069
(304) 293-3640
FAX: (304) 293-3640

WISCONSIN
ST. HIST. LIB. OF WISCONSIN
Government Pub. Section
816 State Street
Madison, WI 53706
(608) 264-6525
FAX: (608) 262-4711

MILWAUKEE PUBLIC LIBRARY
814 West Wisconsin Ave.
Milwaukee, WI 53233
(414) 278-2167
FAX: (414) 278-2137

WYOMING
Served by Utah State University

P U.S. Government Printing Office
Order Form

PLEASE PRINT OR TYPE ALL INFORMATION

ORDER FORM

MAIL TO:

U. S. Government Printing Office
Superintendent of Documents
Mail Stop: SSOP
Washington, DC 20402–9328

Customer's Telephone No.'s

Area Code | Home | Area Code | Office

MASTERCARD/VISA ACCEPTED

Credit Card No.

Date Customer Order Number

Customer's Name and Address

Expiration Date Month/Year

ZIP

Deposit Account Number

TO PLACE YOUR ORDER BY PHONE CALL OUR ORDER DESK AT 202-783-3238, MONDAY THROUGH FRIDAY, 7:30-4 EASTERN TIME

Stock No.	Quantity	Unit of Issue	List ID	☐ Publication	Title of	☐ Subscription	Unit Price	Total

TOTAL ENCLOSED $

SHIP TO: (If different from above)

ZIP

Unit of Issue	Explanation
EA	Each - single copy
KT	Kit of multiple items in a special container
PD	Pad containing multiple sheets
PK	Package containing multiple copies
SE	Set of multiple items
SU	Subscription

[THIS FORM MAY BE REPRODUCED]

GPO Form 3430
(R 11-91)

PRELIM. 13

U.S. Government Bookstores

In addition to the mail order service provided by the Superintendent of Documents, the U.S. Government Printing Office operates 24 bookstores around the country. These bookstores are located in major metropolitan areas across the country. Each store carries many of the Government's most popular publications, along with a selection of other books tailored to suit the interests and needs of its local clientele. They will be happy to special order any Government book currently for sale. All of our bookstores also accept VISA, MasterCard, and Superintendent of Documents Deposit account orders. To find the most convenient Government bookstore in your area, please refer to the listing provided below:

ALABAMA
O'Neill Building
2021 3rd Avenue North
Birmingham, AL 35203
(205) 731-1056
FAX: (205) 731-3444

CALIFORNIA
Arco Plaza, C-Level
505 South Flower Street
Los Angeles, CA 90071
(213) 239-9844
FAX: (213) 239-9848

Room 1023, Federal Building
450 Golden Gate Avenue
San Francisco, CA 94102
(415) 252-5334
FAX: (415) 252-5339

COLORADO
Norwest Banks Bldg.
201 W. 8th Street
Pueblo, CO 81003
(719) 544-3142
FAX: (719) 544-6719

Room 117, Federal Building
1961 Stout Street
Denver, CO 80294
(303) 844-3964
FAX: (303) 844-4000

DISTRICT OF COLUMBIA
U.S. Government Printing Office
710 North Capitol Street NW
Washington, DC 20401
(202) 512-0132
FAX: (202) 512-1355

Farragut West
1510 H Street NW
Washington, DC 20005
(202) 653-5075
FAX: (202) 376-5055

FLORIDA
Room 158, Federal Building
100 West Bay Street
Suite 100
Jacksonville, FL 32202
(904) 353-0569
FAX: (904) 353-1280

GEORGIA
First Union Plaza
999 Peachtree Street NE
Suite 120
Atlanta, GA 30309
(404) 347-1900
FAX: (404) 347-1897

ILLINOIS
One Congress Center
Suite 124
401 South State Street
Chicago, IL 60605
(312) 353-5133
FAX: (312) 353-1590

MARYLAND
Retail Sales Outlet
8660 Cherry Lane
Laurel, MD 20707
(301) 953-7974
(301) 792-0262
FAX: (301) 498-9109

MASSACHUSETTS
Thomas P. O'Neill Jr. Federal Bldg.
10 Causeway Street, Room 179
Boston, MA 02222
(617) 720-4180
FAX: (617) 720-5753

MICHIGAN
Suite 160, Federal Building
477 Michigan Avenue
Detroit, MI 48226
(313) 226-7816
FAX: (313) 226-4698

MISSOURI
120 Bannister Mall
5600 East Bannister Road
Kansas City, MO 64137
(816) 767-8225
FAX: (816) 767-8233

NEW YORK
Room 110, Federal Building
26 Federal Plaza
New York, NY 10278
(212) 264-3825
FAX: (212) 264-9318

OHIO
1st Floor, Federal Building
1240 East 9th Street
Cleveland, OH 44199
(216) 522-4922
FAX: (216) 522-4714

Room 207, Federal Building
200 North High Street
Columbus, OH 43215
(614) 469-6956
FAX: (614) 469-5374

OREGON
1305 S.W. First Avenue
Portland, OR 97201
(503) 221-6217
FAX: (503) 225-0563

PENNSYLVANIA
Robert Morris Building
100 North 17th Street
Philadelphia, PA 19103
(215) 597-0677
FAX: (215) 597-4548

Room 118, Federal Building
1000 Liberty Avenue
Pittsburgh, PA 15222
(412) 644-2721
FAX: (412) 644-4547

TEXAS
Room 1C50, Federal Building
1100 Commerce Street
Dallas, TX 75242
(214) 767-0076
FAX: (214) 767-3239

Texas Crude Building
801 Travis Street
Houston, TX 77002
(713) 228-1187
FAX: (713) 228-1186

WASHINGTON
Room 194, Federal Building
915 Second Avenue
Seattle, WA 98174
(206) 553-4270
FAX: (206) 553-6717

WISCONSIN
Room 190, Federal Building
517 East Wisconsin Avenue
Milwaukee, WI 53202
(414) 291-1304
FAX: (414) 297-1300

U.S. DEPARTMENT OF COMMERCE
TECHNOLOGY ADMINISTRATION

ORDER FORM

SHIP TO ADDRESS

PLEASE PRINT OR TYPE

CUSTOMER MASTER NUMBER (IF KNOWN)	DATE

ATTENTION / NAME

ORGANIZATION	DIVISION / ROOM NUMBER

STREET ADDRESS

CITY	STATE	ZIP CODE

PROVINCE / TERRITORY	FOREIGN POSTAL CODE

COUNTRY

PHONE NUMBER ( )	FAX NUMBER ( )

CONTACT NAME

METHOD OF PAYMENT

☐ Check / Money Order enclosed for $ _____ (PAYABLE IN U.S. DOLLARS)

☐ NTIS Deposit Account Number: _____

☐ VISA ☐ MasterCard ☐ American Express

CREDIT CARD NUMBER	EXPIRATION DATE

CARDHOLDER'S NAME

SIGNATURE (REQUIRED TO VALIDATE ALL ORDERS)

DTIC USERS ONLY

CODE

CONTRACT NUMBER (LAST SIX DIGITS)

ORDER BY PHONE (ELIMINATE MAIL TIME)
8:30 a.m. - 5:00 p.m. Eastern Time, M – F.
Sales Desk: (703) 487-4650
Subscriptions: (703) 487-4630
TDD (hearing impaired only): (703) 487-4639

ORDER BY FAX
24 hours/7 days a week: (703) 321-8547
To verify receipt of fax: call (703) 487-4679
7:00 a.m. – 5:00 p.m., Eastern Time, M – F.

ORDER BY MAIL
National Technical Information Service
5285 Port Royal Road
Springfield, VA 22161

RUSH SERVICE (DO NOT MAIL RUSH ORDERS)
1-800-553-NTIS
RUSH service available for additional fee.

FEDWORLD®
Please call for connect information: (703) 487-4608.

BILL ME
(U.S., Canada, and Mexico only.)
DO NOT USE THIS FORM.
NTIS will gladly bill your order, for an additional fee of
$7.50. A request to be billed must be on a purchase order
or company letterhead. An authorizing signature, contact
name, and telephone number should be included with this
request. Requests may be mailed or faxed.

NTIS HANDLING FEE	
Value of Order	**Handling Fee**
$10.00 or less	$2.00
$10.01 – $50.00	$4.00
$50.01 – $100.00	$6.00
Over $100.00	$8.00

Add $2.00 to handling fee for orders sent outside
the United States, Canada, and Mexico.

PRODUCT SELECTION   ☐ ORDER CONTINUED ON REVERSE

NTIS PRODUCT NUMBER (ORDERING BY TITLE ALONE WILL DELAY YOUR ORDER)	INTERNAL CUSTOMER ROUTING (OPTIONAL) UP TO 8 CHARACTERS	UNIT PRICE	PAPER COPY	MICRO-FICHE	MAGNETIC TAPE ✱	DISKETTE	CD-ROM	OTHER	INTERNATIONAL AIRMAIL FEE (SEE BELOW)	TOTAL PRICE
GAR		$							$	$
GAR		$							$	$
GAR		$							$	$
GAR		$							$	$
GAR		$							$	$

✱ CIRCLE REQUIREMENTS	3480 CARTRIDGE	1600 BPI	6250 BPI	LABELING STANDARD NONLABELED	FORMAT EBCDIC ASCII		SUBTOTAL (FROM OTHER SIDE)	$

PLEASE NOTE
Unless microfiche or other is specified, paper copy will be sent.

Please call the Sales Desk at (703) 487-4650 for information on multiple copy discounts available for certain documents, return policy, and price verification.

Out-Of-Print Surcharge
Effective 4/17/95, an out-of-print surcharge may apply to certain titles acquired by NTIS more than three years prior to the current calendar year; please call to verify price.

International Airmail Fees
Canada and Mexico add $4 per paper copy report; $1 per microfiche copy. Other countries add $8 per paper copy report; $1.25 per microfiche copy. (Paper copy reports and microfiche copies are shipped surface mail unless airmail is specified.)

TOTAL	$
HANDLING FEE PER ORDER (SEE CHART ABOVE)	$
GRAND TOTAL	$

Thank you for your order!
Prices are subject to change.

PRODUCT SELECTION

SIDE 2

NTIS PRODUCT NUMBER (ORDERING BY TITLE ALONE WILL DELAY YOUR ORDER)	INTERNAL CUSTOMER ROUTING (OPTIONAL) UP TO 8 CHARACTERS	UNIT PRICE	QUANTITY						INTERNATIONAL AIRMAIL FEE (SEE REVERSE)	TOTAL PRICE
			PAPER COPY	MICRO-FICHE	MAGNETIC TAPE ★	DISKETTE	CD-ROM	OTHER		
	GAR	$							$	$
	GAR	$							$	$
	GAR	$							$	$
	GAR	$							$	$
	GAR	$							$	$
	GAR	$							$	$
	GAR	$							$	$
	GAR	$							$	$
	GAR	$							$	$
	GAR	$							$	$
	GAR	$							$	$
	GAR	$							$	$
	GAR	$							$	$
	GAR	$							$	$
	GAR	$							$	$

★ CIRCLE REQUIREMENTS	3480 CARTRIDGE	1600 BPI	6250 BPI	LABELING		FORMAT			
				STANDARD	NONLABELED	EBCDIC	ASCII	**SUBTOTAL** (ENTER ON OTHER SIDE)	$

FREE CATALOGS AND INFORMATION

Call (703) 487-4650 and ask for any of the following free titles or check the appropriate boxes below and mail or fax form to NTIS.

☐ PR-827   NTIS Catalog of Products and Services

☐ PR-186   Published Search® Master Catalog

☐ PR-261   Directory of U.S. Government Software for Mainframes and Microcomputers

☐ PR-360-3   NTIS Price Schedule for the U.S., Canada, and Mexico

☐ PR-360-4   NTIS Price Schedule for Countries Outside the U.S., Canada, and Mexico

☐ PR-629   Directory of U.S. Government Datafiles for Mainframes and Microcomputers

☐ PR-746   Directory of Federal Laboratory & Technology Resources

☐ PR-758   Environmental Datafiles and Software Catalog

☐ PR-797   NTIS Alerts (formerly Abstract Newsletters) – customized current awareness bulletins

☐ PR-868   Environment Highlights

☐ PR-888   CD-ROMs & Optical Discs Available from NTIS

☐ PR-936   FedWorld® – Free Access to the Electronic Marketplace of U.S. and Foreign Government Information

4/95
All previous versions of this form are obsolete.

NTIS® is a registered trademark of the National Technical Information Service.
Published Search® is a registered trademark of the National Technical Information Service.
FedWorld® is a registered trademark of the National Technical Information Service.

189

Guidelines and Procedures for Telefacsimile and Electronic Delivery of Interlibrary Loan Requests and Materials

RASD MOPPS Interlibrary Loan Committee—
Approved by the RASD Board of Directors, February 8, 1994

1.0 INTRODUCTION

Telefacsimile (fax) and electronic document delivery (EDD) over the Internet are two methods of communication that have been adapted to the needs of libraries for quick and easy transmission of data. The fastest-growing application of these types of delivery in libraries is as a mechanism for the rapid relay of interlibrary loan requests and/or responses to those requests when they take the form of brief journal articles, excerpts from larger works, and other easily reproduced materials that have been requested through accepted communications channels.

These guidelines address the needs of libraries that use fax and EDD systems in the interlibrary borrowing and lending processes. As such, these guidelines are intended to enhance other interlibrary loan codes and guidelines currently in use and should be used in conjunction with the "National Interlibrary Loan Code for the United States, 1993" (*RQ*33 [Summer 1994]: 477–79), the copyright law (Title 17, U.S. Code), the National Commission on New Technological Uses of Copyrighted Works (CONTU) guidelines on "Photocopying Interlibrary Arrangements" including "Guidelines for the Provision of Subsection 108(g)(2)," and any state, regional, network, or consortium guidelines that may be in effect. These guidelines should be used to expedite interlibrary loan when no state, regional, network, or consortium guidelines apply.

The purposes of these guidelines are (1) to establish uniformity with regard to type of equipment to be used; (2) to recommend uniform practices with regard to equipment operation and administration; (3) to establish guidelines for borrowing and the formatting of requests to be transmitted; and (4) to set guidelines for responses to requests by lending libraries.

RQ 34, no.1, Fall 1994, p.32–33

2.0 EQUIPMENT

2.1 Fax equipment should be digital equipment compatible with the Consultative Committee for International Telephone and Telegraph (CCITT) Group III standards. The equipment should have, as a minimum, features providing automatic sending and receiving, and a document feeder that allows the transmission of multiple pages.

2.2 Each fax machine should have a dedicated telecommunication line to ensure high quality transmission and maximum access.

2.3 Other EDD equipment should be configured to send to and receive from other libraries using the same type of equipment.

3.0 GENERAL GUIDELINES

3.1 In accordance with the library's published lending policy, an interlibrary loan request may be transmitted via fax or electronically to another library. An electronic response and/or delivery may also be requested of that library in accordance with state, regional, or national interlibrary loan codes and the library's published lending policy.

3.2 Each fax or EDD transmission should include a cover or identifying sheet that includes the sender, the receiver, the number of pages being transmitted, and the sender's voice telephone number, telefacsimile number, and/or electronic address. The cover sheet may be omitted when transmitting an interlibrary loan request provided that all identifying information is included on the ILL request form.

3.3 Some documents may not transmit well via fax. These include photographs, detailed charts, maps, and graphs; text including scientific and mathematical symbols, small print, and foreign languages with diacritical, vocalization, or other small marks; and poor quality photocopies. Other electronic document delivery systems may be able to send such material without loss of clarity.

3.4 Unless a specific delivery method is requested, the lending library will determine the method to be used in delivery of the requested material. The lending library should notify the borrowing library when unable to deliver via the requested method.

4.0 BORROWING GUIDELINES

4.1 An interlibrary loan request for a document to be delivered electronically may be submitted through the interlibrary loan system of a bibliographic utility, a local online network, or any other transmission system acceptable to both the borrowing and lending libraries.

4.2 A request transmitted by any electronic method should be typed on a standard ALA Interlibrary Loan Request Form or in a standard free-form format approximating the ALA form (see *Interlibrary Loan Data Elements* NISO Z39.63) and transmitted in accordance with policies and procedures of the lending library.

4.3 A request for electronic delivery should contain the note "Please send to [fax number, or electronic address]" in the borrowing notes field or in a conspicuous place on the request form.

4.4 A rush request should contain the note "Please rush, needs before [mm/dd/yy]" in the borrowing notes field or in a conspicuous place on the request form. Sending a request via fax or other electronic method will not automatically elicit a rush response or delivery. Borrowing libraries should use discretion in requesting rush service except in instances in which local guidelines have been written to accommodate the service by special arrangement or when the policy of the lending library includes rush processing and delivery.

5.0 LENDING GUIDELINES

5.1 The lending library should check interlibrary loan systems, online networks, fax machines, and other electronic methods of transmission at least once per working day for incoming requests.

5.2 Fax and EDD requests should be merged into the normal workflow of the lending library and processed within a reasonable period of time.

5.3 Rush requests should be processed within one working day of receipt.

5.4 When electronic delivery is requested, the lending library should attempt to comply, provided the document is of reasonable length and of a quality that will transmit well.

5.5 Any photocopy of a document produced in response to a request for electronic delivery should be discarded after the transaction has been completed. The lender should mail the original photocopy only in circumstances in which the borrower has received an illegible transmission and requests a paper copy to be mailed.

5.6 A negative response should be made via the same network or transmission method through which the request was received.

5.7 A negative response to a rush request should be sent via fax, electronically, or by telephone within one working day. If the request was sent via an online ILL system, the request should also be updated or forwarded.

5.8 It is recommended that no additional fees or special handling charges be levied by the lending library for a document or response sent via fax or EDD. ∎∎

Interlibrary Loan Policy
(Lending)

T

NAME AND ADDRESS OF LIBRARY

    University of Massachusetts Library
    Amherst, Massachusetts 01003

ADDRESS FOR INTERLIBRARY LOAN SERVICE:

    Interlibrary Loan
    University Library
    University of Massachusetts
    Amherst, Massachusetts 01003

BOOKS:
    Will lend _____ X _____
    Will not lend _____
    Length of Loan _3 weeks' use_
    Renewals _____ usually _____
    Will lend books in print _ X _

PERIODICALS:
    Will lend _____
    Will not lend _____ X _____
    (May lend if article exceeds 50
     pages, in exceptional circumstances.)

MASTERS' THESES:
    Will lend __If 2d copy available__
    Loan period __3 weeks' use__

DISSERTATIONS:
    Will lend _pre-1961 if 2d copy_
    _____available_____
    Will not lend _after 1961_
    Loan period __3 weeks' use__
    Copies available: From University
     Microfilms since 1961

MICROFORMS:
	Will lend:	Will not lend:
Cards	X	
Film	most	
Fiche	X	

NEWSPAPERS ON FILM:
    Will lend __most; 1 week's use__
    Will not lend __Heavily used titles
            (e.g. last 20 yrs.
            Boston Globe)

OCLC SYMBOL	AUM,AUM
NUC CODE	MU
PHONE:	(413) 545-0553
DATE	MAR. 1, 1990

ADDRESS FOR PHOTODUPLICATION SERVICE:

    Interlibrary Loan
    University Library
    University of Massachusetts
    Amherst, Massachusetts 01003

TWX SERVICE:

    Not available.

PHOTOCOPY SERVICE:

    Charge per exposure _$ .20_
    Handling charge ____ .00 ___
    Minimum invoice ___$ 6.00_
    Cost for cost estimate_ None_

MICROFILMING:

    Service available _ No _

HARD COPIES FROM MICROFILM:

    Charge per exposure _$ .20_
    Handling charge ____ .00 ___
    Minimum invoice ___$ 6.00_

BILLING POLICY:

    Invoiced with material.

POSTAGE:

    Do charge _Air mail, first class,_
    _____special handling_____

    Do not charge_ Normally _____

OTHER:
    Loans for library use only: _Microfilm, theses, dissertations; others usually not_

    Service suspended during Christmas holidays: ___ NO _____

COMMENTS:
    The University of Massachusetts/Amherst Library imposes an equivalent service charge
    on loans only to those libraries which charge fees for interlibrary lending. We
    encourage reciprocal agreements to avoid such charges. UMass/Amherst has signed the
    NELINET reciprocal code.

International Lending*: Principles and Guidelines for Procedure (1978) — Major Revision 1987

The mutual use of individual collections is a necessary element of international cooperation by libraries. Just as no library can be self-sufficient in meeting all the information needs of its clientele, so no country can be self-sufficient. If the library service of a country is to be effective methods must be devised to obtain access to material held in other collections in other countries. International lending has as its aim the supply by one country to another, in the surest and fastest way, of documents that are not available in the country where they are needed.

The following guidelines, agreed by the Standing Committee of IFLA's Section on Interlending in 1978 and modified in 1987, represent a major revision of the Rules agreed by IFLA in 1954. While they have no mandatory force, and while every country must determine the ways in which it conducts interlending, the guidelines are strongly urged on individual countries and libraries as a basis for the conduct of international lending. They are preceded by a statement of Principles of international lending agreed in an earlier and slightly different version in 1976 by National Libraries and by the Standing Committee of IFLA's Section on Interlending, and are accompanied by a commentary which seeks to elucidate and amplify certain aspects of the guidelines.

PRINCIPLES OF INTERNATIONAL LENDING

1. Every country should accept responsibility for supplying to any other country, by loan or photocopy, copies of its own publications, certainly those published from the present date, and as far as possible retrospectively. This responsibility may be discharged in various ways, among which national loan/photocopy collections appear to have particular advantages.

2. Each country should have a national centre or centres to coordinate international lending activity for both incoming and outgoing requests. Such centres should be closely linked with, if not part of, the national library where there is one.

3. Each country should aim to develop an efficient national lending system, since national lending systems are the essential infrastructure of international lending.

4. As far as possible, photocopies or microfilms should be supplied in the place of loans of original copies.

5. Fast methods should be used for supplying and returning items. Airmail should be used whenever possible.

6. All requests should be dealt with expeditiously, having regard to accuracy, at all points: the requesting library, any intermediary used and the source library.

7. Standard and simple procedures should be developed and adopted, particularly procedures for requesting items and for reclaiming any payment.

---

*'Lending' is held to include the sending of photographic and other reproductions in place of the original.

GUIDELINES FOR PROCEDURE

1. General

Each library should, within any nationally agreed policy, use the most efficient methods for identifying locations of wanted documents and transmitting requests.

<u>Commentary</u>

1. Speed of supply is extremely important to most users. Every effort should be made to follow routines which are simple and time-saving. International requests often take far longer to satisfy than those dealt with nationally so that should be modified where necessary procedure to reduce delays. All communications should be in clear and simple language and legible to avoid misunderstanding across linguistic barriers.

2. National Centre for International Lending

2.1 Each country (or, in the case of federal countries, each state or province) should have a centre playing an active role in international lending. Its main functions are:

a) to act as a centre for the receipt of requests from abroad and their transmission onward to libraries within its own country when direct access to collections is not possible or accepted;

b) to act as a centre for the transmission of requests to foreign countries from libraries within its own country when direct access is not possible or not accepted;

c) to provide where necessary bibliographical support and expertise to ensure that requests sent abroad reach the required standards;

d) to gather statistical information from within its own country on international loan transactions and to send these figures regularly to the IFLA Office for International Lending.

2.2 Centres for international lending may, and should where possible, also perform the following functions:

a) to perform a coordinating role for national interlending;

b) act as the main national centre for the supervision and construction of union catalogues and their maintenance;

c) to have direct access to significant library collections in their own country;

d) to provide an information service on interlending;

e) to have responsibility for planning, developing and supervising an efficient national system of interlending where this function is not adequately performed by another agency.

<u>Commentary</u>

2. The nomination or establishment of national centres to carry out the functions mentioned in 2.1 and 2.2 is strongly recommended as the most efficient and effective means of carrying out these functions. In those countries where no such national centre has been nominated or established the following recommendations are made:

2.1a Published guides, as comprehensive as possible, should be provided to facilitate the direction of requests by other countries. All libraries within the country should make strenuous efforts to observe the same procedures for handling and when necessary circulating requests received from other countries.

2.1b In the case of loans of originals, individual libraries should accept responsibility for ensuring that no loanable copy of a required work exists in another library within the country before sending requests abroad. See 3.4 below.

194

2.1c The collection of statistics, which is vital for monitoring trends and efficiency, should still be carried out on a national basis.

2.1d Strong coordination is essential if the international requirements and responsibilities of a country without a national centre are to be fulfilled efficiently. A coordinating body may be in a position to fulfil some of the functions of a national centre.

3. Procedure for Requesting

3.1 All requests using paper forms shall be on the forms authorized by IFLA, unless otherwise stipulated by the library to which requests are sent. Requests submitted by telex (TWX) or electronic mail shall conform to agreed standards.

3.2 To ensure that inadequate or inaccurate requests are not sent abroad the borrowing library shall verify, and where necessary complete, the bibliographic details of items requested to the best of its ability, giving the source of reference where possible. Where necessary or appropriate details shall be checked or completed by the national centre.

3.3 Requesting libraries should keep a record of all requests, each of which should have a serial number.

3.4 In the case of loans of originals, all reasonable efforts shall be made to ensure that no loanable copy is available in its own country before a request is sent abroad. Documents that are available in a country but are temporarily in use should only be requested on international loan in exceptional circumstances.

Commentary

3. Requests for loans should normally go through national centres, since otherwise it is very difficult to ensure that there is no other loanable copy in the country, and loans are expensive. It may be decided that it is easier, cheaper and faster to apply direct abroad (for example, when the only known location is outside the country); however, a record of all such requests should be sent to the national centre for information. Requests for photocopies may however in appropriate cases be made direct to foreign libraries, not necessarily in the country of publication.

3.1 Forms should wherever possible be completed in typescript.

3.2 Inadequate requests cause delays, and may have to be returned for further checking.

3.3 Where a request is inadequate because the requesting library has insufficient bibliographic resources to check it, it should be checked by the national centre or centres before it is despatched.

3.4 This is the responsibility of the appropriate national centre when no comprehensive record of national holdings is generally available.

3.5 Fast methods include airmail, telex, telefacsimile, direct computer transmission and electronic mail.

4. Procedure for Supplying

4.1 Every country has a special responsibility to supply its own national imprints on international loan. No country or library is under an obligation to supply a work that has been requested, but all reasonable efforts should be made to satisfy international requests.

4.2 Items shall be sent direct to the requesting library except where, for administrative reasons, it is specifically required that they should be sent to the national centre.

4.3 All documents lent should be clearly marked with the name of the owning library.

4.4 Packages containing items sent in response to requests shall be clearly marked: 'INTERNATIONAL LOANS BETWEEN LIBRARIES'.

4.5 No library receiving a request should normally retain it for longer than one week (two weeks in the case of difficult requests) before supplying the item or returning the request to the national centre or the requesting library.

4.6 When a request cannot be satisfied, the requesting library should be notified at once.

4.7 When the satisfaction of a request is likely to be seriously delayed, the requesting library should be notified at once.

Commentary

4.1 The responsibility of each country to supply its own national imprints is emphasized: without the acceptance of such a responsibility, both availability and speed of supply are seriously jeopardized. This responsibility is an essential element in Universal Availability of Publications.

4.4 Clear statements on the outside of packages are necessary to avoid problems with Customs.

4.5 Difficult requests include requests that require extensive bibliographic checking and requests that are satisfied by making copies of long documents (eg microfilms of books).

4.6 Failure to notify inability to supply or delays in supplying causes further delays and uncertainty
&   in the requesting library. In countries with no national centre, fast procedures should be devised
4.7 to transmit to other libraries requests that cannot be satisfied. If such procedures are not possible, the requests should be returned at once to the requesting library.

5. Conditions of Supply

5.1 Where photocopies are supplied, libraries supplying and receiving them must abide by any requirements necessary to satisfy relevant copyright regulations.

5.2 Original documents when received by the borrowing library shall be used in accordance with its normal regulations, unless the supplying library stipulates certain conditions.

5.3 Items should be sent by the fastest postal service available.

Commentary

5.3 It is recognized that in some cases the use of airmail, although desirable, may not be possible because the cost cannot be borne by either the borrowing or the supplying library. The use of fast methods of transmission is nevertheless very strongly urged, since slower methods may make libraries reluctant to lend and inconvenience the individual user.

6. Period of Loan

6.1 The loan period, which shall in all cases be specifically and clearly stated, shall normally be one month, excluding the time required for despatch and return of the documents. The supplying library may extend or curtail this time limit.

6.2 Application for extension of the loan period shall be made in time to reach the supplying library before the loan period has expired.

7. Procedure for Returning

7.1 Documents lent should be returned by the fastest postal service available. Packages shall be marked 'INTERNATIONAL LOANS BETWEEN LIBRARIES'.

7.2 Libraries returning documents shall observe any special stipulations by supplying libraries with regard to packaging, registration, etc.

7.3 Documents shall be returned to the supplying library except where return to the national centre is specifically stipulated.

Commentary

7.2 Special stipulations may relate to special packaging in the case of fragile documents or registration in the case of rare items.

8. Receipts

No receipts shall be provided either for the supply of an item or its return to the supplying library, unless specifically requested.

9. Responsibility for Loss or Damage

From the moment a library despatches an item to a requesting library until it returns, the requesting library shall normally be responsible for any loss or damage incurred, and pay the supplying library the full estimated cost of such loss or damage, including where requested any administrative costs involved.

Commentary

It is in the interests of all concerned to ensure that all items are adequately packaged. Claims from supplying libraries for loss or damage cannot be seriously entertained if packaging by them has been inadequate.

Supplying libraries are expected to help where necessary with postal inquiries in cases of loss or damage.

10. Payment

Accounting and payment procedures should be minimized. Payment shall be made or waived according to agreements between the two countries or libraries involved. Payment between national centres or individual libraries receiving and providing a similar number of satisfied requests should be waived. Payment may also be waived when the number of items supplied to a particular country or library is so small as not to justify the accounting procedures involved.

Commentary

Simplified methods of payment include:

a) prepaid systems, whereby national centres or libraries buy numbers of coupons in advance, and send an appropriate number of coupons with each request;

b) deposit accounts, whereby the supplying library holds a sum deposited by a requesting library and deducts amounts from it according to each item supplied;

c) flat-rate payments, whereby average rather than individual costs are recovered; or unit payments, whereby charges are made in a limited number of units. Either of these methods may be combined with pre-payment or deposit accounts.

Payment may be made by national centres, which may recover it from requesting libraries in their countries, or direct by requesting libraries, according to the system in operation in the requesting country. The requirements of the supplying library or country, which should be as simple and clear as possible, must in all cases be observed.

Different practices may be applied to loans and to photocopies or other reproductions sent in place of loans: for example, two countries, or a group of countries, may agree to waive charges for loans but not for photocopies.

11. Statistics

Libraries participating in international lending shall keep statistics of requests received from and sent to other countries, and those satisfied in each case. These statistics shall be sent each year to the national centre or national association for forwarding to the IFLA Office for International Lending.

Commentary

The statistics to be collected should include:

1. The total number of requests sent abroad and the total satisfied a) by loan, b) by photocopy.

2. The total number of requests received from abroad and the total satisfied a) by loan, b) by photocopy.

The above statistics should preferably be kept in rank order by country.

Where it is not possible to collect figures for satisfaction rates over all requests, they may be estimated from sample surveys.

A fuller statement of recommended statistics is given in IFLA Journal, volume 3 number 2 1977, page 117–126: International lending statistics.

Guidelines for the Loan
of Rare and Unique Materials

Approved by the ACRL Standards & Accreditation Committee, ACRL Board of Directors, and the ALA Standards Committee, February, 1994.

By the ACRL Rare Books and Manuscripts Section's Ad Hoc Committee on the Loan of Rare and Unique Materials

These guidelines are proposed for adoption by the Association of College and Research Libraries and are published here for broad professional review. The committee's objectives in preparing these guidelines are:

1) to encourage and facilitate interinstitutional loan from special collections for research use;

2) to affirm curatorial responsibility in decisions regarding the loan of special collections;

3) to specify the responsibilities of lending and borrowing institutions; and

4) to ensure the safety and security of items loaned.

This proposal has been reviewed by members of the Rare Books and Manuscripts Section and was endorsed by the section's Executive Committee at its 1993 Midwinter Meeting. The proposed guidelines have also been reviewed by the members of the Reference and Adult Services Division's Management and Operation of Public Services Section's Interlibrary Loan Committee and were endorsed by that committee at its 1993 Midwinter Meeting. It is envisioned that these guidelines will be incorporated as an integral component of the ALA interlibrary loan procedures.

The guidelines

These guidelines are intended for use by libraries, museums, public archives, historical agencies, and other cultural repositories in order to facilitate the interinstitutional loan for research use of special collections, including books, manuscripts, archives, and graphics.

Basic assumptions underlying these guidelines are:

1) Interinstitutional loan from special collections for research use is strongly encouraged but must be conducted in a manner that ensures responsible care and effectively safeguards items from loss or damage.

2) The decision to lend an item rests with the individual exercising curatorial responsibility for that item. Such decisions should reflect an item-by-item consideration rather than broad categorical responses.

3) It is not expected that items of significant rarity or monetary value or items in fragile condition will normally be lent for research purposes.

4) Although personal familiarity and/or direct communications with curatorial staff at other institutions can facilitate the lending process, the loan of materials should not depend solely on personal contacts but should rest on well-defined interinstitutional commitments.

5) A borrowing institution must meet significant criteria in order to provide appropriate conditions for housing and use of rare and unique materials.

Responsibilities of borrowing institutions

Institutional prerequisites for borrowing

The borrowing institution must:

A) Provide a secure reading room under constant surveillance to insure the safety of the materials during use.

B) Have a special collections program, including staff assigned to and trained in the care and handling of special collections.

C) Provide secure storage for borrowed items during the loan period.

D) Provide storage under environmental conditions that meet accepted standards for housing special collections.

Guidelines for initiating a loan request

A) Requests for the loan of materials from noncirculating special collections must indicate that the borrowing institution meets the institutional criteria specified above and that the borrowing institution subscribes to the principles expressed in these guidelines.

B) Loan requests should normally be routed through the respective Interlibrary Lending (ILL) departments.

C) Every effort should be made to locate requested material in a general collection before submitting a request to a special collection of noncirculating materials. When a circulating copy cannot be located, that fact should be noted when requesting the item from a noncirculating collection.

D) Patrons should be encouraged to travel to other institutions for on-site access when their research involves long-term use or large quantities of material, or when distance presents no extraordinary hardship for them.

E) The borrowing institution should describe the requested material fully. Standard bibliographic sources should be used to verify each request. When a request cannot be verified in these sources, full information regarding the original source of citation should be submitted.

F) In addition to full bibliographic description, it is desirable that requests include RLIN, OCLC, or other bibliographic utility record identification number and the call number for each department from which the item is being requested.

G) The request should indicate whether or not another edition, version, or form of material (e.g., photocopy, microform, or photograph) can be substituted for the one specified.

Guidelines for handling materials on loan

A) No copies of borrowed materials should be made without the explicit permission of the lending institution.

B) If copying is permitted by the lending institution, it should be done by special collections staff at the borrowing institution and in compliance with U.S. copyright law. The borrowing institution may, however, decline to make copies in any case and refer the patron directly to the lending institution to negotiate arrangements for copying.

C) The borrowing institution must comply with the loan period established by the lending institution. Unless otherwise specified by the lending institution, the loan period will be thirty days. Renewal of a loan should only be requested under unusual circumstance, and renewal requests should be submitted in a timely fashion.

D) The borrowing institution must abide by and administer any special conditions governing the handling and use of borrowed materials as specified by the lending institution.

E) If a borrowing institution fails to comply with the conditions of a loan, including proper care and packaging of borrowed items, that institution can expect that future requests to borrow special collections materials will be denied.

Responsibilities of lending institutions

A) Institutions receiving requests should be as generous as possible, consonant with their responsibilities both to preserve and to make accessible to their on-site user community the materials in their care.

B) Requests should be considered on a case-by-case basis by the individual with curatorial responsibility for the requested material.

C) Response to a request for the loan of special collections materials should be made within five working days.

D) It is the responsibility of the lending institution to indicate any special conditions governing the use of loaned materials, clearly stating any restrictions or limitations on research use, citation, publication, or other forms of dissemination.

E) Lending institutions reserve the right to limit the volume of material lent and the loan period. The normal loan period for special collections is thirty days.

F) If it is determined that a request can best be fulfilled by photocopying, lending institutions are expected to provide photocopies at a cost comparable to the standard rate within the lending institution.

G) Unless the lending institution so stipulates, it will not be necessary for the borrowing institution to return photocopies from special collections. If the lending institution does wish the return of photocopies, the copies should be clearly marked as loans.

H) Refusals either to lend or copy a requested item should include a specific reason (e.g., fragile paper, tight binding, too large to ship safely, etc.). That an item is part of a special collection is not a sufficient reason.

I) It is assumed that the lending institution will lend rare material at a cost comparable to the standard ILL fee charged by that institution for the loan of general library material. If the costs of shipping and insurance exceed the ILL fee, the lending institution may require additional payment. Before the material is sent, however, the lending institution must notify the borrowing institution of any additional charges and secure the borrowing institution's agreement to pay prior to sending the material.

Liability and transport for borrowed materials

A) The safety of borrowed materials is the responsibility of the borrowing institution from the time the material leaves the lending institution until it is returned to the lending institution.

B) The lending institution is responsible for packing the borrowed material so as to ensure its return in the condition in which it was sent. The borrowing institution is responsible for returning the material in the same condition as received, using the same, or equivalent, packing material.

C) If damage or loss occurs at any time after the material leaves the lending institution, the borrowing institution must meet all costs of repair, replacement, or appropriate compensation, in accordance with the preference of the lending institution.

D) The lending institution has the option of specifying alternative methods of delivery. These methods may include a different system of transportation, insurance, and special wrapping instructions. The borrowing institution can specify that the material be delivered directly to its special collections department. The lending institution can specify that the material be returned directly to the special collections department.

E) If alternative methods are to be employed, delivery specifications must be communicated to the borrowing institution, which must agree to return the material in the manner specified.

F) Verification of transfer and delivery must be made through the respective ILL department, regardless of method of delivery.

G) The borrowing institution will normally assume the costs of all fees associated with the loan. ■

Reprinted from *C&RL News* May 1993 issue

Guidelines for Preservation Photocopying of Replacement Pages

This document was first drafted as part of a Research Libraries Group Preservation Committee initiative. It has evolved into the present guideline through the work of the ALA/ALCTS/PLMS Physical Quality and Treatment of Library Materials Committee.

I. Introduction

Photocopied replacement pages are required when parts of original texts have been removed or lost. Photocopying also becomes necessary when an embrittled item can no longer be used without risking damage, and a paper copy replacement (rather than film) is desired and is not available from a commercial publisher. In each case, it is essential that photocopies be of the highest quality.

Interlibrary loan requests for photocopies should indicate whether the copies will be tipped or bound into an existing volume, or will complete an item for microfilming—since the former requires the use of alkaline paper and the latter does not.

II. Procedures for Making Copies for Tipping-in and Binding

A. Preservation Photocopying

1. All preservation photocopies should be made on paper selected for its permanence. It should be acid-free 20-pound bond, and have a minimum alkaline reserve of 2% by dry weight. Suitable papers include Xerox XXV Archival Bond, Howard Permalife, and University Products Perma-Dur. As paper mills in the United States continue to convert from acidic to alkaline manufacturing processes, the availability of alkaline papers can be expected to increase dramatically.

2. The contrast setting should be adjusted to achieve the highest contrast possible, so that all text and illustrations are captured clearly and any gray cast or streaking in the background is minimized. Photocopies should have consistently dark print quality throughout.

3. Photocopies must be made on an electrostatic copying machine capable of copying on "plain" paper. The machine must be in good operating condition so that images fuse properly. If a freshly-made copy smudges when an attempt is made to erase the image, the machine is not fusing the image to the paper properly and must be adjusted.

4. All preservation photocopies for tipping-in or binding should be copied one page per side of a sheet of copy paper, so that copies can be cut to approximately the same size as original pages. Double-sided copies should be provided whenever the original is double-sided, unless otherwise specified.

5. Every page of the original should be aligned consistently, straight and parallel with the edges of the glass platen of the copier. When making double-sided copies, back-to-back images should be in perfect register (that is, margins should match). Because photocopy machines vary greatly in design, it is usually necessary to experiment with the positioning of pages on the platen to determine the best procedure for producing well-registered double-sided copies. A mask on the platen will eliminate dark borders and allow for consistent alignment. Copies should be made so that the recto and verso of the original are also the recto and verso of the photocopy.

6. When copies will be tipped in, the margin along the left-hand side of the image on the recto must be at least as wide as the left-hand margin on the original, and should in no case be less than 1/4

inch (unless that means that text will be lost along the right-hand side of the page). A minimum left-hand margin of 3/4 inch must be allowed when whole volumes are being photocopied and will be commercially double-fan adhesive bound. A minimum left-hand margin of 1-1/2 inch must be allowed when whole volumes are being photocopied and will be commercially oversewn.

7. If foldouts are larger than the largest size paper that the photocopy machine can accommodate, they should be copied in sections from left to right and from top to bottom. An overlap of at least one inch should be provided between contiguous sections. Sections should align well so that they may be reassembled into a single sheet. The same binding margin as is described in Section II.A.6 is required.

8. Each page of the original text should be copied, unless otherwise specified, and kept in the same order as the original. Graffiti, marginalia, and stray marks may be removed before copying when possible. Extraneous material laid in or tipped into the original text should not be copied.

B. Copying from Reader-Printers

1. Replacement pages for tipping-in and binding can be made from microforms using reader-printers. Commonly available equipment in libraries can produce images frame-by-frame, and is therefore most suitable for copying a small number of pages. The size of the enlargement lens chosen should be as close as possible to the reduction ratio of the film or fiche, so that copies are as close as possible to the size of the original.

2. When copying from reader-printers, Sections II.A.2 and II.A.8 apply. Since most equipment requires that paper specified by the manufacturer be used, and because that paper is typically non-archival, it is necessary to re-copy all copies produced from reader-printers before tipping-in or binding them. When recopying, all procedures in Section II.A. should be followed.

C. Copying from Microfilm using Xerox Copyflo and Similar Equipment

1. The Xerox Copyflo machine can be used to make preservation copies from microfilm. The process prints a roll of paper from a roll of negative microfilm. Alkaline paper as specified in Section II.A.1 is available in rolls. Suitable papers include Howard Permalife and University Products Perma-Dur. The roll of printed paper must be cut into pages and trimmed for binding. Because of cost, it is most feasible to use Copyflo when copying full volumes or full reels of film. When copying, guidelines in Sections II.A.1-3, II.A.6, and II.A.8 should be followed.

D. Binding Preservation Copies

1. A preservation copy should be bound following the *Library Binding Institute Standard for Library Binding,* 8th edition. Double-fan adhesive binding and oversewing are acceptable methods of leaf attachment, provided that the margin requirements cited in Section II.A.6 are met. Unbound volumes should be no more than two inches thick. Those that exceed that limit should be bound in two or more volumes.

III. Procedures for Making Copies for Preservation Microfilming

Volumes are collated for completeness as part of the process of preparing them for preservation microfilming. Missing pages are acquired through interlibrary loan and other sources. It is necessary for copies to be of the highest image quality, so that they will reproduce as well as the original pages when the volume is microfilmed.

A. Photocopying

1. When producing copies for preservation microfilming, guidelines in Section II.A.2-3, II.A.5, and II.A.7-8 should be followed. Other parts of Section II do not apply since copies will not be permanently retained.

202

Guidelines for
Packaging and Shipping Microforms

These brief guidelines are intended to provide advice to those in libraries and elsewhere who have occasion to ship microforms.

A. General

It is the responsibility of the lending library to specify the method of shipment for return of materials.

The lending library may place a limit on the amount of microform material to be lent at one time.

The lending library should spell out conditions of use, whether copying is permitted and what restrictions on copying are to be observed, e.g., only by library staff is a supervised copy service.

If problems should occur, such as film breakage, the borrowing library should not attempt repairs. The nature of the damage should be explained clearly in a note which accompanies return shipment. The library in which damage occurred should expect to be charged if the cost of repair or replacement is substantial.

B. Microfilm

The lending library should pack microfilm reels in their individual boxes, in rigid containers such as corrugated board, with bubble wrap. The film reels should be packed snugly into the outer containers to avoid damage in transit.

The borrowing library should return microfilm in the same type container in which it was shipped. Film should be rewound and secured with wrappers supplied.

C. Flat Microforms

The lending library should place microfiche or opaques in a rigid pamphlet cover with a pocket, inside an envelope. Alternatively a rigid box of the proper size may be used.

The borrowing library should return microfiche or opaques in the container in which they were received, preferably by first class mail.

Guidelines for Seeking or Making a Copy of an Entire Copyrighted Work for a Library, Archives, or User

A library or archives which wishes to make a single photocopy or sound recording copy of a published copyrighted work for a user or to replace a copy or phonorecord in its collection which is damaged, deteriorating, lost, or stolen, must first make a reasonable effort to obtain a copy in its original form at a fair price, in accordance with Subsections 108(c) and 108(e) of Public Law 94-553, the 1976 omnibus copyright revision act.

"Reasonable Effort"

A reasonable effort requires that the library or archives take the following steps:

1. Attempt to determine whether the work is in print by consulting commonly-known trade bibliographic sources, e.g., Publishers' Trade List Annual, Books in Print for printed works, Schwann Catalog, Phonolog for phonorecords.

2. If the work is in print, attempt to acquire it from a library wholesaler or retail outlet, or from the publisher of the work.

3. If the work is out of print and unavailable in its original form from these sources, attempt to acquire the work or a photocopy or sound recording copy from the publisher or other copyright owner (if such owner can be located readily at the address listed in the copyright registration) or from an authorized reproducing service.

4. If the publisher, other copyright owner, or authorized reproducing service is unable or unwilling to supply a copy of the work, or if the requesting library receives no reply to its request within thirty days of the date it is sent, then it may place an order for a photocopy or sound recording copy with a library or archives which has a copy. The "Revised Interlibrary Loan Form," which has been prepared by the ALA-RASD Interlibrary Loan Committee, may be used for this purpose, in which case the appropriate box on that form should be checked, to indicate that all the above-mentioned steps have been taken. Any order form used in its stead should also indicate compliance with these guidelines.

"Fair Price"

1. Original format

    In order to meet the requirement of fair price, an unused copy of a published copyrighted work should be available at a price as close as possible to the latest suggested retail price.

2. Reproductions (photocopy, microform, sound recording copy)

    To meet the requirement of fair price, a reproduction of a copyrighted work should be available on a timely basis (within thirty days) at a price which is as close as possible to actual manufacturing costs plus royalty payments.

The requesting library or archives shall maintain records of all requests it has made for photocopies or sound recording copies to which these guidelines apply, together with records of the fulfillment of these requests, which records shall be retained until the end of the third complete calendar year after the end of the calendar year in which the respective request shall have been made.

Authorized Reproducing Services

The House Judiciary Committee Report on the New Copyright Law (H. Rept. 94-1476) in discussing Subsections 108(c) and 108(e) of the copyright law, specifies that a reasonable investigation to determine that an unused replacement or copy cannot be obtained at a fair price will, in the normal situation, involve recourse to the publisher or other copyright owner, or an authorized reproducing service.

The RTSD Copyright Revision Act Committee has prepared a set of criteria which authorized reproducing services should meet in providing adequate services to the library community.

Publishers, other copyright owners, and authorized reproducing services which receive requests for photocopies or sound recording copies should all be required to meet the following conditions:

1. The copy supplied should be of sufficiently good quality to meet the needs of the user, or of as a good quality as that which the requesting library or archives could ordinarily expect to receive from any supplier.

2. The copy should be supplied, or notification given to the requestor that such copy cannot be supplied, within thirty days of the date of receipt of the request.

3. The price of the copy should be as close as possible to actual manufacturing costs plus royalty payments.

If any of these conditions are not met, the requestor may be considered to have complied with the provisions of Subsections 108(c) and 108(e) of PL 94-553 and may order a photocopy or sound recording of a work from a library or archives which possesses one without further authorization.

While authorized reproducing services should be required to meet the same criteria of quality, service and price as publishers and other copyright owners, there is a great need for better bibliographic information about what titles are available from such reproducing services. This could be done in the following way:

1. Publishers should include in their catalogs in PTLA a list of titles which are available from reproducing services and their prices, together with the names and addresses of these services.

2. Books in Print should include these titles in their regular listing, together with the names of the reproducing services, or they could have a separate listing of these titles.

Prepared by Implementation of the Copyright Revision Act Committee
Resources and Technical Services Division
American Library Association

After revising the Interlibrary Loan form to provide space for copyright representation (AL, Oct., pp. 492B-C), the Interlibrary Loan Committee of ALA's Reference and Adult Services Division prepared the following Records Maintenance and Retention Guidelines for interlibrary loan departments:

This statement deals only with recommended Record Maintenance and Retention Guidelines. Interlibrary Loan librarians have a responsibility to familiarize themselves thoroughly with the provisions of the Copyright Revision Act of 1976 (PL 94-553), particularly Sections 107 and 108, and the provisions of the guidelines drafted by the National Commission on New Technological Uses of Copyrighted Works (CONTU). Guideline #4 states:

"The requesting entity shall maintain records of all requests made by it for copies or phonorecords of any materials to which these guidelines apply and shall maintain records of the fulfillment of such requests, which records shall be retained until the end of the third complete calendar year after the end of the calendar year in which the respective request shall have been made."

Most libraries already keep some kind of record of *all* interlibrary loan requests. That record should continue. However, it must be supplemented by the kind of record described below *for certain kinds of requests.* (See Subsection 108(d) of the law and CONTU Guidelines #1).

1. Form of record

It is recommended that records for periodicals be kept by title. Two possibilities seem workable: 1) a copy of the ALA Request for Loan or Photocopy form, a copy of the teletype request, or other record could be kept; or 2) a card could be set up for each title requested containing essential information including whatever is necessary to link this card to the library's file of request forms.

Note: A library may choose one of these methods or develop its own. Whatever is done it is essential that the library keep a file of requests for these materials, that the file be accessible by title, and that the date of the request be noted.

2. Creation of Record

a. For periodical material: Beginning on Jan. 1, 1978, when a request is made for a copy of an article or articles published in a copyrighted periodical *within five years prior to the date of the request,* the library will either: a) set up a card for the title of that periodical or b) enter a copy of the request form in a file of forms arranged by title. If a card is set up it should include the date of the request and either the name of the requester or the requester's order number so that reference may be made to the complete form if necessary. All later requests for the same periodical title will be recorded in like manner.

b. For material in any other copyrighted work: Beginning on Jan. 1, 1978, when a request is made for a contribution to a collection or for a small part of any copyrighted work, the library will follow procedures based on those described above. The record may be kept by title or main entry.

3. Use of Record

a. Making requests: Before requesting a photocopy, the record will be checked. If a library is using the card system and no card exists, one will be created. If a card does exist, and the number of previous requests filled complies with the CONTU Guidelines, the date and name of requester will be entered. If a library is using the copy system and the number of previous requests complies with the CONTU Guidelines, the request will be made and a copy filed.

b. Receiving material: When a request is filled, this will be noted on the card or copy. If a request is not filled, a line will be drawn through the entry on the card or the copy will be marked "not filled."

4. Contingencies

When a request is made for loan of material rather than a copy, but the supplying library sends a photocopy, a record will be made either by marking on a card or by filing a copy of the form, at the time the material is *received*.

5. Retention of Records

a. Items in this file of cards or copies of forms must be kept until the end of the third complete calendar year after the end of the calendar year in which a request shall have been made. Thus, for a request made on any date in 1978, the record must be retained until Dec. 31, 1981.

b. If a library uses the card method, copies of the form on which an interlibrary loan has been requested must also be kept, in whatever order the library wishes, until the end of the third complete calendar year after the end of the calendar year in which a request is made.

c. Information contained in the records should be summarized before records are destroyed. The summary may be useful for the five-year review mandated by Subsection 108(i) of the copyright law as well as for internal management purposes. Suggestions for the form of the five-year review summary will be made at a later time.

American Library Association, Reference and Adult Services Division, Interlibrary Loan Committee, September 1977

National Network of Libraries of Medicine
and the Regional Medical Libraries

NATIONAL INSTITUTES OF HEALTH
NATIONAL LIBRARY OF MEDICINE
FACT SHEET
A World of Knowledge for the Nation's Health   April 1995

NATIONAL NETWORK OF LIBRARIES OF MEDICINE™

The purpose of the National Network of Libraries of Medicine (NN/LM™) is to provide health science practitioners, investigators, educators and administrators in the United States with timely, convenient access to biomedical and health care information resources.

The Network is administered by the National Library of Medicine. It consists of eight Regional Medical Libraries (major insitutions under contract with the National Library of Medicine), 140 Resource Libraries (primarily at medical schools), and some 4,500 Primary Access Libraries (primarily at hospitals). The Regional Medical Libraries administer and coordinate services in the Network's eight geographical regions.

New programs focus on reaching health professionals in rural, inner city, and other areas who do not have access to medical library resources. The goal is to make them aware of the services that Network libraries can provide. Other important Network programs include the interlibrary lending of more than two million journal articles, books and other published materials each year; reference services; training and consultation; and online access to MEDLINE® and other databases made available by the National Library of Medicine.

Three of the Regional Medical Libraries have been designated Online Centers, to conduct National Library of Medicine online training classes and coordinate online services in several regions.

Following is a list of the Regional Medical Libraries and the areas served by each.

1. Middle Atlantic Region

The New York Academy of Medicine
1216 Fifth Avenue
New York, New York 10029
Phone: 212-876-8763
FAX: 212-534-7042
States served: Delaware, New Jersey, New York, Pennsylvania
ONLINE CENTER for Regions 1, 2, and 8

2. Southeastern/Atlantic Region

University of Maryland at Baltimore
Health Sciences Library
111 South Greene Street
Baltimore, Maryland 21201-1583
Phone: 410-706-2855
FAX: 410-706-0099
States served: Alabama, Florida, Georgia, Maryland, Mississippi, North Carolina, South Carolina, Tennessee, Virginia, West Virginia, the District of Columbia, Puerto Rico, and the U.S. Virgin Islands

U.S. DEPARTMENT OF HEALTH AND HUMAN SERVICES • Public Health Service • National Institutes of Health

3. Greater Midwest Region

University of Illinois at Chicago
Library of the Health Sciences
P.O. Box 7509
Chicago, Illinois 60680
Phone: 312-996-2464
FAX: 312-996-2226
States served: Iowa, Illinois, Indiana, Kentucky,
   Michigan, Minnesota, North Dakota, Ohio,
   South Dakota, and Wisconsin

4. Midcontinental Region

University of Nebraska Medical Center
Leon S. McGoogan Library of Medicine
600 South 42nd Street
Omaha, Nebraska 68198-6706
Phone: 402-559-4326
FAX: 402-559-5482
States served: Colorado, Kansas, Missouri,
   Nebraska, Utah, and Wyoming
ONLINE CENTER for Regions 3, 4, and 5

5. South Central Region

Houston Academy of Medicine-
   Texas Medical Center Library
1133 M.D. Anderson Boulevard
Houston, Texas 77030
Phone: 713-790-7053
FAX: 713-790-7030
States served: Arkansas, Louisiana, New Mexico,
   Oklahoma, and Texas

6. Pacific Northwest Region

University of Washington
Health Sciences Center Library, SB-55
Seattle, Washington 98195
Phone: 206-543-8262
FAX: 206-543-2469
States served: Alaska, Idaho, Montana, Oregon, and
   Washington

7. Pacific Southwest Region

University of California at Los Angeles
Louise Darling Biomedical Library
10833 Le Conte Avenue
Los Angeles, California 90024-1798
Phone: 310-825-1200
FAX: 310-825-5389
States served: Arizona, California, Hawaii, Nevada,
   and U.S. Territories in the Pacific Basin
ONLINE CENTER for Regions 6 and 7

8. New England Region

University of Connecticut Health Center
Lyman Maynard Stowe Library
263 Farmington Avenue
Farmington, Connecticut 06034-4003
Phone: 203-679-4500
FAX: 203-679-1305
States served: Connecticut, Maine, Massachusetts,
   New Hampshire, Rhode Island, and Vermont

For more information about specific Network programs in your region, call the Regional Medical Library in your area at their direct number or dial 1-800-338-7657.

For general Network information contact:

National Network of Libraries of Medicine
National Library of Medicine
8600 Rockville Pike
Building 38, Room B1-E03
Bethesda, MD 20894
301-496-4777

Toll free phone number for all Regional Medical Libraries: 1-800-338-7657

 **Association of Research Libraries,
Transborder Interlibrary Loan: Shipping Interlibrary
Loan Materials from the U.S. to Canada**

A Fact Sheet Prepared by the
Association of Research Libraries
With Assistance from the
National Library of Canada

June, 1995

BACKGROUND

Interlibrary borrowing and lending arrangements between libraries in the United States and Canada have flourished for many years. Many libraries, especially those closest to the border, participate in "cross border" ILL on a regular basis. Electronic ordering systems have increased the amount of cross-border ILL traffic.

However, ILL shipments between the two countries has been problematic. Anecdotal evidence suggests that most problems occur with customs. For Canadian libraries, GST, custom clearance fees, and postal handling fees have been levied on interlibrary loan materials. These fees vary in amount but have been known to exceed $100 to borrow 21 reels of microfilm. U.S. libraries have also been charged custom clearance fees.

This fact sheet will guide U.S. libraries on the most effective methods of shipping and returning materials to Canadian libraries. This fact sheet applies primarily to returnable material. U.S. Lending libraries may find that it is more cost-effective to send photocopies and other non-returnable materials via fax or Ariel. This fact sheet does not apply to other foreign countries, as different shipping regulations apply to materials sent to Mexico or other foreign countries.

I. USING THE U.S. POSTAL SERVICE TO SEND MATERIALS TO CANADIAN LIBRARIES

RATE CLASSIFICATION:
    Send via "Books and Sheet Music" rate.
    Do **not** use "Printed Matter" as that rate includes all printed matter <u>other</u> than books, sheet music, and
        publisher's periodicals.

PACKAGE MARKINGS:
    Mark packages of returnables (books, microform, AV material):
        ATTENTION REVENUE CANADA:
        Tariff/Tarif 9812.00.00
        GST/TSP Code: 51
        International Loans Between Libraries (International Act of 1978)
        No Commercial Value: Any Value Stated is for Insurance Purposes Only

Canadian tariff 98.12 permits books to be imported from foreign libraries for a specified period of time (generally 60 days) without payment of duty and is intended to cover the lending of foreign materials to Canadian libraries.

WEIGHT LIMIT OF PACKAGES:
Maximum weight: 11 pounds
For heavier packages:
    1) Separate material into multiple packages, each weighing less than 11 lbs.
    2) Send via a commercial carrier

COSTS:
Charges are based on weight.

	Surface:	Airmail:
1 lb.	$2.46	$3.12
2 lb.	$4.06	$4.32
3 lb.	$5.26	$5.92
4 lb.	$6.46	$7.52
each add'l lb.	$1.20	$1.60

INSURANCE:
To insure the contents, the package must be sent "parcel post." Parcel post is the only class of international mail that can be insured. Charges for air parcel post to Canada:

1-2 lb.	$5.00 [minimum weight is 1 lb.]
3 lb.	$6.40
4 lb.	$7.80; each additional lb. is $1.40

II. USING THE U.S. POSTAL SERVICE TO RETURN MATERIALS BORROWED FROM CANADIAN LIBRARIES

RATE CLASSIFICATION:
Return via "Books and Sheet Music" rate.
Do <u>not</u> use "Printed Matter" as that rate includes all printed matter <u>other</u> than books, sheet music, and
    publisher's periodicals.

PACKAGE MARKINGS:
Mark packages being returned to the lending library:

ATTENTION REVENUE CANADA:
TARIFF/TARIF 9813.00.00 OR 9814.00.00
GST/TSP Code: 66
Property of <the name of the lending library>; material returned on interlibrary loan

Canadian Tariff 98.13/14 permits Canadian goods that have been exported from Canada to be returned under specific conditions. These conditions include the return of ILL materials.

WEIGHT LIMIT OF PACKAGES:
Maximum weight: 11 pounds
For heavier packages:
    1) Separate material into multiple packages, each weighing less than 11 lbs.
    2) Send via a commercial carrier

COSTS:

Charges are based on weight.

	Surface:	Airmail:
1 lb.	$2.46	$3.12
2 lb.	$4.06	$4.32
3 lb.	$5.26	$5.92
4 lb.	$6.46	$7.52
each add'l lb.	$1.20	$1.60

INSURANCE:

To insure the contents, the package must be sent "parcel post." Parcel post is the only class of international mail that can be insured. Charges for air parcel post to Canada:

1-2 lb.	$5.00 [minimum weight is 1 lb.]
3 lb.	$6.40
4 lb.	$7.80; each additional lb. is $1.40

III. SENDING OR RETURNING PACKAGES VIA COMMERCIAL DELIVERY/ COURIER COMPANIES

When selecting a courier company, it is important to choose one that delivers to the city in which the requesting/lending library is located. The courier company should not be permitted to leave the material at the closest border crossing, which may in fact be in a different province. The fees paid to the courier company should include the prepayment of any customs brokerage fees. If such fees are not paid, the receipt of the material will be delayed and the receiving/lending library will be billed for the brokerage fees.

NOTES

This fact sheet may be reproduced freely as long as proper attribution is made.

The U.S. Postal Service expects to increase international postal rates during the summer. Please check the ARL gopher (arl.cni.org) for an update version when the rates are increased.

IFLA Fax Guidelines

Introduction

The IFLA Section on Document Delivery and Interlending has believed for some time that there should be some international guidelines on the use of fax in interlending requests. Following research into the fax policies of some major libraries and national bodies, staff of the IFLA Office for International Lending produced a paper which highlighted the problems of fax requests and listed solutions to these problems. The paper went on to make recommendations concerning the elements which should be included in fax requests and included examples of the recommended layout. This paper was circulated for comments. The original paper and comments received have now been merged to produce the following guidelines.

The Guidelines

1. *It is important that a request be transmitted according to the policies and procedures of the supplying library.*

   Where a fax number for the supplying library is not known, the requesting library should contact the supplying library by letter or telephone to find out whether fax or electronic requests are accepted and, if so, whether there are any special forms to use or particular rules to follow.

   If the supplying library has a public fax number or a fax number for its interlending section, it may be assumed that the library accepts requests by fax. However, the requesting library should still find out whether the supplying library uses special fax forms or requires special procedures to be followed.

   If there are special forms, the requesting library should use these and complete them as directed by the supplying library. Only one item should be requested on a form (unless the supplying library allows otherwise). Any instructions given by the supplying library must be followed.

2. *If the supplying library does not have its own forms or established procedures, the requesting library may either choose to use forms (its own or IFLA forms) or send its request in free-text format.*

   Whichever option is chosen, the requesting library must ensure that it incorporates various elements in its request and that these are set out in a logical manner, which is easy for the supplying library to use. The order in which the elements are listed below may be used as a guide. Examples of recommended layout are given in Appendix 1. The names of the elements should be included so that it is clear exactly what is being requested thus ensuring the supply of the correct item. These names are, where applicable, taken from the International Organisation for Standardisation (ISO) standard 10161: Interlibrary Loan Protocol Specification.

3. *The following elements should be included on the request form and in free-text requests:*

   a) **Client identifier or client name.** Request identification by client number or name. Some libraries may wish to include an additional request number as further identification.

   b) **Date-of-service.** Date of the transmission of the request.

c) **Requester-id.** Requesting library's name and full address including fax, telephone numbers and electronic address - in case of any queries and for the supply of the item by return fax or electronic delivery.

d) **Need-before-date.** Date by which the item is needed, particularly if the request is urgent.

e) **Call-number.** Supplying library's call number and location within the supplying library, if known.

f) **The full bibliographical details of the requested item:**

loan: generally a monograph which is borrowed and returned

author
title
edition
place-of-publication
publisher
publication-date
series-title-number
ISBN

photocopy: generally a serial article which is copied and kept by the requesting library

title
volume-issue
publication-date of serial volume-issue
pagination
author-of-article
title-of-article
ISSN

g) **Verification-reference-source.** The full bibliographical details or a copy of the entry so that the supplying library can check it, if necessary.

h) **Note.** Any special requirements such as "microfiche required," "English edition only," or "any edition acceptable."

i) **Delivery-service.** The preferred method of delivery such as post, fax, or electronic transmission.

j) **Copyright-compliance.** For photocopy requests. A copyright declaration statement (which will vary in different countries).

k) **Payment-provided.** Payment authorisation or other notation.

l) **Responder-address/responder-id.** Supplying library's name and full address.

m) **Responder-note.** Space for any report from the supplying library.

IFLA Office for International Lending
May 1995

Example A: Loan

Data element	Example:
Client identifier or client name	55-0053
Date-of-service	9 February 1995
Requester-id	National and University Library
	"Kliment Ohridski"
	Bull Goce Delcev No 6
	9100 Skopje
	Republic of Macedonia
	Fax: 389 91 230 874
	Telephone: 389 91 226 846
Need-before-date	Need before: 20 February 1995
Call-number	Call number unknown
Loan	Loan:
Author	Mangold, Peter
Title	National Security and International Relations
Edition	Latest edition
Place-of-publication	London/New York
Publisher	Routledge
Publication-date	1990
ISBN	0 4150 2295 9
Verification-reference-source	BIP
Note	No additional information
Delivery-service	Post delivery only
Payment-provided	Will pay charges
Responder-address	Loan Division
	Library of Congress
	Washington DC 20540
	USA

APPENDIX 1 (continued)

Example B: Photocopy

Data element:	Example:
Client identifier or client name	55-0008
Date-of-service	6 May 1995
Requester-id	Centralna tehniska knijiznica Univerze v Llubljani
	PO Box 90/11
	Tomsiceva 7
	61000 LJUBLJANA
	Fax: 38 61 214108
	Telephone: 38 61 214072
Need-before-date	Need before: 10 May 1995
Call-number	Call number unknown
Photocopy	Photocopy:
Title	Journal of investigative dermatology
Volume-issue	99 (3)
Publication-date of serial volume-issue	1992
Pagination	306-09
Author-of-article	Wiedow O
Title-of-article	Lesional elastase activity in psoriasis, contact dermatitis, and topic dermatitis
ISSN	0022-202X
Verification-source- reference	CIM 33 1992:5157
Note	Note: Urgent request
Delivery-service	Fax only
Copyright-compliance	I hereby request you to supply me with a copy of the item specified above. I have not previously been supplied with a copy of the same material by you or any other library. I will not use the copy except for research or private study and will not supply a copy of it to any other person.
Payment-provided	Will pay charges
Responder-address	Univ of Colorado Health Sciences Center
	Denison Memorial Library A003
	4200 East 9th Avenue
	Denver, CO 80262
	USA

I.F.L.A. INTERNATIONAL LOAN/PHOTOCOPY REQUEST FORM
FORMULAIRE DE DEMANDE DE PRET/PHOTOCOPIE INTERNATIONAL
COPY B EXEMPLAIRE B

Request ref no/Patron identifier	
No de commande/identité de lecteur	
94-9686	

Borrowing library's address / Adresse de la bibliothèque emprunteuse	Needed by / Demande avant	30-4-1995	Quote if cost exceeds / Prix si plus que
Worldwide Searches	Shelfmark / Cot de placement	9050.985	
British Library Document Supply Centre			
Boston Spa, Wetherby, West Yorkshire	Request for: □ Loan ☑ Photocopy □ Microform		
UNITED KINGDOM	Commande de: Pret Photocopie		
LS23 7BQ			

Report/Reponse

Books: Author, title - Livres: Auteur, titre/Serials: Title, article title, author - Périodiques: Titre, titre de l'article, auteur

Trondheim Papers in Applied Linguistics
The clustering of lexical cohesion in non-narrative test
HOEY, M P

	Publisher / Editeur
Place of Publication / Lieu de publication	

Year-Anee	Volume-Tome	Part-No	Pages	ISBN/ISSN
1988	4	-	154-180	0800-3939

Edition	Source of verification/reference / Référence bibliographique/Verification	Hoey 1991 Patterns of lexis in text

Report/Reponse:

- □ Part not held/Volume /fascisule non detenu
- □ Title not held /nous n'avons pas ce titre
- □ Not traced/Ne figure pas dans cette bibl.
- □ Not for loan/Exclu de prêt
- □ Copyright restrictions
- □ Not immediately available. Reapply in.......weeks
  Non disponible actuellement. Renouvelez la
  demande dans...........semaines
- □ Lent until/Prêté jusqu'au.........................
- □ Use in library only/A consulter sur place uniquement

I declare that this publication is required only for the
purpose of research or private study.
Je déclare que cette publication n'est demandé qu'à des
fins de recherche ou d'étude privée

Signature..........................xxxxx.......................

Date..........................16.4.95........................

Lending library's address/adresse de la bibliothèque prêteuse
Gessanthochschul-Bibliothek Kassel
Landesbibliothek und Murhardsche
Bibliothek der Stadt
KASSEL
Germany

 **Interlibrary Lending Suggestions for Foreign Libraries That Request Books and Photocopies from Libraries in the United States**

1.   Abide by the "International Lending: Principles and Guidelines for Procedure (1978) (revised 1987)" found in the IFLA Journal 14, no. 3 (1988), 258–264.

2.   There is no national center for lending in the United States. Currently, the Library of Congress mails books to foreign libraries under certain conditions. Request information from:

> Library of Congress
> Loan Division
> Washington, D.C. 20540-5560
> Telephone: (202) 707-5444
> Fax: (202) 707-5986

3.   Large research libraries in the United States (holdings of 1 million or more volumes) often have a big enough interlending service to lend books or supply photocopies to libraries in foreign countries. Addresses and policies can be found in:

> OCLC (Online Computer Library Center) Name/Address Directory (online)

> Morris, Leslie R. Interlibrary Loan Policies Directory. 5th ed. New York: Neal-Schuman Publishers, 1995.

4.   Check for larger libraries in the following for addresses and size of library holdings:

> American Library Directory. 2 vols. 48th ed. New Providence, N.J.: Bowker, 1995.
>   (An interlending person is often listed.)

> The World of Learning. 1st– . London, Europa Publications, 1947– .
>   (The 46th edition is 1996. Look under "United States: Libraries and Archives: Selected University Libraries.")

> World Guide to Libraries=Internationales Bibliotheks-Handbuch. Ed. 1– . Handbook of International Documentation and Information, vol. 8. Munich and New York: K. G. Saur, 1966– .
>   (Lists university libraries, government libraries, etc.)

> International Handbook of Universities. 14th ed. Paris: International Association of Universities, 1996.

5.   Information on document suppliers can be found in the following:

> Fiscal Directory of Fee-based Research and Document Supply Services. Compiled by Steve Coffman and Pat Wiedensohler for FISCAL, a discussion group of the Association of College and Research Libraries. 4th ed. Chicago: American Library Association, 1993.

6. Use IFLA or ALA paper forms, if sending requests by mail. Include the same information sent on those forms, if requesting by fax or electronic means such as Ariel. For libraries with access, the OCLC PRISM Interlibrary Loan system is an excellent way to approach libraries in the United States.

7. American libraries do not necessarily understand how slow the regular mail is. Be sure to request transmission by fax or electronic means for photocopies, if those services are available. Ask that a book be sent air mail or by a good commercial delivery service so that it does not spend weeks in the mail.

8. Cost can easily be in the $15 to $25 range for services to foreign libraries. The borrowing library is responsible for all charges that the lending library levies. Payment is often accepted in U.S. dollars only. See 3. above for locating the costs for service. The information may apply only to libraries in the U.S. It is a good idea to ask libraries that will be used what the charges and other policies are for foreign libraries.

9. The IFLA voucher scheme may be used by some libraries in the United States. This allows a library to pay another library for international interlibrary requests by using a voucher instead of real money. Further details are available from the IFLA Office for UAP and International Lending:

> The IFLA Voucher Scheme
> IFLA Office for UAP and International Lending
> c/o The British Library
> Boston Spa
> Wetherby
> LS23 7BQ
> United Kingdom
> Fax: +44 1937 546478
> Telephone: +44 1937 546254
> E-mail: sara.gould@bl.uk

10. OCLC Interlibrary Loan Fee Management (IFM) system may also be used as a payment mechanism for libraries using the OCLC PRISM Interlibrary Loan system that agree to use IFM.

11. When returning books to libraries in the United States, mark each package, "International loans between libraries." This precaution may insure that there will be no customs charges.

May 1996   Virginia Boucher

Methodologies for Determining Costs of Interlibrary Lending and Interlibrary Borrowing

Stephen P. Dickson
Virginia Boucher

Interlibrary Lending

Few libraries are able to extract the costs of interlibrary lending activity from their accounting records. Interlibrary lending is a relatively small cost component of library operations, and traditional accounting and budgeting methods do not provide cost breakdowns that cross large budget line items. However, from both inside and outside the library, requests are made to provide the cost of interlibrary cooperation. States often provide reimbursement to libraries for lending materials to other libraries. Accurate costs for a library to provide this service should be known, so that the participating libraries have an idea of the value of the reimbursement program, and so that the state government can set reimbursement amounts. Good cost-information could also be used by state library agencies or interested groups to convince state legislators to establish or increase reimbursement levels for interlibrary lending activity.

The term interlibrary loan is used to encompass both borrowing and lending. Interlibrary borrowing denotes borrowing from another library to meet the needs of the borrowing library's own patrons; and interlibrary lending denotes loans to other libraries.

The purpose of this exercise is to develop a methodology for estimating the cost of interlibrary lending which will allow comparison of the incremental cost among libraries, and make possible the aggregation of the costs of an entire state or number of states, without the need for extensive time-and-motion studies or the use of complex mathematics.

Philosophy

If extensive (and expensive) methods are to be avoided in determining costs, methods must be employed that will be relatively simple to apply. Certain philosophical assumptions must be made, both to create a boundary for the problem and to ensure a degree of uniformity and comparability in application. The major assumptions are the following:

1. *Marginal incremental costs.* Only the *additional* cost of interlibrary lending should be included in the cost determination. Costs that would be incurred even if there were no interlibrary lending are considered costs of operating the library itself and are not allocated to interlibrary lending. This simplifies the exercise by not requiring allocations of other library and higher authority costs. It does, however, address the primary question of the *additional* cost burden to the library for providing interlibrary lending services.

2. *Lending only.* Costs should include only those attributable to interlibrary lending, not borrowing. A major use of lending cost data is to determine the level and extent of cost that libraries are incurring to support this form of interlibrary cooperation. The fund-providers (taxpayers, etc.) who pay the bills are interested in how much of the funding supports "outsiders." State governments often use reimbursement to inter-library lenders to encourage (or not discourage) resource sharing among libraries. Comparative cost data

would allow an equitable reimbursement. Borrowing on the other hand, is a service provided by the library to its own patrons. The assumption for costing, then, is that interlibrary borrowing would continue even if there were no interlibrary lending, and thus it creates no marginal incremental cost.

3. *Filled vs. total requests.* In an economic sense, the output of lending is a filled loan. There is no output resulting from an unfilled request. The cost incurred in processing a loan request that cannot be filled is, however, a real cost to the library. In addition, a state is unlikely to want to reimburse libraries for not filling loans. One solution to this problem is to include the costs associated with processing unfilled requests as a cost of interlibrary lending as a whole. When deriving a per-transaction cost, the total cost (cost of filled plus cost of unfilled) must be divided by the number of filled requests. A more traditional approach is to develop only the marginal incremental cost of completing successfully-filled loans. The methodology of cost-determination herein presented will address both of these methods.

4. *Estimates are OK.* For this methodology to be useful, it must be relatively efficient and simple to apply. Several cost models have been developed for interlibrary loan that involve detailed analysis of costs, stop-watch timing of staff activities, application of mathematical formulae replete with Greek symbols, and other complicated and time-consuming tasks. Such activities can be justified, and are statistically valid academic models that serve a valid purpose. But these sorts of models are not particularly useful to individual libraries or to state officials attempting to allocate scarce resources. Broad input and relative simplicity, which are considered necessary to this methodology, require that some latitude be provided to libraries to estimate their own costs.

5. *Cost-finding.* In *Cost Finding for Public Libraries: A Manager's Handbook,*[1] Philip Rosenberg utilizes a concept that is simpler than complete cost-accounting and yet satisfies the accuracy and comparability requirements of this methodology. The concept is called cost-finding, and is defined as

> a less formal method of cost determination or estimation on an irregular basis. There may be no formal accounting entries during the year to record costs incurred in specific cost accounts. Instead, cost finding usually involves taking available fund financial accounting data and recasting and adjusting it to derive the cost data or estimate needed. (William W. Holder, Robert J. Freeman, Harold H. Hensold, Jr., "Cost Accounting and Analysis in State and Local Government," *Cost and Managerial Accountant's Handbook* [New York: Dow Jones-Irwin, 1979] p. 97).

It is this cost-finding method that has been used in developing the methodology for this exercise; the Rosenberg book is recommended as a primer for those who use it to estimate costs.

6. *Accounting standards.* The credibility that cost estimates emanating from use of this methodology enjoy will to some extent depend upon conformance to generally accepted standards of accounting. Accounting standards for governmental units are largely dictated by the publication *Governmental Accounting, Auditing, and Financial Reporting,* promulgated by the National Committee on Governmental Accounting.[2] This work recognizes that financial accounting data are often inadequate to explain or defend programs that are not organized along financial accounting classifications. If the users of what this book calls "statistical reports" are to be accurately informed, the methodology for assembling the statistical data must be sufficiently structured to be uniformly and consistently applied. The methodology presented herein has been designed to meet this criterion.

Costs To Exclude And To Include

EXCLUSIONS

Based on the above philosophy, certain categories of cost must be excluded from the cost determination process. Costs to be excluded fall into the following categories:

1. *Collection costs.* Costs of acquiring materials for the library collection and for maintaining the collection are excluded. Since these costs would be incurred even if there were no interlibrary lending, no incremental cost is incurred.

2. *Circulation costs.* All costs associated with the circulation of materials are excluded. Materials circulated as interlibrary loans create little additional burden on the circulation system, and hence no marginal incremental cost.

3. *Catalog costs.* Costs of catalog creation, catalog production and catalog maintenance are excluded. No marginal incremental cost is created by interlibrary lending in this area.

4. *Library administration.* Central library administrative costs are excluded because interlibrary lending creates no additional cost in this area.

5. *Overhead.* Building overhead (utilities, etc.) and overhead costs of the parent organization (city, state, university) are no greater than they would be without interlibrary lending activity.

6. *Borrowing costs.* As stated above, costs of interlibrary borrowing are excluded from this methodology.

INCLUSIONS

By definition, all other costs should be included in cost estimation. The following costs, while not necessarily all-inclusive, are to be included.

1. *Staff costs.* The salary and wage costs of all staff efforts on interlibrary lending, along with the appropriate fringe benefit cost-allowance, must be included. This category will constitute a major fraction of the total cost. Fortunately, these costs are usually rather easy to determine.

2. *Network and communications costs.* The applicable cost of telephone, telefacsimile, electronic mail, network fees (OCLC, etc.) must be included. Costs for acquisition or use charges for software packages that facilitate interlibrary loan should be included in this category. It is necessary to adjust these total costs to represent only lending.

3. *Delivery costs.* All costs incurred in the process of delivering the requested material to the requester, to the extent the costs are not charged to the requester, should be included. These costs are packaging, postage, UPS or other commercial delivery charges, courier expenses, telefax, and so on.

4. *Photocopy costs.* Costs of copying materials to be sent to requesters is included. Any income from photocopy charges can be deducted from the total costs.

5. *Supplies costs.* The cost of supplies that would not otherwise be required should be included.

6. *Maintenance and equipment costs.* The cost of rental and/or maintenance of equipment that is required for interlibrary lending should be included. This could include dedicated copy machines, microcomputers, terminals, modems, etc. The acquisition of equipment items presents a problem, since these items will be used over an extended period of time. To allocate the total acquisition cost to the period when the purchase was made could result in the overestimation of costs for that period and the underestimation of costs for subsequent periods. This issue is discussed in the next section.

7. *Training costs.* The cost of training staff to process loan requests should be included to the extent that actual out-of-pocket expenses are incurred. Salary costs of trainees should be included under staff costs. However, costs of training workshops, tutorials, and the like, including related travel expenses, should be included in this category.

8. *Supervision costs.* The salary and fringe-benefit costs of providing direct supervision to lending activities should be included. In large libraries, this could be the major share of a professional salary. In smaller libraries, it could be a rather small fraction of the salary of someone who supervises interlibrary loan in addition to other activities. Costs in this category should be limited to the first-level supervision of interlibrary lending only. Higher levels of supervision are considered to be general library administration costs, and hence not included.

How To "Find" Costs

Using the philosophy and its application from the previous sections, this section will explain the specific methodology employed to find the appropriate cost of interlibrary lending. It is not possible to anticipate all

222

circumstances that could be present in all libraries, so this methodology must be presented at a certain level of generality. Judgment must, and should, be exercised in cost finding. Some arbitrary estimates may be necessary. This is acceptable practice so long as the person making the estimates is the one who has the best sense of the validity of the estimate. As a rule, real costs are better than estimates, and actual cost information should be used when readily available. Using this approach, material misstatements of cost are avoided, and the resulting costs can be defended as fairly representing actual costs of interlibrary lending. Each cost element from the preceding section will now be considered in detail.

STAFF COSTS

1. Identify the staff members who process interlibrary loan requests. Include staff who also have assignments in addition to interlibrary loan and staff who perform tasks for lending such as mail room personnel.

2. Find the annual, monthly, or hourly salary of each of these individuals. Costs will eventually be stated in annual terms, so determine annual salary at the start. Use 2,080 hours per year to convert a full-time hourly salary to an annual basis.

3. Find the fringe-benefit rate that the institution applies to salaries. If this is not known, contact the personnel or payroll office. Benefit rates range from about 12% to 20% of salaries. If no information can be obtained, use 15% as an estimate.

4. Multiply the fringe-benefit rate by the salary to determine the total fringe-benefit cost of each person identified in step 1.

5. Find the percentage of time that each person identified in step 1 normally spends on processing lending requests. Observation, or a short discussion with each person, should be sufficient to estimate this percentage. If this method is felt to be too imprecise, a short period of time-keeping could be used.

6. Multiply the percentage of time for each individual by the annual salary and fringe-benefit cost to find the applicable cost of lending for each person.

7. Add together the individual costs determined in step 6. This sum is the total staff cost. (Note: Several studies of interlibrary loan costs include consideration of the actual productive time of staff, excluding coffee breaks, sick time, vacation time, etc. This consideration is appropriate when building up costs from detailed time-studies. However, this is not a factor in this method, as the total annual cost of the staff does, in fact, include such non-productive time.)

NETWORK AND COMMUNICATIONS COSTS

1. Find the cost of telephone service. Library administration or accounts payable should be able to provide the cost of local telephone service on a per-phone basis. Many organizations can break down long-distance phone bills by major organizational elements (e.g., the library). Some phone systems keep track of long-distance calls and costs on an actual extension basis. A couple of phone calls should produce enough information to allow a reasonable estimate of total telephone cost. The cost estimate will probably be for the whole library.

2. Find the cost of interlibrary lending phone service. The cost of local service should be available. Get a per-phone cost and multiply by any phones used for interlibrary lending (or estimate the percentage of interlibrary lending use of the phone). Some portion of a library's long distance phone bill may be for interlibrary lending. An estimate may have to be made, if better information is unavailable. Convert the cost to an annual basis.

3. Find the cost of network and electronic mail services. If these costs are not readily known, the library administration or accounts payable should be able to provide total costs. If this approach is unsuccessful, vendor price-lists or a phone call to the vendor should get results. Vendors may even be willing to prepare standard cost information for a specific survey.

4. Determine interlibrary loan share of network services. Some of the network devices and charges may be for more than just interlibrary loan. OCLC, for example, charges for first-time use of cataloging infor-

mation and for placing a borrowing request but not for online transactions exclusively related to lending. However, OCLC access equipment may be used largely for interlibrary loan. Modem charges, telecommunication line charges, and terminal maintenance charges, as well as basic service fees and any other charges must be included. Invoices will usually provide this information. Remove from the total network cost those costs that are not related to interlibrary loan, such as cataloging charges. A period of observation of the use of the equipment may be necessary to do this. The net result should be interlibrary loan's cost of network services.

5. Determine lending share of total interlibrary loan network costs. In the example above, some part of the OCLC interlibrary loan cost should be allocated to lending. It may be possible to arrive at the lending share by reviewing the invoices for specific charges. A short period of detailed observation of the use of the equipment may be necessary. If no other method seems to be reasonable or defensible, apply the ratio of lending to borrowing to estimate the amount of cost allocable to lending. The ratio of lending to borrowing is found by adding together the number of lending and borrowing requests in a year, and then determining the percentage that each is of the total. If lending requests are 50% of the total, then 50% of the loan network costs can be allocated to lending.

6. Add all the annual costs of telephone and network services to find the total cost for this category.

DELIVERY COSTS

1. Find the total cost to the library for interlibrary lending postage. Only the outbound lending costs should be included. Mail rooms often keep track of postage costs by user, which in this case probably means the total library. Find, through interlibrary loan records or observation, what percent of outgoing postage volume is for mailing out interlibrary lending materials. Apply this percentage to the total postage cost to find the cost of lending postage.

2. Find the interlibrary lending cost of UPS or other parcel delivery services. These total costs can be found through accounts payable or the library administration. Delivery services may be "demand-actuated," (that is, someone must call for a pick-up). If so, it may be possible to determine directly the percent of the total volume that is generated by interlibrary lending. Interlibrary courier services, if used, will probably be carrying a variety of materials. Outbound interlibrary loans, returned loans, and incoming borrowed materials will all be included. The proportional share attributable to interlibrary lending of such a service can be estimated by applying the ratio of lending transactions to borrowing transactions.

3. Find other delivery costs. Other means of loan delivery should be identified and costs estimated for them. For example, facsimile transmission of material to fulfill a loan request should be counted if there is an additional cost. Staff time to do the faxing will have been counted already in staff costs. Telephone toll charges for faxing may already have been counted in telephone charges. Maintenance and/or equipment rental is better accounted for under maintenance and equipment costs. Fax equipment is probably also used to receive interlibrary borrowing material. There may well be no additional cost to find in the case of telefax.

4. Add up all the delivery costs found in the above steps to determine total lending delivery costs. Some costs of delivery are traditionally billed to the borrower, and should not be included in the cost accumulated here. It may be easier to accumulate all costs, and then reduce the total delivery cost by the amount reimbursed.

PHOTOCOPY COSTS

Find the cost of photocopying material to be sent to fulfill loan requests. See the above discussion on fax costs. If copy costs are reimbursed, the cost should be reduced to allow for that. Most libraries have some cost-per-copy policy for photocopies. Usually, even if the borrowers are charged, they are not charged full cost. Estimate the total number of pages of photocopy made for interlibrary lending in a year. Apply a cost-per-page. If no other information is easily available, use $.07 per page.

SUPPLIES COSTS

Find the cost of specialized supplies that are used only for interlibrary lending. Special paper used for computer terminals in lending transactions, imprinted envelopes, mailing labels, or packaging materials are examples. (It is not worthwhile to cost out pencils and paperclips.) This will be a minor component of total cost, so it is not worth a great deal of effort.

MAINTENANCE AND EQUIPMENT COSTS

1. Determine equipment costs. As stated above, the cost of equipment is a real cost to interlibrary lending. There are many cost-accounting issues that enter into the determination of the appropriate annual charge for costs of equipment used over an extended period of time. For our purposes, the annual-use charge concept best fits the philosophical assumptions. Under this method, which is broadly used in government contracts, an estimated cost of the use of equipment is allocated to cost centers (in this case, to interlibrary lending), even in periods when no new equipment is acquired. Over time, this method will average equipment costs and is less difficult to estimate and administer than methods which deal with specific depreciation costs. To find the appropriate equipment cost for interlibrary lending, these steps should be followed:

    (a) List all the equipment that is used in interlibrary loan. Include a dedicated copy machine (but not the shared use of a general library machine, for its costs will already have been counted as photocopy costs); and any terminals or computers that are used, the costs of which have not already been counted as network costs. Include only extra equipment for interlibrary loan. Do not include desks, chairs, or file cabinets.

    (b) Find the cost of equipment identified as used by interlibrary loan. Invoices, price lists, or property lists should be available within the library.

    (c) Multiply the cost times an equipment-use factor of 0.25. This assumes an average life for a piece of equipment of four years (25% per year of use). Do this even if the equipment is more than four years old, or if it is new and will be replaced in less than four years. The point is to use a single rate for all equipment. Four years is a generally accepted "class life" for office equipment.

    (d) Estimate the percentage of use of the equipment that is attributable to interlibrary lending. As in other cases discussed above, if there is no information to the contrary, use the ratio of lending to borrowing.

    (e) Multiply the percentage from (d) by the equipment cost from (c) to arrive at the use-cost for interlibrary lending.

2. Find the cost of rental and maintenance costs of equipment. Rental and maintenance charges of equipment that have not already been included in other categories of cost (such as network costs) must now be included. Vendor invoices, rental contracts, or maintenance contracts should be available from accounts payable or the library administration. Since these charges are by the month or year, it is not necessary to apply use factors. Once the total interlibrary loan cost has been found, the lending to borrowing ratio can be applied to get the lending cost of rental and maintenance of equipment.

3. Add the use cost from 1(e) to the rental and maintenance cost from 2 to arrive at the total maintenance and equipment cost. (Note that it does not matter if costs are called network costs or equipment costs, as long as the costs are counted only once.)

TRAINING COSTS

Find the out-of-pocket cost, if any, of specific interlibrary lending training. As stated above, staff costs should be excluded. Costs of training seminars, workshops, conferences, and travel to training sessions should be included. If these training experiences were for interlibrary loan in general, and not just for lending, apply the lending to borrowing ratio to find the amount to apply to lending.

Find the first-level supervision cost of lending. Depending on how staff costs were cumulated, these costs may already have been counted. If not, use the same methods described under Staff Costs to arrive at the cost of first-level supervision.

All components of interlibrary lending costs have now been determined, and the sum of the category totals will be the total cost of interlibrary lending.

Finding Cost Per Transaction

All costs found above should be annual estimates. To determine unit cost, that is, the average cost of an interlibrary lending transaction, the annual cost is divided by the annual number of lending transactions. This calculation introduces the issue of the cost of unfilled loans. As stated in the section on Philosophy, two methods have been chosen to address this issue. The first method is to assume that the cost of processing unfilled loan requests is really a cost of the lending activity as a whole and, as such, should be reflected in the per-transaction cost of processing filled loans. A 1982 study by the University of Kansas Libraries[3] used this method to determine their costs per lending transaction. The simple formula below will provide the per unit cost using this method.

Method 1 formula:

$$\frac{\text{total cost of interlibrary lending}}{\text{number of filled interlibrary lending requests}} = \text{Cost per filled loan}$$

The second method is more complex. In this case, only the cost to process filled requests is to be included. This makes it also necessary to determine the cost to process unfilled requests. There is no simple way to make that determination. The only sure way to make a distinction is to do a time-and-motion study to track staff time and other expenses attributable to unfilled requests, or to track specific transactions, accumulating their individual costs. These are not practical alternatives. Two studies reviewed for this exercise specifically addressed the cost of filled vs. unfilled loans. The first is a highly reputable study of costs of interlibrary loans in academic libraries.[4] The second is a study of interlibrary lending costs at the University of Colorado at Boulder.[5] These studies show that an unfilled loan request costs considerably less than a filled loan; the cost of an unfilled loan is 50%–65% of the cost of a filled loan. For this exercise, assume that an unfilled loan costs 55% as much as a filled loan. (Substitute the actual percentage if known.) A formula has been developed to determine the cost of a filled loan transaction, once the cost of all lending transactions has been determined.

Method 2 formula:

$$F = \frac{C}{f + .55u}$$

Where:
    F = Cost per filled lending request
    C = Total cost of interlibrary lending
    f = Number of filled requests
    u = Number of unfilled requests

The formula assumes that the cost of an unfilled request is 55% of the cost of a filled request. (A different cost assumption could be substituted, and the formula adjusted accordingly.) This formula is derived from the relationship of the components which make up the total cost of interlibrary lending (C in the formula). These components are: filled requests (f) times the cost per filled request (F), plus unfilled requests (u) times the cost per unfilled request (U). This relationship can be stated as:

$$C = (f \times F) + (u \times U)$$

To solve for F, the cost of a filled transaction, the formula becomes:

$$F = \frac{C}{f + .55u}$$

An example may more clearly illustrate use of the formula. Suppose total cost of interlibrary lending was found to be $40,000 a year, using the above methodology. Suppose further that there were 15,000 interlibrary lending requests in a year, and that 10,000 of these were filled and 5,000 were unfilled. Entering these values in the formula would produce:

$$F = \frac{40,000}{10,000 + (.55 \times 5,000)}$$

$$F = \frac{40,000}{12,750}$$

F = 3.137 or $3.14 per filled request
U = .55 × 3.137 or $1.73 per unfilled request

Uses Of This Cost Information

It is necessary to address the issue of the appropriate use of the information resulting from the application of this methodology. The total lending costs derived are not to be taken as absolute costs. But even though almost all of the components of cost have been estimated, it is possible to use the results as a fair representation of the cost of interlibrary lending, particularly if the results are aggregated for many libraries. The results may be used to compare relative costs of interlibrary lending of one library to those of another, as a common structure and methodology is used. Costs may be compared among libraries of like kind, such as public libraries or academic libraries. Significant variations in cost-per-transaction among different libraries could be the result of many factors. The nature of the library, the physical location of the collection (many branches, etc.), the administrative organization of the interlibrary loan function, and the degree of automation used, are examples of such factors. On a statewide basis, the *average* cost per transaction obtained from aggregating individual library costs based on this methodology could be used to set state interlibrary lending reimbursement levels. Within the appropriate limits cited here, the methodology should provide credible information of significant value to individual libraries, state librarians, and other interested parties.

Notes

1. Philip Rosenberg, *Cost Finding for Public Libraries: A Manager's Handbook* (Chicago: American Library Association, 1985), 9.
2. National Committee on Governmental Accounting, *Governmental Accounting, Auditing, and Financial Reporting* (Chicago: Municipal Finance Officers of the United States and Canada, 1976).
3. *Interlibrary Loan Costs at KU* (Lawrence, KS: University of Kansas Libraries, 1982).
4. Vernon E. Palmour et al., *A Study of the Characteristics, Costs, and Magnitude of Interlibrary Loans in Academic Libraries.* Prepared for the Association of Research Libraries (Westport, CT: Greenwood Publishing Co., 1972).
5. *Interlibrary Lending Cost Analysis Study* (Boulder, CO: University of Colorado at Boulder Libraries, 1982).

Cost Of Interlibrary Lending

Data Form

Library: _____
    Person completing data form: _____
    Telephone number: _____
    Title: _____

Please refer to Dickson, Stephen P. and Virginia Boucher, "A Methodology for Determining Costs of Interlibrary Lending" for guidance in determining costs for the individual sections of this data form.

A. STAFF COSTS

1. Staff member annual salary _____ plus
   fringe benefit cost _____ equals
   annual salary & fringe benefit cost   _____

   Percent of lending time _____ times annual
   salary & fringe benefit cost _____
   equals cost of lending for staff member 1   _____

2. Staff member annual salary _____ plus
   fringe benefit cost _____ equals
   annual salary & fringe benefit cost   _____

   Percent of lending time _____ times annual
   salary & fringe benefit cost _____
   equals cost of lending for staff member 2   _____

3. Staff member annual salary _____ plus
   fringe benefit cost _____ equals
   annual salary & fringe benefit cost   _____

   Percent of lending time _____ times annual
   salary & fringe benefit cost _____
   equals cost of lending for staff member 3   _____

TOTAL STAFF COSTS   _____

B. NETWORK AND COMMUNICATION COSTS

1. Telephone service

   Local telephone service   _____
   Long distance calls   _____
   Total telephone services   _____

   Lending share _____ (%) times
   telephone services equals
   total telephone costs   _____

2. Electronic mail

   Electronic mail services   _____

   lending share _____ (%) times
   electronic mail services equals
   total electronic mail costs   _____

3. Network services

   Modem charges   _____
   Telecommunication line charges   _____
   Terminal maintenance   _____
   Basic service fees   _____
   Other   _____
   Total network services   _____

   Lending share _____ (%) times
   total network services
   equals total network costs   _____

   TOTAL NETWORK AND COMMUNICATION COSTS   =============

C. DELIVERY COSTS FOR LENDING

   1. Postage   _____
   2. Parcel delivery service   _____
   3. Telefacsimile   _____
   4. Courier   _____
   5. Other   _____
      Total delivery service   _____

   Lending share _____ (%) times
   total delivery service
   equals total delivery costs   _____

   TOTAL DELIVERY COSTS FOR LENDING   =============

D. PHOTOCOPY COSTS

   (Staff costs, supplies costs, and equipment costs may include all the
   photocopy costs, in which case this section should be left blank.)

   Photocopy costs not covered elsewhere for lending   _____

   Minus income from photocopy charges to other libraries   _____

   TOTAL PHOTOCOPY COSTS   =============

E. SUPPLIES COST

ALA forms (no addresses)	Printer paper
Invoices	Printer ribbons
Imprinted envelopes	Typewriter ribbons
Mailing labels	Staplers
Microfiche mailers	File folders
Packaging materials	Other
Diskettes	

   TOTAL SUPPLIES COSTS   =============

F. MAINTENANCE AND EQUIPMENT COSTS

    1. _____ cost _____
       times .25 equals   _____

    2. _____ cost _____
       times .25 equals   _____

    3. _____ cost _____
       times .25 equals   _____

    4. _____ cost _____
       times .25 equals   _____

    Total equipment costs   _____

    Lending share _____ (%) times
    total equipment costs
    equals lending equipment costs   _____

    5. Rental and maintenance costs   _____

    Lending share _____ (%) times
    rental and maintenance costs
    equals total rental and maintenance costs   _____

    TOTAL MAINTENANCE AND EQUIPMENT COSTS   ========

G. TRAINING COSTS

    TOTAL TRAINING COSTS   ========

H. SUPERVISION COSTS

    (Already included in Staff Costs?)

    TOTAL SUPERVISION COSTS   ========

TOTAL COST OF INTERLIBRARY LENDING
(Add all figures with a double line)   ========

Total cost of lending _____ divided by the number
of filled interlibrary lending requests _____
equals the cost per filled loan   ========

Note: This form was designed to compute the cost of lending using method 1 only.

Interlibrary Borrowing

Some libraries wish to know what it costs to borrow a book or obtain photocopy through interlibrary loan. If a similar cost can be derived for acquiring, cataloging, and maintaining a volume, a comparison can be made as to whether it is more effective to borrow or to buy. Knowing the interlibrary loan cost for photocopy can help in determining whether or not to use a commercial supplier or what the financial burden might be if serials titles are cancelled. Of course, there are other considerations such as the time the document is needed, how well an acquisition would fit in with the collection development policy, and the current staffing of the two units. For those who think that interlibrary loan is not part of basic library service, it may be necessary to determine a reasonable cost of borrowing before uniform charges are passed on to the library user. The authors believe that interlibrary loan *is* a basic part of library service.

"A Methodology for Determining Costs of Interlibrary Lending," by Stephen P. Dickson and Virginia Boucher, should be used in conjunction with these recommendations. It starts at the beginning of appendix EE. It can be also found in *Research Access through New Technology,* edited by Mary E. Jackson, pp. 137–159, New York: AMS Press, 1989.

In the PHILOSOPHY section, Filled vs. Total Requests, Estimates are O.K., Cost Finding, and Accounting Standards apply to calculating borrowing costs as well as lending costs. This study is concerned with borrowing only and not at all with lending. Marginal Incremental Costs do not apply here since borrowing is a legitimate and common part of library service, not something that is considered an add on. Some costs of operating the library itself, then, will have to be included.

The COSTS TO EXCLUDE AND TO INCLUDE section will be somewhat different also. Collection Costs and Catalog Costs will not be included nor will Circulation Costs since the latter are such a tiny percentage of the total circulation in most libraries. Lending costs, of course, are not included in the cost of borrowing. The new additions here are Library Administration and Overhead, which will have to be included since borrowing is considered here a regular part of library service.

The list of areas to be included will be as follows for borrowing:

Staff Costs

Network and Communications Costs

Delivery Costs

Photocopy Costs

Supplies Costs

Maintenance and Equipment Costs

Training Costs

Supervision Costs

Library Administration Costs

Overhead Costs

Loan Costs

The HOW TO 'FIND' COSTS section can be used easily by substituting the word "borrowing" when "lending" is used. Remember to use the borrowing share of the total, if actual costs are not known. Photocopy Costs would include the invoices which have to be paid in order to acquire photocopy for library users at your own institution. There will also need to be a category of payments for books borrowed as well as for photocopy. If costs are passed on to the library user, the money paid would have to be subtracted from the total.

Library Administration and Overhead are not easy to calculate. Overhead can include utilities, janitorial service, depreciation on furnishings, and for many, a central administrative cost such as that for a university or a city government. There is some consistency in academic libraries, but other types of libraries vary dramatically in the application of overhead costs. The best way to find the library administration and overhead costs is to talk with the financial officer for the larger entity (city, academic institution or the like). If there is a certified rate, use it. If nothing can be obtained, use 40% of the total direct costs.

In conducting the study, be certain to include any other parts of the library operations where work is done specifically for interlibrary borrowing, such as the mail room or work on an information desk where requests are received.

FINDING THE COST PER TRANSACTION can be done when the total borrowing costs are added together and when the total borrowing transactions are known. These transactions should include the filled borrowing requests, the unfilled borrowing requests (they usually take as much or more work than the filled ones), and the found-in-library requests. In other words, *all* the borrowing transactions are considered here to be equally important and equally time consuming.

The simple formula below will provide the per unit cost using this method:

$$\frac{\text{Total Cost of Interlibrary Borrowing}}{\text{Number of Filled Interlibrary Borrowing Requests}} = \text{Cost per Borrowing Request}$$

It is necessary to address the issue of the appropriate use of the information resulting from the application of this methodology. The total borrowing costs derived are not justifiable as absolute costs. Though almost all of the components of cost have been estimated, it is possible to use the results as a fair representation of the cost of interlibrary borrowing, particularly if it is possible to aggregate the results for many libraries. The results can be used to compare relative costs of interlibrary borrowing for one library to another, since a common structure and methodology is used. Costs can be compared among like types of libraries, such as public libraries or academic libraries. Significant variations in costs per transaction among different libraries should be the result of many factors such as the nature of the library, the physical location of the collection, the administrative organization of the interlibrary loan function and the degree of automation used. An average cost per transaction obtained from aggregating individual library inputs based on this methodology could be used to see if the interlibrary borrowing appears to be "normal" compared to other libraries. An average cost per transaction can also be compared to the average cost for acquiring, cataloging, and maintaining a volume, should that cost be available, to see whether it is more cost effective to borrow or to buy.

Interlibrary Loan Training and Continuing Education Model Statement of Objectives

I. Introduction

The impetus for the development of these objectives arose from a recognition of the continually increasing demand on interlibrary loan personnel along with the apparent lack of guidelines both for training and continuing education purposes.

A national survey conducted by this subcommittee in early 1989 ascertained that a widely felt need for program development existed in the interlibrary loan community. However, the subcommittee believed that, prior to the development of any model program(s), a commonly accepted core body of skills and knowledge was needed on which to base such programs. It was also assumed that such programs would need to be tailored to local and regional needs. In support of this, the committee sought to assist by codifying a core list of knowledge and skills and accompanying objectives for training.

Structure

In our approach, we have taken as our model the language and form of objectives commonly applied in the field of education. The structure of the document provides general goals for the achievement of knowledge and skills in five core areas of interlibrary loan practice: codes, borrowing and lending procedures, copyright compliance and management of interlibrary loan. These general goals are supplemented by *terminal objectives* which describe specific elements of knowledge, competence or skill defined as necessary to achieve the general objective. In many cases, sample *enabling objectives,* which are designed to state in measurable terms the achievement of the terminal objectives, are included. Because of the variety of responsibilities that any staff member may have, these training objectives are defined by function rather than by position, with the exception of the manager who is assumed to have specific role-defined responsibilities. Thus, for the purposes of this document, "staff member" is not defined in terms of any specific job description within interlibrary loan. In addition, the subcommittee would like to specifically acknowledge the important contributions of Virginia Boucher and her Interlibrary Loan Practices Handbook (see bibliography), which provides us with an excellent logical framework with which to organize our own work.

Audience

The intended audience for these objectives is any interlibrary loan staff member responsible for the development of training materials and sequences for new staff as well as planners of interlibrary loan continuing education and training on the local, state, regional and national levels.

Use of the Objectives

These objectives have been created primarily as a guide for the development of new training and continuing education programs. It is anticipated that they can be flexibly applied to the development of both broad and specifically focused programs, with planners developing additional, and in most cases, more specific enabling objectives, based on local policies and practices. For example, planners of a workshop on verification may choose as their instructional goal that participants master the terminal objectives related to the major reference sources for verifying serial holdings within the state or network. Toward that end, the planners would select Terminal Objectives 5 through 9 from the General Objective on ILL Verification, and adapt and/or augment the suggested enabling objectives to measure the success of the training.

In addition, these objectives may be used as an inventory list against which existing programs may be measured. Through comparisons with ideals as well as with current practices, it is hoped that these objectives will emerge as an integral model for the design of comprehensive and uniform interlibrary loan training.

RASD Interlibrary Loan Committee
Subcommittee on Continuing Education
  and Training
Barbara Beaton, Chair; Tom Gilson,
Peggy Jobe, Chris Loring, Helen Moeller
January 1990

II. Interlibrary Loan Codes

General Objective:

The staff member understands the principles of resource sharing through which libraries can responsibly augment the availability of materials through their own collections and how relevant international, national, regional, local or consortia interlibrary loan codes govern interlibrary loan policies and procedures.

Terminal and Enabling Objectives:

T.1   The staff member knows the interlibrary loan codes which apply to his/her library.

    E.1   The staff member can name and locate the texts of all interlibrary loan codes applicable to the library.

T.2   The staff member understands the purpose of interlibrary loan.

    E.1   The staff member can determine if any interlibrary loan request is a legitimate request according to applicable codes and reject inappropriate requests.

    E.2   The staff member can determine when a request or pattern of requests suggests consideration by collection development and/or acquisitions staff.

T.3   The staff member understands the scope of interlibrary loan.

    E.1   The staff member is able to identify and consult sources to ascertain other institutions' lending policies.

    E.2   The staff member can identify the types of material which may not be available through interlibrary loan due to their nature and in such cases consult lending policies before initiating borrowing requests.

T.4   The staff member is aware of the responsibilities of a borrowing library.

    E.1   The staff member can describe his/her library's resources and its bibliographic control and determine which interlibrary loan requests can be filled from those holdings.

    E.2   The staff member can identify and use locations with which his/her library has cooperative resource-sharing agreements before requesting materials from locations outside the state or region.

234

E.3 The staff member can identify when his/her library becomes responsible for damage or loss of material.

E.4 The staff member can identify any conditions of loan the lending library has established, including its fee structure.

T.5 The staff member is aware of the responsibilities of a lending library.

E.1 The staff member can state his/her library's interlibrary loan lending policy and fee structure.

E.2 The staff member can state reasons for not filling requests and the method by which the requesting library is notified of the inability to fill a request.

T.6 The staff member understands the responsibilities of the borrowing and lending libraries regarding the costs of interlibrary loan.

E.1 The staff member can describe the costs a borrowing library assumes when initiating an interlibrary loan request.

E.2 The staff member can describe what procedures they, as lenders, should follow when charges for filling a lending request will exceed what the borrowing library has authorized.

T.7 The staff member understands the duration, conditions and nature of interlibrary loans.

E.1 The staff member can establish the appropriate duration of a loan for borrowed material.

E.2 The staff member can describe when it is appropriate to grant or request a renewal for a borrowed item.

E.3 The staff member of a borrowing library can describe what their obligation is regarding material recalled by a lending library.

E.4 The staff member of a borrowing library knows the followup procedure when patrons' materials are overdue, lost or otherwise not returned within the stated loan periods.

III. Procedures: Borrowing

A. General Objective: ILL Interviewing

The staff member understands how interlibrary loan functions and can use this understanding to answer patron queries and to elicit complete information from the patron.

Terminal and Enabling Objectives:

T.1 The staff member is aware of any eligibility requirements for the use of interlibrary loan at his/her institution.

E.1 The staff member can name the categories of clientele which are eligible for interlibrary loan service.

E.2 The staff member can name appropriate alternatives for those patrons not eligible for interlibrary loan service.

T.2 The staff member is aware of current transmission and delivery methods for interlibrary loan requests.

E.1 The staff member can describe, in sequence, the preferred methods of transmission and delivery for requests.

T.3 The staff member is aware of typical turnaround times for various types of requests.

 E1. The staff member can describe various local and regional consortia collection strengths and typical response times.

T.4 The staff member is familiar with typical loan and photocopy fees.

 E.1 The staff member can describe probable loan or copy charges to patron in advance of transaction, solicit permission from patron and describe institution's procedure for receiving payment.

T.5 The staff member understands availability periods as they relate to interlibrary loan and can counsel the patron about timely pickup of requested materials to maximize use of returnable materials.

T.6 The staff member is able to instruct the patron in the completion of an interlibrary loan request form.

T.7 The staff member recognizes the bibliographic elements necessary to adequately identify a book, periodical, article, newspaper, microform, dissertation or thesis, government publication, technical report, or conference proceeding.

 E.1 The staff member, given a variety of citations for materials in different formats, can correctly complete interlibrary loan request forms for those items.

T.8 The staff member understands the principles of the Copyright Act of 1976 as they apply to interlibrary loan and can counsel the patron as to whether or not the request complies with that Act.

 E.1 The staff member can, given sample requests, determine whether a request conforms to either or neither CCG or CCL guidelines.

T.9 The staff member understands when to suggest that the patron use the material at the owning library rather than requesting through interlibrary loan.

B. General Objective: ILL Verification

The staff member recognizes the bibliographic information necessary to verify and locate a book, pamphlet, periodical, article, newspaper in microform, thesis or dissertation, government publication, technical report, or conference proceeding.

Terminal and Enabling Objectives:

T.1 The staff member recognizes a complete citation.

T.2 The staff member understands that the *form of citation* varies for different subject areas and disciplines and can reconcile these differences with acceptable interlibrary loan practice.

T.3 The staff member recognizes that the *amount of information* required in a citation varies for different subject areas and disciplines and can reconcile these differences with acceptable interlibrary loan practice.

T.4 The staff member is able to identify access points within the citation to be used in verification.

 E.1 The staff member can name the most common forms of main and added entries under AACR1 and AACR2.

T.5 The staff member is familiar with, and can select, the most appropriate major reference tools to verify book, pamphlet, periodical, newspaper, microform, thesis or dissertation, government publication, technical report, or conference proceedings.

    E.1   The staff member can name, in sequence, the appropriate tools for verification of a variety of materials.

T.6   The staff member is familiar with appropriate online databases, indices, abstracts, catalogs, and bibliographies to verify incomplete or incorrect citations.

    E.1   The staff member can name regional and national networks accessible in his/her library, such as OCLC, RLIN, etc.

    E.2   The staff member can search cd-rom and other locally available electronic bibliographic resources.

    E.3   The staff member can appropriately consult with or refer to other staff members with greater expertise in scope and protocols for searching when necessary.

T.7   The staff member understands that form of entry and access points may vary in different reference tools.

T.8   The staff member is aware of major tools such as Sheehy's <u>Guide to Reference Books</u> to suggest alternate avenues of research for problem citations.

T.9   The staff member is aware of acceptable forms of abbreviation for verification in transmitting requests.

    E.1   The staff member can name standard and/or locally acceptable sources for identifying and interpreting abbreviations.

T.10 The staff member is aware of the need to monitor changes in database construction which may alter points of access and search strategies.

C. General Objective: Transmission of Requests

The staff member is familiar with, and can implement, the various methods of transmitting interlibrary loan requests.

Terminal and Enabling Objectives:

T.1   The staff member knows the uses of the ALA Interlibrary request form and the proper completion of the form.

    E.1   The staff member can identify the various data elements of the ALA ILL form and understands their importance in the loan process.

    E.2   The staff member can complete the ALA ILL form with all the necessary information for a successful transaction and follow correct procedures for mailing ALA ILL requests.

T.2   The staff member knows the purpose and uses of the relevant network (OCLC, RLIN, WLN, etc.) ILL subsystem for borrowing requests.

    E.1   The staff member can use the network ILL documentation to determine appropriate policies and procedures.

    E.2   The staff member can format and transmit a request as outlined in the network documentation.

    E.3   The staff member can identify and use additional features of an ILL subsystem when appropriate (e.g. directories, union lists, etc.).

E.4　The staff member can update and respond to system messages to complete borrowing transactions and maintain accurate borrowing files.

T.3　The staff member knows how to use an electronic mail system to format and transmit ILL borrowing requests.

E.1　The staff member can identify the electronic mail system(s) available for ILL use.

E.2　The staff member can format and transmit a request on the electronic mail system according to any applicable policies.

T.4　The staff member knows how to fill a borrowing request via telefacsimile.

E.1　The staff member can operate the telefacsimile equipment.

E.2　The staff member can locate the policies and procedures governing the use of telefacsimile for transmitting requests.

E.3　The staff member can name the data elements to be included on the form used in making the telefacsimile transmission.

D. General Objective: Responsibility for Borrowed Materials

The staff member understands the borrowing library's responsibilities and accompanying procedures for the safe return of materials.

Terminal and Enabling Objectives:

T.1　The staff member knows all delivery options available to his/her borrowing library.

E.1　The staff member can select the most appropriate method for delivery, taking into account speed of delivery, cost, and safety of materials.

E.2　The staff member can identify participants of all document delivery couriers or interagency mail arrangements.

E.3　The staff member can identify any special packaging or labeling requirements for each of these options.

T.2　The staff member knows the proper procedures for packaging materials for safe transit.

E.1　The staff member can select suitable cartons and boxes and pack them to ship various library materials safely.

T.3　The staff member recognizes that materials must be insured against loss or damage.

E.1　The staff member can name policies and procedures governing the insuring of materials being returned to lending libraries and whether chosen delivery method requires additional insurance.

E.2　The staff member can determine the value of the items being insured.

E.3　The staff member can complete the appropriate paperwork to assure insurance coverage.

E. General Objective: Role of National Libraries

T.1　The staff member recognizes that the resources of national libraries are to be considered as a last resort for the identification of locations or the loan of materials for research and serious study.

E.1 The staff member can identify, in appropriate sequence, all options to be exhausted prior to requesting assistance or loan from a national library.

E.2 The staff member can identify the appropriate national library to which a request for assistance or loan should be sent.

IV. Procedures: Lending

General Objective:

The staff member understands and adheres to all applicable policies and procedures in lending material through interlibrary loan.

Terminal and Enabling Objectives:

T.1 The staff member is aware of the relevant policies governing his/her institution's clientele for the provision of materials through interlibrary loan.

E.1 The staff member can determine whether a requesting library is within the scope of his/her library's policy.

E.2 The staff member can describe his/her institution's loan periods for various materials and formats.

T.2 The staff member knows the categories of materials excluded from loan, or with special loan conditions by his/her institution (e.g. rare, reference, etc.).

T.3 The staff member can communicate these policies through any appropriate medium to requesting libraries.

T.4 The staff member understands and adheres to the unique response requirements of the interlibrary loan system(s) or network(s) used.

E.1 The staff member responds to interlibrary loan requests using NISO standard responses.

E.2 The staff member is able to respond within the time frame designated by the system or network in the appropriate manner.

T.5 The staff member understands and adheres to any special requirements of the borrower.

E.1 The staff member is able to determine if the borrower is willing to pay the amount charged by the lender.

E.2 The staff member is able to recognize and describe appropriate handling for requests requiring special treatment, such as time, shipping, or billing requirements.

V. Copyright Compliance

General Objective:

The staff member understands the principles of the Copyright Act of 1976 as they apply to interlibrary loan.

Terminal and Enabling Objectives:

T.1 The staff member understands and adheres to established guidelines for copyright compliance in borrowing practices.

E.1 The staff member can identify appropriate locations for the display of copyright warnings.

E.2 The staff member is able to determine whether a photocopy request is covered by copyright.

E.3 If the item is covered by copyright, the staff member is able to determine whether copying is permissible under CONTU guidelines and so indicate on the request.

E.4 If the request will result in exceeding limits set by these guidelines, the staff member is able to choose an appropriate course of action from the alternatives open to him/her.

T.2 The staff member is aware of guidelines for the retention of records for photocopy requests.

E.1 The staff member can apply these guidelines to the development and/or maintenance of a record retention system.

E.2 The staff member is able to retrieve relevant information from the system.

T.3 The staff member is aware of the responsibilities of the lending library in maintaining copyright compliance.

E.1 The staff member is able to recognize non-compliance in requests received and respond appropriately to the requesting library.

VI. Management of Interlibrary Loan

General Objective:

The manager can administer interlibrary loan for optimal effectiveness and efficiency.

Terminal and Enabling Objectives:

T.1 The manager of interlibrary loan can administer the service within the context of the library's and interlibrary loan service's goals and objectives.

E.1 The manager can locate the library's mission statement, collection development and service policies statement and can describe the role of interlibrary loan within the context of such statements.

E.2 The manager can provide written interlibrary loan goals and objectives that build upon the library's goals and objectives.

T.2 The manager is aware of the interdependence of interlibrary loan and collection development within his/her institution.

E.1 The manager can identify current collecting patterns of the library.

E.2 The manager can describe existing strengths and weaknesses in the collection.

T.3 The manager can solve problems and plan for change.

E.1 The manager can describe his/her planning process for problem solving and for implementing change.

E.2 The manager can identify changes within either the library itself or the interlibrary loan environment as a whole that will affect interlibrary loan policies and procedures and thus require planning.

E.3 The manager can identify interlibrary loan objectives that are not being met and can describe how they will be met in the future.

T.4 The manager is able to analyze and forecast trends in borrowing and lending volume so that staffing and equipment is maintained at adequate levels.

240

E.1 The manager can identify what data are collected in her/his office and justify their collection.

E.2 The manager can describe which interlibrary loan data can be used as measures of borrowing and lending trends and performance.

E.3 The manager can identify, evaluate and implement appropriate microcomputer and/or mainframe programs to aid in the collection and analysis of data.

T.5 A manager can provide thorough and effective training and staff development for ILL employees.

E.1 The manager can describe the steps in the training method that he/she employs.

E.2 The manager can produce a job description for each interlibrary loan staff member.

E.3 The manager can provide and update procedural manuals for each position or task.

T.6 A manager supervises interlibrary loan staff so that they perform effectively and efficiently.

E.1 The manager can provide job performance standards or expectations for all interlibrary loan positions.

E.2 The manager can describe how he/she monitors the performance of each staff member.

E.3 The manager can describe the method of performance review and appraisal that he/she employs.

T.7 A manager can ensure that appropriate record and bookkeeping systems are in place and maintained on a timely basis.

T.8 A manager can ensure that the interlibrary loan service operates in an ethical manner.

E.1 The manager enforces the spirit of the Copyright Act of 1976 as it applies to interlibrary loan operations in his/her institution.

E.2 The manager can identify major sources of information (e.g. ALA Yearbook, Bowker Annual) for monitoring current developments in copyright law which affect interlibrary borrowing and lending.

E.3 The manager can describe when it is appropriate to request material from libraries beyond local and regional resources.

E.4 The manager can determine when a pattern of interlibrary loan requests suggests consideration by collection development or acquisitions staff.

E.5 The manager can apply other ethical considerations, such as confidentiality of patron records, to policies and practices.

VII. Bibliography

Boucher, Virginia. Interlibrary loan practices handbook (Chicago: American Library Association, 1984).

"Guidelines and procedures for telefacsimile transmission of interlibrary loan requests," RQ 30 (Winter, 1990). In press.

Guidelines for packing and shipping microforms (Chicago: Association for Library Collections and Technical Services, 1989).

"International lending: principles and guidelines for procedure," IFLA Journal 14 (3):258–264 (1988).

ORGANIZATIONS

Many organizations occasionally provide information, workshops, or additional training for interlibrary loan and document delivery for the area they cover:

> Consortia
> Library service systems (public library, multi-type, etc.)
> State libraries
> State library associations
> Regional library associations
> Regional networks
> Special interlibrary loan and document delivery groups

Bibliographic utilities provide interlibrary loan information and training:

> OCLC (Online Computer Library Center)
> > OCLC ILL Users Group (meets at ALA conferences)
> RLIN (Research Libraries Information Network)
> WLN

American Library Association (ALA)

> Reference and Adult Services Division, Management and Organization of Public Services Section, ALA

> > At midwinter (January) and annual conference (June) these groups meet:

> > > Interlibrary Loan Discussion Group (welcome to participate)
> > > Interlibrary Loan Committee (welcome as observers)

> > Interlibrary loan programs at annual conference, usually every other year

> Association of College and Research Libraries, ALA

> > At midwinter (January) and annual conference (June) these groups meet:

> > > Copyright Committee
> > > Fee-based Information Service Centers in Academic Libraries (FISCAL) Discussion Group

> Association of Specialized and Cooperative Library Agencies, Interlibrary Cooperation and Networking Section, ALA

> > At midwinter (January) and annual conference (June) these groups meet:

> > > Interlibrary Cooperation Discussion Group
> > > International Networking Discussion Group

Exhibits of products at ALA conferences

International Federation of Library Associations and Institutions (IFLA)

Meetings, programs and workshops at annual conferences, usually in August:
Document Delivery and Interlending Section

PUBLICATIONS

Interlending & Document Supply. vol. 11, no. 1– . Boston Spa, Wetherby, West Yorkshire, U.K.: British Library Document Supply Centre, 1983– .

Preceded by *Interlending Review, BLL Review,* and *NLL Review.*

Journal of Interlibrary Loan, Document Delivery & Information Supply. vol. 4, no. 1– . Binghamton, N.Y.: Haworth, 1993– .

Preceded by *Journal of Interlibrary Loan and Information Supply.*

Library & Information Science Research. vol. 5– . Norwood, N.J.: Ablex, 1983– .

Preceded by *Library Research.*

RASD Update, Reference and Adult Services Division, ALA (occasional information)

RQ, Reference and Adult Services Division, ALA (occasional articles)

Newsletters of appropriate organizations:

OCLC (including log-on messages)
RLIN
WLN
Consortia
Library service systems
State libraries
State library associations
Regional library associations
Regional networks
Special interlibrary loan and document delivery groups

Indexes, CD-ROMs, and OCLC FirstSearch

ERIC
Library & Information Science Abstracts
Library Literature

Listservs

Copyright: Leave subject line blank and send subscribe message, SUBSCRIBE CNI-COPYRIGHT [first name, last name], to:
listproc@cni.org

Interlibrary Loan: This listserv will probably move to Northwestern University in fall 1996. For the present, leave subject line blank and send subscribe message, subscribe ill-1 [first name, last name] to: listproc@usc.edu

PEOPLE

Talk with interlibrary loan and document delivery librarians at meetings of organizations.

Visit an interlibrary loan librarian at another library.

Build a network of people you can talk to about ILL by telephone, fax, e-mail or in person.

February 1996   Virginia Boucher

INDEX

Virginia Boucher is an interlibrary loan consultant who conducts work shops and speaks on interlibrary loan topics in the United States and Europe. She is professor emeritus at the University of Colorado at Boulder Libraries, where she served as head of interlibrary loan for twenty-five years.

Virginia Boucher was a member of the committee that produced the Interlibrary Loan Data Elements standard, ANSI Z39.63. She was awarded the American Library Association's Herbert W. Putnam Honor Award in 1984, the RASD Isadore Gilbert Mudge citation for distinguished contributions to reference librarianship in 1990, and the Colorado Library Association's Lifetime Achievement Award in 1991.